Photograph Adrian Siegel

OLIN DOWNES

OLIN DOWNES
ON MUSIC

A Selection from His Writings
during the Half-Century
1906 to 1955

EDITED BY

IRENE DOWNES

WITH A PREFACE BY

HOWARD TAUBMAN

GREENWOOD PRESS, PUBLISHERS
NEW YORK

DEDICATION

AFTER *my husband's sudden death last August 22, I went, at the end of September, to Nantucket to close our cottage on the loved island. There, when he heard the wind in the pine trees, he always said it was the finest symphony.*

During the long drive across the moors, I thought of the happiness we had known there for a few days in June, a June which was to be Olin's last, when he had plunged into the preparation of the garden and the care of the little fruit trees which he was determined to foster against winds and salt spray.

My first steps led me into the garden. There, shining among the tall grasses, was a small quince tree bearing four golden, fragrant fruits, the first fruition of a long effort, so imaginative, loving, and so hopeful. It suddenly seemed symbolic of a thousand strands in Olin's life and work with music, with human beings, and with gardens. So many things that he had begun, with his heart and mind, bore good fruit. In a far greater sense than I had ever before realized, even perhaps had had any time to realize, his energies had been continuously creative: his responses to life—whether to people, to music, to nature—were of never-ceasing freshness, and these responses were as swift as they were generous.

I began to sense a living continuity in all that he had done; that his gifts to life had not ended with his death, but would, sustained by the impulse he had so greatly given, bear fruit.

I thought of the life-giving inspiration and beauty which he had felt in music, which had found expression in his writings. I hoped to preserve some of these writings in a permanent form.

A few days later, in Nantucket, I received a telegram informing me that Simon and Schuster had approved a plan for the publication of a book of Olin's writings.

This was the beginning of this book.

In a very real sense, this volume is intended for those who love life itself. To Olin, the wonders of nature and of the universe, the pulsing life of humanity, its greatness, its cruelties, its joys, were given expression in the "invisible" art of music, to him the greatest of the arts.

It is hoped that the sum of these selections will be suggestive of the varied and manifold fascinations of music in its many forms. These were encountered in a journalistic career of fifty years during which his communication of these experiences has meant much in the lives of thousands of music-lovers. He once wrote: "The artists, creative and interpretive, give us, the inarticulate ones, something of fulfillment, of release, and of vision that penetrates even the opaqueness of our minds and senses."

IRENE DOWNES

December 1, 1955

PREFACE

By Howard Taubman

(For twenty-five years, as co-worker in the functioning of
the Music Department of *The New York Times,* by day and by
night, Mr. Taubman had exceptional opportunity to gain impressions of Olin Downes. In the autumn of 1955 he was appointed successor to Mr. Downes. Mr. Taubman contributes to
this book the following portrait.—ED.)

OLIN DOWNES

OLIN HAD A SOLID, sturdy body packed with energy. His head,
with its high brow and rough-hewn planes, gave the impression
of granitic strength. When, as he did in his later years, he walked
with his kind of bearish gait, he looked like a remote and for-
bidding man. But the appearance was deceptive. When you sat
opposite him in his office or across the table over a bite of sup-
per, you discovered at once that he was responsive and out-
going. His enthusiasms were torrential, expressed in vivid and
exciting talk. His eyes mirrored the sensitivity of his percep-
tions, the fury of his indignations and the sparkle of his
laughter.

His zest for life was so enormous that he could not, even had
he wished to, detach himself from any phase of it. In the practice of his profession he was fully committed. He loved the art
he served and was a vital, throbbing part of it. His mind and
his ears were constantly alert to any vibrations that had fresh
meaning; his was the eternally open heart.

I often felt, like others who knew him intimately, that his
writings could not imprison the contagious diversity of his

personality. His robust sense of ridicule was infrequently conveyed through the printed page. The reason, I think, was self-abnegation. He was too serious and responsible about music and musicians to wish to use a weapon that would not only be cruel to the victim but would also have the disagreeable result of magnifying the wielder.

He did not mind laughing at himself. The stories that he told with the greatest relish were those in which he was the butt. One concerned his experience as a fledgling forced suddenly to review Geraldine Farrar's first appearance in Boston as Marguerite in *Faust*.

It was the first year of Olin's half century as a music critic. Happy as he was to be earning six dollars a week on the Boston *Post* for the privilege of listening to all sorts of music and performers, he had, nevertheless, to cling to an outside job to help support his family. Evenings he would go to the gymnasium of a Y.M.C.U., climb up a ladder onto a platform encircled with wire mesh like a cage and take his place at a piano. There he would pound out tunes as an instructor led a group of physical culturists in a series of exercises.'For twenty minutes he would set the rhythm to such things as drills with dumbbells and for the remaining forty would play popular selections to amuse the athletes below. The men had their favorite tunes. One would cup his hands to his mouth and cry, "Hey, professor, give us 'Bedelia.' " And, as Olin would recall with a chuckle, "Bedelia" it was.

Olin contrived to keep this job through his first season on the Boston *Post*. He whispered not a word of it to anyone on the newspaper, and his family, on pain of violent retribution, was sworn to secrecy. When he had an evening concert to cover, he arranged for a substitute pianist. As the opening of the Metropolitan Opera in its spring visit to Boston approached, he hoped he would be relieved of reporting the event.

He had not yet covered an opera and, as he remembered with an amused shudder, was rather superior to it, regarding it as something less than a serious art form. Possibly he had some hesitations that in his greenness he would not be able to cope with the alarums of an occasion loudly trumpeted in advance. For here was Miss Farrar, a native of the Boston area, returning to her homefolks as a great prima donna.

The Boston *Post*'s drama critic had been covering opera openings. When Olin approached him, that gentleman observed that he had been doing this chore for fifteen years. "Then I can count on your doing it again?" Olin said with relief, and the drama critic replied caustically, "I guess you can."

A free man, Olin wandered around that afternoon. It was a rainy, muddy Monday, and the young man arrived at the gymnasium looking, but not feeling, bedraggled. About a quarter of nine, a head appeared at the top of the ladder and said, "Hey, professor, the Boston *Post* wants to speak to you on the telephone."

Olin was horrified. How had they tracked him down here? It seems that Mr. Grozier, publisher of the *Post*, had decided that he wanted his new music critic to cover the opera and had so ordered it. Olin could not be found at home or anywhere else. His family, under extreme pressure, had finally weakened and told the office his working address. The managing editor was on the telephone; he snapped his orders. There was iron in his voice, and Olin headed for the Boston Theatre.

The audience was a brilliant one, the ladies in their formal finery and the men in white tie and tails. Feeling painfully conspicuous in his unpressed street clothes, Olin slipped into the theater and sat down beside a woman who had on what he recalled as "perfectly awesome evening attire." She was the wife of the drama critic whom Olin had dispossessed from the seat. As soon as the curtain fell and the lights went up, the uncomfortable Olin went looking for the drama critic and told him he could have the seat back. Olin stood through the rest of the performance back of the brass rail at the rear in a tangle of humanity, trying to catch the sight and sound of the occasion.

Like an innocent, unaware that a critic sometimes left before the final chord was sounded, he remained to the end of the performance. He ran every step of the way to the *Post*. The editor was waiting with the words "Where is your story?" As

Olin gasped, the editor muttered, "Oh, Lord!" Turning to a reporter, he said, "Write us a column of slush for the next edition."

Olin plunged into the task and barely made the last edition. Consumed by anxiety, he turned defiant and belligerent, as he well understood later on. He attacked Farrar's voice and the way she produced it; he laid it down that she was a clumsy and inexperienced actress.

He turned in his copy and walked home, all the way to Cambridge, distractedly, running over in his mind the words in his article and considering their gaucheries. He could not sleep and was up early and at the newsstand. His eye fell on the front page of the Boston *Post*. There was his article in a two-column spread, and over it the headline: OLIN DOWNES SAYS THAT GERALDINE FARRAR IS IMMATURE.

Grim as he felt about the caliber of the piece, Olin could not help remembering that Miss Farrar was twenty-six while he was twenty. He was able to manage a sardonic smile and in later years he could roar over it without shivers of horror.

This incident was part of the "painful progress" of learning his métier. From the beginning to the end of his career, his mind was never closed to learning. Indeed, his eagerness to broaden his compass was one of his most endearing traits.

His education, because of the force of economic circumstances, was far from systematic. He felt that this was a severe handicap. In deepest truth, however, it was an advantage. In his youth he reached out for new ideas, information and impressions with an avidity that made their absorption far more meaningful and lasting than any learning by rote could have been. And even in the years when his eminence was established beyond dispute, he continued to pursue special studies such as a language or a new instrument.

On the Boston *Post* he slowly mastered the techniques of journalism and criticism while continuing to expand his musical horizons. Eager to work, he did not sit by idly when the music season slowed down and stopped. He offered to take on other assignments, and in good time became one of the finest interviewers and feature writers in the business. His fame spread beyond Boston.

In 1923 Richard Aldrich, who was about to retire as music critic of *The New York Times,* invited Olin to come down to New York for an interview with Adolph S. Ochs, the publisher. Olin came, wondering whether, at thirty-seven, he was ready for such a position. On the eve of the appointment he dropped in on a concert of new music by Stravinsky and others conducted by Leopold Stokowski. There were cheers and catcalls, the kind of response that would never have happened in Boston. He was amused and exhilarated. He wrote later privately: "It was just the right introduction, that first evening in New York. Here was the freedom of ideas, here was merciless competition, here was quarter neither asked nor received, here was living. I never lost that sensation. I am one of the abandoned persons who think that New York is the finest city in the world, and the most formidable challenge offered to men of ideas in all America."

And so he plunged into his work for *The New York Times* with an ardor that had not abated when, after more than thirty-one years on that journal, his flying typewriter was stilled. He brought to his labors curiosity, humility, temperament, passion and unremitting enthusiasm.

Of all Olin's qualities the most precious was his remorseless honesty—with himself as with others. If he condemned musicians for malfeasance or misfeasance, he was also ready to call himself to account. An excellent example of this characteristic is the change of mind and heart that he had concerning Honegger's *Jeanne d'Arc au bûcher* and his readiness to admit it. The admission and the reasons for it may be found on page 408.

Writing came hard to Olin. Part of the trouble, I think, was psychological. He believed that gaps in his formal education had handicapped him. Actually, he wrote with a vividness and eloquence that were irresistible.

There was another reason for Olin's incessant struggle with words. This was his unflagging conscientiousness. He was possessed by a demon that drove him to seek to improve and improve. There is a story of his going to hear Yehudi Menuhin when that violinist was still unacclaimed as a prodigy. Olin had his heart set on going to Madison Square Garden that night to see a prize fight; he was an ardent *aficionado* of the ring. He had the tickets in his pocket, and he thought that he would catch a movement of the Beethoven Violin Concerto that the boy, Menuhin, was to play. Then he could go to the fight and return to the office to write the few lines that would be needed to dispose of the infant fiddler.

Olin found it hard to believe that the boy could play with such virtuosity and appearance of maturity. He decided he had better listen to more than the first movement. He remained, of course, to the end. The fight was forgotten. This was a tremendous and yet puzzling experience. Olin sat down and tossed off a review, filled with the glow of his excitement and enthusiasm. He read it over and decided that no youngster deserved this sort of salutation. He laid aside this review and wrote another. This one was calm, objective and flat. The editor was clamoring for copy. The deadline was at hand. Olin blended the two reviews into a third effort. But as he left the office, he was still wracked by doubts.*

If Olin had had no deadline to contend with, he would have spent endless hours on most reviews. His Sunday pieces emerged from days of fierce combat with himself and his recalcitrant typewriter. He was almost never satisfied. He would finish what looked like a fine piece and would instantly tear into it, revising and improving.

The recurrent obligation to meet deadlines was like an ordeal by fire. And yet I know that Olin would not have had it otherwise. We discussed often the arguments for waiting a day before writing a review, and he could see that it would relieve some of the pressure. But in the end he felt that there was no better way than to set down one's reactions in the heat and haste of the moment. No time, perhaps, for the ultimate chiseling of a phrase, but the gain was tremendous. There was time only for honesty and the warm immediacy of the response. There might be occasion in the Sunday article to reflect and ex-

* The excellent result will be found on page 131—ED.

pand, but in the review written to a deadline one had to capture the mood and spirit of an event as one still held them fresh in mind.

The pieces in this volume culled from Olin's immediate and more leisurely reactions are the measure of his vibrant response to music in all its manifestations. Note well the very first review in this book—a perceptive and appreciative discussion of Debussy's *La Mer* when it was still new. Olin responded with similar keenness to the new works of men who are today acknowledged as masters—Richard Strauss, Stravinsky, Prokofieff, Shostakovitch and, above all, Sibelius. It was Olin's passionate advocacy of the Finnish composer, carried on out of a profound conviction that this was music of universality, that did more than any other factor to establish him securely in the United States. Olin never ceased the hunt for the large, authentic voice in music, and he was especially eager to hear it in American music. If much of this volume concerns the music of the twentieth century, it is a just reflection of Olin's contribution to a public sympathy for the output of our own time. And while he was inclined to be modest about that contribution, Olin knew that it was a proud task to be a music critic and he rejoiced when he thought that he had helped to spread an affection for the art he held so dear. Nor did he confine himself to criticism in the performance of this task. He lectured, appeared on the radio, wrote books and, on several occasions, took active leadership in major musical enterprises.

Olin's lifelong devotion to music was a broad and enveloping force. To him music was an expression of life in all its concerns and diversities. To him music was the art that expressed man and his aspirations most profoundly. For him music had a range as wide as life itself. His own range had that kind of breadth.

CONTENTS

Contents

Contents

Contents

Contents

xix

Contents

Contents

xxi

Contents

Contents

Contents

Contents

Contents

Contents

Contents

Contents

Contents

Contents

PART I

CONCERNING 1906

How I Became a Music Critic

This note, written about 1935, was found among
Olin Downes's papers.—ED.

HARDLY a week passes that I do not receive a letter asking how one
becomes a music critic. I can't answer these letters satisfactorily, if
only for the reason that music criticism is so unorganized and so little understood in its purposes and values that there is no accepted
way in which an appointment of this kind is secured—at least no
way with which I am acquainted.

I was twenty years old and in need of money, with a number of
mouths to feed. I cannot profess to a more abstract motive. Music
was my stock in trade. During the season I gave whatever poorly
paid piano lessons individuals would take of me. I played accompaniments in vocal studios at fifty cents an hour, and some of the
teachers for whom I played—confound them—still owe me unsettled
accounts for those services. One of them administered vocal lessons
in place of specie. But that did not help the budget.

Between professional occupations I sandwiched in anything else
I could find to do. In the summer it was particularly tough going.
The lessons and accompaniments practically stopped. I tried for a
job as pianist in a dance orchestra, but was turned down by the
leader on the grounds that I had not the necessary "routine." He
was quite right. But what to do?

It was necessary to get some steady salary. I thought of trying to
get work as a music critic. I knew nothing of how newspapers were
run, or what one did when aspiring to the critic's position. But I had
exceptional luck. I walked in one day, armed with one letter of
identification, but without preliminaries or appointment, to the

3

office of E. A. Grozier, editor and publisher of the Boston *Post*. The chief had not yet come in, and I had enough wits to lie to his secretary and say I had an appointment. By God's grace I sat nearer the door when he entered than she did, and commenced to talk, I imagine rather wildly. He was highly skeptical. "When I took over this paper," he said, "I fired Philip Hale." (Philip Hale was, and is, in my opinion, the most brilliant music critic America has produced. At the time of this conversation, in the Year of our Lord 1906, he was writing for the Boston *Herald*.) "If I could get him today, I'd grab him. . . . But as for you, young man, I don't see that you have either experience or reputation to recommend you."

This was sad but true, and unarguable. I privately gave up, but talked on as a face-saving device before departure. Suddenly he shot a question. "Suppose, young man, that I were to avail myself of your valuable services. What would it cost the paper?"

My God! Could he mean it? Was there a possibility? I answered, with what I now perceive to have been Socratic wisdom: "What I want is an envelope, with something in it, at the end of every week."

"You'll have to tell me how much it needs to be."

Now it was time to think fast. I didn't know newspaper wage scales at all. In previous summers I had done manual and even menial jobs to keep something coming in, and the utmost I had been able to make was five dollars a week. That was for jobs I didn't like. Here was a job I would like, tickets to all the concerts and operas, and the whole of music thrown open to me. Perhaps that should shade the price (and don't frighten him, and make him a reasonable offer). The chief was silent, watching me. I took a deep breath and plunged. "What would you say to four dollars a week?"

The chief turned and looked out of the window down on Washington Street. His shoulders shook. I thought he was coughing. He was laughing. He thumped the desk. "By God, if I didn't want it more than that I wouldn't put it in the paper!"

Like a flash: "Make it five."

"Young man, I'll make it six, and we'll see if you can write for a newspaper." And that, so far as I am concerned, is the only way I know of to become a music critic.

Debussy's *La Mer* Reaches Boston

"... puffing blue rings of smoke ..."

THE program of the sixteenth Symphony Orchestra rehearsal, which took place yesterday afternoon, consisted of Debussy's three orchestral sketches, *The Sea*, performed for the first time here; *Olaf's Wedding Dance*, by Alexander Ritter, the author of the poem affixed to the score of Strauss's *Tod und Verklärung*, also performed for the first time; Liszt's "Mephisto" Waltz, and Berlioz's overture *Le Carnaval romain*.

The feature of the concert was the performance of Debussy's sketches. They are three in number. The first is intended to represent *From Dawn Till Noon on the Ocean*, the second *Frolics of Waves*, the third *Dialogue of the Wind and the Sea*.

Surely Debussy has never penned a more marvelous and subtle score than this, and surely he has never more successfully exercised his incredible skill in the blending of color and the use of strange involved or conflicting rhythms which convey psychological suggestions and impressions in a manner only possible to this inimitable Frenchman. In this music there are rare and precious harmonies, shifting, evanescent play of light and shade, and we are strangely conscious of the indefinable mystery of the sea. This is a wonderful, unique art, and the composer has unquestionably enlarged the musical horizon. But is it a great, vital art? Is it elemental enough to appeal to succeeding generations and differing epochs of thought and expression? Is it not rather a new taste, a rarity, calculated to appeal to the refined sensuousness of a hyper-refined age? To us this music lacks the vast, elemental note, and with its prismatic opalescent hues seems rather the sea conceived by a dreamer lying on his couch in a sumptuously upholstered apartment and puffing blue rings of smoke into the air.

Olaf's Wedding Dance is a rather surprising product when one considers the source from which it came. Ritter we had conceived to be a thinker, a scholar, and somewhat of an iconoclast. Did he

5

intend this waltz to be seriously taken? It is a beer-garden affair, and scarcely worthy of a place on a serious program.

The "Mephisto" Waltz has been dubbed "music of the bagnio," and alleged to be unfit for the chaste ears of a Symphony audience. Yet no one seemed offended yesterday afternoon, and it was warmly applauded. The performance, to borrow James Huneker's phrase, was one of "abounding deviltry."

JANUARY 26, 1908

====

"An Epoch-making Rondo": *Till Eulenspiegel*

Mr. Schelling plays his own suite

THE program of the thirteenth public rehearsal and concert of our Symphony Orchestra was as follows: *Till Eulenspiegel's Merry Pranks*, R. Strauss; Fantastic Suite for piano and orchestra, Schelling; symphonic poem, *Viviane*, Chausson. Mr. Ernest Schelling was pianist in the performance of his own suite, which was given for the first time in America on this occasion.

Many extensive and detailed explanations of Strauss's epoch-making rondo have been published by admiring commentators, a proceeding hardly essential and, indeed, rather harmful than otherwise. Strauss deals with universal types, with basic truths. Let the music, with its laughter and tears, its pity and mockery, its passionate commentary on all things that are, speak for itself.

The *Till Eulenspiegel* is frequently spoken of as a masterpiece of rarest humor. It is all that, and more. The music does not arouse unadulterated merriment; there is more of the grave than the gay in these wanton measures; the note of destiny is sounded; with terrible persistency and ever-growing menace it dogs the Rogue's footsteps to the end. Using marvelously subtle but strong touches, the composer tells the tale. As he proceeds, you insensibly, but none the less deeply, become more and more impressed with the moral that underlies this diverting raillery. The epilogue, in almost Mozartean strains of infinite tenderness, says: "So it was, in the fable I have

6

told you. My story is ended." Was this in earnest? You smile at the thought of some musical drollery, but the smile fades; you have been set a-thinking.

Now, this the music means to me; it may suggest entirely different things to you, but at any rate let not a circumstantial program come between the composer and those he endeavors to reach by his art. An immortal book should not be illustrated; it is sad that Strauss, a profound philosopher and generalizer, should be subjected to such injury.

The performance, finished to the utmost in every detail, was of unusual excellence in many ways. If memory serves, there was not, at least on Friday afternoon, the peppery vigor about the opening section that made the music so gripping when the composer directed it in this city in 1904. Dr. Muck conducted with a sure and dextrous hand, with a subtlety and finesse that came, at the beginning, dangerously near to dissection. By this means, however, every phrase became very significant and suggestive, no point was lost, the evolution of the musical thought became surpassingly clear and apparent, the fateful climax was extremely poignant and telling.

Mr. Schelling's suite was written in 1905–6, orchestrated in 1907, and given its first performance, the composer being pianist, under Mengelberg at the Concertgebouw, Amsterdam, October 10, 1907.

We are not to forget that Mr. Schelling is an American. The finale of this suite is entitled *Virginia Reel,* and the themes are *Dixie, Old Folks at Home, Yankee Doodle,* and an original theme.

The composition is agreeably, often ingeniously instrumentated, and it is written throughout in a symphonic, orchestral style, despite a very brilliant and difficult piano part. At first hearing, Mr. Schelling appears to have written music which, while always refined and in some passages truly imaginative, is not remarkably potential or extremely individual. This composer is a young man, and he already expresses himself in an interesting way. Doubtless, in the course of his future development, he will give us many works of still more interest and durability than the Fantastic Suite.

A man of dreams and introspection, Chausson could hardly have chosen a subject more likely to enkindle his imagination than the legend of Merlin and Vivian. *Viviane* was given its first and only other performance in Boston in 1902. It is to be hoped that such another long interval will not elapse before it is repeated. There is another world, a world into which Chausson readily and gladly escaped; and in the forest of Brocellande there was only bliss supreme and eternal. Hence this music of radiant visions and ineffable tenderness; music that is permeated in every measure with an essence as fragile, exquisite, completely conquering, as the compelling spells that Vivian wove over the enraptured Merlin. These qualities in the music were enhanced by a performance of marvelous delicacy and tonal beauty.

JANUARY 26, 1908

Who Can Succeed Dr. Muck?

Richter? Wood? Weingartner? Mahler?

DR. MUCK at the close of the Symphony season will return immediately to Berlin, there to resume his duties at the Royal Opera. In June the conductor will proceed to Bayreuth to conduct performances of *Parsifal.*

The question of Dr. Muck's successor lays a difficult problem before the management of the Symphony Orchestra, for the number of men among whom a choice may be made is not legion. Of the previous conductors who have served here there is only one, Mr. Gericke having gone into retirement, at all eligible for consideration. That is Nikisch, who was here from 1889 to 1893, and Mr. Nikisch is well known to be extremely kittenish on all matters relating to engagements. Moreover, he is a poor drillmaster, and it is remembered that the technical standard of the orchestra was materially lowered during his regime.

Under later conductors, especially Mr. Gericke, our orchestra developed that superb finish and virtuosity which placed it second to no other such organization in the world today. When Dr. Muck arrived in this city in 1906, he found not an ensemble of some hundred musicians awaiting him, but a wonderfully sensitive and well nigh perfect instrument to be played upon. As we all know, the Doctor proved a very capable performer, the men, meanwhile, rejoicing in comparative immunity from the extra rehearsals which were the rule rather than the exception under Mr. Gericke. This year, however, in addition to materially altering the personnel of the band, Dr. Muck has become the most industrious and implacable of drillmasters. The proficiency of the orchestra is now at another high water mark.

Who can carry on the work? The rare man must be master of routine. Also, with the qualities of a hard and tireless worker, he must unite the broadest scholarship, the faculty of bringing himself into sympathy with music of all schools and periods, and a magnetic, inspiring personality. That is demanding a very great deal, but the Symphony audiences of today are not the audiences of twenty years ago, and they would hardly be satisfied with less. Our critical appreciation and wide acquaintance with every variety of orchestral literature have been the astonishment of every great musician who has visited us of late years. Dr. Muck has found it difficult to meet the widely inclusive demands of his auditors.

The field from which to choose is small. The majority of the great conductors of today, such as Dr. Hans Richter and Mr. Henry Wood in London, or Mr. Mottl in Vienna, are firmly established in European cities. They are practically out of the question. Dr. Richard Strauss, who made a furor when he conducted his own compositions in this city in 1904, is a law unto himself. He usually appears as a conductor of his own compositions, and it is a painful fact that he values America chiefly for its gold—that he does not especially relish our artistic atmosphere.

Felix Weingartner made a sensation in this city when he conducted a colossal performance of Berlioz's *Symphonie fantastique* two years ago. He is a virtuoso conductor of the very highest rank, but is now engaged at the Vienna Opera, and it is questionable, after all, whether what we want is a "star" conductor.

There is Gustav Mahler, now of the Metropolitan Grand Opera Company of New York. Mr. Mahler would be a treasure trove. He expressed his artistic principles with commendable force and earnestness a short time ago, having been accused of nonconformance with tradition. "Tradition," said Mahler, "means sloth!"—a musical Declaration of Independence which will go down in the history of the art. That is the sort of man we need and desire, but Mr. Mahler, unfortunately, is likely to be engaged for some time to come with the opera company.

Mengelberg of Amsterdam, a young man, is making a stir in the musical world. He is reputed to be a leader of indisputable talent and industry, and a man of the highest ideals.

Steinbach of Cologne is said to have been once approached on the subject. This may be so, but it is unlikely that Steinbach will be approached again.

Schnéevoigt, if we may believe the musical journals, is a man of parts. There are a number of lesser lights who have displayed fine abilities, but whether they are of sufficient weight to take place at the head of our orchestra is very debatable. And all this amounts merely to discussion. The question is as yet entirely unsolved. Who will it be?

Dr. Max Fiedler conducted from 1908 until 1912. Dr. Muck returned in 1912.—Ed.

NOVEMBER 29, 1908

Ein Heldenleben and the Tchaikovsky Concerto

"There should have been a twenty-minute intermission."

RICHARD STRAUSS'S great tone poem for orchestra, *A Hero's Life*, was given performance for the second time in Boston yesterday afternoon at the seventh Symphony rehearsal of the season.

Ein Heldenleben was first heard in this city when Mr. Gericke was here in 1901. It was then difficult for the majority of hearers to form any opinions of the work. Strauss was quite new to us seven short years ago. He wrote music which seemed, and seems, to the more conservative of the passing generation, too complicated to retain either beauty or intelligibility.

The hero stands on his own feet. Perhaps there is a touch of the flamboyant about him, yet he elicits your unwilling admiration, and the opening section, which portrays the individual, is splendid, vigorous, soundly constructed music. The second division, *The Hero's Enemies*—they who mock and gibe and snarl at the great man—is a masterpiece of malicious irony. It would not have been surprising to look up and discover the woodwind-players "making

10

faces" just then. The enemies, as depicted by the composer, are surely a hellish crew.

The solo violin represents the loved one in what is to us an unfavorable light. Such a coquette! Such a whirligig! Was this the present Mrs. Strauss in the days of her youth? Perish the thought! The determined wooing of the swain, the ultimate acquiescence of the adored, are so obviously set forth that he who runs might read. The love music which follows has genuine tenderness, though the tenderness is very German, and rather heavy, and inclined toward sentimentalism.

The battle scene has long ere this set audiences by the ears. It is the *ne plus ultra* of magnificent contrapuntal effrontery. Themes are fairly hurtled against each other. The lyric phrase associated with the beloved appears ever and anon amid the brutal shrieking cacophony and the pounding of the drums, sailing smoothly along above or between the other motives. Such sure and prodigious workmanship is confounding! And out of the maelstrom which has served for what technicians call the "development section" we come, firm on our feet. The hero theme is triumphantly hurled out by the brass in the primary tonality of the piece, and the "recapitulation" begins, called by Strauss *The Hero's Works of Peace*. And what are they? Why, *Don Juan, Don Quixote, Traum durch die Dämmerung,* by Richard Strauss! This new material is introduced with consummate skill. But of what avail the simple life? Still the world is scornful. Existence is a delusion. And now comes one of the most wonderful passages of the whole tone poem. In the throes of a diminished seventh chord, while the strings rush up and down a sizzling chromatic scale, the whole orchestra shudders. Is this revulsion, world-weariness? Does the hero say, with Lenau's Don Juan, though from a different point of view: "Exhausted is the fuel, and on the hearth the cold is fiercely cruel"? But this passes, and noble pages of contemplation and sonorous majesty follow.

Works such as this should be heard oftener than twice within seven years. One can only record impressions now. The world moves swiftly. The music was surprisingly clear yesterday. It is absolutely symphonic in texture. Strauss's canvas is large to the point of unwieldiness. He handles his material with freedom, but he keeps well within the tenets of the form perfected by Beethoven. Yet, with all this, the *Heldenleben* seems at a second hearing swollen, elephantine, and curiously out of perspective in spots.

11

What a monstrous effusion it is! You may not like it, it may rouse your most deep-seated artistic antagonisms, but you can hardly pass it by—this ebullient, overwhelming outpouring. And whether Strauss does or does not portray himself in what is generally considered the composer's autobiography, the work is beyond peradventure the product of an egotism so sublime as to be its own excuse.

Tchaikovsky's B flat minor Concerto, with all its barbaric splendor and opulent color, was robbed of its full effect by the preceding piece. Mr. Ossip Gabrilówitsch was in fine fettle, and he had his own idea of the concerto, though it was of little avail to exhausted nerves. There should have been a twenty-minute intermission, for only an Over-man may survive the *Heldenleben* with an appetite for more. The prelude and *Liebestod* from *Tristan and Isolde* brought the concert to an end.

JANUARY 1, 1909

The Sibelius Second.

"It is disconcertingly vital."

THE program of the eleventh concert of the Symphony Orchestra this season last night in Symphony Hall: Symphony No. 2, Sibelius; scene and aria, *Ah! Perfido*, Beethoven; menuetto from Serenade in D, Brahms; three songs with orchestra: *Hymnus*, Strauss; *Die Musikantin*, Max Fiedler; *Er Ist's*, Hugo Wolf; Caprice on Spanish themes, Rimsky-Korsakoff.

The Symphony No. 2 by Sibelius has been given once before in Boston, under Mr. Gericke, in 1904. It was the first work by the Finnish composer to be heard here, and no doubt it was largely for this reason that it did not make so strong an impression as the First Symphony in E minor, given by Dr. Muck in 1907. But the symphony heard last night is a magnificent work.

It is dangerous, too. We should beware of it. It should not appear on too many programs. It might do incalculable harm to art, for it is sufficient to beat down the guard of the cleverest philosophy of esthetics ever formulated by dilettanti!

12

It is disconcertingly vital. It is brusque, direct, unsparing of emphasis, a primeval product, one would say, of the land that gave it birth. For through Sibelius, who thinks in 3-2 time and speaks with the voice of the early gods, a nation becomes articulate. His orchestral style is as individual as his ideas, which are like rough lumps of richest ore. It is as much the result of them as the bed of a river is the passageway worn by the current. The instrumentation is often harsh and thick, and as often again of the highest brilliancy. Gusts of tone in the lower strings, a brass choir that bursts out in golden splendor or chokes with choler, sweet, wild phrases for the woodwind—the shrill skirling of an icy blast, or fitful gleams of lovely sunshine, or, as in the last movement, the long persistent figures for the basses, like the roar of surf.

Destiny has its hand on this music. Its might is unconquerable, but chained and impotent. How magnificently it mutters and glooms! The two middle movements are prodigious beyond compare. The pizzicato of basses which prepares the entrance of the melancholy theme for the bassoons, and the entrance of that theme, is one of the most imaginative and inevitable instances of such procedure in symphonic literature. There is no escaping the mood. And what themes! The long, mournful melody for the strings in the second movement, and the pathetic, aspiring air for the oboe in the following section. Wilde said that no great artist ever sang without the fullest consciousness of the matter and the manner of his singing. Be it so. Whether preconceived or not, we know of few more affecting moments in modern music than the simple moving phrase sung by the pastoral instrument over rich harmonies in the brass—a passage made the more striking by reason of the utter contrast of the flying measures that precede.

Over all is the bleakness, the space, and the eternity of the north. Listening to this symphony, one would say that from that tremendous region shall come all things creative. These melodies seem to spring from the very bottom consciousness of a people—more, of humanity.

It remains to relate the astounding conclusion and its preparation. From the preceding movement the strings rush up, pile Ossa on Pelion, and then walks out—what? A lordly, vulgar, heroic, commonplace tune that from a cheaper soul would serve admirably for the first eight measures of a slow waltz for the summer hotel. But how splendidly this defiance rings out! With what a battalion of brass and rhythm is it flung forth, a gauntlet thrown in the face of man and god! In other hands it would serve for the beer garden. But behold! A voice from Valhalla. The apotheosis of this theme at the last is unutterably superb. The man who can write with such force, such sheer strength and fertility of invention, who can, so to speak, throw manners to the winds and bring back the gods, is quite beyond price in an overcultivated age. The performance of a very difficult score reflected the greatest credit upon Mr. Fiedler and his men.

In this concert Miss Tilly Koenen showed herself one of the great interpreters of song now before the public. She has a great voice, and she has executive ability which is not the property of all lauded concert singers. . . . Mr. Fiedler's song is modern in style and feeling, and an apt expression of the spirit of the poem.

There was a brilliant performance of Rimsky-Korsakoff's Caprice, and the melodious movement by Brahms met with its due reward.

JANUARY 3, 1909

The Young Elman Plays Tchaikovsky

And Another Strauss "Torrential Tone Poem" Is Heard

THE program of the eleventh rehearsal and concert of the Symphony Orchestra was:

Religious Festival Overture on the Chorale,
    Ein' feste Burg ist unser Gott..............Otto Nicolai
Violin Concerto.............................Tchaikovsky
Tone Poem, *Death and Transfiguration*......Richard Strauss

Mr. Mischa Elman, a young violinist of extraordinary talent, was soloist in the Tchaikovsky Violin Concerto, and his was a triumph, a triumph the more gratifying in that it represented the appeal of sane, vital art, which, whether Mr. Elman had been eighteen or fifty, would have exerted the same electric effect upon the enthusiastic audience.

Mr. Fiedler, it is generally conceded, made one of his greatest successes thus far when he placed upon a recent program Richard
Strauss's overwhelming *Hero's Life*, which will be repeated at the
second pension-fund concert of the season. No less remarkable and
more uplifting was the performance of the *Death and Transfiguration*. There is no question of one thing: that Richard Strauss, be
his position what it may three hundred years hence, is beyond
question the authoritative voice of this period; that when he speaks
he voices the wonderful impulses of this generation. No wonder that
he appeals irresistibly to young musicians, to the rising conductor
Mr. Fiedler and others of his ilk, of today. Has there ever been a
more curious age? And that heaven-storming mind, in its dauntless
questioning, would not be balked by anything in the sky above or
the earth below. Is all that within the province of art? Yes, within
the province of art that is growing greater, more profound, more
expressive, more all-embracing every day of these amazing years.
To me such art represents the greatest word, "modernity."

This tone poem is among the earlier of Strauss's epoch-marking
works. He has not wholly escaped Wagner's idioms, or, rather, when
this influence is perceptible, he multiples—the voice, mind you, of
this nth-power generation—he multiplies a hundredfold the emotional stress, for instance, of the dramatic episode that depicts the
final climax of Tannhäuser's struggle with the flesh and the spirit in
Wagner's opera of the name. There is such a vortex of a reminis-
cence in *Tod und Verklärung*.

It requires strong nerves to bear the strain of one of these torrential tone poems. Mr. Fiedler accomplished more than any conductor in our experience with the "Transfiguration" music—a dangerous test of the interpreter. In characters of fire he painted that
soul-picture. Where, or when, are we to stop? Shall it soon be given
to the Over-man whom Strauss is forever prophesying, to drink of
the waters of Life and Death, and to Know?

Perhaps in a few generations the terrible depicting of the death
chamber, the trance of introspection, and the dying man's last conflict with the last grim foe will seem naïve alongside the paintings
of Richard Strauss the second, but for us of 1909 there is little in
any art that goes deeper. Here and there in the score seems to be
a patchy place, where the ends of a tremendous vision did not meet,
where the inspired speech takes for a moment the tones of other
men. But who else could have written the overpoweringly atmos-

pheric beginning, the magnificently militant pages that represent man's struggle with fate, the warning of the trombones, and the psychological transition from death to victory? How very few composers—and conductors—could have so built up the ascending, victorious, rainbow-tinted apotheosis? And what more can we say of Mr. Fiedler's transcendent interpretation than that it was equal to the great modern masterpiece?

APRIL 2, 1909

Pelléas et Mélisande Makes History

"An unforgettable debt to Oscar Hammerstein"

THE Manhattan Opera Company made history last night when Debussy's *Pelléas and Mélisande* was given an incomparable performance at the Boston Theatre with a cast including four artists who created their roles at the first performance of the opera—Mélisande, Miss Garden; Geneviève, Mlle Gerville-Réache; Golaud, Dufranne; Arkel, Vieuille. Mr. Dalmorès took the place of Jean Périer, the original Pelléas, until lately with the Manhattan company. Mlle Trentini was Little Yniold; Mr. Cralde was the Doctor; Mr. Campanini conducted.

Debussy's opera will never enjoy the popularity of *La Bohème*. Plainly, it puzzled the majority of those present—the musicians of Boston were there. It is an intensely dramatic work, but it requires a little time for the crowd from Washington Street to adjust themselves to those wondrous and ineffably delicate values. Now, in the red-pepper hour, as the writer sits with pencil in hand, the helplessness of words descends on him with the weight of the Atlantic Ocean, and to put that experience on paper is like trying to portray the lands one visited in dreams.

It is doubly difficult, unless the mood favors, to enter the subworld of Debussy, for at the outset you must forget the vast and prodigious lore of all modern opera composers; you must forget all about the history of opera, Italian, French, German, resume your cast-off innocence and credulity, and become as open to convictions as a little child. Until then it is waiting in vain, for Debussy is secure in this land of dreams. He will not ask you to come, but if you care to follow you are welcome.

This opera is as new as anything under the sun. It must have—of course it has—its origin somewhere. So has eternity. A tinge, an echo, of Wagner may be imagined here or there, but otherwise one tries in vain to indicate the source of the strange and rapturous art. Perhaps it would not have been as astonishing to the Greeks as it is to us today.

It is always thrilling to contemplate the advent of a new genius. History abounds in incidents of the mildest of mankind suddenly become as the lion in his advocacy and execution of his theories. But here is another of the utterly new things about Debussy, the absolute reticence and self-effacement of his art. It does not flounder, it does not protest. It only stands right there, as unexplainable and as undeniable as the thousands of laws of which it speaks and of which we only suspect the existence in an occasional God-given moment. What wonder, when this is so, that Debussy writes without grievance or proclamation, with the absolute surety and consciousness of truth that is the characteristic of the master?

Debussy chose his libretto as inevitably as he composed. He searched, perhaps unconsciously, for the masterwork, the medium, that he should further rarefy and enhance in tones. His theories, musical and dramatic, had for years been perfecting in him. Then in the fusion of these forces and Maeterlinck's drama came the moment to create. He did so, and, in our humble and rashly premature opinion, he has marked an epoch.

As to his dramatic theories, Debussy said, among other things: "I tried, with all my strength and sincerity, to identify my music with the poetical essence of the drama. Before all things, I respected the characters, the lives of my personages; I wished them to express themselves, independently of me, of themselves. I let them sing in me.

"When listening to a work the spectator is wont to experience two kinds of emotion: the musical emotion, on the one hand; the emotion of the character in the drama on the other. Generally they are felt successively.

"I have tried to blend these two emotions and make them simultaneous.

"Melody is, if I may say so, almost anti-lyric, and powerless to express the constant changes of emotion or life. . . . I have never been willing that my music should hinder, through technical exigencies, the changes of sentiment and passion felt by my characters. It is effaced as soon as it is necessary that these should have perfect liberty in their gestures as in their cries, in their joy as in their · sorrow."

There is expressed the nature of *Pelléas and Mélisande* better than I could put it. It remains to say, with the aforesaid rashness, that Debussy succeeded in his aspiration to a degree that defies description. His technical methods would in themselves justify pages of analysis that are not appropriate at this time. It has been well remarked that he is a de-composer; that is, he separates the strands of harmony, as we know it today, reduces his chords to their lowest terms, and on this foundation erects his own wonderful and hitherto undreamed-of castles.

He uses to a great extent the Gregorian modes, and the whole-tone progressions give him the unlimited scope he requires in modulation. His orchestra is small, smaller than most composers of this day dare employ, though it includes an English horn and a bass tuba. He gets from it hundreds of new effects that are his own, and all of them are beautiful. Dramatic coherence is retained to a very unusual degree by the orchestral interludes that bind the many tableaux together, that reveal and accompany the changing moods of every scene. Three arts are combined as a whole, with a success and effectiveness unprecedented.

This music drama has justly been called "mystic," "symbolic," and a dozen other things. Lawrence Gilman hit on his clever phrase, "sound-wraiths," which he applied to the evasive and haunting motives that are used, though only in a general sense, throughout the score. They are so characteristic and so subtly employed that one feels them rather than hears them; becomes unaccountably aware of their presence. If I had not been acquainted with the piano score, the memory of those impalpable but unforgettable impressions would remain forever.

The play goes on in an unknown land, a land of shadows. The marvelously rich and shimmering orchestra rarely rises above a forte. An exclamation, a gesture, an evasive phrase, a half-finished sentence—so the characters, for the most part, communicate with each other. One would think, then, that this wistful and melancholy puppet show lacked dramatic force and a human note.

It does nothing of the kind. With every tableau that the curtain silently gathers upon, one becomes more moved and engrossed. The music, too, flows with inexhaustible inspiration, with cumulative power and appeal. This music is not music. It is simply a subtle aroma of the drama.

The first act envelops one with a romance and glamour that are so beautiful as to be almost painful. How refreshing in its simplicity is the next scene by the fountain! The scene between Mélisande and Golaud is an example of dramatic verity unsurpassed in the literature of opera. Think of Mélisande's alarm in the dark grotto, and Pelléas's joyous greeting of the moon as she bursts through the clouds.

The third act is simply beyond words. Remember the scene in the vaults, and the transition to the pure air above, so finely intimated by the orchestra.

But act four brings the great emotional climax of the work, and the final scene of this act, as the lovers embrace and kiss in the face of death, is superbly done without brutality, sweepingly passionate with all the eternal glory of the grand impulse and none of its physical taint.

The performance was as near perfection as we may hope to achieve in this world, and that, it should be realized, implies an artistic achievement to which the mounting of so colossal an opera as *Salome* bears no comparison. The scenery was a masterpiece in itself, as was the rapidity and dexterity with which it was so often handled.

Mr. Campanini was a revelation in his reading of that most subtle of scores. So was Miss Mary Garden.

Mr. Hector Dufranne as an actor and singer was superb. Mr. Dalmorès was perhaps a trifle too much of the open air, though a very dramatic and ardent Pélleas.

The other artists deserve praise in equal measure. Mlle Jeanne Gerville-Réache and Mr. Vieuille have magnificent voices. If it were only for this production, Boston would owe an unforgettable debt to Mr. Oscar Hammerstein.

Rachmaninoff Conducts and Plays

"A tall gentleman in a frock coat"

A MEMORABLE concert took place yesterday afternoon when Sergei Rachmaninoff conducted his symphonic poem after Böcklin, *The Isle of the Dead*, and played his Second Piano Concerto at the ninth public rehearsal of the Symphony Orchestra in Symphony Hall. The program was completed by Brahms's *Tragic Overture* and the prelude to the *Meistersinger*.

Mr. Rachmaninoff, a tall gentleman in a frock coat, is a man of surprising, not easily explicable force and personality. In recent years Richard Strauss, Camille Saint-Saëns, Vincent d'Indy have preceded him as visiting conductors. The first electrified his orchestra and his audience. The second received the reward of his achievements. The music of Mr. d'Indy did him more justice than his presence. With a lesser reputation Mr. Rachmaninoff surpassed all these, as far as an individual impression was concerned. When Mr. Fiedler brought him upon the stage, he acknowledged a cordial greeting with a fine dignity and the self-possession of a man of wide experience. Then he led the orchestra in a superb performance with extraordinary authority and magnetism.

Listening to the impressive music, one was the more sensible of the vitalizing power of the man himself. It was not possible to put a finger on a theme and say: "That's Rachmaninoff," but one was immediately seized and absorbed by an overmastering mood expressed with consummate technical and esthetic mastery. That was Rachmaninoff. When he writes for the piano he is only occasionally successful in capturing a good idea. Either, for the most part, he does not write seriously, or else invention, which is not the strongest factor of his compositions, refuses to work for the mere sake of sound or tonal design. He would tax the piano as he taxes the orchestra. The orchestra can respond, and Mr. Rachmaninoff is aware of its resources as are few composers, even today.

There is hardly a composer so utterly and exclusively subjective

20

when he sits down in earnest to express himself. Claude Debussy may frighten the bourgeois, sitting in his tower of ivory, but somewhere, sometime, there is a public to be astonished. With superb, unassumed superiority, Rachmaninoff, self-absorbed, contemplates a great picture, then takes an immense modern orchestra, improvises upon it, talks to himself, quite regardless. It is by fortune, not design, and the grace of an enormous technique as well as an imagination that turns notes to gold, that this music has many qualities which appeal to audiences at large.

Böcklin's pictures have inspired more than one composer, but this is not pictorial music. It is the expression of a strong, latent frame of mind, a characteristic attitude, I believe, on the part of a very introspective individual. The water that surrounds the island is not the River Jordan, but the Styx. The scoring, the consummate skill with which the *Dies Irae*, for instance, is employed, cannot easily be described in print. There is remarkable psychological as well as technical relation between the different sections of the tone poem. Has Rachmaninoff ever been more successful in putting himself upon paper? We should hear other of his works in the larger forms.

The concerto, too, is strong, having similar hallmarks, but widely differing in its construction. The themes, which are cheap in more than one instance, usually have vigor and well-defined contrast. The piece is a monumental example of effective writing for the solo instrument combined with the orchestra. The first movement is especially effective, but there is more than the lust of conquest in these pages. There are beauty and imagination that go far to redeem an occasional sterile or commonplace passage. Mr. Rachmaninoff played as he conducted, with a technique ample to meet the big demands of the work, with a sureness and conviction and enthusiasm that carried all before it. He received an ovation after the last movement.

A Symphony by Halm, a Tone Poem by Strauss

**"The drab music served admirably to set off the
flaming masterpiece of Strauss."**

THE twenty-third public rehearsal of the Symphony Orchestra yesterday afternoon in Symphony Hall. The program: Symphony for Strings, August Halm (first time in America); tone poem, *Don Quixote*, Richard Strauss; Overture, Scherzo, Nocturne, and Wedding March from incidental music to *A Midsummer Night's Dream*, Mendelssohn.

There are a number of good ideas in August Halm's Symphony for Strings, ideas which are most likely to come when the composer stumbles upon them in the course of his journey—"findings," as the French put it. But the symphony is too long and monotonous in its character. Halm may well be praised for the continence of his harmonic style in these days of ear-splitting dissonance, and this was not a little, for the drab music served admirably to set off the flaming masterpiece of Strauss.

Don Quixote has been given once before in this city. It is perhaps the least popular and well known of the great symphonic poems. It is also, perhaps, the most remarkable and individual of them all—a quintessence of the Strauss that has sprawled all over the musical horizon for the time being. The performance yesterday afternoon had much to do with the exceptional appreciation and enthusiasm of the audience. In 1904 Mr. Gericke gave a most musicianly, and in many respects a highly poetical, reading of the monumental work. But we believe that Mr. Fiedler made the music heard more nearly as it passed from the composer's brain. It was notable, too, that in contradistinction to too many recent concerts, the performance was remarkable for its clarity, its balance, and its suggestion; its avoidance of the ultra-realism which has been read into this music. The bleating of the sheep, for instance, was by no

22

means as prominent as on the former occasion—it was merely a small detail, one of many, in a magnificent picture.

And how differently we looked at things yesterday, after an interval of only six years! We even wasted breath then over the poor wind machine. The variation in which that instrument is employed —the flight through the air—is one of the most superb flights of fantasy in one of the most vivid and imaginative compositions in existence. Then recall the variation wherein the Don orates upon chivalry, and the crazy rapture introduced by the harp. The opening pages, it has been well said, are absolutely uncanny in their psychology—the knight going mad. There is another page—where Don Quixote, in a passage of sweeping glory, silences his commonplace squire's objections to chivalry. This is so truly noble, so ardent in the cause of all that is most high, that it may well bring tears to the eyes of those who cherish the truth. The final passages are not less uplifting. They could come only from the man who created the apotheosis in *Tod und Verklärung*.

This performance was one of the greatest that Mr. Fiedler has given in this city. Mr. Warnke gave an exceedingly eloquent interpretation of the very difficult cello part, and one would go far to find the equal of Mr. Ferir, the violist. But why was not the name of the tenor tuba, also, preserved to fame?

APRIL 14, 1911

Two New Americans' Compositions Are Heard

One Has Ten Times the Vitality of the Other

THE twenty-second public rehearsal of the Boston Symphony Orchestra yesterday afternoon in Symphony Hall presented a program of unusual significance, and enthusiasm ran high: the prelude to *Parsifal*; Rachmaninoff's masterpiece, *The Isle of the Dead*, after the celebrated picture of Arnold Böcklin; a *Suite symphonique*, by George W. Chadwick, and Henry F. Gilbert's *Comedy Overture on Negro Themes*, both latter compositions played from manuscript for the first time in this city. Music of an old and a young continent, and music that reflected very clearly its national as well as artistic origin. It is good to say that both of the new compositions by composers resident in Boston and in Cambridge were welcomed with great acclaim. Mr. Chadwick, who conducted his own work, was recalled three or four times. Mr. Gilbert was long in appearing, but the audience, which usually flies to the doors at the sound of the last chord, stayed and applauded until after many minutes the composer bowed from the stage.

The *Parsifal* prelude was given a very impressive performance, and so was Rachmaninoff's tone poem, which now seems one of the great masterpieces of modern music. This piece is superb in its proportions and in the masterly development of the material, the big lines of the structure, and the splendid continuity of the thought. Moreover, and in spite of his formal achievements, Rachmaninoff has written as freely as though he were improvising alone before the great picture of Böcklin. The emotional current is continuous, the expression of moods that vary from human terror and protest to the most exalted hope and faith and the loftiest contemplation. The composition is colored with wonderful richness and "atmosphere," and its form is so tremendous, so durable, that it seems as though the tone poem should live for a thousand years. When Böcklin had finished the second sketch of his *Todteninsel*, at the wish of the Countess Marie von Oriola, he wrote her that his picture "must produce such an effect of stillness that anyone would be frightened to hear a knock on the door." Rachmaninoff has captured this mood with unexplainable success. A moment during the performance might have been prolonged. This was at the place where after immense surges of tone the orchestra subsides, a horn emerges from the mass of rich sound with a single note, sustained very softly, and then the violas take up this note and from it commence to vibrate with indescribable effect the *Dies irae*. This motive is used throughout the composition in a number of forms and with exceeding effect.

Mr. Chadwick's *Suite symphonique* took the prize of $700 for an orchestral composition offered by the National Federation of Music Clubs, which was awarded last month. The suite was first performed in Philadelphia on the 29th of last March. The suite is in four movements, and it is on the same lines as the *Symphonic Sketches*, first played here under Dr. Muck, in which Mr. Chadwick accomplished what he has tried to accomplish in the composition heard yesterday. The *Suite symphonique* is the pale ghost of the *Symphonic Sketches*. It is hollow. The orchestration is skillful, but it does not suffice to conceal a lack of potential musical ideas. One of Mr. Chadwick's most valuable attributes has been his strong native vein of humor and a healthy, rather sentimental sentiment. In this suite the humor is either not humor or it is broad farce. The second movement consists of the smooth evolving of a theme which has superficial characteristics of Scottish folk music, mixed up inexplicably with other material in the form of an intermezzo that is Oriental in character.

Mr. Chadwick probably had his own ideas and good reasons for inserting this contrasting section, but the reasons are not obvious or admissible at a first hearing. The first and third movements of this suite are labored. In the last movement there are occasionally delightful passages, but it is not the opinion of this writer that the composition increases Mr. Chadwick's reputation as a composer.

Next, Mr. Gilbert's *Comedy Overture*—a different story. This overture has ten times the vitality of the work which preceded it, but, as Mr. Chadwick has dressed to the utmost advantage—at least as far as instrumentation is concerned—things which as a rule are impotent, Mr. Gilbert, choking with enthusiasm and sheer musical feeling, has not been entirely happy in welding together the different sections of his overture, in balancing and juxtaposing them. It should be remembered that this overture was not originally intended as a concert number. It was conceived as a prelude to an operetta based upon the charming "Uncle Remus" folk tales of Joel Chandler Harris, and it was—it is, to a certain degree—a potpourri of folk tunes of America. Yet this does not wholly excuse sins of omission and commission. Mr. Gilbert, thanks to Mr. Fiedler's initiative, will hear his music played and he will rapidly gain the faculty of presenting his ideas in their best light.

But it may be said that this work amply sustains Mr. Gilbert in his faith in the availability of the folk music of this country for artistic treatment, and that, in spite of its defects, it appeared to make an excellent impression yesterday. No wonder!

The humor of the opening theme is irresistible; perhaps Mr. Gilbert's humor, also, is a little broad in the rollicking imitations of the theme by the brass. Yet this ripping humor, and the romance, and the real pathos of the theme that used to be sung, according to the composer, by the stevedores and "roustabouts" on the Mississippi, are exceedingly potential and worthy of extended treatment. The composition is bursting with the most exuberant life and energy. Its laughter is reckless and unpolished; its poetry of haunting sweetness. There is then the vigorous fugal treatment of the first theme in "ragtime" rhythm, and the golden proclamation by the brass when the fugue reaches its climax. This is indeed a splendid burst, though it could be scored with still more splendor and sonority. The recapitulation is telling but not well proportioned, and, as the overture stands, there is perhaps too much insistence upon the stirring opening theme—a theme which might well stand as it is if the rest of the overture were better balanced.

When all is said and done, however, Mr. Gilbert has written a piece well worthy of a hearing on a symphony program. It is always the case that we appreciate least what is closest to us, and so a composer who dares to employ a tune of frankly "ragtime" quality may lay himself open to censure. But it would be interesting to compare this tune with the best folk tunes of Europe, which are so frequently treated by European composers, and see which melodies had the most inherent strength.

JULY 29, 1911

═══

Der Rosenkavalier: Two Years Before It Reached the U.S.

"The new thing is not Strauss's music, but his humor."

IT IS necessary to consider briefly the material of the important music dramas which precede *The Rose Cavalier*: *Feuersnot* (1904), *Salome* (1905), *Elektra* (1909). Each of these operas is in one act, in contradiction to Stauss's early operatic experiment, *Guntram*, which is in three. The sweeping, triumphant motive of *Feuersnot* is the arch-romanticism of Kunrad—or of Richard Strauss, for Strauss is there, standing behind his hero. Village burghers and German folk music make the frame for Kunrad's overwhelming desire, form the prelude for his passionate monologue in the darkness that he has brought on by enchantment, and merge into the accompaniment of his glorification by fire. As for *Salome,* Wilde had arranged matters in advance. Never was there a finer libretto, and Strauss found it practically made to his hand. Against the figure of the beautiful princess of Judea and her transcendent passion—and her garment, the Oriental night—is set that of John the Baptist, the "whited sepulcher," as the woman calls him; and, more in the background, the neurotic Herod, his evil nagging Queen, the quarrelsome Jews, the young Narraboth and his untimely death. There then rises in tremendous grandeur the fate-haunted Elektra, surrounded by her blooming sister, the brother who was but the messenger of the gods, and again a queen and king in decay. All of these operas moved straight and swift as an arrow to their climaxes. In *Elektra* Strauss achieved greater heights than in *Salome,* but whether he maintained them uniformly is matter for serious questioning. It may be that the greatness and intensity of his subject threw even Strauss somewhat from his artistic balance. It is certain, at least, that he found voice inadequate for what he had to say, and that after passages of Swinburnian lyricism in *Salome* he resorted again to a complexity and a predominance of orchestral writing which would seem to put *Elektra* back among the symphonic poems.

So much up to the year 1911. In every one of his later operas Strauss discovered new musical expressions and contributed immensely to modern musical development. What can one say of his fourth opera (or his fifth if the early *Guntram,* on Wagnerian lines, is included in the count)?

As Hofmannsthal, Strauss's librettist, turned from the stern and terrible spirits that he had evoked in *Elektra,* so Strauss, recoiling from his encounter with the fates, has devoted his genius to the musical interpretation of a comedy of manners which has for its piquant setting Vienna of the early eighteenth century. This comedy offers a series of very adroit and diverting situations and much excellent dialogue, although Hofmannsthal's comedy is a little marred by exaggeration, overdrawing, a fault not entirely absent from *Elektra.* But what Strauss has to work with is, on the whole, an excellent libretto; the plot, of the order dear to Beaumarchais, makes no overwhelming demands on some subjective phase of the composer's personality, but does give the freest play to his extraordinary descriptive technique, his excess, if anything, of humor which is of Rabelais and of Mozart, and his uncanny appreciation of human nature. This opera is not a symphonic poem, or anything like it. In its musical style, as well as in its dramatic content, it harks back to such works as *Don Giovanni* and *The Marriage of Figaro*. It is in three acts, and the characters are drawn for the ear as well as the eye—from the outside. The composer is to treat not of himself, but of three characters of the first importance, several of the second, and a number of minor personalities who have each their word. We are to watch human nature, the view entirely unobstructed by a creative personality. Strauss in this last opera employs an orchestra nearly as large as the orchestras used in his former works for the stage, but he handles his instruments, as a general rule, with far more economy and restraint.

An ardent love scene between the Princess von Werdenberg—whose husband is absent—and the youthful Octavian opens the opera. Presently appears the Princess's cousin, Baron Ochs von Lerchenau, a pompous old noble and a libertine. He has determined to mend his fortunes by an alliance with Sophie, daughter of the rich merchant Faninal, and he has come to ask the Princess's advice relative to the choice of a Rose Cavalier—one who, in accordance with the custom of the time, shall carry a silver rose to the betrothed as an emblem of love. Octavian has, in the meanwhile, assumed the disguise of a maid, and the Baron, seeing the newcomer, promptly begins a flirtation and succeeds in arranging for a future meeting. The Princess recommends a certain young friend of hers—no other than Octavian—as Rose Cavalier, and the Baron, before departing, leaves the rose to be given to him.

Octavian presents Sophie with the rose and she promptly falls in love with him, her sentiments being duly reciprocated. The Baron displeases everyone by his coarse manners, and eventually Octavian, in the course of a violent dispute, stabs him slightly in the arm. Octavian is unceremoniously sent away and Ochs departs to keep his appointment with the supposed maid. The meeting duly takes place, but certain of the Baron's domestics and creditors, whom he has neglected to pay, have their revenge and interrupt the love scene in a comical way. The police appear and, with the arrival of Faninal, matters are straightened out. Ochs's engagement to Sophie is broken. In his stead, Octavian wins Sophie's hand, and the Princess regretfully renounces all pretensions to his love.

These are the incidents of the comedy. It does not seem unwise, upon comparatively little evidence, to say that Strauss has woven about them a score which, if only as a feat of the finest virtuosity, must command the admiration of musicians and of any who are at all susceptible to the effect of music heard in relation to drama on the stage. Even the bare and comparative_y meaningless piano score is full of felicitous character-sketching and the most witty and epigrammatic musical comment. Here Strauss can indulge as never before his faculty for the vivid and relentless outlinir᷒ ϳf character in a few strokes of the pen: the Princess, both patrician and sentimental, and noble at heart; Octavian, an easier cha acter; the naïve and charming Sophie; the brutish Ochs, who, indeed, is unmercifully treated by both librettist and composer; the gossiping Valzacchi; the mellifluous tenor who warbles some Mendelssohnish phrases to the accompaniment of a flute cadenza; the whole human comedy flashes by. Strauss, as we have said, in former operas united, with wonderful felicity, music and drama. In his latest work he has put his music absolutely at the service of the stage. He will break up the most promising phrase unless it is the exact and complete revelation of the moment. His virtuosity in the employment of the waltzes, minuets, etc., might have been expected. But unless one had borne in mind such early works as his octet for wind instruments and some phrases of *Till Eulenspiegel* and of *Don Quixote*, he could hardly have been prepared for the most fortunate lyric invention, to say nothing of humor that bubbles or fizzes or—and we say it sometimes with regret—laughs a horselaugh of the most unbuttoned, Rabelaisian variety.

The Rose Cavalier, however, so far as reading goes, seems more remarkable for newness of style than newness of themes. This does not in the least imply that the music lacks point or vitality, any more than the fact that Stevenson wrote in the same tongue as Thomas Hardy would imply that either man lacked ideas. Strauss has, it may be said in passing, brought music closer to literature than any other composer up to his time, and he has evolved a prose of marvelous force and richness and flexibility. In each one of his earlier operas Strauss treated of a subject which appealed to him strongly on subjective grounds. In every case, up to *The Rose Cavalier*, new subjects evoked new musical thoughts, which in turn begot new technique as their inevitable manner of expression. *The Rose Cavalier* stands square on the shoulders of the operas which preceded it, but in its musical material pure and simple, it seems a summing-up and an amplifying of all that Strauss discovered in those operas, rather than the birth of newly created music. In its operatic style it is nearer *Feuersnot* than the celebrated works which came later. Certain melodic fragments may be traced to the lyric music of *Salome*, although in these instances Strauss has skillfully withdrawn the flavor of the eroticism that glows in the latter opera. Nor, probably, would the motive of the silver rose—a curious and exotically colored succession of chords that flash about for a passing instant in unrelated tonalities—have been as it is had not Strauss written the strange, cross-related harmonies that he penned when he thought of death and fate in *Elektra*. It seems paradoxical, in fact, to find a number of those grim progressions gaily employed in comedy. There is a highly humorous instance in act two when the Baron, holding converse with Sophie, proclaims his disgust for certain homely virtues, over rasping harmonies like those which accompany Elektra's first appearance on the stage and her terrified spring backward. The music of *The Rose Cavalier* acknowledges all these origins. In addition, Strauss has further enriched his vocabulary by the invention of melodies designedly Mozart-like in style, astonishingly fresh and simple in outline and harmony. And Strauss has never been happier in his treatment of voices. His characters really converse. The inflection of the voices, in many instances of ensemble, seems absolutely spontaneous and as natural as the feeling supposed to be represented—which of course it is not, the phrases having been fashioned with the greatest care. If there is anything really new in *The Rose Cavalier*, it is this. In the second act, for instance, Sophie, fresh from a convent and waiting innocently for her bridegroom to appear, voices her emotions in a manner that is almost laughably naïve and genuine. Shortly afterward comes the rapturous duet with Octavian, which should prove one of the finest moments of the opera. It is late in the day for such objections, and yet there are those living who will claim, in spite of the songs and many other works and passages in all the works of Strauss, that he cannot write melody. In *The Rose Cavalier* Strauss has often set to work deliberately to write melody, though this melody must disappear the instant that dramatic requirements command. It can hardly be denied that he has succeeded. The opening scene of the opera, and the scene at the last between Octavian, Sophie, and the Princess, are surely pretty strong evidence of that fact.

Yet the importance of Strauss's latest music lies not nearly so much in this as in the other fact of his newest artistic attitude. Strauss employs musical phrases as we employ verbal phrases and adjectives. Adjectives have their equivalents and their slight variations of meaning. Strauss, born littérateur that he is, knows thoroughly the dangers and the virtues of alliteration, of rhyme, of blank verse, and all the other devices of literary workmanship. He employs such devices, in music, with incredible ingenuity and force. The greatest authors in the world use the same words a great many times. It is not necessary, in the least, to claim that as absolute music the music of Strauss is new. As a matter of fact, much of it is, though scarcely any of it is new in the sense that Chopin, Debussy, Mozart are new. The new thing in *The Rose Cavalier* is not Strauss's music, but his humor, his wide humanity, and his expression of those qualities of himself. The significance of Strauss is greater, not lesser, because he is cultivating, not a fresh kind of melody, but a fresh art—and where is there today an art of similar dimensions and possibilities?

OCTOBER 21, 1912

Mme Calvé in Recital with Her Husband

"The true and final test of conjugal affection"

MME EMMA CALVÉ, assisted by her husband, Galileo Gaspari, tenor, and Emiliano Renaud, pianist, gave a concert yesterday afternoon in Symphony Hall. Mme Calvé sang the stances of *Sappho*; the Habañera from *Carmen*; "*In questa tomba*," Beethoven; some old French folk songs; and, with Mr. Gaspari, the duet from the second act of *Carmen*, and the scene from *Cavalleria Rusticana* between Turiddu and Santuzza, the scene which begins with Turriddu's exclamation, "*Tu qui, Santuzza.*"

The concert was well attended and the audience enthusiastic, as it is sure to be on such occasions. Mme Calvé, when she is in the vein and chooses to prove herself, is well nigh incomparable as an interpreter of music of dramatic or sensuous appeal. Her singing

31

was very uneven yesterday afternoon, nor was this to be wondered
at. The ensemble performance must have disconcerted her, as her
support was anything but adequate. A concert with a tenor husband, especially when this tenor whoops as Mr. Gaspari whooped,
for instance, in that telling moment of the final duet—such a concert must indeed be the true and final test of conjugal affection.

Mme Calvé sang the stances from *Sappho* with a breadth and
grandeur of style which recompensed for much. The music is impressive only when it is sung in this manner, and but few singers
now before the public can do it justice. Then there were the French
folk songs, which Mme Calvé has made especially her own, which
she sang with her customary eloquence, and which display to such
advantage the various registers of her voice. As sung by her, these
songs stand in the memory. Mme Calvé, with her usual graciousness, added half a dozen encores. Mr. Renaud opened the concert
with a Tchaikovsky-Liszt Polonaise, of which he gave a brilliant performance. Some might differ with his treatment of the Schumann
Toccata. He played the Liszt *Légende, St. Francis de Paule,* with the
appropriate coloring, and in response to hearty applause he added
a pleasing encore.

NOVEMBER 16, 1912

Dr. Muck Conducts the Sibelius First

It Dwarfs the Rest of the Program

A GREAT work was given yesterday afternoon in Symphony Hall—a
memorable performance—and the music made an ineffaceable impression. This was the First Symphony of Sibelius, which Dr. Muck
had already introduced here with pronounced success in the season
of 1907–8. The program of the fifth public rehearsal of the Boston
Symphony Orchestra also included Tchaikovsky's rarely heard
Piano Concerto in G major, played by George Proctor; an *Overture solenelle,* by Glazounoff, an empty and brave-sounding piece,
and Chabrier's orchestral rhapsody on Spanish dance tunes, *España.*

This is a veritable conflagration of genius, yet the second half of the program, interesting as it was, was dwarfed by the first. Chabrier's remarkable piece would have been heard to far greater advantage in other surroundings, and earlier in the afternoon. Tchaikovsky's concerto and its musicianly performance came as an anti-climax.

In speaking of music such as this symphony and other orchestral music of Sibelius, it is difficult to avoid superlatives, and superlatives are not needed in the defense of music which is so rapidly coming into its own, and which will be so firmly established on all orchestral programs a decade hence.

This man happens to be a Finn, but he is a patriot for all the world. He lives in the north. So do others, but they have not caught its accents primeval. Others have diverse matters of which to speak. Sibelius is only himself, and his birthright. Few, indeed, can boast so grand a heritage, such a wealth of melody, mastery of material, originality of style.

There are those who will be offended by the uncompromising strength, the brutal directness, lack of courtesy, in this music. It is certain that Sibelius did not think of a rondo or minuet when he wrote the two last movements of the First Symphony, music as wild and fantastical as music could well be. The orchestra rages or exults savagely. Far indeed from evening dress and Symphony Hall.

This symphony flies by as though it were composed in one breath. Movement succeeds movement, as it were, in one breathless haste. There is so much to be said, there is such necessity for saying it; for the composer is in deadly earnest. Then there is the exceeding freshness and pungency of coloring. Think of the moment when the second theme of the first movement appears, a gleam of light in the gloom. There the violins, in a high register, shimmer out, and the harp supplies an unusually rhythmed accompaniment, while the lovely tripping phrase smiles through. This short and unambitious theme is in itself a conclusive demonstration of genius. And so are the measures immediately following, as, in accordance with a formula of long standing, the wind instruments call to each other with fragments of the first theme. The means are orthodox, the result unbelievably elemental. Then the brass instruments storm and protest among themselves. There are the sudden bursts of that intense brilliance which is surely one of the characteristics of northern landscapes. There is the bleak song of the clarinet, over the rolling drums, that opens the work, and the wild, headlong rush, the rhythmic shock of the first theme.

This symphony is not quite so matured and individual a piece as the Second Symphony of Sibelius. There the idiom is still more personal. In the First Symphony there are passages in the development of the melodies evidently culled from textbooks. They are few, and they give place quickly to whole new conceptions, passages that are like great nuggets of new precious metal. Consider the slow movement, and its dramatic climax; the barbaric scherzo; the mad vigor of the finale, with its alternating theme, lovely and simple, a little orthodox in its curve, wholly unorthodox in its unfolding and its remarkable orchestral coloring. The last movement is, of the four, probably the finest, irresistible in its sweep and power, grandly tragic, the climax of all that has gone before. No wonder that Dr. Muck was recalled.

Mr. Proctor's performance was creditable to him as a pianist and as a musician, and this was especially the case in the last two movements of the concerto. He sang the sensuous melody of the middle movement with sentiment that gave the phrases genuine appeal, yet avoided the dangerous approach to sentimentality which is inherent in this music. The finale was exciting and Mr. Proctor was recalled.

The performance of Chabrier's piece was on the same remarkable level as the remainder of the program, and Dr. Muck is to be greatly thanked for introducing the music of both Chabrier and Sibelius in Boston.

NOVEMBER 1912

Harvard Musical Review

American Composers and Critics Take Stock from Schoenberg to "Ragtime"

THE second issue of the *Harvard Musical Review* for November contains leading articles by Edward Burlingham Hill '94, "Modern Music and Its Critics"; George A. Burdett '81, "A Russian Duet";

Gilbert Elliott, Jr., '13, "Modern Music and the Young American"; S. Foster Damon '13, "Modern Popular Music." There is published a song, *Stanzas of Music*, a setting of the lines of Lord Byron, by George Foote '08. In addition to the customary editorials, there are reviews of Arnold Schoenberg's *Harmonie-Lehrer*, published last year in Vienna and Leipsig; of Massenet's entertaining memoirs, *Mes Souvenirs*; of Oliver Hueckel's English version of the text of *Die Meistersinger*. As a frontispiece, there is a late and interesting picture of Claude-Achille Debussy.

Mr. Hill summarizes the most recent and important manifestations in modern music. He then discusses the desirable attitude of the critic of today toward these developments. He finds that contemporaneous musical criticism is considerably broader in its scope and character than in former years. But there are stragglers in the procession. These, unhonored and unnamed, are gently castigated. Mr. Hill, himself a reviewer of the highest reputation, believes that the critic should be more objective, more respectful in his attitude toward those composers who are masters of their craft, possible prophets for future generations. "For the critic's profession in its intrinsic nature is assimilative." So is the composer's until he commences to compose. So is a critic's until he sits down to formulate his criticism. Criticism, of course, has value only in ratio to the strength and distinction of its subjective element. It would be interesting to discuss this article at greater length than is now possible.

Mr. Elliott considers the possible future of the young American composer. He draws attention to the uncommon breadth of his horizon, the catholicity of his taste. The point may well be emphasized. The greatest asset of the American composer, as well as the American critic, is the cosmopolitanism of his education, the freshness of his point of view.

Mr. Damon's article on modern popular music takes up an important phase of the same question: the popular music of America and of other countries. Mr. Damon makes only passing mention of what is, in fact, the most promising sign of American musical independence which has yet appeared: Henry F. Gilbert's *Comedy Overture on Negro Themes*. Here is the rollicking humor, the nervous energy of the race; here is the great poetry of a new land. Mr. Damon quotes the definition of "ragtime," an inadequate definition in an inadequate work—*Grove's Dictionary of Music and Musicians*, edition of 1908—as "covering the ground pretty well." An adequate inquiry into the nature, origins, and development of ragtime has yet to be written, and, if written ably, would be read with interest and treasured in the archives of those who thirst for information on this question.

And what will Mr. Hill say to George B. Weston's review of Schoenberg's harmony lexicon? Mr. Weston quotes several ingeniously horrible chords which appear to support his argument sufficiently well. Yet, as absurd as these chords seem, we side somewhat with Mr. Hill on this matter. We would like to know more of Mr. Schoenberg, for he has not been downed, up to this time, by either critics or publishers; he has lasted some years in Austria and Germany, has recently crossed the English Channel, and has now aroused the curiosity of America.

The second issue of this magazine is a decided advance on the first. The editors have before them an exceptional opportunity. The *Harvard Musical Review* is an auspicious sign of the flourishing state of the music division of this university. Its editorial policies will be subject to no outside influences of any kind. There is free field for the zealous discussion of living musical issues; and the Division of Music at Harvard is a large one, with many promising members. In addition to those who have already published, there are doubtless many yet to be heard from—young men with ideas and convictions. Young men should be formidable. A more subjective attitude in these articles would be approved by us, if not by Mr. Hill (!), even if this were necessarily at the expense of the soundest premises and correctness of style.

There is doubtless material in plenty for the waiting presses, and the readers of the magazine will look forward to issues which will present matter of constantly increasing interest and value.

Kreisler Plays the Beethoven Concerto

"Then the violin sang like ten instruments instead of one."

THE feature of the public rehearsal of the Boston Symphony Orchestra yesterday afternoon in Symphony Hall was Fritz Kreisler's memorable performance of the Beethoven Violin Concerto. This was surely one of the greatest interpretations of the work which have been given in Symphony Hall. More than ever was Mr. Kreisler's supremacy as an artist impressed upon the listener; higher than ever he rose in the esteem of a public which has long welcomed him. The violinist was delayed in beginning the second movement, on account of the storm of applause which broke out as soon as he had stopped for an instant. His reading was as virile and as true in its sentiment as could possibly be desired; it was a reverent interpretation of a masterpiece; yet it was also notably subjective, the expression of a great artist deeply versed in classic interpretation, but with something of his own to say.

Mr. Kreisler's performance must stand at the head of his achievements in Boston. Technically it was, of course, thoroughly finished, with always the suggestion of reserve force and dexterity, but the playing of the cadenza may well have appeared to many the culminating point of this performance. The part-playing was a marvel of virtuosity and musical feeling. Then the violin sang like ten instruments instead of one, and this portion of the movement became, as it should be but as it rarely is, the magnificent capstone of the whole structure. The slow movement was nobly sung. Sentiment of the loftiest, simple and pervasive enough to make every hearer akin. And not the least part of this performance was Dr. Muck's accompaniment, played as by brothers-in-arms, directed as if Dr. Muck had done nothing but rehearse with Mr. Kreisler for the last fortnight. At his first performance of this concerto this season with the orchestra in another city, there was no rehearsal at all.

The program, a goodly program, was cordially applauded. No symphonic music is more dramatic than Beethoven's Third

"Leonore" Overture. In few of his pages has Mozart surpassed the musical interest and finish of workmanship which he displayed in the finale of the "Jupiter" Symphony. Dr. Muck respects the period and the school of this music, yet he, like other progressive conductors of today, finds this music full-blooded, masculine in its character, despite its grace, ravishing the ears with the purity of its orchestral coloring.

NOVEMBER 27, 1912

The Boston Opera Opens with Offenbach

"A most happy choice"

THE opening of the fourth season of the Boston Opera Company last night at the Boston Opera House easily takes rank as the most significant and successful first night in the history of the institution. *The Tales of Hoffmann*, the work chosen for the intial performance, was a happy choice on account of its unique qualities and its popular appeal. The manner in which it was mounted offered something wholly new in opera in this country, and the performance was an earnest of equally fine things to come. The cast follows:

Hoffmann	Edmond Clément
Lindorf, Coppelius, Dappertutto, Dr. Miracle	Vanni Marcoux
Spalanzani	Ernesto Giaccone
Maître Luther	A. Sillich
Crespel	Ramon Blanchart
Andrès, Cochenille, Pitichinaccio, Frantz	Luigi Cilla
Nathanael	Paul Saldaigne
Hermann, Schlemil	Edgard Bourquin
Stella	Myrna Sharlow
Giulietta	Elizabeth Amsden
Olympia	Bernice Fisher
Antonia	Louise Edvina
Nicklausse	Elvira Leveroni

Grand Corps de Ballet
Conductor, André Caplet

No opera could have been better chosen to represent at its best the remarkable art of Josef Urban, the new stage director at the Boston Opera House. *The Tales of Hoffmann* is a "fantastic" opera in the fullest meaning of the word. It consists of a prologue, three acts, and an epilogue, the three acts connected, apparently, only by the figures of Hoffmann and his servant, Nicklausse. But in reality these acts have the closest affinities. Although the relation is now generally understood by the public, this relation has never been so remarkably set forth on the stage; nor have there often been presented on the operatic stage in this city such marvelous harmonies of color. Only a master could have juxtaposed the magnificent colors in the Venetian scene with such superb effect, nor were the other scenes a whit below this so far as the entire success in the carrying out of the artistic conception was concerned.

Mr. Caplet had collaborated thoughtfully with Mr. Urban in presenting the work, and thus for the first time the active work of production had gone on under the intelligent and co-operative labors of two principal heads. The result was evidence indeed of the success of the method. There were, of course, the usual features of an opening night. In this instance, its social and artistic brilliancy was especially notable.

This opera is remarkable for many things, but principal among them are the extraordinary effects gained by the simplest means. There are few composers who excel Offenbach, when he is at his best, in this. With a tap of the drum he can evoke awe and terror, and a note of the horn, if you are listening, will evoke for you more moonlight than whole pages of orchestral splurge by modern masters. The same thing is true of the voice parts. How simple and unsophisticated the melodic curve, yet how characteristic of the individual and his expression of the moment.

Offenbach's opera is to be taken far more seriously than many more pretentious masterpieces, and yet, at the same time, it is inexhaustibly entertaining. This happy union of two elements seems almost to have been lost with Offenbach and his generation.

The libretto of *The Tales of Hoffmann*—two of the scenes being laid in no specific period, and one in no specific period or place— gives the stage manager every possible opportunity. He is unhampered by traditions. Mr. Urban's scenery made an immediate and unforgettable effect. The scene in the wine cellar was not merely typical of a German wine cellar of former days, it was a poetic harmony of many striking or subdued colors, like a picture by some Dutch master. The daring and consummate skill with which colors that might have been supposed to be antagonistic were brought together wrought a result that was one of the greatest possible pleasures for the eye.

The casting offered Mr. Marcoux exceptional opportunities as an actor and as a singer in his various roles of Lindorf, Coppelius, Dappertutto, and Dr. Miracle. As Coppelius he was a crabbed, fantastic figure, at once ridiculous and sinister. But it was as Dr. Miracle, clad in a black robe, with white head and his supernatural height, that he made an unforgettable impression. This was, in fact, Death, and the worm was his brother. Miracle danced a fiendish fandango and rattled his vials of poison in the face of the horror-stricken Crespel. Nor must there be forgotten the manner in which this dark figure melted into a fearful shadow in one corner of the room, nor the sudden appearances and disappearances from the scene: through the windows, the walls, the doors, from nowhere he started out, and he disappeared as a shadow itself through the casement. And finally the figure which crept behind the unhappy Antonia while a voice as from her own soul hurried her to her end.

Mr. Clément took the part of Hoffmann with a distinction which had been expected of him. His facial expression and his sensitive gestures were a quick index to his inner state. Mr. Clément was invariably the master of his idiom, a distinguished artist who found the inflection and the color for every musical phrase.

Miss Fisher as Olympia did herself exceeding credit, and Miss Amsden was an appropriately sumptuous figure as the courtesan of the second act.

Mme Edvina's voice has a girlish quality which becomes the part of Antonia, and the climax of the act found her a dramatic exponent.

These and other parts were taken in a manner to do the greatest justice to the excellent supervision of all parts of the operatic productions which go forward under Mr. Russell. The incisive orchestral performance, with Mr. Urban's splendid stage pictures and the charm of the new opera added to the repertoire, made a most auspicious opening of the new season.

Mary Garden Is Seen as Tosca

"... will cause considerable discussion in this amiable
and respectable city"

AN OPERA of viciously realistic type, by a modern Italian composer,
was given last night at the Boston Opera House, and the three principal parts were taken by artists of the French school of acting and
singing. This had a very pronounced effect upon the character of
the performance. The opera was Puccini's *Tosca*; the principals
were Mary Garden, Charles Dalmorès, and Vanni Marcoux. The
performance was swift and terrible. No one who was present will
forget it. Some will remember it unpleasantly. As the composer set
out with sensational aims, the performers cannot be fairly accused
of similar purposes. They were carrying out to the fullest possible
extent the intentions of the originators of the music drama, and
their art was so great that in spite of its horrible realism it was as
subtle as it was brutal and sweeping in its dramatic power.

Those present supped their fill of horrors by the time that the
second act came to an end. After the curtain fell, half of the audience split their gloves in admiration of the superb performances on
the stage and the other half still sat, past speech, breathless, as they
had been through the entire act.

Three rare artists understood each other thoroughly. More unity
of intention, more masterly collaboration on the stage, would hardly
have been possible. So that as the drama progressed it gained continually in atmosphere and momentum. At last it seemed that the
actors had been borne out of themselves, that they, like their audience, were in the grip of frightful and overmastering emotions. As
an example of realistic dramatic art, then, this performance was almost incomparable.

Everything—song was the least consideration—was sacrificed
wholly and entirely to dramatic effect. Mr. Marcoux was the cold
and terrific Scarpia in the flesh, the distinguished voluptuary and
tyrant at whose voice Rome trembled, and Mr. Dalmorès was the

most youthful, impetuous, and heroic Cavaradossi that has been seen on the Boston stage. Meanwhile Miss Garden, never more beautiful, never such a mistress of tragedy, tore traditions to tatters and threw to the winds the precepts of singing teachers. To a public grown finical and avaricious of new sensations, she gave more sensations in the course of an act than the majority of them had experienced, in all probability, in the course of months of opera-going.

Tosca is a work of genius. In it Puccini has expressed, probably for the first time in music, actual physical pain, the actual throb of tortured flesh. This is one of the things that he has accomplished; therefore, *Tosca*, in one sense, at least, stands by itself in the literature of music drama. Others have written strange music, but for elementary brutality, expressed in sound, commend us to this monstrous, masterly score.

The opera—or melodrama—was given for all it was worth. Miss Garden's Tosca, which she sang for the first time in Paris last summer, was, as might well have been expected, quite a new conception. This Tosca was, in the first place, more of a French than an Italian woman. She might be, according to Sardou, an empty bauble of fate, but if she was vain, trivial, and capricious, she had also elemental passions, quickly roused. And so the first scene with Cavaradossi was more than a scene of accusation and coquetry. When Tosca saw, as she supposed, the features of her rival on the canvas, a storm of passion was loosed and the woman was elemental in her rage. In the second act it was the extraordinary grandness and dignity, the classic greatness of gesture and poise on the part of Miss Garden that lifted a scene which is so revolting and so sordid in its nature to a height of great tragedy. Even in the most physical moments there was felt pity for a tortured woman, and a certain grandeur in suffering. Even in its intense realism and a certain theatrical quality essentially French, this figure on the stage was like a figure out of the great old French tragedies.

Miss Garden did all that could possibly be done to make the *"Vissi d'arte"* a logical resting-point for the drama. She did give it meaning and exceptional significance, and Mr. Marcoux made the moment the more plausible. The song is a wretched sop to the public, a trap for applause, a retardation of the drama. The development of this role, the individuality of the conception, the absolute sequence and logic of it, all were beyond praise.

Mr. Marcoux's Scarpia is far greater than it was last year, although its frankness and brutality have now reached a point which will cause considerable discussion in this amiable and respectable city. Last night, according to his idea of his part, Mr. Marcoux was unsurpassable. Cruelty, power, tortured desire were writ large upon the face and the bearing of a distinguished personality, and in how masterly a manner was all this set forth! What acting, what diction, what inimitable art prevailed throughout, and made the more telling the multiplying revelations of atrociousness! Mr. Marcoux surpassed himself, and his Scarpia was one of the greatest impersonations ever seen in opera in this city.

Mr. Dalmorès—vocally the part has been far better represented here—as Cavaradossi was a youth of noble and impetuous nature, disdaining baseness, defiant of tyranny, a poet and a lover, and his scene in the second act with Scarpia must be recorded as one of the memorable scenes which have been witnessed at this theater.

Mr. Moranzoni, who conducted the orchestra, was likewise brutal, drastic, nerve-racking. The opera is of that character.

DECEMBER 12, 1912

A Rameau-Debussy Concert

With Mary Garden, George Copeland, and André Caplet

A CONCERT of the most exceptional interest was given yesterday afternoon in the Boston Opera House. Mary Garden; George Copeland, pianist; Mme Florence de Courcy; Messrs. Diaz, Lipmann, and Sampieri of the opera company took part in the performance of music by Rameau and Debussy. André Caplet conducted, and to him must be credited performances of extraordinary virtuosity and sensibility.

Miss Garden gave supreme exhibitions of her art. Back of her and of the orchestra hung a cloth of gold, with the white design of the fleur-de-lis and a counter figure in blue, and the singer, clad likewise in white, was herself as an embodiment of the angel, the

43

blessed damozel, who leaned out over the golden bar of heaven and wept for her earthly lover.

The performance of Debussy's cantata *La Demoiselle élue,* perhaps the most beautiful choral work in a small form that is known in modern music, was only one of the features of the occasion, and the performance of this luminous and exquisite music was rarely poetic. Rameau, first, was represented by his overture to *Zaïs,* music from the ballet *Les Indes galantes,* and a trio for men's voices from *Hyppolyte et Aricie.* In addition to the cantata of Debussy there was a performance of the two dances, *Danse sacrée et danse profane,* originally scored by the composer, if we remember rightly, for harp and a small number of strings, also published in a piano arrangement, and yesterday played by the strings of the orchestra, with a piano part played by Mr. Copeland.

Mr. Copeland played the piano pieces *L'Égyptienne,* by Rameau, and the two pieces of Debussy, *Hommage à Rameau* and *Pagodes,* as solos. For the orchestra there were two of the *Nocturnes*: the first, *Nuages,* and the second, *Fêtes.* Miss Garden sang two of the *Ariettes oubliées*: *C'est l'extase langoureux* and *Voici des fruits, des fleurs.* Finally, Mr. Caplet's ingenious and characteristically Debussyian orchestration of Debussy's piano suite *Children's Corner* brought the concert to an end.

Mr. Caplet had arranged this program, and he has never conducted with more distinguished success. His exceptional feeling for this music, his profound scholarship and knowledge of orchestral resources had never been revealed to such advantage. For an orchestra in its fourth year to give such performances of such music, music which is exceedingly difficult to catch in its mood and its techniques, was an achievement of which more mature conductors than Mr. Caplet might well be proud. These orchestral performances alone, especially those of the *Nocturnes,* would have made the concert memorable.

Boston *Première* of the Sibelius Fourth

"Audacity which according to at least the majority will be
ridiculous, and perhaps to a small minority sublime"

THE Fourth Symphony of Jean Sibelius was performed for the first
time in Boston yesterday afternoon at the public rehearsal of the
Boston Symphony Orchestra in Symphony Hall. This symphony is
in certain respects the most remarkable work which has yet been
produced by one of the most original and interesting composers of
the present period. It is, for instance, the extreme of northern impressionism, and this is very far from the delicate impressionism of,
let us say, a Debussy, with his tone pictures of moonshine, floating
clouds, the summer night on the sea, the rain falling in a garden.
Silbelius speaks of gray skies and silent expanses of lakes and forests, of bristling crags and winds and supernatural sounds in a wild
land. And, if he ever knew, he has now forgotten how to please.

The Fourth Symphony is the soliloquy of a man alone with
nature, bitter against fate, cursing the heavens. Sibelius had ere this
given offense by reason of the brusque and unvarnished character
of his superb music, but in this last symphony he has developed the
gentle art of making enemies to a point hitherto unsuspected by
even his most enthusiastic admirers.

The Sibelius of the Fourth Symphony is a hundred miles away
from the composer we in Boston have known up to this day, and,
bold and virile as is his earlier music, there is little in any of it that
has been heard here to account for the extremely advanced manner
of the new work. Here the composer has elaborated harmonic
idioms of his own which place him in the very vanguard of the
leading innovators of today.

Look at the work on paper and, looking, "hear" the music if you
can. There are very few indeed who will be capable of this feat.
Sibelius juxtaposes not only instruments but harmonies, not only
harmonies but keys, with a mastery and audacity which according
to at least the majority will be ridiculous, and perhaps to a small

minority sublime. His absolute mastery of his medium, at least, is apparent on every page. We have here not a young experimenter dabbling in modern effects, but a mature artist who expresses with absolute precision exactly what he wishes to say. It is easy to believe Mrs. Rosa Newmarch, quoted in the program book as remarking that the Fourth Symphony was composed in the midst of nature. We can also feel reasonably sure that there was not a grand piano handy; that the composer heard strange new harmonies which he was evidently able to put down accurately and immediately on paper. Uncompromising, powerful, and imaginative the music is.

Whether, in exchange for a surprisingly individual manner hardly hinted at before, Sibelius has not sacrificed other most valuable features of his earlier style—the splendid, long-breathed themes, the breadth and power of structure, the simple yet haunting harmonies—is a matter yet to be decided. Sufficient for the day that Dr. Muck, so far as one could judge, gave an admirable performance of a singular and most interesting work, and that to him attaches the credit of first introducing that music in this city.

DECEMBER 19, 1914

───

Schoenberg's Five Pieces for Orchestra in Boston

"Wonder and bewilderment"

YESTERDAY afternoon in Symphony Hall, at the eighth rehearsal and concert of the Boston Symphony Orchestra, Dr. Karl Muck, conductor, a polite and well-intentioned audience laughed outright as the first of Arnold Schoenberg's Five Pieces for Orchestra was played for the first time in this city. The other four pieces appeared to excite only wonder and bewilderment. After the last had come to an end, some ten isolated Schoenbergers applauded persistently for a few minutes in one corner of the hall.

Dr. Muck's gestures had spoken for themselves. He had rapped peremptorily on his conductor's desk as he opened the score. As each piece came to an end without resting on any chord familiar to anyone in the audience, he raised his baton, and proceeded without a pause and rather grimly to the next "piece." At last he bowed several times to his orchestra, as to courageous, skillful colleagues who had performed a difficult and dangerous task, and, ignoring a few well-meant handclaps from the audience, marched off the stage apparently in an unamiable frame of mind.

No one need have been surprised at this. Dr. Muck, in response to the oft-repeated persuasions of some admirers of Schoenberg, one of the latest composers to make a sensation in Europe, had finally decided to play music for which, it is said, he has little admiration, for the sake of any who might wish to hear it. The strain of the rehearsals must have been considerable, since the music is not only intricate in its rhythms and its polyphony, but also, for the most part, very ugly. That it was possible to rehearse it at all with any results is at least as much of a wonder to us as rehearsals of Richard Wagner's *Tristan and Isolde* must have seemed to nearly everyone back in the seventies.

There was much curiosity about this music, although curiosity of a rather sensational order. It was known that of all masters of discord whom Europe has produced in the last fifty years, Schoenberg was one of the most extreme in his tendencies. There had been reports of rioting in concert halls of Germany at performances of his works. In Chicago, where the Five Orchestral Pieces were performed last year, there was either amusement or, as yesterday afternoon in the lobbies, outspoken irritation with such music.

This music, for the greater part, sounds very horrible. The sonorities of the orchestra are so intense in pitch and quality that it is a physically taxing experience for the ear. At a first hearing, the only pieces which conveyed any definite impression to this reviewer were the third, an impressionistic effect of pronounced individuality and, if you can look at it that way, of a very subtle beauty; and the fourth piece, a piece which really communicates sensations of terror, or horror. The first piece appeared to ordinary ears, unattuned to the intensities of Schoenberg, simply laughable, and so it was received. The last piece was also very terrible, physically hurtful—and this is but sober statement of fact.

It should be added that at first hearing much music now accepted has seemed very ugly and very incomprehensible; that Schoenberg's music, with all its strangeness, gives the impression of sincerity and clearly defined intention on the part of the composer. Furthermore,

Schoenberg has long since proven his technical acquirements as a composer. For ourselves, we can only say that at present this music is so disagreeable that, whatever its merits, we cannot find the courage to wish to hear it again. At the best, it appears as the music of raw and tortured nerves.

For us this music, however original and masterly in workmanship, is exceedingly unhealthy and disagreeable, having neither the grandeur of cleansing tragedy nor the uplift of a great composition that makes all men akin.

The other important features of the concert were Dr. Muck's detailed but imaginative readings of the "Faust" Overture of Wagner and the "Surprise" Symphony of Haydn.

FEBRUARY 1, 1915

The Russian Ballet Invades Boston and Conquers It

"There was more excitement in the air than the
Boston Opera has seen in many a day."

THE Russian Ballet directed by Sergei Diaghileff performed for the first time in Boston last night in the Boston Opera House. This remarkable organization and its unique achievements had been emphatically heralded in advance, and as a result an unusually brilliant audience taxed the seating capacity of the theater, which had been sold out hours before the performance.

There were even garments à *la* Bakst! There was more excitement in the air than the Boston Opera has seen in many a day. It may be said at once that the audience, despite the regrettable absence of such dancers as Nijinsky and Karsavina, was not disappointed. The evening was a constant increase of excitement and approval, which reached its climax after the superb performance of *Scheherazade*, the last word in all that is gorgeous and intoxicating in Oriental art.

After each ballet there were repeated curtain calls for the artists. Twice, as the curtains rose—the first time on the beautiful setting of

48

The Midnight Sun, and the second time on Bakst's painting of the interior of a harem, a setting in which blacks, purple, oranges, reds, greens, and a hundred other violent colors are combined with the most astonishing audacity and vigor—the audience burst into applause, and as the performance of *Scheherazade* continued and the music and the rhythms of the dancers became constantly wilder, applause threatened more than once to break out and defeat the orchestra.

The ballets presented were *The Bird of Fire,* by Igor Stravinsky, stage settings and costumes planned by Govoline, dances by Fokine; *The Enchanted Princess,* music by Tchaikovsky, setting by Bakst; *The Midnight Sun,* ballet designed by Léonide Massine, with decorations and costumes by Lemenoff, music by Rimsky-Korsakoff; *Scheherazade,* Persian tale in one act, by Bakst and Fokine, music by Rimsky-Korsakoff.

It was an admirably representative program, displaying more than one aspect of the art of the modern Russian ballet, an art in which Russia now leads the world.

The Bird of Fire is a setting of fantastical folk legend. *The Enchanted Princess* is a ballet in the conventional European style. *The Midnight Sun* is one of the most distinctive and delightful of spectacles offered by this organization, with its accompaniment of naïve and beautiful chants and its very old and picturesque Russian costumes. *Scheherazade,* the ballet which established the fame of Bakst in Paris, had been slightly "toned down" to suit the censors, but it remained substantially and inevitably the original work of musician and stage artist. It made an immediate and sweeping success.

It was James Huneker who said that sedition might be incorporated in the four walls of a symphony and the police be none the wiser. Mr. Huneker might have added: "within the four walls of a palette." There is that in the color scheme of Bakst which is itself far more elemental, if less realistic, than any possible antics of dancers on the stage. The scene is as completely of the Oriental imagination as the strange music of Rimsky-Korsakoff, and as the world-old tale of events which led the Shah Shariar to take unto himself a new wife every night and bowstring her at sunrise. The colors, the dancers, mingling in an ordered and rhythmic confusion, are indeed of the land and the people who "would contract immensity to the limits of desire."

The scene is the interior of a harem—staged with remarkable

perspective. The Shah and his brother consult. They announce their departure on a hunting expedition. The wives arm their husbands, profess their grief at the departure, and only by secret signs to each other indicate their pleasure at this event and its opportunities. The men depart, the eunuchs are dragged forth, and are cajoled by the laughing women until they unlock with the great keys that hang from their belts the doors of cells which are seen at the back of the stage.

From each cell leaps a slave. The slaves and the women pair off, but Zobeide, the favorite, remains alone, restless, dissatisfied. At last, very reluctantly, the head eunuch unlocks the last door, and out bounds a gigantic Negro.

The music quickens; the dances become madder. Figures and colors whirl before the eyes. Now and again a solo dancer emerges from the group and lends more movement and abandon to the scene. The colors of the walls and the costumes are, in the majority of cases, of the strongest and most unqualified hues, which combine and recoil, as it were, with equal violence and ardor.

The dancers do not perceive the silent entrance of the brothers and their soldiers, with swords drawn. Suddenly, as the orchestra crashes out that enigmatical motive which is in itself an apostrophe to the eternal and inscrutable East, they stop, petrified at the doom which confronts them. The Negro slave writhes in terror on the ground.

The carnage begins. The women, pursued by the soldiers, fall on all sides as the swords slash in the air. Finally, Zobeide is discovered, crouching and unharmed. She implores pardon. The Shah is about to grant it when his brother points to the dead slave. Thus reminded, the Shah with a gesture condemns his favorite, who kills herself with a knife given her by one of the soldiers.

When Bakst and Fokine first put their conception on the stage and took for its musical embodiment the famous symphonic suite *Scheherazade* of Rimsky-Korsakoff, the widow of that composer made loud complaints, first, as to their conscienceless pirating of her husband's music; secondly, because of their alleged mutilation of the score. The only mutilation of the score noticed last night by this reviewer was the omission of the third movement of the suite, *The Prince and the Princess,* and this omission was made in America, not in Paris and London, where an amorous scene was enacted to that charming music.

The mimed drama was evidently devised with the greatest intelligence and forethought by the artists of the stage, and the music, which is frequently fragmentary and episodic in the concert room, now seems as if it had been composed by Rimsky-Korsakoff, nearly half a century ago, to accompany this extraordinary scene.

What music it is! How it must have astonished the European world back in the eighties when, as if with one stroke of a magician's wand, Rimsky-Korsakoff exorcised the soul of the East and painted the land of mosques and deserts, of palm trees and bulbuls, as it had never before been painted in tones. And how stirring is this music today, especially, be it emphasized, when so marvelously translated by Russian scenic art! The pounding rhythms, the crooning of wind instruments, the pomp and the savagery, and ever and again the solo violin, the voice of Scheherazade, telling another tale: "Once upon a time . . ."

As for Stravinsky's music, it may, or may not, as commentators in New York have agreed, be less mature and characteristic of the later Stravinsky than the music for *Petrouchka*, the ballet which will be seen later in the Boston engagement; it remains that this score of *L'Oiseau de feu* is a well nigh perfect masterpiece of its kind. It is wedded indissolubly to the action and the scene, which it fits like a glove. A movement, a gesture, an incantation, sounds of nature, which here seem to be mysteriously in league with sinister and powerful factors of the drama—any one and all of these things find the most immediate and intimate echo in his music, music of essentially fantastical and racial quality. The sounds heard in the forest as the curtain rises are not the sounds heard, for instance, in the Arnold Arboretum, nor anywhere, in fact, but in that forest which the imagination of the Russian folk fills with creatures and events of its own devising.

Stravinsky's dance music is marvelously free and classic in its rhythms. Far indeed from the banal stuff of Tchaikovsky in *La Princesse enchantée!* His music that tells of the dawning love of the prince and the virgin he has discovered in the forest is of the most charming tenderness and purity. The bridal music at the end is an equally happy employment of elements rhythmical, melodic, and harmonic, found in the folk music of Russia. Russian themes, which could not possibly be thought of as anything but Russian, pervade the score. The orchestration is a triumph of all that is transparent and beautiful, rich, endlessly varied in color, and invariably composed with the acme of reserve force and good taste. Welcome, indeed, such a scene and such a composition.

The performances on the whole were of exemplary brilliancy, though *The Bird of Fire* was not presented with all of its possible effects. Here was the only occasion when the absence of Nijinsky and Karsavina was directly felt, for the reason that *The Bird of Fire* lays far more stress upon the individual talent than any of the other spectacles seen last night.

The dancer who mimes the bird must have a transcendental technique and much imagination. In other words, she must have genius, and must re-create, as she dances, the conception of composer and stage artist. This Mme Maclezova, a skilled and experienced executant, cannot do, and hence one of the crowning features of the ballet fell short of its complete effect, painstaking and intelligent though she was. More effective by far was the delightful dancing of Mme Lubov Tchernicheva, the captive princess. Her dances were all that was graceful, naïve, and virginal. Mr. Cecchetti was thrice admirable in his suggestion of puissance and malignity as Kastchei. Mr. Massine was wholly in place as the Prince Ivan.

The performance of the *Scheherazade* was a worthy conclusion of the evening. Mme Flora Revalles, the Zobeide, accomplished wonders by reason of the suggestion and reserve of her acting. In its imperiousness, its subtly amorous quality, this impersonation was a remarkable piece of art. Mr. Bolm, the Negro slave, danced wildly and with a power and abandon appropriate to this role.

The music was admirably performed last night. Mr. Ernest Ansermet, the conductor, has under him an admirable orchestra, and he directs this orchestra with the most sympathetic comprehension of the music—witness his reading not only of the *Scheherazade* music, but also of the gorgeous, barbaric march, *The Delights of Power*, from Rimsky-Korsakoff's "Antar" Symphony, and a very difficult and wonderfully made score of Stravinsky.

A Romantic Program: Berlioz—Liszt—Schumann

The "Revolutionists" of the 1830s a Century Later

A PROGRAM of uncommon interest was presented by Dr. Muck yesterday afternoon at the twelfth concert of the Boston Symphony Orchestra in Symphony Hall. Dr. Muck, having recovered from his recent severe indisposition, was again at the helm.

The first performance at these concerts of the first of the twelve symphonic poems with which Liszt revolutionized modern music, *Ce qu'on entend sur la montagne*, proved a matter of far more than merely historical interest, and the seldom-played overture of Berlioz, *Rob Roy*, prefaced happily the remarkable score of Liszt. This in spite of inequalities of workmanship and because of the youth and romanticism of the writing. This overture was first performed in 1833. The first sketches of Liszt's symphonic poem were made in the same year. The first performance of Schumann's "Spring" Symphony, which brought the concert to an end, took place in 1841. A "romantic" program, a revival of the gorgeous music of the thirties.

Liszt's symphonic poem is startling in its eloquence, color, and impetuosity, and its astonishing prophecy of later scores. Shades of Zarathustra! The famous enigmatical conclusion of Strauss's tone poem suddenly smote our ears.

Was it with deliberate intent that Dr. Muck thus unmasked a composer whom he is far from admiring *in toto*? For there in the concluding measures of Liszt, large as life, were the wavering tonalities, the plucking of double basses—Liszt varies the effect, very interestingly, with the kettle drums. The mystic and philosophical mood was so completely depicted that we almost wondered whether the final page of Strauss had been tacked to the score of the early symphonic poem of Liszt. There should be a footnote in Strauss's score in this place: "After the symphonic poem *Ce qu'on entend sur la montagne*"! A feature of Zarathustra which Strauss's partisans

53

and commentators have ignored! Nor has the composer, apparently, taken the pains to enlighten them.

But this symphonic poem is notable for other things than a foreshadowing of a special effect by Strauss. The writing is exceptionally vigorous and sincere. Few of the scores of Liszt have so much richness of color, although there are scores which present finer tone color to the ear. Taken as a whole, the work is full of inspiration, and must have seemed at the time of its first performance in 1847 a heaven-storming piece of audacity. The themes are not transformed as freely and as cleverly as they are in other compositions by Liszt; the final section of the tone poem is too long, and you have the spectacle of a composer endeavoring assiduously to lift himself up by the bootstraps. "Ahem, ahem"—somehow the great roll, the thundering sentence, will not come. But, if you will except this passage, and if you can tolerate the bombast of the earlier Liszt, you have a piece of music aglow with ideas and enthusiasms that seem very young and more than half convincing today.

Berlioz's overture has precisely these same qualities, although the employment of the tune *Scots Wha Hae wi' Wallace Bled* is rather naïve than effectual; the romantic flavor of that must recompense for occasional weaknesses of workmanship. But it is a brave piece of music, and there is the quotation, the most beautiful page in the work, of the viola solo from *Harold in Italy*, a theme which obsessed the composer's imagination and haunted him through many years.

These two performances were of exceptional brilliancy, but in no wise more remarkable than the performance of Schumann's symphony. All that a great musician could do to aid a composer who was none too expert with the orchestra was done, until the symphony glowed with unbelievable color and the passion of spring. Symphony or not, as some say of this work, it held a worthy place on the program yesterday, and at the hands of Dr. Muck, Schumann received his righteous reward.

===

Three Boston *Premières* for Sibelius

And Spalding Plays Beethoven

THREE compositions by Jean Sibelius were played for the first time in Boston yesterday afternoon at the concert of the Boston Symphony Orchestra, Dr. Karl Muck, conductor, in Symphony Hall: *Pohjola's Daughter*; *The Oceanides*; *Night Ride and Sunrise*. Albert Spalding played the Beethoven Violin Concerto. The overture to *Egmont* brought the concert to an end.

All of these pieces of Sibelius are nature sketches. *Pohjola's Daughter* is inspired by the charming episode of *Kalevala*, the Finnish epic, in which the aged hero, Vainomoinen, encounters the daughter of Pohjola sitting on a rainbow. She weaves and laughs at his suit. She coquettishly suggests several tests of the hero's wisdom and valor. But his achievements are of no avail, and the sledge-ride is resumed.

The music starts in the manner of a legend, with a sort of recitative for the cellos, which later becomes a persistent accompanying figure that suggests the ride. The vigorous rhythm is developed with constantly more force and momentum. The brass choir throws out a wild call. This call is in the major key, and thus contrasts effectively and joyously with the minor tonality that has preceded and the intentionally monotonous rhythm of the ride. Then comes the meeting with the daughter of Pohjola. There is laughter in the woodwind, and dialogue which becomes more and more strenuous. There is a humorous suggestion of the anger of the enraged minstrel, and again the music of the ride returns.

Again are heard the defiant fanfares of the brass, and a new theme, sensuous and full of melancholy—the longing, one would say, of him whose years and wisdom are increasing, for young arms and laughter. This melody, flung across the darkly colored pulsating orchestra, is not quickly forgotten. It is in its color, its suggestion and exceedingly ingenious manipulation of short figures that this piece makes its effect. And the effect is superbly imaginative and

55

suggestive of the ruggedness and sadness of northern nature. There are colors not found in the orchestra of composers other than Sibelius. There is the emotion of one inspired by the nature about him and the legends of his own land.

In the *Oceanides* Sibelius is still more of an impressionist. This piece, too, has true imagination, but not such distinctive material, throughout, as the piece that preceded. Yet there are prodigious pages. There is the feeling of the vasty deep, of the thresh of waters and the sough of winds, of the song and the crash of great waves. Few composers could be so simple and elemental in feeling.

In *Night Ride and Sunrise* there are fantastical measures in the transition from the mood of suspense and darkness and agitation to the calmness and majesty of the rising sun, and at the last there are superbly simple and imaginative effects of color in the orchestra. But again, in the latter section, there is a tendency to harmonic commonplaceness. The earlier pages—those of the "night ride"— have the suggestion of that which is mysterious, even sinister, and of grotesque shadows.

Mr. Spalding in his performance of the Beethoven concerto showed his sincerity, his musical understanding, and a fine, clean-cut technique. It was a sane and satisfactory performance, and a performance by a young man too reverent toward his art to do other than place himself wholly at the service of the composer. Mr. Spalding was heartily applauded and recalled.

MARCH 24, 1917

Three Boston *Premières* for Bloch

And Friedberg Plays Brahms

Three Jewish Poems, by Ernest Bloch, who directed the performances of his own works, and a memorable performance of Brahms's B flat Piano Concerto by Carl Friedberg, were distinguished features of the concert of the Boston Symphony Orchestra, Dr. Karl Muck, conductor, yesterday afternoon in Symphony Hall.

The music of Bloch took everyone by surprise on account of its emotional depth and its novelty of color and accent. A number of new works of greater or lesser importance have been heard at the Symphony concerts this winter. None has made such a distinctive impression. No others have revealed, as we believe these *Jewish Poems* reveal, a new and important figure in the modern musical art.

Mr. Bloch, turning his back on precedent and the set formulas of European schools of composition, has essayed to write music which shall be fundamentally and distinctively Hebraic. He has succeeded in this in an astonishing degree. We feel that this music, not the most mature achievement of the composer, is in some respects tentative and experimental. As much is admitted by Mr. Bloch in the notes which he himself contributed to the program book. But these characteristics are of negligible import in view of the originality and eloquence, and what one might call the essential naïveté of true art, revealed in these pages. This is unmistakably the music of a new man with something wholly his own to say, who composes not because he makes up his mind to do so, but because he must.

How did Mr. Bloch discover this freshness of idiom, this deep and fundamentally racial manner of speech? He does not believe that a composer who wishes to express the spirit of his race has necessarily to make use of folk songs for such a purpose. He has gone deeper than this. It is true that his music has Oriental characteristics of rhythm and melodic outline, but there is the heartening conviction on the part of the hearer that this Orientalism comes from inside out, rather than from outside in. The composer has not found these rich and fascinating idioms because of a deliberate search for that which would be externally indicative of his quest, but because such forms of expression were forced into existence by the driving power of his own emotions and ideas, and by the birthright inherited from his forefathers.

This music has the warmth, the melancholy, the sensuality, the prophetic fervor of Hebraic literature. It is at moments harsh and austere, of a passionate intensity, or it has Oriental grace and languor.

Technically speaking, there are Oriental rhythms conspicuous for their suppleness and variety; harmony that is intentionally simple, and often rugged and harsh; unusual and very effective

57

schemes of orchestral color; and a manner of melodic ornamentation which, as it glides rapidly through chromatic intervals, gives the impression of intervals smaller than those of the accepted scales of Western Europe—an ornamentation which is as a diaphanous veil thrown about the main thematic fragments. This latter is observed particularly in the first movement. Other passages furnish a direct contrast in the breadth and simplicity and long line of the themes.

Of the three movements, *Danse, Rite,* and *Cortège Funèbre,* the first is perhaps the most tentative in its form and instrumentation. But it is enormously rich in material and suggestion. Thus the first theme, stiff and archaic in its steps, giving an extraordinary impression of the antique, yet having a wealth of the characteristically chromatic embellishments. Other short, wailing motives, which glide through half-tones that might as easily as not become quarter-tones, set over monotonous rhythms, and interrupted by outcries and dialogues of wind instruments, make the material of this movement. The second movement opens with a grand simplicity and tenderness, and then, following impressive trumpet calls, a passage of fiery and majestic utterance that might well be the adjurations of the prophet in the temple. The last two movements—the Ritual and the Funeral Procession—are movements which, in spite of occasional thickness and lack of balance of instrumentation, would remain monuments to the talent of the composer, had he left nothing else to the world. The exceptional force of this music is startling. It was the more startling yesterday, as it was so unexpected, and so novel in its forms of expression.

Mr. Bloch was called back to the stage repeatedly. The orchestra as well as the audience, impressed by his music and by the simple dignity of the man on the platform, joined in the applause.

Mr. Friedberg, in playing the Brahms concerto, displayed not only phenomenal virtuosity in dealing with a work which is one of the most ungrateful in existence for the pianist, but a never-failing beauty and sonority of tone and a true nobility of conception. Dr. Muck and Mr. Friedberg collaborated in a wonderfully clear exposition of the contents of a complicated symphonic work, and for once this work stood revealed at its full stature. They understood the rugged, heroic spirit of the opening, the demoniac scherzo, the haunting poetry of the slow movement, and the humor and vigor of the finale. Orchestra and pianist out-vied each other. Not in seventeen years at these concerts had this concerto been so superbly presented. More performances of this kind would bring about a more general appreciation of the rather formidable Brahms of the B flat Piano Concerto than now generally obtains. The audience was quick to appreciate the wholly exceptional qualities of the performance. As a matter of record, the concert opened with a performance of Sinigaglia's noisy overture to *Le Baruffe Chiozzote*, performed with exemplary precision and brilliancy.

APRIL 14, 1917

Debussy's *Images* and Schubert's C Major

Is Debussy's expression of nature more fundamental than Schubert's?

THE complete set of Debussy's *Images* for orchestra was performed yesterday afternoon at the concert of the Boston Symphony Orchestra, Dr. Karl Muck, conductor, in Symphony Hall. The *Images* include the *Gigues,* heard for the first time in Boston yesterday; the three pieces—*In the Streets and Waysides, Perfumes of the Night,* and *The Morning of a Fete Day*—which are called, collectively, *Ibéria;* and the *Rondes de printemps.* Schubert's long and beautiful Symphony in C major completed the program.

Both Debussy and Schubert feel nature intimately, and whether Debussy's expression of nature is more fundamental, or as much so, as Schubert's is a matter cheerfully left to posterity to decide. But this may be said: in writing pieces essentially and typically French in their clarity, simplicity, frankness, and masterly arrangement of detail, Debussy has evolved new practices of harmony and form which have already had an important effect on composition.

He is, if you like, an impressionist. That is, his effects are effects of rhythm and color rather than of melody, which is in a sense the musical equivalent of line. But he is not an impressionist in a slapdash manner. His effects of color are achieved by a marvelous care and certainty of method. That the multiplicity of detail neither annoys nor distracts us is only the proof of the mastery of the composer and the sincerity of his method. A thousand brush strokes as an evocation of "perfumes of the night"!

As for form, there is unquestionably present in these pieces structure of the utmost delicacy and logic. There is another kind of form than that which consists in the slavish repetition and contrast of stated melodies. That form is rhythmic form—the arrangement and development of rhythm. Underlying the apparently thoughtless clash of harmonies and scraps of phrases used with the true instinct of the "decadent" is the juxtaposition and the fruitful interplay of rhythmical motives. They give the music its substance and its life, and they represent that god of the classicists, "development"—"development" which is here a true germination of elements inherent in the musical body.

But let us not talk of technique. This is only the machinery of Debussy. This only serves to convey, as simply and as obviously to those who will lend an unprejudiced ear as the method of Schubert, Debussy's impressions of nature, his memories of songs that echo along the highways and byways of Spain, the thrumming of guitars, the shouts and the colors of a fete day, and the marvelous song of spring.

Dr. Muck gave a performance of the *Rondes de printemps* that must be classed with the greatest he has given in Boston, so subtle was its feeling, so spontaneous its expression. We cannot but believe that such a performance would have delighted the composer, for it was as Debussyish in its clearness and its just relation of detail as it was in its haunting song, its rhythmic life and exuberance.

When Dr. Muck chooses to exert his remarkable rhythmic gift— the gift which he abused, as we felt, in the slow movement of the Schubert symphony—he can improvise like a master on his orchestra. This orchestra in the performance of Debussy's piece rushed forward, or hesitated for an instant, or slackened its pace so naturally that it was indeed as the inevitable impulse of the music.

The performance of Schubert's symphony was very brilliant, but at times tonally rough, which is a thing hard to agree with in Schubert as in Debussy or Chopin or Mendelssohn. In the tonal sense, Mr. Wilhelm Gericke was the never-to-be-forgotten interpreter of this symphony. He was not as dramatic as Dr. Muck in the climax of the second movement. He was not as modern in his feeling, and let us admit that a touch of modernism such as Dr. Muck displayed in the climax referred to is impressive and true to the composer's meaning. But Gericke was incomparably beautiful and successful in attaining the Olympian beauty and repose which underlies the most brilliant passages of this symphony, this explosion of genius. In its performance there should never be a hint of roughness, or undue capriciousness of rhythm, as in the slow movement. The orchestra should be radiant and glowing, but never hard. For the C major Symphony is one of the most beautiful and classic works, despite its romantic undercurrent of feeling, that exist in the world today. The audience applauded all performances with exceptional warmth, recalling the conductor, who, in acknowledgment, summoned the orchestra to its feet.

JANUARY 22, 1918

Boston *Première* of the Mahler Second

"Now it is deeply impressive . . . now theatrical, bombastic, and tedious."

GUSTAV MAHLER's Second Symphony was given last night in Symphony Hall for the first time in Boston by the Boston Symphony Orchestra, Dr. Karl Muck, conductor; a chorus of 350 voices, rehearsed for this occasion by Stephen Townsend; Merle Alcock, contralto, and May Peterson, soprano, assisting soloists.

The symphony, which has been called the "Resurrection" Symphony, is one of vast dimensions, requiring an hour and forty minutes in performance. The orchestra was considerably augmented to meet the enormous demands of Mahler's score. At the close of the performance there was an ovation for Dr. Muck and the performers.

One is immediately impressed, first by the broad and simple outlines and the profound sincerity of the composer in this work, and then by the curiously incongruous characteristics of the music. Now it is deeply impressive, as in the choral conclusion of the last movement; now it is theatrical, bombastic, and tedious in its reiteration of unimportant themes. Now the harmony is pungently modern—

61

although this is comparatively seldom the case—while most of the time it is so simple as to be old-fashioned. In fact, there are no measures in the work which show a pronouncedly original quality of musical invention.

The themes tell because of their broad outlines, their passionate sweep, or because of instrumentation which is not only effective but at times crudely sensational. The composer is frankly indebted to Wagner and Bruckner. Probably neither the suggestion of the sleep motive from *The Valkyrie* at the end of the first movement, nor the quotation of certain progressions from the "Love-death" of Isolde in the duet between the contralto and the soprano where reference is made to the welcoming of death, is accidental.

From Bruckner are derived certain broad progressions, but also, alas, some of the tireless reiteration of thematic material, which was at times the strength but more often the weakness of that master whom Mahler adored. But at least, as regards passionate feeling and symphonic intention, the first and last movements of this work avow the vision and the intense conviction of the composer.

This is not the case with the rest of the work. After the opening movement, which alternates between deep gloom and mystical exaltation, and presents thematic material referred to again in the finale, we have in the following section a happy and naïve tune, a sort of *ländler*, in which the composer is wholly at his ease and felicitous in his invention. But this gay little tune has neither the substance nor importance to justify its so frequent repetition, or the unsuccessful efforts to give it variety of effect by changes of instrumentation. What is obvious, of course, is that in alternating his dramatic opening and this *ländler* the composer had in mind a definite program which he has not given us. But that does not excuse or condone the fact that as music pure and simple and as a movement of a dramatic symphony the music is at first pleasing and then trivial.

Between this movement and the next there is too little variety of character, although the third movement has a certain grotesquerie which the second has not. Then suddenly the alto voice is heard in a charming, tender song, *Thou red, red rose*, from *Das Knaben Wunderhorn*, an expression of faith in the mercy of God and the hereafter.

The last movement commences with orchestral pandemonium, then a mystic call from horns offstage, then again pandemonium, in which motives of the first movement are treated in various guises, including that of the plain chant, the *Dies irae*; and after much of this and of reiterated preparations for the "resurrection" music, the chorus with the two solo voices sing Klopstock's ode *Auferstehen, ja auferstehen*, which Mahler heard sung at the funeral of Hans von Bülow in the church of St. Michael. The simplest harmonies are employed. The chorus sings for the greater part without accompaniment, the orchestra supplying joyous interludes, and the solo voices woven in from time to time. The effect is very simple, beautiful, and full of feeling, and moved the audience profoundly.

A spirit of devotion was to be felt throughout this performance, which for its brilliancy and eloquence will long be remembered. As for the work itself, it does not make a very durable impression. Both Mrs. Alcock and Miss Peterson sang admirably. Mahler the dreamer, the humanist, the philosopher, the mystic, was to be felt and admired back of this music. But we believe the music itself will be shelved long before the memory of the man and his potent services to his art will be forgotten.

NOVEMBER 28, 1919

Monteux Conducts Griffes and Chausson

"Mr. Griffes is a man to watch with care."

AN AMERICAN composer, Charles Tomlinson Griffes, made his first appearance on a Boston Symphony program at the concert which Mr. Monteux conducted yesterday afternoon in Symphony Hall, a program which will be repeated tonight. Mr. Griffes was not the first American to appear on these programs. Nor will he be the last. But it is an important fact to note that this man, aged thirty-five, has really produced a remarkably interesting score.

The title of the work is *The Pleasure Dome of Kubla Khan*. The subject is, of course, that of Coleridge's poem. When he wrote the music, Mr. Griffes states in the program book, he was thinking principally of the "stately pleasure-dome," the "sunny pleasure-dome with caves of ice," the "miracle of rare device." . . . "The gardens with fountains and 'sunny spots of greenery' are next suggested.

From inside come sounds of dancing and revelry which increase to a wild climax and then suddenly break off. There is a return to the original mood suggesting the sacred river and the 'caves of ice.' "

This is the simple program of the piece. It is a program simple enough not to bother anyone listening to the music who is fearful that he may be thinking of an Oriental dance when the composer means him to think of "caves of ice." The imagination of the composer and the hearer is left quite free. That the composer has real imagination, feeling, and, above all, a sense of color is clearly shown. That he has less melodic originality at present is also evident. Who has real thematic invention at the age of thirty today? How many great composers have had it at that age? Comparatively few.

Nor is Mr. Griffes's orchestration wholly original. He knows his Stravinsky, for example, extremely well. The opening is richly suggestive of the opening of the *Firebird*—the persistent tremolo replacing Stravinsky's figure work in the lower strings, short staccato chords of bassoons and piano—if the ear may be trusted—fixing the impression in the mind. The score is plainly derived from ultramodern Russia and ultra-modern France. But with a difference. The difference is that of weak imitation and a young tone-painter with a sense of color which is inherent, rather exotic in character, and absolutely fascinating to the listener. In his mind's eye this composer sees a picture which he paints boldly. His Orientalism is not a mere arpeggio for an oboe or pounding on a drum. It is the Orient conceived by a young modern. And if the thematic contours of this work are not marked by great originality, they are marked by life, by definite direction and at least a strong intention of form.

Above all, there is enormous spirit and contagion in this writing. Feeling this spirit of the composer, it is hard to be overcritical of sources of effects. He has, too, some effects of his own—very ingenious and striking developments of hints given him by older composers; and with all this, the music is personal, individual in quality of imagination, and indicative of a broad and catholic appreciation of music of many schools.

We maintain that this is more than enough to start with, and that it is difficult not to enjoy this transitional music of a composer of talent and of astonishing technical resource. Mr. Griffes is a man to watch with care.* He is not a mere objectivist and a man of ultra-

* Griffes died April 8, 1920, less than five months later.—ED.

refinement in his music, like John Alden Carpenter, for example. Nor is he a man possessed of the broadly nationalistic ideals in the music of Henry Gilbert.

But he is a young American, full of spirit and receptivity, astonishingly progressive, as shown by the texture of a score of a man who was musically educated in composition in Germany; he has temperament in great abundance; he loves to write. Hence it gives one great pleasure to think that out of a sparse harvest another important American composer is coming to maturity. This piece greatly pleased the audience.

The opening piece was Chausson's admirable Symphony in B flat, which was given a wonderful performance by Mr. Monteux. The work had never before in Boston been heard to such advantage. Never before had the solemn introduction merged so inevitably into the calmly joyous allegro. Never before had the instrumentation been so beautifully clear and transparent, nor the long flowing lines of the first theme of the allegro been done such justice. Of course, Chausson did not reach his complete development as a composer even in this, one of his most complete works.

The symphony is principally of German classic mold, and the cyclic form imposed on the already existent mold by César Franck. There is conventional development of motives in the opening movement, battledoring and shuttlecocking of fragments about, ordinary sequences, etc. But the broad, virile stride of this movement, its luminous color; the melancholy of the slow movement; the change to a spirit of hope and thankfulness, so subtly and admirably brought out by Mr. Monteux; and the brilliant finale, of a quality best exemplified by pages of Franck, made a very strong impression and intensified regrets that such a fine and pure musical nature as Chausson's should have met its untimely end.

Mme Louise Homer, gifted with a contralto voice which does not wear out, a natural simplicity and breadth of style, was heard at her best in familiar music which gave much pleasure to the audience: *Nature's Adoration*, Beethoven; "*Ombra mai fu*," otherwise known as "Largo," Handel; *Heart Ever Faithful*, Bach; aria, "*O don fatale*," from *Don Carlos*, Verdi. She was applauded to the echo.

The concert ended with that extraordinary *Bourrée fantasque* of Chabrier, scintillatingly orchestrated by Felix Mottl. The other music had talent. That piece has genius.

Petrouchka: "the Certainty and Recklessness of Genius"

Fountains of Rome: "pure, Italian, patrician"

ULTRA-MODERN music, prefaced by one of the earliest compositions of Felix Mendelssohn, made the program interpreted by the Boston Symphony Orchestra yesterday afternoon in Symphony Hall. The Mendelssohn composition was the Octet for Strings (Opus 20). It was completed in the composer's sixteenth year. It served to display the splendid tone of the string choir of the orchestra, and possibly, also, Mr. Monteux played it to take the curse off the peppery discords of Stravinsky's music to the ballet *Petrouchka*, which came at the end of the program.

Between these two compositions stood the supreme offering of the afternoon, the symphonic poem *Fountains of Rome*, by the young modern Italian, Respighi, wisely repeated after its success when performed for the first time in Boston at the Symphony concerts of two weeks preceding.

Stravinsky's music was heard for the first time at these concerts, and the performance was masterly from every standpoint. This is music intended first of all, of course, to go with a stage spectacle.

Having seen the ballet, which was given in this city a number of times by the Ballet Russe, the writer again found the music deeply impressive because of its vitality, its dramatic characterizing power, its rough popular humor, the scraps of Russian folk music so vigorously employed, and the extraordinary originality of both harmony and instrumentation.

How much this music meant to many unacquainted with the stage spectacle, it is not easy to say. They probably often wondered what it was all about, while other hearers who had also been beholders saw before them the riotous throng at the fair in the admiralty market place, the dances of peasants, players, traders, and the like; the two organ-grinders; the old magician at whose bidding Petrouchka —symbolizing, it is said, the Russian people—dances and mimes; the pains and smarts of Petrouchka, beaten, writhing, and groaning, while wind instruments sound discordant; Petrouchka's struggles against the vile Moor and all his evil; and the fair again, the merriment growing wilder, and finally, in the pale light of the dawn, the ghost of the murdered Petrouchka frantically waving its arms over the top of the magician's booth.

The score is a marvel of genius, genius which creates with the certainty and the recklessness and prodigality of inspiration; which can do anything with the tonal materials employed. The work hangs together even in the concert room without explanatory evolutions and gestures on the stage. The conclusion, the eerie, ghastly music of Petrouchka's end, puts the hearer under a spell even when he is far from the theater. Above all, there is felt continually the back-·ground of life, the commotion, the bustle, the clattering tongues of the crowd, the wildness and extravagance of drunken dances, of legendary songs shouted out by revelers.

.The imperishable memory of the concert remains that of the masterpiece of Respighi. Here is a beauty unutterably pure, Italian, patrician, a beauty which is the product of centuries of culture and art, and of a land where beauty itself finds its valued home.

The work is as original and racial as it is unforced and unerring in the achievement of impressionistic effects by Respighi's wondrous orchestra.

FEBRUARY 19, 1921

═══

Boston Hears the *London Symphony*

And Thibaud Plays Mozart

VAUGHAN WILLIAMS' *London Symphony* was played for the first time in Boston at the concert of the Boston Symphony Orchestra, Pierre Monteux, conductor, in Symphony Hall. Williams, an Englishman of forty-nine years, benefited in his style because of his contact with Ravel and other modern composers, although he is sincere and authentically English in his idiom in this symphony. He has allowed to appear a programmatic explanation of his music.

The symphony is in four movements. The first, one finds, may be taken as expressing London at dawn—the flowing of the Thames, the striking of "Big Ben" in Westminster tower, the noises of the Strand. The second movement is inspired by the thought of Bloomsbury in the foggy twilight of a November day, the Bloomsbury of poverty, of shabby streets and hollow gentility. The third movement, in carnival vein, is Saturday night from a bench of the Temple Embankment. The last movement, in the nature of an apotheosis, speaks of poverty, the march of the unemployed, the tragedy, the poetry, the enigma of London.

There is feeling and mood in this symphony, which is too long and padded. At least it is music by a composer sincere and sensitive to the atmosphere of his town. There is the echo of the din of city streets, the gaiety and vulgarity of the "pub," the smack of folk tune or, rather, street cry here and there, as in the delightful quotation of *"Sweet lavender, who'll buy my lavender?"*

The first movement seems by far the best. The introduction is imaginative—the grayness of dawn, the silence of the river, the distant chime of the clock, and the pages following, which are weird and exciting. The slow movement has poetic atmosphere, though it is long-drawn-out. There is animation and vitality in passages of the third movement, but it is patchy, and the last movement peters out. It would have been better, it seemed to us, had Mr. Williams condensed his material and written a symphonic poem in one movement.

On the other hand, it is recognizable that here, at least, is an Englishman with infinitely more consciousness of his locality than that shown by the pinchbeck Londonism of Edward Elgar. And the themes are not merely quoted. They are treated sympathetically, and are often given a special significance. At other times there is mere manipulation and treading of water.

Orchestrally there is felt the influence of Stravinsky. Since the Stravinsky of one decade is not the Stravinsky of another because of his incredibly rapid evolution, let us be explicit: the Stravinsky of *Petrouchka*, whose color scheme and rhythmic and instrumental effects haunt Mr. Williams until at times he becomes imitative. The performance was a triumph of fine nuance and brilliant virtuosity, thanks to Mr. Monteux.

Jacques Thibaud, violinist, gave an unforgettable performance of Mozart's E flat Concerto. One is tempted to say that this concerto could not be played with greater art. We shall hesitate to go into a concert hall when another violinist than Mr. Thibaud performs it. The perfection of line, the classic grace and continency of expression, and at the same time, the warm quality of the tone and the expressive singing of lovely melodies constituted a veritable revelation of Mozart. Mr. Thibaud was warmly applauded. The applause should have been frantic in order to be proportionate when one recalls an occasion not many weeks ago in which a young violinist played in a manner decidedly superficial and received more recalls, longer applause than did Mr. Thibaud yesterday. *"Sic transit . . ."*

Chabrier's wild and dramatic overture to *Gwendoline* ended the concert, and its superb performance was exhilarating beyond expression. Chabrier was first a temperament, then a musician, though a very gifted one, to boot. Who makes the orchestra blaze as he? Who evokes from the instruments a nobler tumult, a tumult more elemental, as he thinks of the storm-swept coast of ancient Brittany, of the invaders from the north? Then there is the sensuousness and the foreboding intensity of the love music. And then, alas, there is the atrocious musical parody of Valhalla—the climax, where Chabrier not only falls short but falls clean to the ground with the barrel-organ ditty which he gives his dying Harold and Gwendoline as, expiring in the flames, they sing of Valhalla. It is a caricature of nobility, with a Wagnerian appoggiatura to it which only increases the disgust one would feel if the whole business were not so stirring that the one who listens can only choke and applaud.

NOVEMBER 25, 1921

Boston Hears Orchestration of *Verklärte Nacht*

"Dramatic, impassioned . . . and a tendency to be prolix"

THE feature of the seventh program of the Boston Symphony Orchestra, Pierre Monteux, conductor, played yesterday afternoon in Symphony Hall, was the first performance here of Schoenberg's sextet *Verklärte Nacht* (*Radiant Night*) as arranged by the composer for string orchestra.

This work was first performed in Boston in its original shape as a string sextet at a concert of the Kneisel Quartet in Steinert Hall in 1915. The composer has since scored the composition for full string orchestra, and has made some changes in the music.

The change from six strings to approximately sixty is well justified by the results, for this is less a string sextet than a symphonic poem, and furthermore Schoenberg, in using many stringed instruments, has provided or discovered an amazing number of effects which often suggest those of a full orchestra.

The poetic basis of the music is the text of Richard Dehmel: "Two mortals walk through a cold, barren grove. The moon sails over the tall oaks, which send their scrawny branches up through the unclouded moonlight. A woman speaks, she confesses, to her companion whom she loves, a mortal sin. A man speaks. Let her not burden her soul with guilt. See, the moon's sheen enwraps the universe. Together they are driving over chill waters, but a flame from each warms the other. They sink into each other's arms. Their breaths meet in kisses in the air. Two mortals wander through the wondrous moonlight."

For the Schoenberg of today this music is perhaps old-fashioned, even though he has touched up the outpouring of an earlier period. To us who listened yesterday it is extremely beautiful and romantic music. It mirrors the sheen of the moon. The musical dialogue is dramatic, impassioned. True, it is long-drawn-out. The composer has so many ideas, so many masterly transformations of his musical material to offer, that there is over-richness and a tendency to be prolix. But the audience listened fascinated by the simplicity and eloquence of his speech, by its rich harmonic color, its emotional accent, its clear and cohesive succession of mood pictures.

The remainder of the program consisted of Brahms's *Tragic Overture*, Weingartner's version of Weber's *Invitation to the Dance*, and Tchaikovsky's Fourth Symphony. At times, in the music of Brahms, there is a noble, Greek-like mood which few composers have ever attained. The lack of sensuousness is most appropriate, and the classic clearness of style is the only one, perhaps, wholly suitable for such an expression. At other times there is conventional procedure, a regularity of sequence and repetition of theme which weaken greatly the effect of really grand thoughts. Wein-

gartner's treatment of Weber's piece, with all its gratuitous counterpoint and the equally gratuitous and sometimes cheap effects of
instrumentation, is for us atrocious and very inferior to Berlioz's
orchestration of the same music. Poor Weber. He once wrote a
simple and delightful piano piece, *Invitation to the Dance*.

OCTOBER 28, 1922

Vaughan Williams' Fantasia on a Theme of Tallis

"A composer suddenly reminded of his heritage"

ONE walks about Boston today and goes up on Beacon Hill, looks
at old buildings and landmarks, recalls this and that episode of
the history of great America, and then perceives, let us say, Boylston
Street, and wonders whether a present like ours can ever have an
atmosphere, or approach in artistic or dramatic significance the
times that are with us no longer. And then one walks into Symphony Hall and hears the Fantasia on a theme by the old English
composer Thomas Tallis, by the modern English composer
Vaughan Williams, played by Mr. Monteux and the Boston Symphony Orchestra, and wonders still more a similar thing—namely,
whether there will ever be a time as fit for music-making as the age
which produced that haunting old tune and moved Vaughan
Williams, who is living today, to string it out into such beautiful
music.

Vaughan Williams' Fantasia, for double string orchestra, was the
crowning feature of the third Symphony program of the season. It
is singularly beautiful music, practically a set of free variations on
a lovely and archaic tune by an Elizabethan composer. But here at
last are developments which do not aim merely to astonish the
hearer, which spring inevitably, not merely from the musical structure of a chosen melody, but from the emotional moods which that
melody has inevitably provoked in the breast of a sensitive creative
musician.

The opening, once heard, would never be forgotten, with the

antiphonal responses of the one orchestra to the other, the sense of dim, far-off, ineffably beautiful things. The composer adheres both in spirit and letter to the harmonic character of the old music, and the result is the effect of an ancient cloistral gray, of something at once noble and shadowy and beautiful and austere.

Mme de Staël made the celebrated remark, now bromidic, about music being frozen architecture. Searching in vain in our mind for some simile to give the reader an impression only to be realized, probably, by the hearer, it seemed to us that the spirit of old architecture was in this music, the expression of a composer suddenly reminded of his heritage, feeling profoundly the beautiful and tragic past of his land. This composer retrospects not merely through the past years of his own life, but the very life of the country that bore him. He finds, at the moment of creation, more living companions in the ages past than in the bus-drivers and the clerks and the money-changers of the present.

Vaughan Williams, of the *London Symphony*, the song cycle *On Wenlock Edge*, and this Fantasia, is indeed a poet and an English composer to be reckoned with. Of the Fantasia the orchestra gave a superb performance.

An equally brilliant performance was given by Benno Moiseivitch, piano soloist of the occasion, when he introduced a work of far less merit—the Tcherepnin Piano Concerto. It is a virtuoso's piece. As such, Mr. Moiseivitch gave it a memorable interpretation.

The program opened with a classic—Mozart's E flat major Symphony, delightfully played—and came to an end with what is still modern—Liszt's *Battle of the Huns*, after the picture of Kaulbach. Acknowledging the customary Lisztian bombast, it is a fine-sounding piece of music.

How did the man do these things, with all his piano-playing and *fêtes* and letter-writing and *amours* and the rest of it? To answer that may explain how his symphonic poems, with all their tawdriness, keep their place decade after decade on orchestral programs, and how wonders are achieved by genius.

A Composition of Towering Imagination:
Bloch's *Schelomo*

"The Jews' savage love of justice"

A COMPOSITION of towering imagination and, at times, of an almost agonizing intensity of feeling—Ernest Bloch's *Schelomo* (*Solomon*), a Jewish Rhapsody for violoncello and orchestra—was performed for the first time in this city at the concert of the Boston Symphony Orchestra which Pierre Monteux conducted last night in Symphony Hall.

Because music goes so much deeper than speech, and because we are no Shelleys or Shakespeares, it is very difficult to give an idea of the wildness and the grandeur of this music in certain places, the utter despair of other pages, the vehement passions, the Oriental gorgeousness of color. Let Mr. Bloch speak for himself. He can do it better. In the program book he said: "It is the Jewish soul that interests me; the complex, glowing, agitated soul that I feel vibrating through the Bible; the freshness and naïveté of the patriarchs, the violence that is evident in the prophetic books; the Jews' savage love of justice; the despair of the Preacher in Jerusalem; the sorrow and immensity of the Book of Job; the sensuality of the Song of Songs. All this is in us, all this is in me, and it is the better part of me. It is all this that I endeavor to hear in myself and transcribe in my music."

Perhaps Mr. Bedetti, the admirable first cellist of the orchestra, is not as thankful as we are for a really great piece of music for cello and orchestra, for the piece is very difficult to play. It is difficult alike for soloist and for orchestra, and equally full of ideas for each of them. The orchestral part and the cello part have quite different roles, closely as they fit together. The cellist is the narrator, the exhorter. The orchestra establishes a mood and background and, more than that, rises to tremendous heights of prophecy and gloom when feeling seems to have accumulated to the point where the voice of the solo instrument can go no farther.

73

We don't know of any piece of music we have heard for a long time which has the originality, the depth, the powerful dramatic feeling of this one. Free in form, the freedom is that of a master. The emotion, as Mr. Bloch himself has truly remarked, is more than that of an individual. It is racial, ancestral; it is the voice of sages and prophets, which never dies, resounding in the soul of the peoples for unnumbered ages.

Two other living composers represented by first performances of their compositions at these concerts were Arthur Foote, *Nightpiece*, for flute and orchestra, and David Stanley Smith, *Fêtes galantes*, for orchestra with flute obbligato. Mr. Foote's piece is very simple and charmingly written. Played with exquisite art by Mr. Georges Laurent as soloist, it appeared as a model of what a composer who knows his business and also knows exactly what he is going to do can accomplish. Mr. Foote would not attach unwarranted importance to a piece of modest pretensions, but the audience had reason to rejoice in that very modesty and simplicity shown in a composition written surely and with unfailing good taste.

Mr. Smith's *Fêtes galantes* purports to be Watteauesque. It is Debussyesque, too, and the strain of a waltz in it could probably be characterized by some other "esque." It is overlong, and the effect is of spinelessness, in spite of repetitions of parts and sections.

The remaining performances were of the highest quality. What sparkle and verve in the music of Mozart! And what music! An overture* written with no more thought, presumably, than of supplying a curtain-raiser. And the man who wrote it condemned by all the crowd of pretenders and mediocrities in the city with him.

If the music of Bloch was upsetting because of its power and intensity, it was followed by the symphony so truly, so persistently, almost, in D major, of Brahms. And this symphony is lovely. It makes one think of the tender figures of Botticelli's picture of the spring.

* The "Marriage of Figaro."—ED.

———

Roland Hayes Impresses Boston Symphony Audience with His Musicianship

But Balance of Program Is Pretty Dull

ROLAND HAYES, the first colored singer ever to appear with the Boston Symphony Orchestra, was soloist at the concert conducted by Mr. Monteux yesterday afternoon in Symphony Hall. In seasons, a singer has not had so enthusiastic a reception at these concerts.

Mr. Hayes sang first the aria *"Un aura amorosa"* from Mozart's *Cosi fan tutte*, and an aria from Berlioz's *Flight into Egypt*; then, for his second group, two spirituals with orchestrated accompaniments, *Go Down, Moses* and *By-and-by*.

He sang Mozart yesterday with astonishing fineness of nuance and style. His diction and phrasing were for all musicians to admire. The quality of the voice was particularly fine in piano passages and in passages of fioritura. Once in a while the quality of the singing voice of his race would slightly color the classical contour of Mozart's music. This color was heard much more, and, of course, most appropriately, in the Negro spirituals.

The first of these, *Go Down, Moses,* was sung with the tone and the manner of one who prophesies. The second spiritual, much less familiar, was the voice of the old woman near her last days, resigned, full of faith and the knowledge of the weary load soon to lighten. The hearer thought irresistibly of Mr. Hayes's mother, who died only a few days before her son returned here from his last European tour and to his success of yesterday afternoon in Symphony Hall.

Mr. Hayes is an extremely thoughtful and sensitive interpreter. A voice not overlarge serves him well, and was handled yesterday with a restraint which revealed thoughtfully and eloquently the intentions of the composer. It is not surprising that his diction was commended unanimously by European critics. It was admirable in the music of Berlioz as well as in the Italian text of the aria of Mozart. Delicacy and justness of effect were constantly in evidence, in spite of an occasional huskiness due, no doubt, to momentary conditions. It was by these means that Mr. Hayes showed himself the artist, and not by shouting or straining after big effects. He was recalled times without number after the last spiritual.

The orchestral compositions were Dvořák's Second Symphony in D minor, which on the whole is a bore—kapellmeister music, music in which the naïve Bohemian composer hides himself far from his fields and forests in a German studio and emulates the dullest moments of Johannes Brahms; a new piece by Albert Roussel, *La Ville rose*, an interesting and individual expression in which the composer fights happily shy of Debussyish softness and impressionism; and Moussorgsky's immature and vulgar music *A Night on Bald Mountain*, after the manner of Liszt and Berlioz, well coated over by the masterly orchestration of one Nicholas Rimsky-Korsakoff.

PART II

Pablo Casals Appears with New York Symphony

"He glorified the music."

PABLO CASALS appeared with the New York Symphony Orchestra, Walter Damrosch, conductor, yesterday afternoon in Aeolian Hall. The fact is mentioned at once, although the appearance of a soloist at an orchestral concert seldom calls for a leading position in a report of it. Yesterday, however, Mr. Casals's performance became the central feature of the occasion. He played the Boccherini Cello Concerto in B flat, which, with the possible exception of the slow movement, is not more nor particularly less distinguished than other of this composer's work for stringed instruments. But Mr. Casals glorified the music, as he would have glorified a composition much inferior, by his style and consummate musicianship. He was more than a soloist. His performance rose to the dignity and value almost of an enduring work of art. It held something for every listener to find beauty in and to learn from and to remember. After the concerto, audience and orchestra acclaimed the interpreter. It is not often that an artist reaches the heights attained by Mr. Casals in seasons past, yet continues to grow.

One other moment of the concert stands out, with Mr. Casals's playing, and that is the finale of Glazounoff's Fifth Symphony. Movement after movement of this symphony goes by, the music being principally in the vein, as the program notes remarked, of a "Russian Mendelssohn." There is also a fragment of a Russian Wagner, and general tedium of commonplace motives and unjustifiably spun-out developments. Suddenly the finale bursts forth, unexpectedly, inexplicably, with a barbaric vigor and fury that could not possibly have been foreseen from anything that went before.

79

The old saw comes to mind: "Scratch a Russian and find a Tartar." The mood, the wildness of the rhythms, the tumultuous clamor as of hordes that make the earth shake to their tread, are maintained with a magnificence, a boldness of gesture, that would seem to give this finale a place by itself among Glazounoff's later compositions. Here Glazounoff is far more the composer of the early tone poem *Stenka Razine* than the polite symphonist and writer of ballad music of the later years. For one moment, in the Fifth Symphony, Glazounoff is his own man again.

The symphony is very effective for orchestra, and was enthusiastically applauded by the audience. The performance of a noisy piece, Tchaikovsky's *Marche slave*, brought the concert to an end.

FEBRUARY 1, 1924

New York Welcomes *Le Sacre du printemps*

"Unprecedented energy, definiteness, and power"

To PIERRE MONTEUX and the Boston Symphony Orchestra fell the task, superbly executed, of introducing to the public of this city Igor Stravinsky's *Sacre du printemps*, as the work is most commonly known, last night in Carnegie Hall. This work, which created a riot when it was first performed by Mr. Monteux and the Russian Ballet in Paris in 1913, has been more discussed than any other composition of Stravinsky.

The audience, knowing this and fearing more through the many articles of a descriptive kind which had appeared in the daily press, came prepared for the worst, to listen to the new music. After the first part of the score had come to an end, there were a few hisses—whether in indignation or to suppress premature applause was not easy to tell. After the second part had ended, it was apparent that a majority had enjoyed themselves. The applause of this majority was long and loud and, to all appearances, most sincere. It repeatedly acclaimed Mr. Monteux and the gentlemen of the orchestra.

Misleading things are always said about a work with such a sensational history. Two false impressions had been spread abroad concerning this music: first, that it was unequaled in ugliness and fearfulness generally; and, secondly, that it was completely unprecedented among Stravinsky's compositions. Both these reports, as Mark Twain would have said, seem greatly exaggerated. The music, filled as it is with a primitive and at times vertiginous energy, has pages of a rare and highly individual beauty. The score is obviously a logical evolution of the style of Stravinsky, following naturally indications contained in *The Firebird* and *Petrouchka*. There are a number of passages in *Sacre du printemps* which could come straight from both these earlier works. In fact, it contains in one place a quotation, almost exact, of the music of the magician Kastchei from *The Firebird*.

The expression, however, is greatly intensified. It is done principally by means of the force and individuality of the counterpoint, and also by rhythms that have at times a well nigh hysterical shock and fury. There is the effect of complete abandon of mood and manner in this music. We believe that it is thought and written with the most exact precision, with enormous power, and with an uncanny knowledge—prescience—of the capacities of a greatly extended orchestra.

And it is music, not mere sound to accentuate or accompany something done in the theater. This should be emphasized, as Stravinsky has emphasized it in various statements. *Sacre du printemps* is not an accompaniment for a ballet. The ballet was the accompaniment or the representation, after the conception, of the music. Its scenario will serve as a description of the general tenor of the score, which, however, might be fully as well comprehended if it simply bore as general title *Sacre du printemps—The Rite of Spring*, or, in a more exact translation of the Russian title, *Spring Consecration*.

The scene on the stage when the work is thus performed is, first, of a dance of youths and maidens in the springtime, a ceremony of incantation in primitive fashion, with vigorous stamping of the ground. There follows the mock abduction of a maiden; *Spring Rounds*; *Games of Rival Towns*; an old man, a celebrant, who prostrates himself and kisses the earth. In the second part, after an orchestral introduction called *The Pagan Night*, there are preparations for the ancient pagan sacrifice of a human victim to Spring; the choice of the victim; her glorification; the *Evocation of An-*

cestors; the sacrificial act of the victim, who must dance herself to death.

Long before the scenario of the ballet existed, as Stravinsky told Michel Georges-Michel, he had conceived the "embryo theme" of the score. "As this theme," said the composer, "with that which followed, was conceived in a strong, brutal manner, I took as pretext for developments, for the evocation of this music, the Russian prehistoric epoch, since I am a Russian. But note well that this idea came from the music; the music did not come from the idea. My work is architectonic, not anecdotical; objective, not descriptive construction."

That is the story—and, we believe, the sincere story—of the musical evolution of this extremely interesting and exciting creation. As far as appraising its ultimate value is concerned, that is a responsibility fortunately visited upon neither audiences nor reviewers of the present. Their responsibility is to react honestly to what they hear, and, in the case of the newspaperman, to record it. The inspiration of this music seems to us profound and genuine. And Russian, which is another sign of its authenticity, for when a composer speaks most truly he is most likely to express not only himself but his native land. The Russianism in the music is not superficial. It does not depend upon the use of a Russian folk song here and there, or some familiar idiom of popular Russian music. It is much more fundamental than that.

What stands out technically and emotionally in this work, and gives it a place significant, as it seems today, in the history of the modern development of an art, is its unprecedented energy, definiteness, and power. No orchestra that we have heard throws off such heat, such sonorities, such galvanizing, rhythmical force as this orchestra of Stravinsky.

The remainder of the program consisted of the Mozart "Jupiter" Symphony, given a performance different in kind but not in standard by Mr. Monteux and his now highly perfected orchestra, and the Sibelius Violin Concerto, which Mr. Richard Burgin, concertmaster, was courageous enough to play and interpret with splendid sincerity, expression, and fire. His appearance was not the least significant element of a program laden with riches.

Rhapsody in Blue Introduced in a Historic Whiteman Concert

"... apology is herewith indignantly rejected."

A CONCERT of popular American music was given yesterday afternoon in Aeolian Hall by Paul Whiteman and his orchestra of the Palais Royal. The stage setting was as unconventional as the program. Pianos in various stages of deshabille stood about, amid a litter of every imaginable contraption of wind and percussion instruments. Two Chinese mandarins, surmounting pillars, looked down upon a scene that would have curdled the blood of a Stokowski or a Mengelberg. The golden sheen of brass instruments of lesser and greater dimensions was caught up by a gleaming gong and carried out by bright patches of an Oriental backdrop. There were also, lying or hanging about frying-pans, large tin utensils, and a speaking-trumpet, later stuck into the end of a trombone—and what a silky, silky tone came from that accommodating instrument! The singular assemblage of things was more than once, in some strange way, to combine to evoke uncommon and fascinating sonorities.

There were verbal as well as programmatic explanations. The concert was referred to as "educational," to show the development of this type of music. Thus, the *Livery Stable Blues* was introduced apologetically as an example of the depraved past from which modern jazz has risen. The apology is herewith indignantly rejected, for this is a gorgeous piece of impudence, much better in its unbuttoned jocosity and Rabelaisian laughter than other and more polite compositions that came later.

The pianist gathered about him some five fellow performers. The man with the clarinet wore a battered top hat that had ostensibly seen better days. Sometimes he wore it, and sometimes played into it. The man with the trombone played it as is, but also, on occasion, picked up a bathtub or something of the kind from the floor and blew into that. The instruments made odd, unseemly, bushman sounds. The instrumentalists rocked about. Jests permissible in musical terms but otherwise not printable were passed between these friends of music. The laughter of the music and its interpreters was tornadic. It was—should we blush to say it?—a phase of America. It reminded the writer of someone's remark that an Englishman entered a place as if he were its master, whereas an American entered as if he didn't care who in blazes the master might be. Something like that was in this music.

There were later remarkably beautiful examples of scoring for a few instruments; scoring of singular economy, balance, color, and effectiveness; music at times vulgar, cheap, in poor taste, elsewhere of irresistible swing and insouciance and recklessness and life; music played as only such players as these can play it. They have a technique of their own. They play with an abandon equaled only by that race of born musicians, the American Negro, who has surely contributed fundamentally to this art which can neither be frowned nor be sneered away. They did not play like an army going through ordered maneuvers, but like the melomaniacs they are, bitten by rhythms that would have twiddled the toes of St. Anthony. They beat time with their feet—*lèse-majesté* in a symphony orchestra. They fidgeted uncomfortably when for a moment they had to stop playing. And there were the incredible gyrations of that virtuoso and imp of the perverse, Ross Gorman. And then there was Mr. Whiteman. He does not conduct. He trembles, wabbles, quivers—a piece of jazz jelly, conducting the orchestra with the back of the trouser of the right leg, and the face of a mandarin the while.

There was an ovation for Victor Herbert, that master of instrumentation, when his four Serenades composed for this occasion were played, and Mr. Herbert acknowledged the applause from the gallery. Then stepped upon the stage, sheepishly, a lank and dark young man—George Gershwin. He was to play the piano part in the first public performance of his *Rhapsody in Blue* for piano and orchestra. This composition shows extraordinary talent, just as it also shows a young composer with aims that go far beyond those of his ilk, struggling with a form of which he is far from being master. It is important to bear both these facts in mind in estimating the composition. Often Mr. Gershwin's purpose is defeated by technical immaturity, but in spite of that technical immaturity, a lack of knowledge of how to write effectively for piano alone or in combination with orchestra, an unconscious attempt to rhapsodize in the manner of Franz Liszt, a naïveté which at times stresses something unimportant while something of value and effectiveness goes by so quickly that it is lost—in spite of all this, he has expressed himself in a significant and, on the whole, highly original manner.

His first theme alone, with its caprice, humor, and exotic outline, would show a talent to be reckoned with. It starts with an outrageous cadenza of the clarinet. It has subsidiary phrases, logically growing out of it, and integral to the thought. The original phrase and subsidiaries are often ingeniously metamorphosed by devices of rhythm and instrumentation. There is an Oriental twist to the whole business that is not hackneyed or superficial. And—what is important—this is no mere dance tune set for piano and other instruments. It is an idea, or several ideas correlated and combined in varying and well-contrasted rhythms that immediately intrigue the hearer. This, in essence, is fresh and new and full of future promise.

The second theme, with a lovely sentimental line, is more after the manner of some of Mr. Gershwin's colleagues. Tuttis are too long, cadenzas are too long, the peroration at the end loses a large measure of wildness and magnificence it could easily have if it were more broadly prepared; but, for all that, the audience was stirred and many a hardened concertgoer excited with the sensation of a new talent finding its voice and likely to say something personally and racially important to the world. A talent and an idiom also rich in possibilities for that generally exhausted and outworn form of the classic piano concerto.

Mr. Gershwin's rhapsody also stands out as counteracting, quite unconsciously, a weakness of the program—that is, a tendency to sameness of rhythm and sentiment in the music. When a program consists almost entirely of modern dance music, that is naturally a danger, since American dances of today do not boast great variety of step or character; but it should be possible for Mr. Whiteman to remedy this in a second program, which he will give later in the season. There was tumultuous applause for Mr. Gershwin's composition. There was realization of the irresistible vitality and genuineness of much of the music heard on this occasion, as opposed to the pitiful sterility of the average production of the "serious" American composer. The audience packed a house that could have been sold out twice over.

=

Paris Preview of the Boston Symphony's New Conductor

"Mr. Koussevitzky will be a formidable rival . . ."

Paris, May 30

IT IS probable that Serge Koussevitzky, when he comes to America next season as conductor of the Boston Symphony Orchestra, will not give programs of the extremely brilliant and ultra-modern quality that he has been giving this spring in Paris. Mr. Koussevitzky has been told that Americans do not like too much pepper where orchestral music is concerned, and he is inclined to be cautious in this direction. Moreover, he himself is a man of very catholic tastes, who is not by nature an exponent of any one school, past or present, or clique, wherever it may be. Here he arranges lists calculated to appeal to a highly sophisticated public, alert for the latest musical sensation and for composers who, whatever their eventual importance in history, are representatives of the most "advanced" tendencies in this art. For America Mr. Koussevitzky plans carefully balanced programs of classic and modern music, with a good admixture of new compositions, only a few of which he is willing to announce before he reaches Boston; it is not only in Paris that conductors strive to anticipate each other in the production of new works. He hopes, however, that when he does perform unknown compositions in America he will find a following for them. This was said in a conversation with a certain wistfulness and naïveté. Mr. Koussevitzky has yet to discover that in Boston it is customary to keep abreast of everything of importance that is produced in the field of orchestral music, and that the public in New York often accepts what it gets when it finds no means of becoming articulate as to what it wants. But these are things that concern the future. Let us consider a typical Koussevitzky concert in Paris, such as the final concert of his spring series, which took place at the Opéra on the evening of May 29.

In this city Koussevitzky is the conductor of the hour. He is, of course, a storm center of friends and enemies, of the intrigues and rivalries of the various sections of the musical community of Paris. A man of considerable financial resource as well as of commanding personality, his concerts are now packed to the doors. Each one of them, apparently, provides an irresistible sensation or two for an ordinarily surfeited public. Successful men being envied and hated in this sparkling metropolis as much as or more than anywhere else in the world, it follows that each Koussevitzky concert is attended by a considerable number of polished malcontents who do their utmost to secure tickets without paying for them and are very indignant when they cannot do so; and who, having secured seats either by astonishing ingenuity and effrontery or by most reluctantly parting with money, greatly relish the privilege of "roasting" the conductor while the music is being played, with that peculiar Gallic wit and venom which distinguish the choicer spirits of the capital. The others are supporters of Stravinsky, of various stripes. Some are self-interested in the matter. Others will do anything to see and be seen on important public occasions. Then there is the host of foreign visitors—who cannot, however, rob the Parisian audience of that peculiar theatrical flare and glitter which still distinguish it at the height of the season—and there are the genuine musical enthusiasts, thickest in the uppermost reaches of the house, where they still honor tradition by making voluble comments upon the performance or any other matter which happens to interest them. Thus the individual who leaned over the rail of the highest gallery while Koussevitzky was bowing and bowing again to the applause. "Hurry up," he yelled, "with the music, so that we poor people can hear it all before the last subway"—sensible advice, duly heeded. In a word, it is a Paris audience. Even the applause and "bravos" have a certain distinctive timbre, that mixture of sudden enthusiasm and theatrical pretense which no other circumstances provide; and Mr. Koussevitzky, with a triumvirate of composers— Florent Schmitt, Serge Prokofieff, and Igor Stravinsky—who are likewise prominent in the public gaze, is monarch of what he surveys.

A half-hour or thereabouts after the time announced for the beginning of the concert, Koussevitzky enters, steps quickly through the orchestra to his stand, raps for attention, and commences without more ado the Corelli concerto. There are strong divisions of opinion here, as there will be in America, concerning his conducting; but there can be no question of his arousing keen public interest as man and musician, and, whether or not one agrees with his conceptions, it is hardly possible, after listening and talking to him, to doubt his sincerity. On the conductor's stand he is a figure to watch as well as to hear. Tall, with dark hair which is graying, with nervous hands and face which sensitively reflects his mood, and with a degree of bodily command that pertains to few conductors, Koussevitzky plays, obviously but not the less effectively, on his orchestra. He has no mannerism or particular gestures that a single concert fixes in the mind, but does appear to embody in every movement what he finds in the music. With a chorus of some good qualities and others by no means so good, and an orchestra which Mr. Koussevitzky will not prefer to the Boston Symphony, he secured the most expressive and, at times, volcanic response to his wishes. And at such times the conductor was a figure to remember—erect, imperious, his face working with his own emotions; a hand of which the fingers themselves are eloquent, suddenly bringing out an outburst of tone from the chorus; a glance which, sweeping over the orchestra, brings equally sudden and dramatic results. Koussevitzky has the stamp of a leader. As a musician he is evidently endowed with a temperament that can on occasion sweep everything before it. In all that he does there is an authority, a quenchless enthusiasm, and a big sweep which, even if he were less sincere and individual as a musician, would be a compelling force for public success. It is predictable even now that in more ways than one Mr. Koussevitzky will be a formidable rival in America for a conductor whose name also ends with the sound of "ski." No more than that conductor is he in the habit of allowing an audience or an orchestra to stagnate under him.

To return to the concert and the program: Florent Schmitt's evocation of Pan, *La Tristesse de Pan*, as it is hardly necessary to say, is a musical reincarnation of a certain faun who wakens from his slumber, not in a Debussyan heyday of his existence, but some quarter of a century later. His amorousness has a sensuous beauty which appropriately and no doubt intentionally leans more to Debussy than to the more mordant character of the talent of Schmitt. But it is a good piece of music, and the original composition stands orchestral transformation so well that one suspects Mr. Schmitt of thinking for orchestra when he wrote for the piano and finding relief in at last casting his conception in the orchestral mold which his creative nature intended.

Sept, ils sont sept, the violent and undeniably effective composition of Prokofieff, followed. It would have sent an audience accustomed to New York orchestral programs scurrying for the doors. For this Prokofieff is a bold and bad young man. How his music will sound ten years hence is an open question. How it would have sounded under a conductor less temperamental and less sympathetic to its nature than Koussevitzky it is hard to say. But on the evening in question and under the circumstances the work made a powerful impression. It is huge and rather horrible and primitive.

This is the most effective composition of Prokofieff that we have heard. Composed as early as 1917, the score remained in Russia until recently recovered, forwarded to Paris, and performed by Koussevitzky for the first time anywhere. It is music which would have delighted Hector Berlioz, and perhaps it is more than that. There is the sensation of the atavistic. Man trembles before the terrible and the unknown. The chorus is one seething tumult of outcries and supplications, reinforced by exceptional orchestral combinations and harmonies as jagged and unbeautiful as the gargoyles on Nôtre Dame. The task of the solo tenor, admirably executed by H. Fabert, requires a manner sometimes verging on speech, or yells, instead of song, and this with a dramatic intensity that will tax him physically as well as emotionally, to say nothing of maintaining rhythm and pitch against complicated opposing forces. The voice glides through intervals that cannot be reduced to notation, and with a barbaric wildness difficult to describe. Few could have equaled M. Fabert in his task. The orchestra thuds and seethes and erupts. A strange piece with a physiognomy all its own, and a remarkable conclusion.

One listened to that crude, savage, half-articulate music and glanced upward at the loge where Prokofieff was sitting—Prokofieff, the front of whose head is bald, whose face, nevertheless, seems incredibly young and very cerebral, like a being who has come from another age or planet, groomed and dressed in the style of today, to examine a world upon which he may have sinister designs! A queer fellow, who seems to be delving, musically, in a certain hinterland of the human consciousness, listening to what he has discovered there with as much calmness and detachment as if he were a scientist discussing the theory of evolution.

He rose from his seat and bowed as humbly as you please to enormous applause, as the composition came to an end—a sudden hush that falls over chorus and orchestra, an effect of utter prostration and helplessness in the presence of unfathomable mystery. The murmurs of the chorus are heard distantly, from far off, through the exordium of the orchestra. A curious business!

Now came Stravinsky, a small man, extremely self-possessed, who played his concerto exactly as we knew he would before he even entered the hall—with a clean-cut, electrical vigor that had no softness or sentiment in it, with a precision and rhythmical force inseparable from the composer of *The Rite of Spring*. His finger technique was as clean as a steel blade, and his musical thinking, as composer and performer, was as clean as that, too. Again, in this concerto, he has done a new thing, and this by means of a style that is essentially classic. There is an opening theme in the manner of a chorale. It is developed fugally, with great vigor and life, and with many a fine grinding dissonance, broadly speaking, after the manner of Bach. The treatment is lengthy and elaborate, incisive and full of contrapuntal resource. The slow movement has more lyrical qualities, though not very much of sensuous beauty. The finale resumes contrapuntal procedure. Toward the last the composer makes bold employment of syncopation somewhat in the manner of American ragtime, in which, as we know, Stravinsky and other leading European composers have been much interested. With more and more rhythmical force and accumulation of healthy power the concerto comes to an end. It had an electrifying performance, particularly on the part of Stravinsky himself, who played with unending technique and endurance, attacking great chords in a manner veritably suggestive of the paws of a Russian bear, though always with a poise which is one of the astounding qualities of his musical nature. The concerto is one of many new departures of Stravinsky. The *Symphonies d'instruments à vent*, which Stokowski played last year in New York, was another. The concerto bears out the supposition that Stravinsky has become more and more capricious in his musical output since *Sacre du printemps*, and less and less aware of his own artistic destiny. From *Oiseau de feu* to *Sacre du printemps*, via the incomparable *Petrouchka*, his way seems perfectly clear, after which this humble commentator cannot follow the singular and unpredictable divagations of Stravinsky's muse. . . .

Words of Mr. Koussevitzky, outlining his attitude on the subject of orchestral programs, modern and classical music, will be of interest to those who attend his concerts next winter. "I would like to make it clear," said the conductor, "that I am neither modernist nor classicist in my musical preferences. The works of the great classic masters are absolutely indispensable to me, as musician and in my life. No one would less willingly be without them than I. But music is not a static art. Music is continually being made which is an expression of the period in which it appears. It is as necessary for us to know what is being done as it is to know and admire what has been done. As for the value of new works, the conductor uses his best judgment in producing them. He must leave the rest to the judgment of time."

NOVEMBER 8, 1924

===

Jeritza Appears in *Tosca*

"It assumed, incredibly enough, the character
of high tragedy."

THE performance of *Tosca* given last night by the Metropolitan Opera Company, with Maria Jeritza in the title role, was a repetition of a familiar but none the less sweeping triumph for that singer and the company which employs her, for it would be difficult to conceive of a performance which, as a whole, moved more swiftly, with more unerring dramatic logic and cumulative power, to its conclusion. This production is a striking illustration of what an interpretation great in virtually all its parts can do for an opera which is not in itself of enduring worth. For once, Puccini's drama was more than a noteworthy achievement in sensationalism. It assumed, incredibly enough, the character of high tragedy, and it held the audience breathless from the first scene to the last.

Mme Jeritza's incomparable impersonation was not the only cause of this effect. Mr. Scotti was the Scarpia, famous in this role for many long years, but not the Scarpia that we knew a few seasons previous. Last night the figure seemed more sinister than before. The Scarpia that crouched a little—almost, at moments, with the effect of deformity—that shook and trembled with the violence of his own rage, was a more evil apparition than the proud and domineering force of the figure we remembered.

There was a full-throated tenor in Mr. Fleta, who seems to have developed as a singer since last season, and who filled his part with a reasonable imagination of the theatrical fitness of things. Mr. Ananian was an excellent Angelotti, a highly realistic picture of the hunted fugitive. Minor roles were admirably taken. And, finally, there was the masterly conducting of Mr. Serafin.

As for Mme Jeritza's impersonation, this is the most distinguished and original presentation of the role we have seen. It is gloriously sung. It is compact of tone of every shade of color and feeling, physical beauty of the highest type, and eloquence of bodily line and rhythm that would envisage, if music and text were lacking, every emotion.

It begins quietly, with apparent simplicity; it develops gradually and with irresistible power. It becomes at last such a picture of a woman racked with suffering, desperate in the last extremity, that one forgets all Puccini's obviousness, all his stage tricks, his sobbing banalities, and feels the pity and truthfulness of the interpretation as strongly as he feels the inadequacy of words to describe it. This was a memorable performance. Those whose privilege it was to behold it will have memories. When great artists arrive in future years, they will say: "But I heard Maria Jeritza in *Tosca*."

JANUARY 11, 1925

Brailowsky as a Poet of the Piano

"A much abused phrase but for once deserved"

REPEATED hearings of the performances of Alexander Brailowsky strengthen the impression that he is in very fact a poet of the piano —a much abused phrase, but a phrase for once deserved. Mr. Braillowsky is born to play this particular instrument, and he gives a poignant beauty and glamour to even very simple compositions that he interprets with its aid. Naturally, for a pianist of such temperament and quality, the music of Chopin holds a particular appeal. Playing a program of his compositions yesterday afternoon in Carnegie Hall, Mr. Brailowsky refuted the suspicions felt by more than one music-lover that the day of the piano is passing, and convinced his audience all over again that Chopin is the incomparable composer of music for this instrument.

Mr. Brailowsky might have been equally successful as a violinist or performer on the oboe, but we very much doubt it. He has a sheer instinct for the secrets of the piano. He knows intuitively the colors that the pedal can evoke; he summons a brilliancy in bravura and a liquid beauty of tone in singing passages which, while they have been cultivated, are inborn and can never be merely acquired. He seems to have escaped the toughening results of the terrible routine the professional pianist must undergo; he re-creates his music with all the freshness of feeling and imagined beauty that it must have had for him when first the eyes fell on the printed page and straying fingers hinted at the wonders it contained.

He has, too, or had yesterday, a remarkably fine sense of proportion. In a previous concert he played with more extravagance and abandon. Yesterday Mr. Brailowsky was more continent in his effects and obtained them by the most simple and sincere means. There were perhaps two compositions in which he lapsed into the commonplace or virtuotistic; these were the F major Waltz, which is trivial enough in any event, and, rather strangely, the G minor Ballade, in which there were even a few technical shortcomings. But these moments were exceptions. For the greater part of the afternoon the performances were of the most exceptional eloquence and poetic atmosphere.

To play two of the most familiar nocturnes—those in G major and E flat—in a way that made every note a thing of intense beauty, and the whole a really haunting memory, is an almost incredible accomplishment for a hardened concertgoer to encounter. Then there was the archness, the simplicity and caprice of three mazurkas, none of them ranking with Chopin's most individual and emotional contributions in this field, but all of them typical and characteristic of this form which Chopin refined and glorified from the folk music of his country. Came the heroic Chopin of the Fantasy and the C sharp minor Scherzo, both works given interpretations which took away all the commonplaceness that hackneyed past performances had encrusted upon them, and made them inspiring experiences. The performance of the great A minor Étude was in similar vein—retaining, with all its force, the beauty that Chopin never crushed or distorted.

Mr. Brailowsky repeated a delightful performance of the study in thirds, so beautifully accomplished that the listener remembered only that beauty and was unaware of the phenomenal display of technique. The third study, the one in G flat of the first set, was done just as well. Nor was the performance of the early and relatively unimportant Andante Spianato and Polonaise less distinctive. The music had an elegance, a tonal loveliness and sparkle which became the ideal realization of its style. Mr. Brailowsky played encores—no doubt a great many. Superlatives are dangerous, but it is not easy to speak coolly in reporting the accomplishments of a true and rare artist.

FEBRUARY 1, 1925

Stravinsky Visits America at Forty-three

"A case of arrested development"

THE New York public has been particularly favored this winter in its opportunity to gain an authoritative impression of the music of the most widely heralded composer of the day—Igor Stravinsky. Visiting America for the first time, Mr. Stravinsky has personally directed performances of a number of his most important compositions. He will appear this week as soloist in the performance of his own Piano Concerto with the Philharmonic Orchestra, Mr. Mengelberg conducting. We have already heard orchestral and chamber-music programs of works dating from Stravinsky's student days to that singular experiment in music of an "abstract" and "architectural" quality, the *Octuor* for wind instruments, heard last Sunday night in Aeolian Hall for the first time in America. We have not heard *Noces*, a work of relatively early origin and a number of later revisions, and one which impressed this writer as an expression highly individual and Russian to the core when he heard it last summer in Paris; but, after all, this is not a work that illumines any unknown aspect of the composer's creative personality. We have not heard and probably never will hear the one-act opera *Mavra* or *Le Rossignol* in operatic form, but the symphonic poem *Le Chant du rossignol* contains much of the musical substance of the work for the stage, and there have been heard here in previous seasons such works as the Concertino and the pieces for string quartet, the Japanese songs, the elegy for Debussy, *Symphonies d'instruments à vent*, and there have been performances by three conductors of the *Sacre du printemps*. The offerings of two New York musical seasons, in short, have provided an ample representation of Stravinsky at every stage of his career.

He is now forty-three years old. He has not originated a new score of major importance, or nearly approximating the *Sacre du printemps*, in twelve years. The outlook for a worthy successor to the last-named composition, it must be admitted, is not auspicious. The works that have followed it have been, for the most part, of a restless, experimental nature. Now Stravinsky is writing nursery songs; now he is writing "ragtime"; now he has abjured all but the "purest" and most "classical" conceptions of music, as exemplified in the *Symphonies d'instruments à vent* and the rather lamentable *Octuor* for wind-players. The listener asks himself: "Who, what is the essential Stravinsky?" Every time he writes he is someone else, which is not the habit of great masters. A Wagner writes *Tristan* and follows it with *Meistersinger*, but there is no mistaking the authorship of either opera. This restlessness and instability is the most unfortunate and disquieting feature of the Stravinsky question—if it can be called that, for there is little question that the bewildering rise of Igor Stravinsky from apparent creative nonentity to the position of composer of the *Sacre du printemps* has been followed by a decline fully as rapid and destructive of the high hopes of those who believed that in him there was a prophet of a new age. The trouble is that Stravinsky appears to have been precisely the opposite of a prophet of a new age; he seems to have succumbed utterly to the aimlessness, the superficialities and pretenses of this one.

At a time when most composers are beginning to find themselves and formulate a personal idiom, he had set the world by the ears with his savage primitive spring song and was looking about, a tonal (or, rather, polytonal) Alexander, for fresh worlds to conquer. His artistic development had been incredibly rapid and arresting to the public gaᴢe. There is hardly a historic parallel to his development in the five years from 1908 to 1913, or from his twenty-sixth to his thirty-first years. Who, from the composer of such works as *Scherzo fantastique* and the *Fireworks* of 1908, would have dreamed of the exquisite fancy, tenderness, and exotic spell of the score of *Oiseau de feu* that came two short years later? There are liveliness and crackle in the earlier works, but no feeling or atmosphere perceptible. The two scores are brilliantly perfected mechanisms. But the youth who writes music for the fairy tale of *The Bird of Fire* is a poet and a genius. Like other young poets, he is still discarding certain powerful influences, but in the main he shows here the freshness of feeling that his years and sensibility give him and the sense of race that a true creative artist can hardly be without. The music of *Oiseau de feu* is not only that of a young master coming into his own; it is as truly of Russian folklore as the fairy tale that provoked it. It seemed indubitable, when that work appeared, that another poet had been born, to re-create in individual forms of his own the heritage of beauty and legend bequeathed him by his people.

This score in itself would have designated Stravinsky as a man to be watched in his art, but, again, who would have prognosticated *Petrouchka? Petrouchka* came in 1912. There was, if anything, a bigger distance between *Petrouchka* and *Oiseau de feu* than there had been between *Oiseau de feu* and the earlier student pieces. There was a technique infinitely more daring, audacious, absolutely sure in its application, and there was a completely different emotional point of view. The composer of *Firebird* was a poet enamored of an ancient folk tale. The composer of *Petrouchka* had gone out, like Moussorgsky, to the people. He had seen life with open eyes, without fear and without illusion. There is little tenderness and certainly no sentimentality in *Petrouchka*, but a stinging vigor and whirl of life. Life treats roughly the poor puppet, and his agony is conveyed in hard, clear, unemotional accents which become more tragic and provocative of pity than all the maudlin tears that would have been wept by an orthodox opera composer. Then there is a final touch—the eerieness and grotesquerie of Petrouchka's end, when his ghost is seen waving its arms in frantic and helpless protest over the showman's booth at the fair—

Petrouchka, the superfluous one, laughed and blotted out of existence. There is more than burlesque or mere irony in this conclusion. There is the feeling of silent, inscrutable forces which surround our existence. This work, in fact, and not the notorious *Sacre*, may prove to be Stravinsky's most perfect creation, and to present in the most striking manner the elements of the dramatic trinity—the crowd, the man, the unfathomable mystery that envelops them. At any rate, it is between *Oiseau de feu* and *Petrouchka*, and not between *Petrouchka* and *Sacre du printemps*, as many felt, that the real break of Stravinsky with his youthful past took place. In *Oiseau de feu* he is essentially the disciple of Rimsky-Korsakoff and Glinka. In *Petrouchka* he forgets affiliations possible to him only in certain early, soft, and impressionable years. He turns to Moussorgsky, finding in him his real musical ancestor and one from whose influence he never fought free.

No doubt other influences made themselves felt with Stravinsky. It could not be otherwise with an ear and a brain so acute as his. Among these were certainly Debussy in the earlier stages, then Ravel and Schoenberg. But these did not turn him aside; rather they perfected and rounded out his style and helped him to the perspective and the complete grasp of technical resources necessary to produce the score of *Sacre du printemps*. The germs of that score were in *Petrouchka*, although they underwent evolution of which no one who knew *Petrouchka* had dreamed. The style is perfectly consistent, especially in the rhythmical developments and the carrying out of the element of polyharmony; and the use of folk song is of particular value to a man with so little melodic invention as Stravinsky. No need to expatiate upon the music, which could have been composed only at this time, in this nervous and destructive age, expressing, as it does, stark and elemental things which had not hitherto found their way into the tonal art. This is in all probability one of the most important, as it is one of the most typical, of modern scores. Incidentally, the score has been a treasure house to a generation of composers only slightly younger than Stravinsky himself. Its precise value will be settled by time. Meanwhile, it is not easy to deny the author of that work a place high among the prophets. And there—so far as all the evidence that can be weighed at the present time indicates—Stravinsky has stopped. Refinements of technique, sudden complete changes of esthetic, bizarre experiments empty of the impulse of beauty and feeling, seem mainly to have occupied him. The same kind of deterioration has been noted with other moderns, particularly with Richard Strauss and Debussy. They suddenly failed at the height of their powers. But they had produced much more than Stravinsky when this took place, and each of them had passed his fortieth year. The case of Stravinsky's arrested development is an instance of earlier decline, but it seems to bear a similar stamp and is very probably due to similar things. Few indeed are the artists today who stand success and its material rewards without losing sincerity and creative force.

FEBRUARY 6, 1925

Stravinsky Introduces His Concerto; Mengelberg Conducts Schubert

"It may be a little early for the critical brotherhood
to bury Stravinsky."

WILLEM MENGELBERG and Igor Stravinsky were the predominating features of the concert given by the Philharmonic Society last night in Carnegie Hall. There were other "features" of the occasion. Thus there was a symphony in C by one Schubert, and there was heard— barely heard—an atrociously vulgar overture by Tchaikovsky ("1812") in a swollen instrumental version wholly unnecessary and in bad taste for such an occasion. But these were secondary considerations. The audience wanted to watch Mr. Mengelberg, to look at and to listen to Mr. Stravinsky as soloist in his first New York performance of his piano concerto.

This piano concerto is undoubtedly the most important and individual composition of Stravinsky's present "period." In the melodic sense there is not an original idea in the score. But as the expression of an individual temperament it is an amazing and electrifying development. With the exception of the middle movement—the least distinctive, the least individual of the four—the composition is almost purely contrapuntal and rhythmical in its nature. There is no love for melody as that word is traditionally defined; there is little "harmony," if by "harmony" is meant blocks of chords instead of combining melodic lines. There is no emotion, but ruthless, driving energy, and a spirit that is imperious and sardonic.

The orchestra of double basses, wind instruments, and percussion first discourses what may be called by courtesy a chorale. It is a rather cheap tune. Indeed, the impression is that the composer in conceiving this concerto thought of one chorale tune as being about as good as and no better than another—just as a contractor who was to erect a large building would consider that no one brick was better than another for his purposes. The chorale theme which opens the first movement of the concerto is planned apparently simply to provide a working basis, a lump of raw material from which to fashion an extended musical structure.

It is an unlovely passage. The piano enters impatiently with a vigorous rhythm, punctuated on off-beats and measures by chords of a shrieking dissonance, which click on the ear as a whip would flick over the flesh, and now the movement is fairly started. It plunges forward on its own irresistible way. The counterpoint may by a stretch of definition be said to echo the style of Bach or Handel, but it is not quite so. It is more brutal; it takes the bit in its teeth and rushes forward with apparently complete recklessness of consequences. The listener is caught in the current and whirled along with it. The force and impetus of this movement, which in advance of the finale already hints at syncopation of the "ragtime" variety, grows and accumulates to the last emphatic measures.

The slow movement is as a bad imitation of the slow movement of a violin sonata by Bach. There is a false melody, a melody with no real juice or life in it, a wraith of a melody, chilly as the grave. It is handled restlessly, moodily, by orchestra and solo instrument, and the final measures of this movement become bases for the next one. In the finale Stravinsky returns to the contrapuntal manner, but with more boldness and rhythmic abandon than ever. Behind this abandon, however, is the absolute certainty of the master.

The Bachlike figures begin to undergo bewildering transformations. An energetic but dignified motive is now distorted, jazzed, caricatured, and turned into a musical weapon of derision. The pace is always more headlong, until a fragment of the opening chorale makes a forlorn reappearance, to be dismissed with a few

99

measures ripped out by the piano, with which the piece comes to an end.

This concerto made a very strong impression. A number laughed outright at some of its tonal grimaces and contortions, but it was very evident that the work had stirred a majority of the audience. Its rhythm alone, and the magnificent virtuosity of Mr. Stravinsky's performance—he seemed to have endless speed, power, precision at command, and was in fact himself a complete rival orchestra— would have made a sensational effect. Mr. Stravinsky is no con- ductor, but there are very few pianists who could have given the performance he gave last night, even granting the very advantageous position of the composer interpreting his own composition.

The question then comes: is this music? This question is not easy to answer. Would the concerto wear? That is quite doubtful. Is there really any such thing as music which has no echo of the passions of the human heart? Perhaps. If so, then Stravinsky may really be on the track of a new music, abstract, classic in its con- ception, a music that derives its existence and its vital force simply by the conflict of opposing melodic lines and the propulsion of conflicting rhythms. But as the expression of an extraordinary brain and a certain phase of modern temperament this piano con- certo is without a parallel. It is probably only one more step in the present path that Stravinsky is exploring, from which he may very well—and shortly—turn away.

But it is a work which reminds the listener that Stravinsky is no ordinary man, that he is an artist of prodigious force, and that it may be a little early for the critical brotherhood to bury Stravinsky. He is now in a state of restlessness and transition of which this severe, unfertile stuff encountered last night is a very characteristic symptom. Stravinsky may never discover his goal. It seems that he has been led into dangerous side-paths of late, paths as interminable as they are futile. But one thing is certain: he will have more to say before the end comes.

Mr. Mengelberg, conducting the Schubert symphony, that marvel of Dionysian beauty, glorified himself, if he did not invariably glorify the composer. We have heard the introduction of the sym- phony given a serenity of a spirit which was not present last night. We heard last night details of instrumentation that seemed unim- portant and climaxes of a needlessly noisy quality. But, on the other hand, there was the extraordinary authority and orchestral control of Mengelberg. The proper instrumental balances in this symphony are difficult even for experienced conductors to attain. This was the best-balanced performance of the symphony, in the tonal sense, that we ever heard. And when Mengelberg rose to his height, and whether or not one agreed with him—he was Mengelberg. The climax of the slow movement, and the wonderful respiration of the cello phrases that follow the pause, present a case in question. This was incomparably eloquent, so that the listener merely wondered and reveled in the effect, and forgot until too late to ask himself whether the score justified such a procedure. It was true creative interpretation.

FEBRUARY 15, 1925

Advice to the American Composer

"What our young musicians should not do"

PRETENSE, pose, the fear of being considered outside the pale of cultivated society, are disagreeable traits in an individual, but are even more objectionable when encountered in an art. They appear in an art in two principal ways—the way of bumptiousness and bravado, which is simply the opposite pole of self-depreciation, and the way of sycophancy and snobbish emulation of some favorite model.

Examples of both these phases of self-consciousness and affectation were furnished by American compositions performed at the recent concert of the International Composers' Guild in this city [New York]. There was gawkily pretentious music with no results of particular importance save the flourish of thundersticks, and there was imitation of imitations of recent examples of European musical sensationalism. It was not a happy exposition of American talent and initiative. In fact, it was a rather striking example of what our young musicians should not do.

It is curious, and it is a pity that these things should be noticed in young Americans. It is singular that they do not turn with enthusiasm and relief to their own environment and express the color and zest of the life about them, which, as artists, they should be able to feel. But no. It takes an Englishman to write a "London" symphony, and a composer of the French school to hymn in his own way his praise of the speed and the power of a locomotive. Americans, believed to be uncommonly endowed with initiative, self-reliance, and a wholesome freedom of convention, turn to the Milhauds, Stravinskys, or even Marinettis, for guides, philosophers, and friends. Americans have justified their reputation for resolution and common sense in many fields, but when they adventure in music they suddenly become timorous, imitative, and unsure of themselves. As we have said, they show this uncertainty in many ways, some of them bumptious, noisy, and self-assertive, but they very seldom show a desire to be, rather than to seem, or a real determination to get at the roots of their art and discover themselves in the process.

At the bottom of it all, in this country at least, seems to be the laziness and evasion of the dilettante. There is no reason today why a young American musician should fail to find himself and develop his state save a lack of creative energy, faith, and devotion to his task. In former years it was not so. Time was when an American had to go to Europe and sit at the feet of European minds and European conventions in order to achieve any degree of artistic development. Musical technique was made in Germany, and later in France. There was little expert instruction or artistic stimulus here. The American went to Europe and took the consequences, which were not particularly helpful to the development of original music in his own country. But that stage has been passed. In our leading cities there is plenty of competent teaching and artistic contact. The tools of the artist are procurable at first hand, but the conscience and resolution of the artist are different matters. Yet the position of America in thought and in world affairs, and the cultural horizon of the American, are infinitely broader than they were twenty-five years ago, and the time for the American spirit to be creative as never before should be at hand.

But the average young American who has had the advantage of special education in his art remains singularly uncertain, emotionally underdeveloped, intellectually a conglomeration of indeterminate matter. His unsureness and lack of self-knowledge are shown clearly in the course he usually follows in his studies. He has, in the first place, the complacent belief that someone or something can turn him into a creative musician. He does not seem to know that composing can only be learned and never taught. Creation comes from the will to create, and this will can never be conferred. Until there is the potency and the invincible will to give new forms to impressions and experiences of life, all the teaching in the world is without value. The man with real perception of life and beauty, and a real intention to serve these things in his art, is not calculating or palavering with teachers as to which, where, or how he will express himself. He has a purpose fixed from the beginning, and he is always using his will and his imagination to absorb useful materials and come nearer his goal.

Or else the budding composer exhibits the attitude, very common today, of ignorant, arrogant contempt for what the great masters of his art have created for posterity, and the invaluable store of technical knowledge which has been laboriously accumulated for him through the centuries. He does not even know that the score of a Beethoven symphony holds incalculable treasure for a sincere and adventurous spirit. But these scores will not yield their secrets to poseurs or dilettantes. They are there for the man who is not afraid to bow the knee to greatness, who will take what the immortal master gives him as one spirit receives that which is his right from another—not as a thief would steal or a menial accept a present, but as one who stands erect and walks with kings, nor loses the common touch.

The question of what manner of music an American will evolve is of secondary importance at the present time. He must look deeper than he does, and have far more modesty and courage than he has shown, to do anything worth while at all. The reward of those who do not fear to be themselves is already evident, though on a limited and superficial scale, in the production of certain of our composers of popular music. Their lesson is by some wrongly interpreted. They have not written expressive music merely because of an interesting patois of their own which they have evolved; they have written music which in some cases is rich in vitality, humor, and certain qualities of the people because they wrote it naturally, without affectation or pretending to be something they were not. Their best music, in its way, rings true, stirs the listener, and towers high by the side of the compositions which discreetly or ostentatiously ape other cultures and other composers' styles. But the day is yet to come for the American composer as a type to discover himself and his country in his art. That day will put forever to shame the puerility and pretense of our musical present.

APRIL 2, 1925

===

A Myra Hess Recital

"An incident probably without a precedent"

AN INCIDENT probably without a precedent in the concert annals of this city occurred at the end of the piano recital given by Myra Hess last night in Aeolian Hall. Miss Hess had completed her program as announced, and had played as an encore a composition of Scarlatti, when someone in the hall called out "Bach!" The name was taken up by many others in different parts of the auditorium until "Bach" could be heard from every part of the house.

The compositions of Bach do not customarily serve as encores at piano recitals, nor has Bach ever enjoyed the reputation of being food and sustenance for the encore field. But it was Bach last night who figured as the most popular composer of the Hess program. She responded to the demands of her audience with a prelude and fugue from the *Well-Tempered Clavichord*. This was not enough. The cry came again, "More Bach," and was taken up as before. Miss Hess played another one of the preludes and fugues of the "Forty-eight" before the audience was satisfied. She then played two more compositions of Scarlatti and finally two études of Chopin, thus adding half again to the length of her program—a program which had opened with four of the chorales of Bach in arrangements for piano by Busoni, and, in the instance of the chorale *Herz und Mund und That und Leben*, arranged by Miss Hess herself. It may be said here that there are few more promising signs of the times, musically speaking, than the manner in which Bach is constantly gaining in the esteem of the public.

The remainder of the printed program, in addition to the Bach compositions, consisted of four Brahms intermezzos, the E flat

Rhapsody of the same composer, and the Schumann *Symphonic Studies*. The poetic intermezzos are well suited to a pianist of Miss Hess's sensitive feeling and fine adjustment of values. The Rhapsody was good to hear again. It reflects in the opening, perhaps, the influence of Schumann, but it quickly becomes unadulterated Brahms, as in the dark and mysterious color of the C minor passage; in the passage in A flat over the pizzicato bass, which is as the breath of spring; in the ominous preparation and magnificent reannouncement of the main theme of the Rhapsody, and the smashing coda which brings the end.

This piece was given a spirited performance. So were the Schumann *Symphonic Studies*, particularly those of the more poetic character, such as the one with the impressionistic accompaniment which precedes the ringing finale. But one questions whether in music that demands abundant physical weight and vigor as well as ·a boldly dramatic or impassioned style, Miss Hess does herself the utmost justice.

One of her great distinctions is the fact that she plays with a woman's sensitiveness and intuition—not with a lack of deep feeling or of broad line, yet not, on the other hand, as a woman trying to equal the muscularity and physical power that are commonly qualities of a man. It is precisely in Bach, especially the Bach of the suites and the *Well-Tempered Clavichord*, in Scarlatti, in composers distinguished by aristocratic purity of style and eloquence without strain or turgidity, that Miss Hess excels and appears with special distinction among her colleagues. All of the performances of last night were technically brilliant, musicianly, and sincere, but probably the wishes of the audience led it aright to the music of Bach, which seems part of the birthright of a singularly accomplished pianist.

Vladimir de Pachmann's "Farewell" Recital

"He has achieved and forgotten more than many a pianist ever knew."

VLADIMIR DE PACHMANN's farewell recital, or the occasion announced as such, took place last night in Carnegie Hall. Mr. de Pachmann must have been pleased by the size of his audience and the reception extended him, for the hall was packed and many sat on the stage, and enthusiasm ran high.

The pianist was rarely in the vein. The G minor Ballade combined lyrical beauty with wildly dramatic declamation. It made its effect in performance through the cunning with which Mr. de Pachmann marshaled his physical resources, and by means of well-contrived proportions and contrasts which made a greater emotional effect than could have been achieved by mere physical force. As a technical accomplishment as well as poetic interpretation, the performance of the A flat major Étude of Opus 10 was a notable instance.

In the second group were the D flat Nocturne, the Preludes—which Mr. de Pachmann professed to need his music to play—in E minor and F sharp major, three of the mazurkas, and the F major Waltz. In the third group came the E flat minor Polonaise, the F sharp major Impromptu, and the B flat minor Scherzo. The performances, especially of the nocturne, of the E minor Prelude, and of the B flat Mazurka, had the loveliness and melancholy that inhere in supremely beautiful things.

The polonaise of the final group, like the ballade, was played in a manner within Mr. de Pachmann's scale of dynamics, yet the introduction has seldom been more ominous or the following outbursts more defiant when they came. The pedaling of the curious impromptu, one of the most original pages in Chopin, was particularly significant, while the performance of the scherzo must reluctantly be characterized as balderdash. It can be dismissed with other of Mr. de Pachmann's foolings as a thing not to be taken seriously or kept in the memory against exquisite manifestations of his art.

Certainly the masterly interpretation of Mozart's C minor Fantasia, one of the greatest compositions for piano in existence, would in itself have done much to justify the occasion. For when Mr. de Pachmann is greatest, the listener is under the spell of music which seems to have escaped human thralldom; music of a charmed rhythmic life; song that floats on the air with a delicious grace and waywardness past the telling. Then it is realized that this extraordinary man, a virtuoso, at seventy-six, of astonishing qualities, and on occasion a great poet of his instrument, has achieved and forgotten more than many a pianist ever knew.

The audience was naturally loath to leave the hall, and Mr. de Pachmann, at a late hour of a particularly impressive "farewell," was still playing encores.

OCTOBER 27, 1925

Première of Honegger's *King David*

"Junk of all kinds from the scrap heap of Debussy, Stravinsky, Bach . . . even Mendelssohn and Wagner— nothing is missing, and quite cleverly served up."

AN AUDIENCE which included many of the socially and musically elect of this city gathered last night in Town Hall for the first performance in America of Arthur Honegger's "symphonic psalm," *King David*, by the Society of the Friends of Music. It may be said at once that this work, which has had unusual recent popularity in Europe, was very cordially received. At every opportunity there was prolonged applause. It is not often that a new work by a young modern is given such a welcome.

The history of this composition, by a musician who is emerging from the onetime band of six terrible infants of French music to a position where he threatens to outrival all of his former associates in the favor of the public, needs only the briefest recapitulation here.

Honegger composed music, which he scored for a small orchestra, for the drama of Renée Morax, *Le Roi David*, produced at the Jorat Art Theatre of Mézières, June 11, 1921. The music was written very quickly—in two months' time. Its success incited the composer to recast his score for large orchestra and for concert performances.

In this form he employs chorus and three solo voices, tenor, soprano, and contralto; a large modern orchestra; and a spoken part for a narrator, who tells the tale, sometimes ceasing for the musical interludes, sometimes with the music of orchestra, chorus, and soloist as a background for his recitation.

Roi David is short, concise, soon over. There is one extended musical movement, which makes the second part of a tripartite creation—the *Dance before the Ark*, which is Oriental, climactic, and highly effective. The rest of the score, for the greater part, is mosaic, and a singular mosaic indeed, but of that more later.

The career of David is put before us almost as rapidly as if it were a scenario for a movie. The text is pared down to essentials, with a brevity and, as it were, an emphasis of headline that would please a city editor. We see, in rapid flashes and captions, David as a shepherd; David the leader and slayer of Goliath; David pursued by Saul; David as king, lover, penitent; David the prophet; David's death and the coronation of Solomon. All this with the strength and imagery of the Old Testament for a basis. The music combines what is barbaric and archaic with all the ingenious devices that harmony, tone color, and eclecticism—to be sure, an undiscriminating eclecticism, but nevertheless eclecticism—can bring to bear. The result is now cacophonic, now mellifluous, very seldom original or sincere, but usually plausible, novel and interesting in orchestral color, and calculated at the least to be entertaining.

Something for every taste! And why not? The public of the twentieth century is a nervous one, a scare-head, taxi-driving, illustrated-magazine public. It is unwise to try this public too much—indeed, it is almost impossible to do this and have *"réclame"* and success. Mr. Honegger is abreast of the age—was abreast of the age, obviously, even before the days when that excellent tonal farce concerning the Pacific locomotive—*Pacific No. 231*—was a good joke. *King David?* It depends upon how you take it.

We repeat, there is everything for every taste in this score. There is an old cast-off shoe of Handel's (see the chorus *"Loué soit le*

Seigneur"). There is junk of all kinds from the scrap heap of Debussy, Stravinsky, Bach—by all that is holy, a chorale of Bach!— even Mendelssohn and Wagner—nothing is missing, and quite cleverly served up. Polyharmony here, eastern melismata there; now a disarming simplicity of the diatonic persuasion. Once in a while a real musical idea, and one piece that must have taken some time and thought to compose—the aforesaid *Dance before the Ark*, commencing with beautiful and mysterious tonal premonitions, leading, with substantial progress and development of parts, to a wild and imposing climax. Even this, after all, is exterior emotion, but it is a structure with genuine ideas for a basis, notwithstanding its theatricalism. That is more than can be said of most of the work, barring a few passages of genuine charm, such as the *Song of the Handmaid*, the lament and the song of the Daughters of Israel, music for David's death. But what a superficial, hastily flung together mélange it is! What an artificial and sensational contraption! As for Orientalism, there is a French composer named Florent Schmitt who years ago made an amazingly dramatic setting of the Forty-seventh Psalm; we forgot, until now, to mention him among Mr. Honegger's contributors. And there is a composer named Ernest Bloch; there is more that is profoundly and superbly Semitic in one page of one of his psalms for solo voice and orchestra than in all the trumpeting of Honegger.

The performance, conducted by Mr. Artur Bodanzky, enlisted the services of the large orchestra and chorus, and Miss Queena Mario, Miss Marion Telva, Armand Tokatyan, and, as narrator, Léon Rothier—artists of the Metropolitan Opera Company. Too much could not be said in praise of Mr. Rothier's superb declamation, his diction, his enunciation, the quality and pitch of the speaking voice, which now and again verged upon song, the thrilling dramatic eloquence. Mr. Bodanzky had prepared the production with devotion.

Of this production much had been said in advance. Expectations of a masterwork ran high. But it was not a masterwork that came to view. One assisted, instead, at the American *première* of a "best seller."

'A Silver Anniversary for Gabrilówitsch and the Philadelphians

The Tchaikovsky Concerto and Beethoven's Fifth

TWENTY-FIVE years ago—or, to be exact, November 16, 1900—the Philadelphia Orchestra gave its first public concert. With it appeared as soloist Ossip Gabrilówitsch, the brilliant young pianist then making his first American tour. Last night the same orchestra, the same soloist, the same program were heard in Carnegie Hall, and the hearing was memorable.

The program last night consisted of Goldmark's "Spring" Overture; Beethoven's Fifth Symphony; the Tchaikovsky B flat minor Concerto, played by Mr. Gabrilówitsch; and the orchestral music that accompanies the entrance of the gods into Wagner's Valhalla.

Mr. Stokowski interpreted Beethoven's symphony in dead earnest. There was no thought of the conductor, only of the ruggedness, the sublime heroism and pathos of the music. There was regard for every note and every sign the composer made in his score, and at the same time a flaming conviction which gave white heat to the interpretation. A detail—the broadening and emphasis of the four-note motive in its repetitions—was a slight and wholly justified departure from tradition. Again Mr. Stokowski commanded his orchestra despotically; again Beethoven stood foursquare to the universe, the most passionate revolutionist of them all, the warrior and prophet of a new era. No orchestra could have excelled, and few equaled, the technical qualities of this performance. For the precision of which this orchestra is capable is equaled by its flexibility and sensitiveness; and, as we have said, Mr. Stokowski stood at the right hand of the composer.

The final distinction of this concert, which placed it apart from other events of the kind, was Mr. Gabrilówitsch's performance of the concerto. The work is familiar, but in twenty-five years of orchestral concerts the writer has not heard it presented with the breadth, the fire, and the nobility of conception that characterized it last night. This impression was due in part to Mr. Stokowski, who collaborated with the most admirable musicianship; but the concerto, after all, is in the hands of the pianist, and Mr. Gabriló- witsch gave of it a fabulous interpretation. We say "fabulous" be- cause this was the kind of playing, in its great lines, its unlimited power and rich musical feeling, that is said to have been frequent in a former day—which it certainly is not in this one. A Rubinstein might have performed the Tchaikovsky concerto as Mr. Gabriló- witsch performed it, with a giant's grip of its material, a mastery and imagination which made the piano as potent an instrument as the orchestra, and one with almost as many sonorities and colors at command. For once the lordly opening theme had its proper breadth; for once the peroration of the last movement had suffi- cient majesty.

Pianist and conductor, by the most felicitous treatment of line and detail, gave the composition the coherency which it may easily lose, and by subtle fluctuations of pace, rhythm, and phrasing made every measure an engrossing experience. They held back or flung themselves forward with equal judgment and equal impetuosity; they balanced orchestra and piano with a skill probably the result of deliberation, but ostensibly instinctive and inspired. When many pianists and many concertos have been forgotten this performance will be remembered. They brought Mr. Gabrilówitsch back to the stage for recall after recall. It delayed by many minutes the end of the concert.

FEBRUARY 5, 1926

Bruckner's Eighth

"Probably his strongest and greatest"

IT WAS remarked some days ago in these columns that the present fashion of playing symphonies without pause or opportunity for applause between the movements might be injurious rather than helpful to the effect of the music. A case in point is the perform- ance of Bruckner's Eighth Symphony given by Otto Klemperer yesterday afternoon in Carnegie Hall with the New York Symphony Society. This is probably the strongest and the greatest of the Bruckner symphonies. It need hardly be said that it is entirely too long, that there are useless repetitions, and that there is evident the curious impartiality with which an extremely gifted composer is equally willing to dally with an idea that is trite and commonplace or another idea of the most exceptional nobility. To Bruckner it often seems one and the same thing! There are, however, fewer poor ideas and more great ones in the Eighth Symphony than in any other of the grandiose orchestral compositions of Bruckner that we know; and, relatively speaking, there is more conciseness. But when a symphony in four movements lasts more than a solid hour it is unreasonable to give the audience no point or occasion for an instant's relaxation.

This is unjust to the audience and unjust to the symphony. Movement by movement, the Eighth Symphony is not an experience to be rejected. The first movement is strongest in its structure and perhaps the most dramatic in its nature. The themes have the energy and amplitude of Bruckner in a vigorous and creative mood. There are passages of rending dissonance and power in its development that he perhaps never surpassed in this vein—witness the three great tonal crises achieved with fragments of the main theme. The occasional wandering and quibbling, the sudden curious descents from great peaks of inspiration to the maundering repetition of a stale and weak platitude can be passed over when they are surrounded by such visions and splendors.

The scherzo would be an exceptionally fresh, jocose, Beethovenish affair, with a quiet contrasting section of pastoral loveliness, if Mr. Klemperer had not been set upon giving it with all the repeats, a process no doubt logical because of the proportions of the other movements, but one that became wearisome to the flesh. The slow movement, with its poignant beauty and its lofty, mystical feeling, has a parallel in certain phases of César Franck, though Franck is lucid where Bruckner is portentous and involved, and the scores of Franck, a Belgian, are the antithesis of the wholly German style of Bruckner. It is in their utter simplicity, the touching naïveté of their conversations with God that the two musicians have relationship, and certainly Bruckner is in no place more unworldly, more apt and exalted, than in these touching pages.

In the finale he falls far short of the preceding movements, though he starts bravely enough and there are signs and portents in his heavens. Commencing in grand and dramatic style, he soon relapses into reiteration, bombast, and commonplace. And here is a signal instance of injustice done the composer by not permitting the expected pauses between the movements. After three gigantic sections of the symphonic structure have been shown, the fourth, which at the best is an incomplete and crumbling affair, is played, to the disillusion and irritation of those who have listened until the ears may be incapable of the vivid recording of new sensations. Bruckner is judged by an audience reduced to desperation by over an hour of his idiosyncrasies. The audience, which has not been able to register approval earlier in the performance, applauds faintly and thus apparently damns a work which, on the whole, it may highly approve. Mr. Klemperer's interpretation yesterday was one that had much breadth, virility, and feeling. It was highly creditable to him as a conductor and to his capacity for devotion to Bruckner's genius.

The soloist at this concert was Harold Bauer, who played the Beethoven G major Piano Concerto with the pellucid beauty of tone and clarity of execution that this work, unique among all Beethoven's compositions in the form, requires. Not many pianists can play, when they choose, so simply, and capture an audience. Mr. Bauer richly merited the long applause and the number of recalls he received. A performance of Wagner's *Meistersinger* prelude opened the concert.

FEBRUARY 20, 1926

===

Première of Carpenter's *Skyscrapers*

"Without posturing or pretentiousness"

THERE was an event last night in the Metropolitan Opera House of perhaps more importance than the debuts of young prima donnas, however exciting these may be—namely, the first performance on any stage of the ballet *Skyscrapers*, the music by John

Alden Carpenter, the scenic settings by Robert Edmond Jones, the dances directed by Mr. Samuel Lee. This is one of the most interesting of the productions given this season at the Metropolitan, and it is auspicious for the development of a specifically American art form. *Skyscrapers* is a free fantasy on certain phases of American life. These are symbolized by fantastical scenery and by choreography based upon American dances, as Mr. Carpenter's score is based upon "jazz" rhythms.

There is an admirable synthesis of these elements, there is a play of imagination, and transformation of common and even vulgar sights and sounds of the life in an American city into forms of distinction and artistic suggestiveness. It is all accomplished, finally, without posturing or pretentiousness, with deftness, humor, technical skill, and a light touch.

The fundamental underlying motive is the work and play of the masses of any great city. The stage curtain rises to disclose a second curtain which, as it were, hits and dazes the eye—a symbolic design of dizzying converging lines of black and white. On each side of the stage are huge blinking lights. The curtain of black and white, to whistling and clanging sounds in the orchestra, gives place to stage designs suggestive of the confused and prodigious architecture of a great city, with its streets and passing crowds for a half-illumined background seen to the right or left of a towering skyscraper. Back of it loom other huge and lofty shapes, and at the foot of it are gangs of laborers, one group with sledges, another of steel riveters, and others higher up on the span—all delving, and forging the great structure over them. The suggestions of color are admirable throughout. There is singular use of light and shadow. The garments of the workers glint, and they have a steely hue.

The scene changes quickly to another setting—two doors of a factory, or some other great absorbent of labor, and at one side a time-clock. Workmen and workgirls troop in, to mark their time and disappear in murky gloom. A few linger to embrace and "jazz" or "strut" for an instant to Mr. Carpenter's engaging rhythms—and the factory has devoured them.

And now another scene. This is "a Coney Island"—any Coney Island. The workers are at play.

The three solo dancers are Albert Troy, the "Strutter"; Rita de Leporte, "Herself"; and Roger Dodge, the "White Wings," or street-cleaner.

They disport themselves with a rare gusto and with a technique exhilarating in its unconventional and popular derivation.

The ensemble now disports itself as a parody on scenes that take place at any summer beach resort. A band plays discordantly. Showmen ballyhoo their wares. A carousel is wheeled into the center of the stage, and its pillar revolves in one direction while the chorus prances, as the horses of the merry-go-round, in the other. The carousel slowly comes to a halt; the horses slow up, droop their heads or remain as if stopped in mid-air. And so on. One episode follows another quickly. Great distorting mirrors amuse the crowd, which is continually forming and re-forming in fresh shapes and rhythmical groupings.

The small hours of the early dawn arrive. "White Wings" falls asleep and dreams. Coney Island is shrouded in shadow. A chorus of some twenty Negro voices sings some wordless but, as it were, half familiar refrain and the workers awake. The jazz in the orchestra quickens, there is a gradual return to the opening scenes—the factory doors, the winking lights, the whistling and clanging, and finally the gang of labor at the feet of the great buildings and scaffoldings of new structures to arise.

And this motive of labor is pictured with singular impressiveness at the end. Back of the groups that have been until now the center of attention are seen huge shadows of other workers, bending and swinging, plying their sledges. Their shadows become more tremendous and more monstrous, till they tower threateningly to the skies. Some of them stretch immense limbs, others open their arms as if in entreaty, and the curtain falls.

The pantomime ballet, or by whatever name it may be called, is an art form that is uncommonly flexible and a fertile field for artistic expression. The great revelation of the possibilities of this modernized form came with the Ballet Russe of Diaghileff. Its productions were Russian. Sometimes they were arbitrary adaptations of certain well-known scores to an interpretive choreography. Mr. Carpenter's ballet has a distinctively local and even racial quality.

There are some reservations on purely musical grounds. They lie principally in the direction of a lack of very striking inventiveness in the score. The technique is superb, though the procedure as well as some of the rhythmical ideas themselves savor strongly of Stravinsky. The workmanship is so fine, and is imbued with such a spirit, that it conceals itself.

Mr. Carpenter might reply to the criticism of a lack of substantial musical material in his score by saying that he had not tried to be ponderous or to attempt dramatic commentary, but to entertain and amuse. But his intention, in spite of his lightness of touch, is more thoughtful than that. What he has done is to invent some fairly fetching jazz tunes of his own and to include some scraps of familiar popular songs, such as a suggeston of the *St. Louis Blues*, a quotation, for the movement of the carousel, of a phrase from *Massa's in the Cold, Cold Ground*, and a trumpet parody of *Yankee Doodle*, as, in the last delirious ensemble, Mr. Troy lifts his hat and steps about with a sweep and a fling that make him a pinnacle of the ensemble—and all this with a dexterity and a use of frequently complex rhythms in a manner so dextrous and apparently spontaneous that it is only afterward, with a blink of the eyes, that the listener realizes he has been listening to 5-4 and 7-4 and "off-beats" and cross accents that the composer, in the most guileless manner, drops from his sleeve. The inclusion of saxophone, banjos, and percussion instruments is done well and in a manner that enriches without exaggeration. And what a pleasure, what an exhilaration, to listen to an American composer of Carpenter's discernment, taste, and virtuoso mastery of his idiom!

The ballet was very well received. The composer and his two coadjutors appeared before the curtain to acknowledge the applause.

DECEMBER 3, 1926

Mengelberg Conducts the Mahler Fifth

"The most pathetic thing about the music is its complete sincerity."

CERTAINLY one of the most pathetic figures in the music of the late nineteenth century, the aftermath of Wagner and Liszt, is Gustav Mahler. Mr. Mengelberg and the Philharmonic Orchestra performed his Fifth Symphony, heard for the first time at their concerts, last night in Carnegie Hall. The year before, the same leader and orchestra had made known Mahler's Second Symphony. The

Second is less ambitious, relatively speaking, than the Fifth, and is fresher in invention. The Fifth is more tremendous in architecture and more tragic in mold, although half is spirited and joyous, and the symphony progresses from the tragedy of a funeral march to a rollicking finale in the rondo style.

When these things are said, there is little new to add, because, after all, the Fifth Symphony has the same defects that one finds in other of Mahler's orchestral works. Its ideas are commonplace, as are its harmony and key-successions. The orchestration is either swollen or suddenly thin or bizarre. The symphony is prolix and tiresome; the composer never knows when he has said enough, or else is simply unable to desist. Furthermore, and although Mahler specifically denied and objected to a story or "program" being found in his Fifth Symphony, much of it is theatrical, bombastic, sentimental. In the slow movement alone is there the impress of a man communing with himself and not merely jumping about from one place to another. But here, again, the melodic thought is so ordinary, however well planned the arch of the themes, however serious and lofty the style! The last movement is lively and brilliant but, like the rest of the work, restless, vacillating, persistent with a brave show and a certain futility. Be it noted that the symphony was received with enthusiasm in spite of its length and its defects. But it is easier to credit Mr. Mengelberg's performance of the finale for this result than it is to ascribe it to the composition.

The most pathetic thing about this music is its complete sincerity, its impotent self-torture, and the fact that a sudden, swift change in the world's thinking has pushed it so far back and away from us. With its frenzies and introspections the race to come has little or nothing to do. It is one extreme of the scale of which the works of Schoenberg and his disciples represent the other. Mahler cannot escape Wagner and Liszt, and the pernicious megalomania which they left behind them: Schoenberg and his disciples, as Mr. Gilman pointed out the other day in an admirable article about Anton Webern, attempt to deny the same ancestry, and suffer intensely, uselessly, in so doing.

Mahler, for the modern musician, is principally an old story, and one that has little contemporaneous meaning. Mahler, for the psychologist and psychiatrist, would be an utterly fascinating problem. Mahler read Dostoevsky, and would have been understood by him. Mahler's attempts at solutions, his recoiling before indecipherable enigmas, his gropings and questionings, which in themselves rendered him unable to create symphonies, make him an intensely significant and even imposing figure in music. He attempted things greater than he could do, and failed. His spirit, not his music, commands respect and admiration, while he seeks vainly, by means of funeral marches, battle fanfares, Vienna waltzes, rondos, fugues, and what not, and with the aid of an immensely enlarged orchestra, to find the creative goal. But he is helpless, and certainly his music will perish.

As this music is important for its causes rather than its contents, so should its performance take more account of inner spirit than details of execution. Mr. Mengelberg was heard to better advantage in the rollicking finale than in the portentous funeral march. This writer remembers the same march as played by Wilhelm Gericke with the Boston Symphony Orchestra, and later by Karl Muck. Muck's opening movement was stern, tragic, looming gigantic; Mr. Mengelberg's was sentimental, almost languishing. With the former it was the first movement that stood out unforgettably against the sky; with Mr. Mengelberg it was the virtuoso effect rather than inspiration of the symphony that was observed by the listener. The work had been long and carefully prepared; the performance was often brilliant, and warm-toned, if somewhat overstressed, in the slow movement; but its qualities, most of the time, were exterior.

After the music of Mahler the opening motive of the Beethoven C minor Piano Concerto rang out like the hammer of Thor; it cleared the air with its incredible simplicity and concision—a man master of his soul as well as of his task! At the same time, the concerto is mostly old-hat. Mr. Friedberg played with commanding authority and with a tone that was brilliant and brittle rather than sensuous. His musicianship commended him. He played in the slow movement with a continence and tonal beauty he had not previously summoned. He used the Reinecke cadenza in the opening movement, which testified "unsolicited" to the sincerity and the classic feeling of that composer. What can any pianist do with the finale, the poorest part of the work, like all the finales of Beethoven's concertos? The audience cordially recalled Mr. Friedberg. In this there was reason, but a dose of late and overelaborated Mahler, followed by a work of the early Beethoven, was a good deal, even for courageous concertgoers.

═══

The Importance of *Wozzeck* Assessed

"What is Schoenberg? Where are he and his disciples
bound?"

RIOTOUS scenes accompanied a performance of Alban Berg's opera
Wozzeck in the Prague National Theatre. They surpassed the demonstrations at the *première* of the opera in Berlin, December 14,
1925. On the 29th of last November the Prague authorities inter-
vened and ordered the production stopped. In that city, in Vienna,
in Berlin, where Schoenberg has accepted an appointment at the
Academy, musical factions are active. The Schoenberg and anti-
Schoenberg parties do not confine their activities to the newspapers
which advance or oppose their cause. Berg, with Anton von Webern,
stands today among Schoenberg's most favored pupils and exponents. No doubt, aside from the character of his opera, he could
not have escaped the consequences of this artistic relation. A manifesto signed by leading musicians, artists, and intellectuals of Prague
protests against the official intervention and stresses the "organized"
character of the disturbance in the theater. *Wozzeck* has created
trouble wherever it has been given. An opera that creates disturbance is not necessarily of artistic value. An examination of text and
piano score of *Wozzeck* gives more than one possible reason for its
explosive effect. But it is unusual music, not to be estimated from
such superficial acquaintance; the score is curious in construction
and significant of the effect of Schoenberg and his ideas in dramatic
music.

In New York the firm of Schoenberg, Webern, and Berg is known
principally for chamber music. Orchestral pieces of Schoenberg,
his *Pierrot lunaire*—which has strongly influenced Berg in writing
for the voice—and some of the songs, including excerpts from the
Gurrelieder, have also been heard. But the movement of which he
is the leader also concerns itself very seriously with the stage. The
more radically minded of European musicians go so far as to say
that it opens new paths in the rubbish-strewn terrain of opera, a

form which has shown no fresh signs of life since Debussy's *Pelléas et Mélisande*. At any rate, Berg's treatment of the musico-dramatic form and his musical tendencies are fully exemplified in his late and provocative work.

The Schoenberg school of composers insists on its theory of music that is "absolute," i.e., purely musical, polyphonic in texture and owing nothing to outside materials or ideas. "Music," says the master of atonality, "describes the adventures of themes." Then Schoenberg industriously sets to music the verses of *Pierrot lunaire*, the *Gurrelieder*, and much other verse; he composes scores to subjects which are not only extra-musical but, in the opinion of many, of a neurotic and highly unmusical nature in their character. Is it not patent that from the moment a composer sets a poem to music or produces an opera, he ceases to write "absolute," or "pure," music? The fact seems fairly obvious, the questions which decide the value of a song or opera being the worth of text and the music, and the suitability of these different elements to each other. Berg, confronted with this problem in *Wozzeck*, undertakes a method that is at least novel in theory in the attempt to combine "absolute" and "dramatic" forms of expression.

He endeavors to preserve in his opera the elements of long-established musical structures, those which have laid the foundations of instrumental and symphonic music, such as the suite, sonata, fugue, and various dance forms. It is true that these forms are present in the score of *Wozzeck* rather in inner construction than in precise outer aspect. They are treated, in fact, so freely and in such a co-ordinated manner that it is not readily perceptible to the eye or the ear where the boundaries of one form end and those of another begin. It is constructive principles native to pure music that Berg claims to have built upon, rather than the exact observance of principles laid down by classic masters. Therefore it is that the music of the first act of *Wozzeck* includes in its design a rhapsody, a military march, a cradle song, a "passacaglia," with twenty-one variations. The first scene is described as in the form of the suite, containing a sarabande, gigue, gavotte, and "double." The second scene is accompanied by a fantasy on three chords. The theme and variations of the fourth scene accompany the conversation of a doctor who keeps returning to one subject with which he is preoccupied.

The second act is described as a "symphony" in five movements, divided into a sonata movement, a prelude and fugue on three themes, a slow movement for chamber orchestra—the orchestra being identical with that of Schoenberg's Chamber Symphony—a scherzo and rondo. The music of the third act consists of six "inventions," to wit: a set of variations and fugue; a movement on one note, i.e., on a pedal point; a movement in a rhythm—meaning a polka for piano; a movement on six notes, heard now as a chord and now in melodic succession; a movement in a key—from an atonalist—otherwise an orchestral interlude in the key of D minor, with atonalic frills and furbishings; and, finally, what might be freely construed as a toccata!

More evident to the unaccustomed eye than those classic divisions and subdivisions is the interrelation of many of the parts of the score, and, at least on paper, the general continuity of the musical fabric. Essentials of the old forms there may be in fact as well as theory, but for the greater part of the opera there is musical unity and also brevity for scenes that are usually short and that succeed each other with very brief intervals. There are modern "symphonies" which would last longer than the final act of *Wozzeck*, with all its details. Brevity, concentration, flexibility are characteristics of dramatic music which have created much dissension.

And what is the drama to which this score is fitted—or which is fitted to this score? *Wozzeck* was the last dramatic work of Georg Büchner, a genius who died in 1837 at the age of twenty-four. It is feverish and insurrectionary with the spirit of the 1830s, a story of humble, tragic lines, with psychological and pathological elements that could have come from the pen of a Wassermann or an epileptic Russian. Wozzeck, an ignorant soldier, weak of will, a prey to impulse and circumstance, adrift in a world that he cannot understand, is the servant and sport of his captain and the subject of medical experiments by the dishonest doctor of the regiment. Wozzeck has been for three years the lover of Marie, to whom he gives all his earnings for their child. But Wozzeck's mistress tires of her brooding and irascible lover, becoming the easy conquest of the drum major who struts past. Wozzeck attacks him in the barracks, but is knocked senseless while his rival laughs. Marie is first scornful, then repentant, but too late. Wozzeck meets her on a lonely road by a lake and cuts her throat. He returns to the scene of his crime, converses with Marie's ghost, and kills himself. The doctor and the captain appear. Did they hear a cry from the water?

They decide that they were mistaken and renew their walk. "This story is told to the little child, who quietly goes on with his games."

The music of the opera is "atonal." Save in special instances, the old system and the old ideals of tonality are abandoned. The scenes and the music are condensed to their utter essentials. From the singers, who, like the players, have hideously difficult parts (the Berlin *première* of *Wozzeck* was preceded by 137 rehearsals), the composer asks not song, but the *"Sprechstimme,"* the half-song, half-speech of Schoenberg's *Pierrot lunaire*, with cries, groans, and whisperings as additional stimuli. The orchestra is employed variously, sometimes for stunning crashes of tone and elsewhere for subtle and subdued effects of color. In its dimensions this score would have satisfied a Strauss or a Mahler. It requires all the customary wood and brass instruments in groups of four, adding to the orchestra before the stage a bass clarinet, a contra-bassoon, a contra-bass tuba, and most of the pulsatile instruments that are procurable. In addition there is music back of the scene—military music by wood, brass, and percussion, and music for the scene in the inn which asks, among other things, for clarinet, harmonica, accordion, and guitar. But these are exterior characteristics, interesting only as they point to the mind and the tendencies of the composer. They point straight back from Berg to his master, and from Schoenberg back to the nineteenth-century romanticism toward which a notable group of modern German and Austrian composers turn. The orchestral style has evidently, to judge from competent report, many subtleties that Mahler and Strauss did not dream of. That is a new technical position, of great importance in so far as it extends the expressive boundaries of music, but not the answer to the riddle "What is Schoenberg? Where are he and his disciples bound?" The dimensions of Berg's orchestra and the subject he chose, the creation of a late romantic, a successor in Germany of E. T. A. Hoffmann, appear as an indication of his true tendencies. With all the experiments, theories, and divagations, the Schoenberg school stems from the great romantics of the nineteenth century, and is not a new parturition of the twentieth. Berg is part of the time perversely economical of instruments and notes, but he orchestrates, at the climaxes of *Wozzeck*, in what Paul Stefan calls "the grand manner," with the sensuousness and color of an earlier time. These tendencies of a past period are cited by certain commentators as proof that the Schoenberg school has come to the end of its tether. It is not necessarily so. There is no important art which has not its origins in that which has gone before, and *Wozzeck* seems to have made a very considerable effect on more than a few radicals or Schoenberg adherents. Its oppressive but highly dramatic atmosphere is conceded by critics who do not approve the nature of the work or the ideas of the composer. "For Berlin and Germany," says Adolph Weissmann, "*Wozzeck*, for some time to come, has now shifted the burden from concert music to the field of opera. . . ." That *Wozzeck* is undoubtedly the most remarkable attempt in the field of opera since Debussy's *Pelléas et Mélissande* may or may not be a localism, but certain it is that the opera has had a surprisingly energetic public reaction and has proved of steadily increasing interest to modern European students and composers.

AUGUST 7, 1927

Maurice Ravel: Man and Musician

"I don't particularly care about this 'sincerity.'
I try to make art."

Paris, July 20
SOMETHING much older than himself looks from the eyes of Maurice Ravel. It is the spirit of an experienced and ironical race. He is urbane, Parisian, and very swift. He came into the room before one knew he was there, examining everything, the furniture, the ceiling—everything seemingly except his company, which he was examining closest of all, talking very rapidly the while to the air.

His dress was exceedingly plain, fastidious, exotic. And now he sat in a very charming garden known to a few, fussing with his food, sampling a Ravelian liqueur, saying the most monstrous things in phrases that poured out so swiftly that seconds flew by before the full and awful import of the words sank into a slower brain. A real Parisian, an artist, French to the bottom of his soul, on his native heath, and in the most capital fettle. A hummingbird would have been maladroit in his company! M. Ravel grinned behind his lips, shot quick glances which took in everything, guyed the millennium, and roasted the universe. It is unfortunate that so much of his conversation must go unquoted. Alas for pidgin French, hence imperfect communication! Alas, above all, for the inability to reduce the suavity, the *politesse*, the glitter of Maurice Ravel to dull and ponderous Anglo-Saxonism! It is a violence, a crime, and, besides, an impossibility, since this Ravel is as incorrigibly himself as Paris or France, which, whatever their outward semblance, change in nothing essential. What they know they knew before our age was in swaddling clothes. They are not going to change all that for any newfangled bourgeois contraptions. Just try to instruct Ravel. His guest looked and listened, finding it difficult to take eyes from a face which had at moments the very look of some old portrait of a Rameau or a Voltaire, or to keep from shouting at the Gallic felicity, the Gallic irony, breeding and point and smack of him. That's what he was—in his kind a complete and supreme creation.

But we are here to talk about music, and when there is talk of music and Ravel it is time to be serious. How still he has stood, yet he has fashioned his style and followed his self-appointed path, how far he has traveled, in the last several decades! How deliberately this most conscious, most naturally artificial of composers! Ravel has achieved by degrees a style always more isolated from other influences, yet true to itself, although he has gone to various sources for his materials. Nothing passed him that he wanted, and nothing came from his hands without the stamp of a new mind and a fresh artistic purpose upon it. The nature behind the purpose? That's another matter, and Ravel would say that it had nothing to do with the composer.

We had made some remark about a composer's sincerity. He regarded us with fatigue. "I don't particularly care about this 'sincerity.' I try to make art." He said he had been working four years at the violin-and-piano sonata which he will play next season in America—three years in taking out the notes that weren't necessary. "And now for something else." There is a piano concerto in the making, but Ravel has never in his life hurried himself in his work, and it will not be finished in time for America. He will be heard in compositions of a more intimate nature.

"Of course," he added, "if I ever did a perfect piece of work I would stop composing immediately. One just tries, and when I have finished a composition I have 'tried' all I can; it's no use attempting anything more in the same direction. One must seek new ideas."

The violin-and-piano sonata has a second movement of "blues." "And I take this 'blues' very seriously," he said, with an air of engaging candor. And then becoming serious: "Why have not more of the important American composers turned to this 'blues' material and to other music of popular origin which has come to you from so many different sources?

"Do you know my early sources of musical education? They were several. You know, I was born near a border, and that I have Spanish as well as French blood. . . . Well, in my childhood I was much interested in mechanisms. Those machines fascinated me. I visited factories often, very often, as a small boy with my father. It was those machines, their clicking and roaring, which, with the Spanish folk songs sung to me at nighttime as a berceuse by my mother, formed my first instruction in music!"

Times change. Only a few years have gone by since the first performances in America of a certain piano piece, *Jeux d'eau*, by the young Maurice Ravel. This piece was regarded by some tolerantly, by others with distrust and suspicion. Today, already, others are young and Ravel is in a position which some describe as "classic."

It makes one blink. *Jeux d'eau* indeed! The wonder is not that ears surfeited with discords unimagined at the time of its appearance find the piece an antitoxin, but that it retains for us so much of its early iridescence—another testimony to the facture and distinction of Ravel's art. He has left that far behind, so far as evolution of style is concerned, yet not for an instant has he severed the connecting thread. For *Jeux d'eau* read now *Ondine*, that shimmering love picture which is the fulfillment of the youthful idea, and hardly surpassable in its genre, with the newer departures (anticipated nevertheless in certain of the *Miroirs*) of the *Gibet* and the Hoffmannesque *Scarbo* from *Gaspard de la Nuit*.

Fantastic as you please, but always form, form, form, present in the small works and in the biggest and freest ones—in the macabre shadow and blaze of the orchestral *Rhapsodie espagnole*, in the satirical opera *L'Heure espagnole*, or the big piano trio, or the songs great or little. And whether or not we agree with these works, or find in all of them the same measure of inspiration, we are certain to discover an artist of sovereign conscience and clearness of aim, who has never repeated himself or written a careless or redundant measure.

It is a great deal to say.

As for the latest Ravel, he will be heard and estimated this winter. It will be worth while, as the phrenologists say, to examine his bumps! How he will appear to the future is a question that is, happily, for others to decide. Ravel has survived notably those rapid and feverish fluctuations of musical taste and fads, which follow each other in Paris as quickly and unreasonably as the changes in hats, and in the period of post and ante Debussy finds himself secure and distinguished in his métier. A rising and belligerent generation, after flinging a few missiles at him, Parisian fashion, is now inclined to render respect. It would have been otherwise had Ravel been a romantic or an impressionist. In that case the present day in Europe would have been chilly for him; but a romantic he never was. As it is, his environment is neither hostile nor unpropitious. Perhaps it is the reproach of a period of hardness and cerebralism that this is so: it is a matter to be seen. But it is something to be as secure, as imperturbable, as consistent in direction as Ravel has proved to be. He has said little, worked, and followed his destiny. There are not many such craftsmen, artists of such firm traditions and conscience. Technically he is amazing; creatively he is seen in some widely differing manifestations. He belongs, at heart, to the thin and proud ranks of those ancestors who learned and forgot nothing.

SEPTEMBER 25, 1927

The Strauss Festival at Frankfurt

"Today a composer without a faith, a destiny,
or a destination"

Frankfurt, September 2

THE most interesting things about Richard Strauss are those which will never be told, either by the composer or by his most officious biographer. They do not deal with the musician of today; they concern rather his interior progress. A better term might be his tragic metamorphosis. What has become of the early Strauss? What is the inside story of the man and artist, the descent from the heroic and magnificent music that once he flung on paper to the pedestrian and bourgeois manifestations of today? It is no use ascribing this *volte-face* merely to age, or speculating upon the disastrous effect a materialistic modern environment may have upon a creative spirit. Nor is it wholly just or fair to Strauss to say that he has merely reverted to type and fulfilled the promise of certain streaks of vulgarity and sensationalism which soon showed themselves in his music. These qualities did betray themselves early in his career, but they were visible cheek by jowl with the energy, romanticism, and fierce intolerance of the commonplace which gave his music such sweep and splendor.

The presence and the potency of a heroic idealist were not to be denied. When Strauss penned the noble, sardonic, and pathetic pages of his *Don Quixote* there were those who believed he was mocking his own quixotry in the music of Sancho Panza. That he had dared greatly, and never hesitated to attack the heavens in search of a star, and sometimes come back empty-handed, he must have known. But one does not think of *Don Quixote* as mockery. Strauss was both Quixote and Panza, and he saw to it that the spirit of the Don triumphed. What is it that has robbed the composer of a similar victory? Other great composers, and even composers of modest rank and aspirations, as they aged, came nearer, within themselves, to the promised land. They may have lost the power to forge white-hot music, but they retained a perception of beauty and a faith to sustain them. Strauss seems today a composer without a faith, a destiny, or a destination.

These things were borne upon an observer in a rather melancholy fashion in the course of the week of Strauss operas, performed with their creator in the conductor's chair, as the conclusion of the remarkable musical exposition which Frankfurt has been holding all summer. The "Richard Strauss *Festspiele*," which began on the 20th with *Salome,* ended on the 29th with *Frau ohne Schatten,* The impression of disillusion and weariness was strengthened rather than weakened by the composer's demeanor. (Not that it is wise to judge Strauss by a single performance. The old volcano erupted at least once during the festival, and then there was a sensation.) Strauss would appear in the orchestra pit, looking neither to right nor left, acknowledging perfunctorily the wild applause which broke out the instant he was visible. He would bury his nose in his score and go about his conductor's business in a way that promised a secure performance as certainly as it secured a dull one. Dull most of the performances were. What Strauss feels today as man and musician is not for a traveling commentator to determine. No doubt he is weary of conducting. He received, of course, the handsome fees which he always exacts for his services. The festival had every exterior glory, but it rang hollow. After each act Strauss had to appear before the curtain. His expression said plainly that he valued public applause and the idolatry that a large section of the German public still bestows upon him at their true worth, and felt them to be of very little moment. It is rather sad. Personally Strauss is a simple, modest, entirely unassuming man, impatient of compliments or sycophancy, desirous of plain communications with plain people. It may be attributing to him a complexity of disposition which he does not possess, but, unless it is sheer imagination, he preserves with all his affability a complete aloofness; if there are regrets and bitter disappointments within him they are kept where they belong, back of the deep eyes and the fine forehead and a face that has brooded. The man is likable, as his friends testify. The conductor is most of the time a routine kapellmeister, and, in flashes, the man of genius. The composer seems to have buried himself.

And so the Strauss week was, in its way, a disappointment. It had given hope of a new perspective and a better understanding of the composer, perhaps even a glimpse of new and vital qualities in his style. As a matter of fact, it served principally to confirm the gloomier order of suspicions. Here were the six operas of Strauss, from *Salome* onward, in a row: *Salome* for a beginning, then *Elektra, Rose Cavalier, Ariadne auf Naxos, Intermezzo,* and *Frau ohne Schatten.* The last three operas are unknown in America. The ridiculous fuss and feathers raised over the Metropolitan *première* of *Salome* in 1907 frightened that institution so much that it has never since dared to repeat the performance. Hammerstein, after the burst of morality had subsided, gave *Salome* many times, proving the impulsive and exaggerated character of its opposition. Hammerstein also produced *Elektra*, with the incomparable Mazarin in the title part, but this opera proved strong meat for singers and audiences, and so it has been shelved, although it possesses certain passages which must rank as summits of Strauss's dramatic genius, and has exerted an influence upon modern German music which is more powerful than could have been foretold when it appeared. The only Strauss opera that has held the stage in America and gained a strong position in the repertory there is the *Rose Cavalier*, with its rococo setting and theme. *Ariadne*, which followed *Rose Cavalier*, is yet more stylistic and artificial, although it has enough of distinction, perhaps, to cross the seas, and would certainly be more entertaining than some of our operatic novelties past, present, and promised for the near future. But from the work which followed *Ariadne* in date of production, that cheap skit *Intermezzo*, that accumulation of everything ugly, inane, and devastatingly commonplace, may heaven deliver us! This from the composer of *Eulenspiegel* and *Tod und Verklärung* and *Zarathustra*!

It would be interesting and perhaps amusing, on sociological grounds, to see what would happen if this piece ever got as far as America. Perhaps the same opera-goers who quivered at the neuroticism of *Salome* and now exult in the sadistic revels of a Scarpia, or the perverse and sensational conclusion of an act of *The Jewels of the Madonna*, would applaud it. Might even arise a Comstock to greet the appalling domestic scenes of the bickerings of a German wife and conductor—the latter avowedly Strauss in disguise—as a sign of Straussian regeneration and a glorification of hearth and home! Stranger things have happened. It was Wilde who remarked that where some catch an effect, others catch cold. O shivering Watch and Warders! Strauss might at least have stopped at the *Sinfonia Domestica*. He lived, if not to blush, to commit *Intermezzo*.

Then there is the sixth opera, which completed the Strauss week of Frankfurt—*The Woman without a Shadow*. This work is a very different story, though an unfortunately long and involved one. The music is fresher, finer in feeling and texture than any other score Strauss has made for the stage. This is especially true of the first act. The explanation is probably in the subject itself, which is a symbolic fairy tale of a vague and complicated character, and in the fact that Strauss conceived the music years ago when he was in his creative prime, although he revised and elaborated it, with too good a will, in a later period. The principal trouble, indeed an insuperable obstacle to the proportion and effect of the opera, is its impossible libretto.

Two husbands, the one a king, the other a poor dyer, have wives who have no children. A woman without a child is a woman without a shadow. The woman the king has married is half human and half of another world; his falcon pursued her and wounded her when she had the form of a gazelle, while the king was hunting. The queen wishes a shadow. There is much symbolical argument about the penalties of having no shadow, among which are the declaration of invisible powers that without a child the king shall in three years be turned to stone; and the penalty of the woman who is willing to part with her shadow, her right and potency for offspring, as the wife of the dyer sells her shadow to the queen and refuses her sorrowing husband the happiness of parentage. And much more of the same sort. Little fishes frying in the pan speak with the voices of the unborn children, and these are seen in a vision. There is a fearful storm. The dyer and his wife sink in a cataclysm to a nether region. At last both couples fetch up in a temple, where they seek truth and deliverance from sin and are reunited in happiness and forgiven for their sins which have caused so much suffering. This will give an idea of the sort of thing that Strauss attempted to set to music. More than that is required in the creation of a good opera.

It is more pleasant to remember a closing scene of the Strauss Festival when the young Strauss merged for an instant with the older man and an audience rendered thunderous homage. This was on the occasion of a final concert given at noon on the 30th in the music hall of the exposition, when the Banda Municipala of Madrid and the organist Professor Wilhelm Kempf of Stuttgart rendered the musical entertainment. It opened magnificently with the C minor Organ Passacaglia of Bach. It proceeded with performances of Spanish music by the band, conducted by its leader, a short, stout, elderly man, a master of his task, Lamote de Grignon. Strauss had conducted this band in a performance of his *Don Juan*, in a special arrangement, of which he most justifiably approves, by Mr. de Grignon. Strauss was to conduct this piece as a final performance of the exposition.

Before he did so he was informed of the fact that in his honor there was a newly named Richard Strauss-Strasse in Frankfurt.

Whether the warmth of his greeting and the obvious pride that was shown in him by the faithful Frankfurters stirred Strauss or whether it was the superb responsiveness and fire of the players under him may not be known, but he rose from his seat in the audience, took the stage at a jump, and launched that band of wild Spaniards into an electrifying performance. The tone poem is astonishingly well arranged for the wind instruments; effects of strings as well as brass are excellently and imaginatively contrived. Naturally, at the climaxes the special sonorities of brass and wood were useful. Strauss, when he began, stood as he usually does when conducting, quite stiff and still, his left arm hanging straight at his side. But in a moment he forgot himself. He was leaning forward, exhorting the orchestra, molding every phrase and gradation, spurring and reining that band at will, leading it up to climaxes of a shattering intensity. It was the act of not only a conductor but a creative master. And it was the old—rather the young—Strauss as he was when he first achieved that still magnificent tone poem. At the end everyone lost his head except a newspaper photographer. De Grignon rushed frantically from the wings. He and Strauss fondled, kissed, and babbled over each other. The photographer, with unsuspected magnetism and will power, caught them on the fly and forced them to freeze in that attitude for a moment, which was brave, for the two men were genuinely angered. Then the crowd rushed forward and the men were centers of a mob, and in the face of Mr. Strauss was that for which his audiences had looked in vain through the progress of the festival.

NOVEMBER 26, 1927

Menuhin Makes His New York Debut at Eleven

"It seems ridiculous to say ..."

THERE was an extraordinary demonstration when the eleven-year-old violinist Yehudi Menuhin played the Beethoven Concerto with the New York Symphony Orchestra last night in Carnegie Hall.

The hall was crowded to capacity with an audience which had gathered with curiosity rather than belief that a child could adequately interpret such a composition, even if he were able to deal with its technical demands. But when the boy touched the strings it was evident that an exceptional musical intelligence and sensibility, as well as uncommonly good technical groundwork, were behind the performance. There was the silence that betokens the most intent listening until the cadenza of the first movement, when applause broke out and threatened to stop the performance.

Master Menuhin's interpretation of the slow movement and the finale was, if anything, of a finer quality than his playing of the first, perhaps because of the complete mastery of the situation that he had gained by that time. He felt and he conveyed very beautifully the poetry of the slow movement, and his playing of the finale was of refreshing taste and simplicity. In this place, especially for modern-minded audiences, the music verges perilously on the conventionalities of Beethoven's period. Last night the finale was another story. When it finished, hardened concertgoers applauded, cheered, and crowded to the stage. The orchestra applauded as loudly.

The stature of the performer being slight, he was finally led to the conductor's stand, from which he waved his acknowledgments to the players and audience. Still the audience would not go, and Fritz Busch, the conductor, led the soloist back again to the stage.

It would seem, therefore, that that object ordinarily loathed by reviewers and serious lovers of music—the infant prodigy—is not wholly a thing of myth.

Master Menuhin has a technique that is not only brilliant but finely tempered. It is not a technique of tricks, but one much more solidly established, and governed by innate sensitiveness and taste. It seems ridiculous to say that he showed a mature conception of Beethoven's concerto, but that is the fact. Few violinists of years and experience known to this public have played Beethoven with as true a feeling for his form and content, with such healthy, noble, but unexaggerated sentiment, with such poetic feeling in the slow movement and unforced humor in the finale.

His tone is surprisingly sonorous, refined, and rich in color. This was the case even though a boy whose small hands made it difficult for him to tune his instrument, which he frequently passed to the concertmaster for this purpose, was playing on a Grancino fiddle, three-quarters size. This violin had limited capacities, yet the tone carried to the uttermost limits of the hall. Now and again there were indications of a sagging string, but these incidents did not impair the quality of the performance.

For the cadenza of the first movement Menuhin played the one by Joachim, which is very difficult. His fluency, confidence, and aplomb might well have been envied by older players. It was at the end of this cadenza that the audience first threatened to "hold up" the performance. But it was in the two last movements—in the slow movement, which is the great test of a musician's sincerity and depth of feeling, and in the finale, so surely and delightfully performed—that a boy of eleven proved conclusively his right to be ranked, irrespective of his years, with outstanding interpreters of this music. It is a pleasure to add that he appeared genuinely absorbed in his task, and not in the sensation he was creating. From the first concerts of a career which began at eight, Master Menuhin, who is now a pupil of Enesco, has been carefully and admirably trained, and protected by his parents from educational "forcing" or public exploitation.

DECEMBER 27, 1927

An Evening with the Beethoven Association

A Critic in Danger of Enjoying Himself

WHEN the Beethoven Association gives a concert of the kind offered its audience last night in Town Hall, the professional reviewer of music is in danger of forgetting his business. His business is—or is supposed to be—the judicial, pontifical, pragmatical estimation of compositions and performances.

At these concerts, or most of them, he is in danger of enjoying himself! Enjoying himself, he is at one with the audience and also with the distinguished performers whom the Beethoven Association is accustomed to assemble for the service and the glory of the musical art. These are the happy occasions when the barriers of formality, adjudication, arbitrary standards, and differences of taste, which too often characterize public concerts, disappear.

Last night was an instance in point. There was a list of artists uncommonly well suited to the purposes in hand. They interpreted a program principally of familiar music with a gusto felt and shared by the audience. There were two items of special interest: the first, the Violin-and-Piano Sonata of Ravel, which has been played here but which is still for practical purposes a novelty; the second, a score that should be more familiar than it is, namely, Bach's Triple Concerto for three harpsichords and strings, in the superb arrangement of Harold Bauer for three pianos. The interpretation of this composition fairly brought down the house. The audience rejoiced in the superb music and in the spirit and the various distinctions of the performance.

The performers were Harold Bauer, Myra Hess, Harold Samuels, pianists; Yelly d'Aranyi, violinist; Marie Roemart Rosanoff, cellist. Miss d'Aranyi had already shown herself a violinist of very exceptional qualities. She proved them anew on this occasion. In fact, it was the glowing tone, the vivid temperament, and the technical brilliancy of this artist which, with Miss Hess's excellent treatment of the piano part, made significant the rather weak Piano-and-Violin Sonata, Opus 105, of Schumann.

It was an evening of a high prevailing standard of ensemble which does not always obtain even when distinguished artists meet together. Sometimes this ensemble reached the most brilliant heights, as for example the performance of the first movement of the Bach concerto and the beautiful interpretation of the Ravel sonata by Miss Hess and Miss d'Aranyi.

It is in the second movement of this sonata that Ravel very wittily employs rhythms and idioms derived from American "blues." It may be said that few if any of the other serious European composers have been so successful as he in parodying the swing and twist of American dance music. It may also be said that fewer still have taken jazz rhythm, intervals, etc., as raw material and worked over this material with such ingenuity, technical cunning, and laughter as Ravel. But the middle movement of the sonata is by no means its only amusing page. The composer entertains himself with certain insignificant ideas—the importance, as it were, of being Ravel! This sonata is not much more serious or weighty than the Sonatina for the piano, but it is a model of workmanship and taste and modern devices, including parallel harmonic planes employed in an engaging and laughably felicitous way.

The performance was one of the most delightful finesse and balance. It has not been often this season that an audience has listened to such sensitive and reciprocal interpretation.

The Bach concerto, even if played less comprehendingly than it was by Messrs. Bauer and Samuels and Miss Hess, would have made an impression. As it was, the swing of the opening measures decided the evening at once for the concerto. There was a well nigh ideal blending of timbres, contagion of spirit and of rhythm. The slow movement was not so perfect as regards precision of attack and complete unanimity of intention, but what music!

This is certainly one of the greatest slow movements of a concerto that Bach wrote. The framework is of towering strength, in the majestic phrase that moves about in the fashion of a passacaglia, the independence of the part-writing, the aptitude for astonishing modulation. But this is the technique. It is the mood that is expressed with especial significance. For the music is not only of romantic reverie but, in places, of deep melancholy. Here is Bach the poet, the dreamer, the author of the Chromatic Fantasia and also of the music of the *Passions*. The other movements are Bach in vigorous vein, and the finale is very rich, vital, and surprising in its contents.

But it is the slow movement that haunts the memory, that might be Bach's portrait of Rembrandt. This dwarfed everything else on the program, even the Brahms Trio, Opus 101, played so well by the Misses d'Aranyi, Rosanoff, and Hess. It was Bach who brought salvo after salvo of applause from a delighted audience.

Beecham and Horowitz Make a Joint New York Debut

"The performance triumphed immensely in spite of these things."

THE deeds of a new conductor, a striking figure among the "guest" leaders who are deluging America this season, and the power of a young virtuoso of brilliant technique and overwhelming temperament to fairly stampede an audience, were memorable features of the concert given by the New York Philharmonic Society last night in Carnegie Hall.

The conductor was Sir Thomas Beecham, making his first bow to an American audience. The pianist was the Russian Vladimir Horowitz, who also made his American debut on this occasion and by his sensational, if by no means impeccable, performance caused most of the intermission to be occupied in applauding and cheering him and calling him back to the stage. It has been years since a pianist created such a furor with an audience in this city. At the end of the concert there were many recalls and more cheering for Sir Thomas.

To what extent all this excitement was due to other elements than the purely musical will be revealed by later concerts and recitals. Certainly both artists have reason to be pleased with the reception. Sir Thomas, of course, was the first to confront the audience. When he appeared he was urbanity itself, confidence, poise. A man of some height and of a stocky build, groomed and mundane, he surveyed the audience and the hall with deliberate interest while the audience surveyed him.

The guest was evidently master of the situation, and apparently in excellent fettle. He conducted without score, as many of the leading conductors of the day do. If he had had a score before him, there might have been smoother co-operation with the pianist in the performance of the concerto. But this question need not here detain us. What is more important is the fact that Sir Thomas Beecham quickly proved himself a musician of unusual enthusiasm, magnetism, and purpose, and that he provided a program refreshing in its contents as in its execution.

This program offered for the first time in America three pieces of delightful music from the inexhaustible treasure house of George Frederick Handel. They all came from Handel operas which are quite unknown to this generation—the overture to *Teseo*; the musette from *Il Pastor Fido*; the bourrée from *Rodrigo*. There was another first New York performance, *The Walk to the Paradise Garden* from Delius' opera, also unknown here, *A Village Romeo and Juliet*, and still another first Philharmonic performance, the *Chasse royale et l'orage* from Berlioz's *Les Troyens*. The remaining pieces were the Mozart Symphony in C major (Köchel 338) and the Wagner prelude to *Die Meistersinger*. A program too long for American custom, and, if anything, too full of good things! But what a list! And there are conductors who play warhorses season in and season out in this city and profess it difficult to find unfamiliar music worth while for their audiences. Sir Thomas has been for many years in England a beacon light for musical progress, a man utterly intolerant of routine, mental laziness, or blind tradition.

He is not a virtuoso conductor, in the ordinary sense of that term. Not that he lacks the gesture eccentric or impetuous. Quite the contrary. This is the most athletic conductor America has seen for many a season. He is energetic and to the point. His movements, as he conducts from memory and strides about his rostrum, are careless of the audience. Sir Thomas is making music. His beat for the superb opening of the *Teseo* overture was a beat and a sweep of the arm which evoked from the men the big curve, the splendid stride, of Handel's magnificent stately phrases. Sir Thomas's rhythm and line, as they might be called, changed with the character of the music. Now he was as the strong swimmer breasting the tide, or he crouched like a panther, ready to spring upon a piece of counterpoint the instant that its head projected from its lair. Pleasantries aside, he gained the results that he wanted from the men. He always conveyed the big line and the rhythmical breath of the music, conducting with entire authority, without affectation, with a directness and vitality which brought an immediate response from the listeners.

It may even prove that Sir Thomas Beecham is a musician first and a conductor afterward. It would not be at all bad for Philharmonic audiences if future concerts should show this. The musical health of his interpretations would commend them if they had not other distinctive qualities. As a matter of fact, while he did not fuss and fret over details, he showed a mastery of nuance when the occasion warranted, as in one of the Handel pieces, where he gave three successive shadings to certain repeated figures—a forte, a piano, a pianissimo, and from that point to the end a fine diminuendo which merged into silence. But none of this was finicky or superfluous or for purposes of exhibition. It seemed inevitable, inherent in the music.

There was the same sincerity and regard only for the task in hand in the interpretation of the music of Delius, which abounds in characteristic qualities of that extremely sensitive and imaginative composer. The interlude is sensuous, impassioned, and of a fine texture. Does it rank among Delius' greatest pages? That also is a question for future performances to answer. Certainly it was music worth the hearing, and to those who heard it for the first time the interpretation seemed fortunate, revealing.

Then came a more debatable piece of conducting, with Mr. Horowitz's performance of the Tchaikovsky B flat minor Concerto. It was quickly evident that either conductor and pianist had not sufficiently rehearsed to the point of thorough understanding, or there were differences of conception which would not down in their ideas of the concerto. No doubt the former explanation is the one. In any event, the pianist at the beginning wanted a faster tempo than the conductor conceded, and there were many pages when the two seesawed in their ideas. Despite this and some imperfect balances, sometimes the fault of Mr. Horowitz, he made a tremendous impression on the audience. His treatment of the work was a whirlwind of virtuoso interpretation. Mr. Horowitz has amazing technique, amazing strength, irresistible youth and temperament. If one judged his tone only by the first and last movements, it would be described as very brilliant, very strong, but hard.

In the slow movement, however, there was another quality which showed that the pianist could sing and could evoke beautiful colors with the pedal of his instrument. But there could be many reservations about this performance, as, for instance, tempos, already referred to, sometimes too slow, usually too fast; the many places in which Mr. Horowitz played accompanying passages with unnecessarily loud and prominent tone; the prevailing scarcity of understanding between him and the conductor. The performance triumphed immensely in spite of these things. It was big playing, however it were picked to pieces. It would have overwhelmed the audience if Mr. Horowitz had played much worse and far more inartistically than he did—which truth is rather tragic. He would have triumphed, in any case, by his electrical temperament, his capacity for animal excitement, and his physical capacity for tremendous climax of sonority and for lightning speed. Very possibly Mr. Horowitz is a great musician as well as virtuoso. The first movement of the concerto implied as much. But he has that to prove. What is to be recorded is the wildest welcome that a pianist has received in many seasons in New York, the appearance of a new pianistic talent which cannot be ignored or minimized, however it is estimated artistically, and a concert of many and spectacular attractions. As has often been said in these columns, one concert does not make a conductor or a virtuoso either. Half a dozen hardly suffice to test a new leader. But within the limits of a single concert there was no question of the triumph.

JANUARY 14, 1928

Jeritza Essays Carmen

"Constantly increasing wonder, if not delight"

A VAST audience assembled last night in the Metropolitan Opera House to attend the American debut of Maria Jeritza in the role of Carmen. This gathering looked and listened with constantly increasing wonder, if not delight, in her performance. Those who expected novelties of interpretation were not wholly disappointed.

The American public has seen Carmens and Carmens—the Carmens of historic greatness, Carmens mediocre or worse. But last night's Carmen stands in a niche of its own. It tended, upon the whole, to the realistic. When Carmen entered, she roughly jostled a man in the chorus. She sang her entrance music while maintaining a cigarette in her teeth. She sprawled in a wheelbarrow when she sang the Habañera. The Seguidilla was delivered in a different position—lying backward over a table. And Carmen, her back to her captor, danced a kind of Hawaiian hula while she mocked the amorous man. All this occurred in the first act, which was perhaps the best part of the impersonation.

Mme Jeritza's second act was not exactly as eventful as this; nevertheless it maintained the flavor of novelty as well as conspicuous ineptitude in action and song. Mr. Tibbett, not particularly well cast as the Toreador—although he sang much better than his vis-à-vis, and displayed a much finer mastery of French diction— did not intend to be entirely outdone in stage business. He jumped onto a table in delivering the second verse of the Toreador song, bestriding this improvised podium masterfully, illustrating by obvious movements and gestures his narrative of the bullfight.

The opera was otherwise burlesqued in the course of a ramshackle performance. Mme Jeritza sang very badly, with a poor tone quality and a lack of resonance, and without apparently the slightest regard for pitch. In this respect other members of the company entered into the spirit of her performance. There was a prevailing joyous spirit of disregard for key all over the stage. As for style, for French—! Mme Jeritza's French would have been repudiated in the Franco-Prussian War. Mr. Johnson's enunciation and pronunciation, decidedly open to criticism, were models by the side of it. He was in poor voice and seldom did justice to his music. Only in the last act did he stir and impress his listeners by the return of his wonted artistry and eloquence in song. In the third act the singing that received the applause of relief, if not of acclaim, was the mediocre delivery of Micaëla's air by Miss Fleischer—a triumph, again by comparison.

The principal spot of virtue in this curiously infelicitous representation was the singing of the chorus, practically the one reminder of great past performances of Bizet's opera by the Metropolitan. The audience found good reason to approve, especially, the chorus of children, who represented the urchins of the first act. But the methods of Mme Jeritza seemed to be infectious during a performance extremely unfair to a great music drama. It is surprising that a singer of her experience, intelligence, and observance of tradition in other roles should have been willing so recklessly, ineptly, crudely, to violate every principle of technique, style, and even effective stage presence as she did on this occasion. *Carmen* stands many different treatments and many different conceptions of the principal part, but there is a line to be drawn between that which is individual and artistically daring and that which cannot be justified by any sound principles of taste or logic. Mme Jeritza's Carmen is the poorest thing that she has done on the Metropolitan stage. She is apparently unfitted for this role, by physique, style, technical accomplishment, or appreciation of the nature of the opera.

JANUARY 16, 1928

====

The American Debut of Maurice Ravel

"He has disdained superficial or meretricious success."

A LARGE and brilliant audience assembled last night in the Gallo Theatre to do honor to Maurice Ravel, who appeared for the first time in this city in a chamber-music concert of his own works. When Mr. Ravel came on the stage to play his own Sonatine for piano, the audience rose to greet him. They applauded him at every possible interval. He played encores after his Sonatine—the Habañera, arranged by himself for the piano, from his *Spanish Rhapsody* for orchestra, and the *Pavane pour une infante défunte*. He accompanied Greta Torpadie in the singing of his *Histoires naturelles* and the *Chansons madécasses,* for voice, flute, cello, and piano, and he played his late Sonata for Violin and Piano with Joseph Szigeti.

The *Introduction and Allegro,* for harp solo, flute, clarinet, and string quartet, was played by Carlos Salzedo, the Hart House Quartet, Arthur Lore and Henri Leon Leroy.

The precision and the taste of Ravel's workmanship, the complete technical mastery of his medium, the care with which each different musical idea was worked out complete, impeccable in form and style, were striking manifestations of the art of a composer whose works rebuke the pretense and dilettantism so fashionable in many quarters of Paris today.

The String Quartet, carefully and zestfully performed by the Hart House Quartet, is a good point of departure in an examination of Ravel the composer, because it is the work in which he has his feet firmly on his own ground, after preliminary acknowledgment of the influence of Debussy. The *Histoires naturelles*, fashioned with a cunning that equals their humor, are, in the first place, a continuation of a French esthetic and satirical tendency that can be discovered as early as Rameau and Couperin in French music, that reaches modern manifestation in certain songs of Chabrier and Chausson, and anticipates the pseudo-originality of such songs as Poulenc's *Bestiaire* and other ingenious imitative expressions by members of the late *"Six,"* beside whom Ravel is a very great and classic master.

Miss Torpadie gave highly intelligent and commendable performances of these songs. The Sonata for Violin and Piano is a work in the lighter vein, in which Mr. Ravel, a most serious artist and workman, may be heard asking: "Why be serious?" But his take-off of "blues" in the second movement is by no means the only felicity of this entertaining piece, which is truly Gallic, decorative, and witty, and fashioned as by an expert jeweler.

The audience hearkened attentively, appreciatively, to these compositions, to the ironically barbarous *Chansons madécasses*, and to the brilliant coloring and wheedling, scintillating effects of the *Introduction and Allegro,* so admirably conceived for the modern harp and for various combinations of its tone with that of other instruments.

Nothing could have been more typical of the precision, economy, and refinement of this music than the slight, aristocratic, gray-haired, and self-contained gentleman who bore himself with such simplicity on the platform, well content, as it were, to give an accounting of what he had done, and to leave his listeners to their own conclusions. And, indeed, his achievement speaks for itself.

Never to have composed in undue haste; never to have offered the public a piece of unfinished work; to have experienced life as an observant and keenly interested beholder, and to have fashioned certain of its elements into exquisite shapes of art that embody the essence of certain French traditions, is a goal worth the gaining. Mr. Ravel has pursued his way as an artist quietly and very well. He has disdained superficial or meretricious success. He has been his own unsparing critic. The audience was appreciative of the opportunity to welcome the man and the composer.

First American Stage Performance of *L'Histoire du soldat*

"The unmistakable success of last night was the success
of the poem"

WHAT may be technically described as a brilliant and highly representative audience attended last night in the Jolson Theatre the first stage performance in America, at the hands of the League of Composers, of Igor Stravinsky's *L'Histoire du soldat*. The audience heard the piece with every evidence of enthusiasm, and indeed it is highly effective in the theater. A suite made from the music that Stravinsky produced for this "story" of the soldier, which he described as one to be "read, played, and danced," was performed several seasons ago in New York. The music then missed fire, which was quite logical, since it hardly exists as an organism without its specific applications to the poem and the stage spectacle. The unmistakable success of last night was the success of the poem, written or at least translated in a kind of doggerel jingle admirably suited to its subject; to the ornate stage settings, which were too ornate; to the virtuoso performance of the dancers, which was too elaborate and professional; and, by no means least, to the biting musical commentary of Stravinsky.

Obviously this commentary is a degenerate and eviscerated product of the composer who once wrote the score for *Petrouchka*. But it is in precise accord with its theme, excellent for punctuation of the spoken narrative and for the pantomime on the stage, and even for instrumental interludes that mock and jest and jeer—all this with consummate skill, with a few instruments, with a technique which makes of each instrument a solo voice and an agent of dramatic narrative. The music feels as if Stravinsky had written without enthusiasm, certainly without faith and without pity, employing to the full his capacity for terse statement, for caricature and a certain ironical fantasy. Again, a perfect harmony with his theme and, as a component part of his tale, an eloquent medium.

The theme is one born, perhaps, of war-weariness and disillusion

143

in Europe—Ramuz wrote his poem in 1916—but it has as its basis a conception even more universal and timeless than that of war, which has found expression in ways great and small, as far apart as the *Faust* of Goethe and the opera *Wozzeck* of Alban Berg, which in recent years has created some disturbance in Europe. It is the theme of the man, the devil, and the fate of the man's soul. Ramuz's idea is cast in the cheap, popular ballad vein, intentionally banal, and with despair for its conclusion. The devil finds the tired and bewildered soldier wandering home from the wars, and bargains with him for his fiddle, his one salvation. The devil deceives the soldier, plays with him as a cat with a mouse. For an instant the unlucky man escapes the domination of the fiend, but only for a moment. Foolishly, without foresight, without reflection, he is in the net again. Stravinsky's drums, solo, thud and bang the rhythms of a weary march, and the play's over.

The setting and manner of performance are unusual. Last night they followed only partially the methods of European stages. The story is spoken by a reader seated at one side of the stage. What the reader relates is danced and mimed. The reader delivers his address in the first, second, or third person, as the whim appears to seize him, and without the conventional inflections or changes of tone when he speaks for the different characters. Most of the time he is the impassive reader of a tale, but sometimes he is the friendly adviser of the man struggling in fate's net, or even deeply sympathetic with him.

On the stage are three figures: the soldier, impersonated last night by Blake Scott; the devil, represented by Jacques Cartier, appearing by courtesy of Oscar Hammerstein; the princess, who last night was Lilly Lubell. The reader was Tom Powers, present through the courtesy of The Theatre Guild. He sometimes changed and sometimes cut the translation of Rosa Newmarch. And so, through five rapid scenes, the piece sped on. The pantomime was directed by Michio Ito. The stage settings and costumes were the creations of Donald Oenslager. Pierre Monteux, guest conductor of the Philadelphia Orchestra, was the interpreter of Stravinsky's score.

The music for this is written over ordinary and banal rhythms and figures of musical speech. It parodies some vulgar tunes, and the music for the delivered soldier and his princess, in their bridal

chamber, is a parody of the old Lutheran hymn *A Mighty Fortress.*
There is much polytonality and other choice forms of a modern
dissonance and rhythmical horseplay. The most extensive music
is the *Royal March*, played for the celebration of the meeting of
the soldier and the king's daughter. There is music in the rhythms
of the tango, waltz, and of course ragtime for the wedding. These
are designations of the main section of a score which is one of
separate lines rather than colors, and fragments of music whittled
down to the smallest essences.

The best proof of the effectiveness of all this, of the ingenuity
and subtlety of the score and the brusque and colloquial character
of what may be termed by courtesy a poem, lies in the fact that a
representation quite too far in spirit from the original did not
vitiate its effect last night. Last July in London the writer saw a
performance of *L'Histoire du soldat* by the Arts Theatre Club, a
performance commended by Stravinsky and instructive as comparison.

The orchestra was not in its customary place, below and in front
of the stage. It was on the opposite side of the stage from the reader.
There was a theater within a theater, a little square, hardly big
enough for an immense burly soldier to move about in. This stupid
and tired soldier became gigantic and the center of observation. His
uniform was not highly colored, as last night, but was a common
service garb, frayed and worn. The devil had no brilliant colors
to identify him. On the contrary, he looked a harmless elderly
gentleman, perhaps an attorney out for a walk in the country, pursuing his favorite hobby with a butterfly net.

Everything in the background was dull, drab, and realistic. But
there was a highly grotesque and medieval episode when the devil
appeared, as a growling dog, in the princess's chamber and was
dragged from the room by the tail. Admitting the artistic and entertaining dancing of Miss Lubell and Mr. Blake last night, as also
the brilliant performance of Mr. Cartier, it remains that a stiff,
wooden dance of the princess by Lopokova was more fantastical and
characteristic. The reader last night followed the methods of a
Chinese property man. In London he was attired as a soldier on
leave, and there were moments when his gestures were identical
with those of the devil's victim. The effect was almost macabre,
ghost-like. One who looked and listened might have wondered if

the narrator was not telling a story about himself, and if the soldier, the devil, and the princess were not all figments of the imagination, called forth by the strange and fascinating tale.

The performance last night was too ornate, too gorgeous in setting, too virtuotistic in style, and by so much deficient in grim, sardonic, dramatic quality. Of its kind, however, it was brilliant, well co-ordinated, logically carried through. It introduced a work which could be treated in many different ways and be successful on the stage. It also convinced one again that Stravinsky's natural bent is the ballet and the theater.

This performance was followed by a repetition of the delightful score of Manuel de Falla's *Retablo de Maese Pedro*, staged with the puppets of Remo Bufano. Nothing could have been a better prelude for the beautiful and inspired music of Falla than the bitter, bare music of Stravinsky.

All in all, a brilliant evening, a fresh record for the energetic and enterprising League of Composers.

MAY 30, 1929

━━━

Toscanini's *Lucia*

"The ministrations of linnet-headed coloratura sopranos"

Milan, May 8

IT HAS been an exceedingly great pleasure to this reviewer to encounter a certain aspect of the genius of Arturo Toscanini with which Americans of this day and generation can scarcely hope to become familiar on the other side of the water. This aspect is not that of the conductor of symphonies nor yet that of the interpreter of *Tristan und Isolde*, or *Götterdämmerung*, or *Ariane et Barbebleue*, or any of half a dozen other masterpieces of music drama which Toscanini re-created for Metropolitan audiences in bygone years. Those achievements are written large in the operatic and symphony records of the golden metropolis.

But have the music-lovers of that favored metropolis, by any chance, heard Toscanini conduct an old, outmoded opera long since consigned to the ministrations of linnet-headed coloratura sopranos to their audiences, and disgustedly relegated by musicians and reviewers who profess to know anything to the ash heap of hoary antiquities? It is an opera composed by one Donizetti. Its name is *Lucia di Lammermoor.*

Believe it or not, that is an opera worthy of respect. There are reasons when a work lasts as long as *Lucia*, and Toscanini makes them most clear. When *Lucia* is performed in America, as in most other places, it is purely as a vehicle—which lumbers and creaks with the weakness of age—for sopranos who pipe trills. When mounted with care, even with imagination in its action and scenic settings, and approached earnestly and reverently, as Toscanini approaches everything he contemplates as an artist, it becomes a beautiful and affecting experience.

Suppose *Norma* at the Metropolitan had not been conducted by Serafin or sung by Ponselle. What would have been its fate? But in most theaters *Lucia* is handed over to second- or, preferably, third-rate conductors, an inadequate orchestra, and routine singers, or worse. One visitor at La Scala sat absorbed through three hours of this opera, engrossed by its aristocratic style, by the curve of Donizetti's phrases, his surprisingly dramatic touches of orchestral commentary, and the actual poignancy of much of his music.

Well, there was Toscanini near by and in perfect profile, his eyes blazing, his lips moving, with deep shadows in the lines of his face cast up by the light of the conductor's desk. He was singing with the orchestra, as he always does when he leads, directing the players less with his hand than with his piercing eyes, fashioning every note and phrase, as completely "on fire" as if he were conducting *Tristan* or *Otello.* The emergence of certain orchestral phrases—as, for instance, at the moment of Lucia's fatal signing of the marriage contract—and the intensity of the orchestral utterance were as unexpected as they were thrilling to hear.

Again and again the orchestra assumed such significance that one acquired a new idea of Donizetti, for it was obvious that he was not lacking in the sense of dramatic import when he chose to exert it. And always there was the governing principle of infallible taste. Certain tempos, which at every other performance we heard were slow and syrupy, became quickened to a pace that eliminated the sentimentalism with which certain passages commonly reek. This music came nearer to a Bellinian character than to the vulgar, exaggerated Italianisms of the decline of the Donizettian school. There were constant changes of dynamics and frequent broad alterations of tempos where other conductors would merely have maintained a uniform pace.

It was immediately evident that every singer was held as in a vise to Toscanini's ideas. This was particularly necessary, one would say, in view of some of the singers. For instance, Aureliano Pertile's ardent and expansive temperament would seemingly have made him do all sorts of things if permitted, but, as it was, he sobbed the hero's anguish with a sincerity and fire which would, nevertheless, degenerate into sheer bombast if uncontrolled.

Yet within a just limit there was marvelous accompanying as well as directing. With Madama dal Monte—who, if she has not a voice of unequaled beauty and brilliance, interpreted her music with the most admirable intelligence and style and with equally admirable clearness and finish of her coloratura—Toscanini fairly breathed. The smallest punctuation of her phrases, the slightest occasional pause or retard which gave a true emotional inflection to a passage commonly considered one of mere ornament, was reflected instantaneously as in a mirror by the orchestra.

Thus, the whole interpretation of the opera, which included only one first-rate musician among the singers, was a notable example of emotional sincerity and finished style. When the music became utterly conventional and routine, as from time to time it does, the listener was still absorbed by its delivery, which had not a dull moment.

The journey toward Milan, long and uncomfortable like many European journeys, was worth while a dozen times over for this experience. Of course, an opera is likely to gain by being heard in its natural environment. This is true, at least, of all but the very greatest masterpieces. The audience of La Scala has obviously degenerated as regards brilliance of display and manners, just as opera audiences in all places have degenerated in these respects since the war. But it was an Italian audience, the members of which could not refrain from singing under their breath with the singers or the orchestra.

It was obvious also that this was a gathering that paid more exacting and more critical attention to song than our audiences do, and that the singers were fully aware of that fact. The chorus was not equal in quality nor perhaps in technical resource to the chorus of the Metropolitan. The orchestra was inferior, too. For all that, the orchestra played with superb warmth and elasticity of phrase. The chorus acted as well as sang. The scenic settings were of a color, depth, and artistic quality which have not been equaled in America.

Another thing: the tempo of the city and the theater are more leisurely than ours. The performance proceeded swiftly, with punctuality and dispatch, yet was enjoyed with a certain deliberation and completeness of sensation that can hardly be experienced in a restless American city. All these things are most important in hearing an old opera.

Tomorrow night they give *Falstaff*, but with how good a cast there is no telling at this time of writing. But we could have been well content if a visit to Milan meant nothing but the Scala-Toscanini production of *Lucia*.

JUNE 30, 1929

═══

Boris as Moussorgsky Originally Wrote It

"And here is Moussorgsky in frock coat and spats. . . .
But we knew another composer."

Moscow, June 15

THERE are many musicians and musicologists who remain indifferent to the contrasts alleged to exist between the *Boris Godunoff* of Moussorgsky and the *Boris Godunoff* of Rimsky-Korsakoff. Arturo Toscanini knows of them. But it could not be discovered that Mr. Toscanini had read the score in the new edition of Paul Lamm, issued by the Publishing Department of the Russian State. Mr. Toscanini knows, of course, the 1874 Bessel edition, which is so much more authentic than that of Rimsky-Korsakoff, but which is still very far in content from the original.

When the two versions of Moussorgsky and Rimsky-Korsakoff are compared, the differences are glaring. The changes of dramatic structure and also text would be in themselves sufficient to necessitate the complete overhauling of any *Boris* production that aimed justly to represent Moussorgsky. It cannot be claimed that there are no essential differences between a version of opera which cuts whole scenes and episodes, adds passages that were not composed by Moussorgsky, and makes many changes of harmony, of melodic line and rhythm. The *Boris* of Moussorgsky is one thing and the *Boris* of Rimsky-Korsakoff another. They are not the same work. Which score is the better of the two is logically matter for discussion, but the differences are great and inescapable. Sometimes, at the hands of Rimsky-Korsakoff they are of benefit to Moussorgsky. More often they give him injurious misrepresentation.

These differences are emphasized by the printed music, but printed music is never an accurate index to the effect of a work in performance. This is even truer of opera than of instrumental compositions. Where an experienced student or practical musician can judge in the large of the thematic material, development, and instrumental values of a symphony, he cannot do the same with a musical work for the stage. The proportions of an opera are almost impossible to calculate with exactness in advance. Puccini, a practical man of the theater, never turned in a score without having rehearsed it with stop-watch and cardboard figures on a cardboard stage, and there probably has never been an opera which remained unaltered in preparation for performance. In other words, the only way to gain an idea of the effect of the Moussorgsky *Boris* was to go to Russia and hear it. It is the greatest and most important interpretative achievement of that country in music since the revolution of 1917.

The contrasts are accentuated rather than diminished by the stage performance. Certain variations in the two scores would naturally pass with little notice from the casual opera-goer, but other departures of Rimsky-Korsakoff are astonishing. He is eternally the schoolmaster who knows better than anyone else what should be done. He has the incorrigible zeal of the specialist—of the surgeon who will find some reason to operate even when an organ is in a healthy condition. He starts with his blue pencil from the very beginning. Little notes in the prelude that mean nothing one way or the other are meticulously altered. Rhythmical accents that mean much more and are very characteristic of Moussorgsky are "corrected," systematized. The instrumentation of the prelude is made clearer and more sonorous, and Rimsky-Korsakoff adds a little counterpoint. The Moussorgsky version of these pages is not strong. Rimsky's orchestra has here more color and sound. Combined with the opening chorus, it also "sounds," but Moussorgsky's scoring is here bolder, wilder, and more in consonance with the dramatic intention of the music.

And what does Rimsky-Korsakoff do to the music of his opening chorus? In its original form it is an immediate index to the directness and unconventionality of Moussorgsky's genius, as also to his profound sympathy with Russian folk music and the keenness of his ear. It is written by him in measures of 3-4, alternating with 5-4. Two measures of 3-4 give place to one measure of 5-4. Three measures of 3-4 and one measure of 5-4 are repeated, after which eight measures of 3-4 conclude this period with one measure of 5-4 and one measure of 3-4. There is a total of twenty-one measures. This is too much for Rimsky. He contrives to level it off by a new subdivision of measures, twenty-six of them in 2-4 rhythm and seven more in 3-4. What is better or more efficacious than arithmetic—multiplication, division? And our good teacher is infallible in his figures. He comes out on the same accent as Moussorgsky! Just the same, it is a little surprising, particularly from a composer who knew folk song and who wrote the 11-4 chorus in *Snegourochka*. And the spaciousness and rhythmical elasticity of phrase which Moussorgsky desired is gone. Russia has partly disappeared. We are on the German border. And here is Moussorgsky in frock coat and spats, a cane in his hand, a flower in his buttonhole—fit for gentlemanly society. But we knew another composer.

The same kind of thing is done and done again by Rimsky-Korsakoff in other pages. Could he have been entirely sincere in wishing to help Moussorgsky when he did this? His deeds and his words prove that he was, but the document makes it hard to accept their evidence. Details need not trouble us, but there are bigger as well as smaller things in the Rimsky edition which differ from Moussorgsky. Rimsky-Korsakoff surely will not give him his lead. As for harmony, what is one to make of the changes in modulations, in chords, in key color? The music for Marina, the Pole, whom Moussorgsky could portray only by the same means his predecessor Glinka used to characterize a Pole in his *Life for the Czar*—namely, by a mazurka—is bad enough in all conscience. What are we to say when the one mark of distinction that the opening chorus possesses, a double pedal for the lower parts, is calmly rubbed out and insipid major harmonies in parallel thirds substituted? The master disciplines the refractory and now helpless pupil.

This is one side of an argument which has two. In other places Rimsky-Korsakoff has repeatedly carried out Moussorgsky's wishes in ways in which the latter was unable to help himself—ways imperative for the success of the opera. Nor is Rimsky-Korsakoff lacking in psychological insight. Listen to his golden brass when Boris announces his high resolve as the newly appointed ruler of the Russian people, or the introduction to Boris's soliloquy in the first act. Sometimes he more than meets Moussorgsky on his own ground. Elsewhere he is far from him. When Boris cries out that his powers are failing and that he feels as though body and soul were crumbling within him, Moussorgsky has an extraordinary effect gained by different instruments taking up in turn the tones of a chord which he builds gradually from the bottom. Rimsky pooh-poohs this as a childish idea. But performance of the passage as Moussorgsky wrote it contradicts him. On the other hand, there are times when Moussorgsky wants something and does not know at all how to get it. He then writes measures which sound weak and appear on paper so weak, tentative, and unsure that it seems a conservatory student of orchestration would have known better than to write that way. Probably he would have known better, which is not the same as being a Moussorgsky. It is certain that fanatical indignation with Rimsky-Korsakoff for his editing of Moussorgsky seems as wide of the mark as it is to minimize his editorial misrepresentations. The truth is between the two extremes, with many grievances on the side of Moussorgsky. In his orchestration there are some superb heights and some yawning gulfs of ineffectiveness. These empty spaces do not exist with Rimsky-Korsakoff, and of course when he is confronted with a problem that he really understands he is unsurpassable. The scoring of the coronation scene is a case in point. Moussorgsky's is weak beside it. Perhaps one should speak with a certain caution of this, remembering the smallness of the chorus and orchestra at the Stanislavsky Art Studio. Rimsky-Korsakoff has also extended the great chorus of acclaim by thirty-nine measures, and it is excellently done. It is more conventional, if you like. Yes, and the episode is more conventional with monumental music. Unfortunately, a final test of the power of this passage could not be made, since the dates of the Leningrad repertory made it impossible to hear it on the big operatic stage and with the full orchestra.

There is room for endless comparisons between the two scores. At the end it boils down to the fact that the music of *Boris* as a whole is far superior, far more dramatically truthful and modern in texture in Moussorgsky's original version than in the Rimsky-Korsakoff editing, and that the Rimsky-Korsakoff orchestra as a whole is probably more effective if not as original as Moussorgsky's. But the strength and meat of the music and the drama are in Moussorgsky's original conception and execution of his work, which cannot be known for what it really is in Rimsky-Korsakoff's version. In the two passages which are given only in Russia—the first version of the scene in the Czar's apartments, and the scene before St. Basil's—the orchestration as a whole is highly original and striking.

The scene before the Cathedral of St. Basil is well contrived in Stanislavsky's little theater. The stage there is very shallow, and yet there is the impression of verisimilitude in the appearance of one of the gates of the cathedral, with snow hanging on balconies and arches and a stairway which the guards, then the Boyars, and at last Boris descend. The beggars at their feet are grouped with all the saliency made known in America by the Moscow Art Theatre. The dialogue is extraordinarily effective, and the scene is the quintessence of Moussorgsky. It takes such singing actors as these to convey for the technique of a stage of today the color and atmosphere of an episode conceived fifty-five years ago. At the last moment, when the idiot answers Boris, refusing to pray for him, the stage is gradually darkened on a group that has the effect of a fresco, in which every figure is etched and shrouded, and every shadow and every rugged surface in itself an interpretation. In a larger theater the same scene would be presented in a larger way. In a small theater every small stroke of the composer-dramatist is felt, unforgettably.

How should *Boris*, in the light of the new documents, be staged? It is remarkable how difficult it is to add or subtract very much from Moussorgsky's first draft of the opera. This first draft did not include the scene of the Kromy revolt, which should certainly be added to it, since it is splendid music and splendid opera. The episode of the chiming clock, a supplementary feature of Moussorgsky's second version, should be added to the stark simplicity of the first. The Polish scenes of the second version, in the ideal production, would be dispensed with. The choral measures added to Pimen's scene in Moussorgsky's second version should be retained, and Pimen's narrative of the murder of Dmitri, contained in the first version, would give this scene the climactic point which is otherwise lacking.

Imagine a *Boris* with a first act as Moussorgsky first wrote it, including the odd thirty measures which for some reason were lopped off of the opening scene, and with the addition of Rimsky-Korsakoff's scoring and extension of the coronation music. Then would follow the scene between Pimen and Grigori, with restorations as noted. Then the scene at the inn, with or without the hostess's song. The first version of the act in the Czar's apartments, as they give it here, is far simpler, more concentrated, more starkly dramatic, emphatic of the psychology and the plight of Boris, and, as it happens, nearer Pushkin, than the scenes as Moussorgsky altered them. Add here one portion from the second version, the episode of the chiming clock. The children's songs of the second version could be used if desired for operatic entertainment, but had far better be sacrificed to make way for the longer monologue of Boris. The episode of the parrot is an interruption of music and drama and should be abolished, as Boris's aria would be automatically abolished by the use of the music and orchestration of the first version. If the audience cannot relinquish the polonaise or the love duo of the Polish act, let the conductor make a potpourri of them *à la* intermezzo in *Cavalleria Rusticana.* Atrocious? Yes, but not as atrocious as the distortion of the opera by these scenes is now. For the last act, three scenes—the scene before St. Basil's, the scene of the Kromy revolt, and the scene of the death of Boris. *Boris* would then last no more than three hours and a half. Honest folk could get to bed and an epochal masterpiece have its rightful proportions.

As it is, the opera will endure. Its lines are so great that they cannot be obscured. Even when they are twisted and broken off short in such a way that the work resembles a house which has been repaired and added to by a half-dozen crazy carpenters, it is massive and indestructible. But Moussorgsky has a right to be judged not only by what he actually wrote, but by his opera as he first planned it, for himself and not for managers and prima donnas. This can be done. The world moves, in spite of all signs to the contrary. *Boris Godunoff* waited nearly forty years for recognition. It has waited fifty-four years to be made available in its authentic form to the public. Given another fifty years, we may yet hear and see it in its fine integrity.

JANUARY 3, 1930

Mengelberg Conducts Bach and Strauss

And Harold Samuels Performs a Novelty— a Mozart Concerto

MR. MENGELBERG, recovered from his recent regrettable indisposition, conducted the concert given by the Philharmonic-Symphony Society last night in Carnegie Hall. The soloist was Harold Samuels, the pianist, who on this occasion played not Bach, but Mozart.

An extraordinary symptom of the return to classicism, which has made the music of Bach such an important factor in latter-day programs, is the recrudescence of the Mozart piano concertos. Mr. Iturbi, Mr. Gabrilówitsch, and now Mr. Samuels have elected to play Mozart at symphony concerts, a proceeding which a few years ago, would have been attempted once or at most twice a season, but certainly not three times. How is it that these Mozart concertos, which have nothing to do with the modern prescriptions for success in the concert hall, grow, apparently, on performers and audience? There is no sumptuous or frenetic orchestration, there are no pulsing climaxes, no hair-raising passages of bravura to leave the audience agape—nothing but very pure Mozart melody, very clear Mozartean form and orchestration. And the audience exults. It exulted last night with Mr. Samuels.

He plays the A major Concerto with a simplicity that would baffle lesser musicians, with the sincerity of the artist as sure of himself as a man as he is sure of himself as an interpreter. Mr. Samuels, it might be said, did not once raise his voice. He sang the melodies deliciously, his legato playing being as remarkable for its smoothness—the smoothness that Mozart sought and commended —as his staccato was for crispness and cleanness. His fast movements sparkled, and his slow movement sang with an intensity of beauty and a contained loveliness which gave the music its complete due, while there never was overemphasis or disproportion. This was a rarely simple, completely sincere and masterly performance of a very beautiful piece of music, each of the Mozart piano concertos having beauties all its own. The same form, the same general scheme of instrumentation prevail in the A major as in the E flat Concerto played by Messrs. Iturbi and Gabrilówitsch. But the A major Concerto is another world of beauty, and Mr. Samuels initiated his audience into this glamorous realm with a fineness of feeling and a perception of symmetry that once more acclaimed Mozart as a unique genius in the whole literature of music.

Mr. Mengelberg opened his program with the D major Suite of Bach. His fast movements and his dance movements had the sturdiness, the two-fisted energy and jollity, of good old Bach, who wrote great music as coolly as a carpenter turns out his daily handiwork or a shoemaker addresses himself to his last. The air, almost too celebrated, which Wilhelm popularized through his transcription was not so fortunately stated, for the conductor was inclined to drag the tempo, and the cadences were sentimentalized. This oily sentimentality is anything but advisable in Bach, and by so much was the beautiful air disfigured. Few indeed are the conductors who are willing to let such a passage speak for itself, and Mr. Mengelberg last night was, unhappily, not an exception to the rule. Elsewhere his vigorous rhythms and his grasp of the music did it honor.

The audience applauded this performance heartily, as it was later to applaud two popular works of Richard Strauss: the brilliant and sadistic dance of Salome from the opera of that name, and the tone poem *Don Juan*.

FEBRUARY 8, 1930

Prokofieff Introduces His Second Piano Concerto

And Koussevitzky Conducts the *Scythian Suite*

IT WAS the turn of Serge Prokofieff at the concert given by the Boston Symphony Orchestra, Serge Koussevitzky, conductor, last night in Carnegie Hall. Mr. Prokofieff, who is scant of hair but tall, blond, with an appearance of boyishness, figured on the program as composer and also as pianist in the performance of his Second Concerto, heard for the first time in this city. Mr. Koussevitzky gave an amazingly brilliant performance of the Prokofieff *Scythian Suite*. Suite and concerto evoked storms of applause. The composer, after both performances, was repeatedly called out, bowing from the platform. Mr. Koussevitzky, who greatly admired Mr. Prokofieff's talent, signaled the orchestra to rise in his honor, while the conductor himself applauded. All this bordered on unconditional triumph. Those who had reservations were silent and outnumbered.

It has not always been thus. Mr. Prokofieff, who will be thirty-nine years of age next April 24, has already been for a considerable period a storm center of modern music. Fifteen years ago, with the *Scythian Suite* already to his credit, he was the terrible infant of contemporaneous composition. When he came to America for the first time he took much castigation from the press, but he always had a lesser or greater number of fanatical admirers, and there were not lacking those willing to take up cudgels for him. What more does a composer need for fame? Mr. Prokofieff may or may not be a great composer of tomorrow. We don't know about tomorrow, and shall not try to. At present he occupies a position before the public for which less sincere composers would be willing to resort to any trick or make any sacrifice. He is a figure conspicuous in the musical talk of the day.

There is no question that his music is of contemporaneous inspiration, in spite of the intentional, if not deliberate, barbarisms of the *Scythian Suite*. Tribal ceremonies, sacrifices, dances, lamentations, fighting, and salute to the rising of the sun—these things may emanate from atavistic sources in the subconsciousness of the composer, but they are as modern as Flaubert. The battle with the Evil God, as portrayed by Prokofieff, is as impersonal and as metallic as the battle with the armed elephants in *Salammbô*. And just as the characters in *Salammbô* are figures and not characters, men as yet only a few centuries removed from beasts and therefore capable only of action and unaware of the conscious reasonings and emotions of men, so is this music hieratic and unemotional, done in hard surfaces, savage without hate or fear, since its existence has nothing to do with these feelings. But here are force, severity and hugeness of line, and a feeling of terror in the presence of unknown things. And the spirit of this unemotional music saves pages already old-fashioned in workmanship, in rhythmical periods and formal character, and music not wholly sufficient unto itself, since there are purely reiterative and repetitive measures which are actually dance and would be in their real place as accompaniment of dance.

But the final pages—those depicting the sunrise, with the harmonies that shatter like the points of a thousand spears against the sustained tones of the trumpets, are—if not among the greatest—among the most brilliant pages of recent musical literature. These things were impressed upon the listener in the most exceptional way by the masterly performance of Mr. Koussevitzky and his men. It is hard to believe that Mr. Prokofieff has ever had a more brilliant interpretation.

The piano concerto is more advanced and more absolutely musical in its intention than the early suite. It is pure musical form. The first movement has lyrical ideas which are clear, melodic, and of a flowing beauty, and they are subjected to delightful and astonishing treatment. In later movements are stretches intentionally symmetrical and conventional in form. They are worked out largely on the basis of rhythm, though contrapuntal devices are also employed. There is little of a lyrical nature after the first movement. The second, as the program book tells us, is a kind of *"moto perpetuo"* for the two hands playing in octaves against the orchestral part, the whole having the effect of a rapid technical étude.

There is the insistence upon so-called "pure" form, rhythm, design. As a matter of fact, for record of a first hearing, this writer finds many of these purely musical ideas purely monotonous and undistinguished. He finds commonplace figures overworked; variation, frequently ingenious but in the end monotonous, rather than development of germinal motives; a good deal of banality and not very much musical fertility or intensity. Mr. Prokofieff, for his part, played the piano with ample technique and tonal power, and with the rhythmical pulse so essential to this music.

Prokofieff was introduced with an air of innocence by Mozart's *Kleine Nachtmusik.*

A fascinating concert, whatever the pros and cons, with the novelty of material that so many orchestral concerts in New York lack, and a standard of orchestral virtuosity which has not been surpassed, if it has been equaled, this winter in New York City.

The Passing of Cosima

"The beating of great wings"

FOR a long time before her actual death, Cosima Wagner had departed the land of the living. The catastrophe of the World War not only put an end to the Bayreuth of the older Wagner generation, but its strains and tragedies sapped her strength and snapped her nerves—she was already seventy-seven years old—and when the Festspielhaus reopened its doors in.1924, Cosima Wagner was a ghost of the past.

She could not attend performances. She was only accessible at Wahnfried to the fewest favored visitors. The body outlasted the mind, although as late as 1927 Cosima had short lucid intervals. At those moments a chance mention of some figure of her past would cause her to rejoin, and for a few moments a connected narrative would follow, then to be succeeded by incoherence or silence. In 1919 newspapers suddenly announced that she had died. A flood of articles and reminiscences began to pour into the newspapers and periodicals until, as suddenly, the report was authoritatively denied from Bayreuth. But now Cosima, daughter of Liszt and the Comtesse d'Agoult, wife of Hans von Bülow and Richard Wagner, has gone. We know a good deal more of her past and see it in a broader perspective than we did in 1919. The picture gives plentiful opportunity for criticism, but it is, above all, a picture of a great woman and a great age, of which the last vestige, so far as Wagner and his very important part in that age are concerned, has gone from us.

None of the people intimately bound up with Wagner's later years were less than great people. Most of them, beginning with Wagner himself, have been abundantly documented. Cosima has come in for her share of the accounting, and there are many people today who remember her in the active years of her management of Bayreuth. And yet it is probable that the real Cosima is known less than any of the other dramatic figures of the Wagnerian past.

It is probable, furthermore, that she will remain the most enigmatic and by no means the least significant of them all, largely on account of one striking quality, or lack of it, which is implied by her history —her essential lack of imagination.

Cosima Wagner was probably the most brilliantly gifted woman of her day. Nietzsche, whom she was principally instrumental in estranging from Wagner, bore witness to it—he and a thousand others. She was ugly, especially in her youth, but they say that Anton Rubinstein was only one of many who, aside from Wagner, were fascinated by her. She took strongly after her mother, the Comtesse d'Agoult, in her pride and strength of purpose, her masterly silence concerning herself, and her immense capacity for direct and ruthless action. She completely understood Wagner's ideas. She set about their realization with the same intentness, devotion, and ferocity which had characterized her possession of the man— once her purpose had been aroused, once she had set out upon that course. But imagination? It is a somewhat different thing. Imagination creates and objectifies. Wagner had this quality supremely. He objectified in his art all of his conceptions and all of the experiences which they engendered—the conception invariably coming first, as an accurately documented history of any one of his masterpieces will show.

Also he objectified himself and the incredible power and naïve unscrupulousness of all his purposes in his innumerable letters and literary effusions. Cosima also could write, but it was not revelation of what was transpiring within. Such a woman acts, but never explains herself. Besides, Cosima was a born aristocrat, if not a snob. She took after her mother in this as in other matters, and would never have acknowledged the necessity of explaining anything. She would write a libretto, based upon the *Oresteia,* for her young husband, Von Bülow, to set to music. Later she would pen a monograph upon her father, Liszt, directions to translators of Wagner's texts, or a blue-stocking letter or a literary essay descended directly from the manner of her mother, who, like George Sand and other women of the forties, had to write, and did so, as we know, under the name of Daniel Stern. Cosima was very cultured and could talk with anybody in a brilliant way. But the creative and visualizing imagination which was so transcendently the quality of her husband was never hers. What was deepest in her she never betrayed, perhaps never knew herself, and it was just this which made her so powerful, so ruthless, so scornful of weakness even in Liszt, her own father. It was her energy and laconism which made her life so extremely concentrated and effectual and formidable, and made her the more or less inscrutable figure she will always remain.

She made enemies by the score, usually, strategically speaking, in the right places—not in the wrong ones, like Wagner. She reckoned shrewdly in these matters. She aroused either intense dislike or slavish devotion, and there were few in whom she could not instill the fear of God. Of course, she utterly changed the complexion of Wagner's life, once she had him and Bayreuth in her hands!

Something to work with and for! Bayreuth, the dream of Wagner, who wished to democratize music and art, who was banished from Dresden in 1849 as revolutionary and Bolshevist, with Bakunin and company, running for his life! Bayreuth, become the headquarters of aristocracy, the salon of intellectual and titled Europe. The D'Agoult had her salons; the Von Bülows had a salon on a small scale when they were married in Berlin; but here was a salon of Valhallan dimensions, where the gods and the moneyed Nibelungs of the world mingled and bowed to the greatness that was Wahnfried's, a salon worthy of Cosima's steel.

All that hadn't entirely vanished in 1924. In fact, Bayreuth, when it reopened its theater, was a hotbed of aristocracy and reaction, with the old flag of the German monarchy floating over the Festspielhaus, and the grafs and gräfins, the dukes and earls, incognito! Some of them, it was said, were "wanted" by a republican Germany that didn't quite dare to put forth its hand and grab them. Monarchism and separatism were too incipient just then in Bavaria. It was an amusing and an exciting day—July 22, 1924—with an electrical undercurrent. Old carriages and liveries, not mere automobiles, sweeping by; subdued recognitions, salutations, reunions, some obviously accompanied by deep feeling and all permeated by an inescapable flavor of a majestic past. For a side detail, Karl Mephistopheles Muck and Ferdinand of Bulgaria snickering in a corner of the courtyard. Passion that suddenly blazed into flame at the end of the opening of the *Meistersinger* performance, when Hans Sachs makes his concluding address, to the magnificent music, concerning the situation of the German people and the refuge of German art. The audience rose and remained standing, tears in the eyes of those in the house and those on the stage. The curtain fell, and simultaneously some ill-advised person began to yell *"Deutsch-*

land über alles." The audience, standing, sang verse after verse of
the hymn, and it was a wonder that sabers didn't flash in the air.
You could feel the flash if you didn't see it. This was thy doing,
Cosima! This, in Bayreuth, vision of the socialistic and revolutionary Wagner, become a veritable asylum and nucleus of dis-
guised or tolerated political émigrés. Cosima's work, social as well
as artistic, had endured, and she unconscious of it at the time and
already, as we have said, out of the land of the living. That was
six years ago. Since then Bayreuth, too, has bowed to change and
responded willy-nilly to currents of a new day.

And yet—a good deal, we fancy, will be said in the immediate
future about Cosima. A good deal more, we think, will be said still
later. Greatness does not fade so easily, and after all, in all the
tangled tale, there is heard the beating of great wings, and there is
felt the presence of something which has more than a topical interest for humanity.

APRIL 23, 1930

Schoenberg's *Die glückliche Hand* Is Found Decadent

And *Le Sacre* Is Found Better without Choreography

DIE GLÜCKLICHE HAND (*The Hand of Fate*), an opera
in pantomime with a leading voice part and chorus. Music by
Arnold Schoenberg. Produced by the League of Composers and
the Philadelphia Orchestra. At the Metropolitan Opera House.

The Man.............................Ivan Ivantzoff

Mimes
The Chimera........................Olin Howland
The Woman......................Doris Humphrey
The Stranger......................Charles Weidman
Two Workmen.............John Glenn, Charles Lasky
Chorus from the Curtis Institute of Music

Followed by

LE SACRE DU PRINTEMPS (*The Rite of Spring*), ballet
by Igor Stravinsky, now performed for the first time here with
stage action.

The Chosen One.....................Martha Graham
The Witch..............................Anita Avila
The Sage..............................Gould Stevens

Men and Women Dancers
Conductor, Leopold Stokowski

Whatever the ultimate value of the works presented and whatever
the qualities of the performances as regarded complete fidelity to
purposes of the composers, it is certain that two of the most interesting events of the New York musical season of 1929–30 took place
last night in the Metropolitan Opera House. These were the productions by the League of Composers and the Philadelphia Orchestral Association, under the leadership of Leopold Stokowski, of
Arnold Schoenberg's twenty-minute "opera" or macabre melodrama *Die glückliche Hand* and Igor Stravinsky's *Sacre du printemps*, given in its original form, which is that of the ballet.

The opera house had been bought out by the public, at special
prices, days in advance. There was long applause last night, and
Mr. Stokowski made a speech before the curtain in which he thanked
the audience for its support, and observed that he and a certain
number of his colleagues were working in artistic directions which
the compositions of Schoenberg and Stravinsky typified. These
directions were the synthesis in the theater, on the basis of a rhythmical polyphony, of all its resources of drama, music, lighting, the
dance, etc., in new ways that accorded with modern thinking and
that were to eventuate, it was hoped, in an American form of art.
Mr. Stokowski solicited further public support for experiments of
this kind. He had reason to be encouraged by the curious and
tolerant attitude of last night's brilliant audience.

The works performed had indeed the character of original and
fruitful experiment. Nor could two modern compositions have been
more significantly contrasted. The composition of Schoenberg's—
which appears to be musically meager but is undeniably atmospheric and original in its combination of music, color, and other
theatrical ingredients—is highly decadent in a very interesting meaning of that word, and in an extreme of pessimism, looking, in fact,

toward death. In this it seems to us the antithesis of anything "American." At least, we hope so.

On the other hand, the music of Stravinsky is certainly that of life, on however primitive or brutal a plane, and last night, after the murky, Poesque creation of Schoenberg, it fell upon mind and senses as a rejuvenation, indeed a rebirth, from a fertile soil, of new force and horizons of power. How magnificent the primitivism of this music, its stark, hidden, explosive strength and its profound growth from the soil! *Sacre du printemps* is more than a title, it is truly the essence of the music. It may be added here that Stokowski appeared last night as the conductor of conductors to unleash its elements.

But let us take the program in its order. As one by one we hear the representative compositions of Schoenberg, a lonely and singular figure in modern music, he documents himself the more completely. There are two important elements, for artists and psychologists, in the work performed last night. The first is its technique, the second its psychological basis. The least important feature is the hollow, asthmatic, despairing music.

The drama is simple. A Man is seen, emerging from darkness, an evil creature astride of him—a chimera, its talons in his neck. The Man is deluded by the apparition of Woman, symbol of his dream and desire. She forsakes him for a rich lord. The Man for a moment draws himself up to the height of his powers, by a single blow of his arm turns a piece of metal into a diadem, flings it contemptuously from him, and then, once more cozened by the Woman, falls for the last time, the prey of his fate.

The technical significance of the work, the practical methods by which phantasmagoria of the mind and soul are indicated, is found in the very subtle and pliant combinations of sounds and colors—at least in the original intention of the composer, not fully realized last night—also in various nuances and mergings of speech and song, in pantomime and drama, line and rhythm, and symbolic representation. These things, very carefully synthesized, are certain to affect the future evolution of opera, which will have to find a point of departure from the antiquated fashions of other days or lose its hold upon the public, as unquestionably it is doing. For these features alone *Die glückliche Hand* is a significant study.

But there is something far more interesting, and of significance in its bearing upon the position in art of Schoenberg, the man and the musician. It appears as more than a casual coincidence that *Glückliche Hand* in the person of Schoenberg (though he now lives in Berlin) emanates from the same Vienna which is the home of Freud.

For we believe that Freud could find no more interesting and provocative subject for his studies than his fellow citizen of former days, and we believe that the Freudian standpoint is necessary to explain Schoenberg's music. It is certainly music of "suppressions," of highly involved and egocentric impulse, and none the less poignant, even impressive, for that reason.

It is decadent music, not merely of a man, but of a period, which bears within itself the seeds of its disintegration. And the correlation of man and period might well be sought in the psychoanalytic examination of Schoenberg himself, his neuroticism, his pessimism, his exasperated passion which is without force or evocative power, his consciousness of oppression, his vain and extremely involved ways of attempting to make his music potent and articulate while every day its "complexes" multiply and its potency declines.

This from a man who commenced in music as a poet, a romanticist, a Wagnerian, and who appears today more than ever as an aftermath in essential elements of a past period, not the harbinger of a new one. Indeed, the impression one gets of this dying art is akin to the thought of some struggling creature left by a receding tide, perishing on strange sands.

When Schoenberg composed *Die glückliche Hand*, his second dramatic work, in four years from 1909 to 1913, he was active in many ways, and especially as a painter. In this opera he is for us everything but a creative musician. His sincerity is unquestionable; his workmanship, on paper, is of a ghastly complication and meticulousness, not only in thematic treatment, but in the most careful and somewhat indirect methods of orchestration. He has very interesting scenic conceptions. He has compiled his own very brief text and left to orchestra, actors, and stage director the carrying out of its implications. Perhaps after repeated hearings the last pages of choral lament might affect the listener strongly as musical expression of tragedy and despair. And here and there a detail would be noted, in the orchestral commentary, blending with a striking ingenuity with gesture or vocal inflection.

Schoenberg directs a great many changes of light in his score, and many more colors than were turned on the stage last night.

Mr. Stokowski has remarked publicly that theaters at his disposal in New York and Philadelphia had not sufficient lighting facilities to illustrate adequately the composer's ideas. Robert Edmond Jones, however, whose business these matters were, has stated personally that he has employed lighting for Schoenberg's drama exactly as he wished, and has not been conscious of limitations imposed by theater equipment.

There was also different action. Much was done by means of shadows cast by the principal participants, especially by the malignant and sinister figure of the Chimera. That monster was in truth hideous, if less mysterious and fortuitous in action and more like a horrible insect than we had pictured from reading the directions in the score. But the setting and the shadows, with the six masks staring from the darkness at the beginning and end of the play, and the employment of simple dimensional scenery, did measurably achieve the implied effect. Doris Humphrey was admirable in her pantomime as the Woman. Ivan Ivantzoff's intelligent and highly dramatic use of voice and gesture as the Man bore adequately the principal burden of the dramatic representation—a most thankless and difficult task. Olin Howland's Chimera, according to the action agreed upon, fulfilled excellently its purpose. Charles Weidman's Stranger was equally in place.

Of the performance of *Sacre du printemps*, with a truly imaginative setting of Roerich and a new choreography, on the whole appropriate if not invariably interpretative from the musician's standpoint, it is not time to speak now. As a musical listener, the writer prefers Stravinsky's music without any spectacle. But if dancing there must be, it can be said that much was accomplished last night —especially in movements when the dancers wove a kind of polyphony and choral movement, and when the black-vestured participants entered the scene to watch with frantic solicitude the fatal dance of the Elect, interpreted by Martha Graham—to approximate the character of the score. Stravinsky wrote it for a ballet, but that does not lessen the difficulty of its choreographic interpretation. The scenery, particularly memorable for the iron twilight of the beginning of the second part, and the orchestra, conducted by Mr. Stokowski with thrilling incisiveness and nervous power, made, for some, the real essence of the occasion. But students and critics of choreography might have it otherwise.

The Friends of Music Dare a Performance
of Janáček's Festival Mass

"The music is fantastically, impractically, and
inarticulately original."

IF THIS world were an ideal one and composers of great, imperfect
works, justly destined to be unsuccessful, were given their due—
then the Friends of Music would quickly give a second performance
of Leoš Janáček's Festival Mass, which they produced yesterday
afternoon in the Metropolitan Opera House.

This mass, so far as a very fleeting and imperfect acquaintance
with its pages and one individual's reaction to it are concerned, is
great and partly incoherent music. It is so different from a Roman
mass that its crude, primitive, Hussite conception of the ritual will
shock the esthetic sensibilities of many people wholly unprepared
for it, as it will merely puzzle or bore others. It is very stark, barbaric stuff. Steel rings in the music, and ancient racial voices. Count-
less generations are back of the work that old Janáček wrote in
his seventy-third year, shortly before the end, as also ancient religious ceremonial of a Slavic race, which has no more to do with
the ritual of the Greek Church of Russia than with the Catholic
Church of Rome. The origins of the mass are of a more unknown
character; for that reason, and for its barbaric emotion and its
barbaric sound, it seems even more ancestral, mysterious, remote
from conventional things.

Meanwhile, although there are suggestions of Moussorgsky and
perhaps of other composers that Janáček knew and subconsciously
sympathized with, the music is fantastically, impractically, and inarticulately original. Sometimes one thinks a little of Bruckner,
Janáček's master, in the reiteration of certain musical figures. But
this is a parallel rather than a tendency held by the two in common.
Janáček's thinking is wholly different from Bruckner's in this work,
which is certainly the truest and most original expression of his
genius that is known to us. (The opera *Jenufa*, performed in a

recent season by the Metropolitan Opera Company, is much less creative.)

Janáček writes almost entirely in a harmonic style, dispensing with the old contrapuntal forms and nearly all of their devices. He writes harmonic combinations which are not suggested or endorsed by anybody. Solo and choral passages are harmonically so bold and uncompromising that, lacking the printed music, the listener might well wonder if the musicians were not wholly mistaken or miraculously off pitch and key with each other. Yet the logic of this procedure is clear, even if it is not practical in sonorous effect or organic in the accepted harmonic sense. And these characteristics add to the savage, energetic, yet mystical accent of many pages. Similar unpredictable originalities are found in the instrumentation, which has sometimes a wonderful brilliancy and glow—veritable bursts of color—of its own. In other passages it is wholly ineffective, almost ridiculous, for thinness and poor spacing.

The same thing in invention. Sometimes, in a magnificent burst, the composer takes an amazing flight. Then he suddenly seems to halt, perplexed, entirely at sea. Then he fumbles about, manipulates some formula or other, dwells upon an idea which leads nowhere, till light breaks again and once more, heroically, prophetically, he soars to the sun.

The form of the mass is wholly unconventional. The conclusion no more follows tradition, with its organ and orchestra postludia, than anything else in the piece. This is a huge, tremendous work, a conception only half expressed; one which only partly realizes a vision that must have dazzled the composer. This composition can hardly hope for success with the public or a permanent place in the repertory, which, concretely speaking, it does not seem to deserve. But it is an inspiring composition. The man who penned it was incipiently a master, as he shows by his boldness and fearlessness, and by the vision he projects in spite of technical and stylistic disabilities. But his gifts never came to full flower.

Mr. Bodanzky and his forces had rare courage in producing this music, which should be heard again. In the performance of the Festival Mass the soloists were Editha Fleischer, Karin Branzell, Dan Gridley, Friedrich Schorr, and Louis Robert, organist. The performance of a difficult score, too little known for an appraisal in detail to be possible, was obviously distinguished by intelligence and devotion.

The Festival Mass was preceded by other Czech music—Smetana's prelude to *Libussa* and the Four Biblical Songs of Dvořák, sung by the admirable Editha Fleischer. A large and interested audience was assembled.

MARCH 13, 1931

New York *Première* of Bartók's Fourth String Quartet

"Strong, passionate, stark"

A CONCERT of new and old music, labeled collectively "first performances in New York," given by the New World String Quartet last night in the concert room of the New School for Social Research, introduced as the major item of the program the Fourth Quartet of Béla Bartók. There are no available records of previous American performances of this work.

This is curious, since the Fourth Quartet is one of Bartók's finest compositions in that form—perhaps the most complete, concise, yet free and highly individual in expression. There are five movements, and a theme stated in the first movement is transfigured in the last. The music may be called racial, though it does not advance the facile Hungarianisms of other scores. It appears as a distillation from racial sources. It is strong, passionate, stark in its strength, stripped to the bone. Yet there is much color, and in spite of the precision and economy of the score it has a rhapsodic essence and is highly emotional.

Sometimes, when a composer is growing toward a certain point and when his procedure is partially experimental, his music may lose a degree of conviction and consistency of style, and this may puzzle even warmly sympathetic listeners. We have heard earlier works of Bartók than the one played last night which were dryer and less spontaneous in character, and gave less the sense of spontaneous and completely individual expression. Here is no hesitation, uncertainty, or inconsistency, and Bartók, as in other works, makes virtuoso employment of the many effects of which the string quartet is capable.

In doing this he appears to be actuated by racial temperament, but in spite of its exotic accent the music is classic in clarity, balance, and insistence on sheerly musical ideas. The opening measures announce a powerful idea in a powerful way, and there is no sagging or hesitation from that moment until the last. In the broad perspective the five movements become almost three, since the two fast movements which precede and follow the lento make an effect almost that of a three-part form. The lento itself, beginning with mysterious sustained dissonances dropped like a veil of color through which the song of the cello is presently heard, is of a mystical beauty. The first and last movements are bold, extended in development. They announce and they sum up the essence of the composition.

Would that other string-players made so admirable a program as the musicians of last night. Bartók's ultra-modern music was followed immediately by a Symphonia of Isaac, a Ricercare of Vecchi, and a Fantasia of Gibbons. Then there was played the second movement alone from Schoenberg's Third Quartet, which, thus isolated, was placed in admirable relief for examination.

Was it the excellent arrangement and contrast of the program's material which made the listener so appreciative? The one movement of a Schoenberg quartet could be listened to with a degree of concentration that it would not have been possible to give the whole work. As a result, the exceptional unity of the movement and the relative conservatism of its polyphonic scheme were doubly manifest, one listener remarking that if she heard that music again she feared she might like it. This apprehension was shared by the writer!

Then, very properly and wisely, Bartók's arresting composition was repeated, as important works should be, whenever possible, at one and the same concert. This quartet, as also the movement of Schoenberg and in a lesser degree the music of the old composers, was played with exceptional understanding, sympathy, and musicianship.

====

Stravinsky's Violin Concerto Is Found "A Futile Thing"

Yet It Is the "Real Sensation" on a Varied Stokowski Program

BEFORE anyone knew what had happened, Leopold Stokowski had leaped upon the conductor's stand last night in Carnegie Hall and launched the orchestra into a shrill Cuban dance by one A. G. Carturla.

There were two dances by this Carturla, who was born at Remidios, Cuba, in 1906, and who lives there today. Furious, tonally bifurcated music was this, projected by the blond one with the racket of a thunderbolt.

The first piece was over almost before it began. The audience had barely time to quiver before the second dance was on. It came to an end, in turn, with an abruptness that positively stunned the auditors. They, stupefied, took a silent moment to gather their wits and applaud. No one had had time to find out what he thought of the music.

Swiftly Stokowski resumed his incantations. This time the audience had abundant opportunity to appraise the music, for it was long and mostly slow. The composer sat in a box over the stage and bowed repeatedly when the piece was finished. He was Efrem Zimbalist, the violinist. His symphonic poem *Daphnis and Chloë* was heard for the first time by the audience. The tone poem possesses, among other attributes, certain graceful and unpretentious ideas and a solo flute. But we prefer Mr. Zimbalist the composer in smaller forms.

Mr. Stokowski was on the loose. The long hands were cutting figures in the air. Came another novelty, Darius Milhaud's Concerto for instruments of percussion. This concerto has two movements, the first nervous and jumpy, the second "sustained and sad." The piece, it appears, was suggested to Milhaud by the professor of the battery of percussion instruments of the Etterbeek School of Music in Belgium. It may be said that those instruments of per-

171

cussion, which include bass drum, tenor drum, kettle drums, snare drum, tambourine, tambourin de Provence, cymbals, rute, castanets, triangle, rattle, metal block, and gong, are accompanied by a less powerful but none the less acidulous orchestra consisting merely of flutes, piccolo, clarinets, one trumpet, one trombone, and strings. It is tedious and empty music.

By the side of this emptiness a very brilliant performance of a piece that has been played before in the city, the *Soviet Iron Foundry* by Alexander Mossolow, was stirring. This piece generates noise and rhythm. Steel plates, which aroused the curiosity of the audience, are needed in the score. The horn-players, whose parts are prominent, are asked by the composer to stand when they play. In this sense the performance of last night was not spectacular, but it had electricity, and it relieved tedium.

All this was prelude to the real sensation of the evening, the first performance in New York of Stravinsky's Violin Concerto, with Samuel Dushkin, who has first performing rights of the piece, as soloist.

The concerto is short, lasting fifteen minutes or thereabouts. Through an interviewer—none other than Guido Gatti, the distinguished Italian musicologist—Stravinsky has ingenuously stated his views concerning the proper length of concertos. "The duration of a composition," he says, "can no longer be measured by those of the past." For a Mozart the invention of the theme "presented the maximum effort." The rest of the half-hour was easily filled by means of repetitions, refrains, and cadenzas. But today all that is changed. "Now every measure is the result of an enormous condensation of thought, so that sometimes in a whole day's work I just manage to write two or three measures; proportions have changed, and a concerto of fifteen minutes is already a monumental work."

No doubt it is with Mr. Stravinsky. We could go further. If there were ten measures of real theme in the concerto heard last night, it would be still more monumental. But, then, Mr. Stravinsky does not concentrate on his themes, does not consider them "the maximum effort." With him "the maximum effort" seems to be to string out conceptions which are the apotheosis of nothing by two or three measures and call it a day.

The concerto is a futile thing, not redeemed by its obvious technical skill and cerebrality. In the first and last movements, rhythms are juggled in a lively fashion. In the two middle movements, entitled *Aria I* and *Aria II*, the style is more sustained. There is a motto figure, or chord, of three notes. Stravinsky's technical knowledge is to be noted everywhere, and is not the least evident in the intricacy and skill of the difficult passages for the violin and the manner in which the violin and orchestra are balanced. Mr. Dushkin played the violin part with commanding skill, with the authority of a complete knowledge and a virtuoso's temper. For this writer, the concerto joins the lengthening list of the stillborn compositions of the later Stravinsky.

The classic of the concert, the composition of proved mastery, was Moussorgsky's *Pictures at an Exhibition*, as orchestrated with a wizard's cunning and a singular comprehension of their Russian fantasy and hugeness by the manikin Ravel. This work provided the orchestra and the virtuoso leader with opportunity to manifest their most striking qualities, and conferred upon the program a body and significance of material previously lacking.

JANUARY 8, 1932

Lotte Lehmann Triumphs in Her Debut

"If she had sung the song backward it would have been
hard to keep cool. . . ."

THE audience that gathered in Town Hall last night to hear Lotte Lehmann's first song recital in this city was not only impressed, but thrilled. It has been a good many years—more years, at least, than the writer has spent in this city—since any local song recital has offered such excitements and distinctions. Singing songs by Brahms, Schubert, Schumann, Mme Lehmann swept her listeners from their feet. She has a voice of magnificent range and color. Above all, it is an intensely communicative voice, one that stirs with feeling and that immediately affects those who hear it. She herself is a woman of superb temperament and capacity for the expression of great and varied emotions.

173

The moment that the first song, *Von ewiger Liebe,* had ended, the audience knew that a great artist was present. The outburst of applause was a spontaneous and most impressive tribute. This first impression was not lessened but intensified as the concert proceeded. To claim that every song was perfectly sung would be exaggeration. That is a thing that never happens. But in sum the vocal and interpretive gifts of the singer surpassed the highest expectations which had been awakened by the reputation that preceded her. At this time Mme Lehmann is a member of the Chicago Opera Company. She came to America after sensational successes in opera in Vienna and other cities. Her Fidelio, for example, has been acclaimed as the greatest interpretation of this part to be seen today on the lyric stage. But not all opera singers can face the test of concert performances. There were moments last night when Mme Lehmann was operatic, and when, as an interpreter of song, her temperament got the better of her and she stepped from the frame. But even when she did this—at least in the early groups, in moments such as the final measures of Schumann's *Ich grolle nicht* —she was so puissant, noble, and impassioned in her style, supplementing interpretation with such vocal resource and such a wealth of nuance, tone color, and all-conquering sincerity, that if she had sung the song backward it would have been hard to keep cool and refuse to be moved by what she did.

Mme Lehmann is not only a singer; she is a musician. Above all, she projects emotion and dramatic meaning, whatever she undertakes. In her groups of German songs, excepting certain items by Richard Strauss, she was on her native heath. She sang songs which have become household words in such a way as to resurrect every wonderful thing which familiarity had caused us to take for granted or to accept as a matter of course. At her height she displayed interpretive genius—nothing less. Some songs, such as the Schumann *Nussbaum* and *Aufträge,* had such an effect that one is willing to go some time without hearing them sung by other singers. Such a performance as this cannot fail to bring the art of lieder singing to a higher estate than it has enjoyed in these parts for a considerable period.

There were some technical flaws. Some might take them as indication of defective technique. We do not believe this. Mme Lehmann impresses us as a singer with a prodigious technique at her command. When technique failed her, or the technical standard sank for a moment, it was because of emotion not entirely under control, or a scale of proportions not good for a concert hall. Thus, when certain tones were attacked without complete preparation they came out slightly off pitch, or there would be an undue acceleration of tempo to a climax and a passing poor focus as in the voice of Death in Schubert's *Death and the Maiden*. In other places a phrase was unwisely separated from its fellows for the sake of dramatic effect and forgiven by the audience because of the thrilling emotional impact. But passing imperfections and personal exceptions to tempo, such as the slow tempo of Brahms' *Schmied* or the disproportionate conclusion of *Ich grolle nicht*, are small beside the accomplishments of the evening. Indeed, it is almost impertinence to dwell upon these minor matters in the light of the sensuous beauty, the variety of moods, the individuality of the performances. There were phrases never to be forgotten by those intimate with these songs and their innermost meaning.

Some of them had to be repeated, and this was almost regrettable, because in an inspired moment the thing done twice is never done the same. Yet it was the necessary concession to a wildly enthusiastic audience. It would be a pleasure to speak in more detail of the earlier performances of the evening, but that is not possible here.

It must be added that Mme Lehmann was not so fortunate throughout her recital. If she had sung the whole evening as she sang a group of French songs by Hahn, Chausson, and Fauré, she would have been accepted as a highly intelligent artist but not a great deal more. This group was a noble experiment by a woman who in the recital field is pre-eminently a great interpreter of German lieder. Mme Lehmann was outside the mood of these songs.

Did this interruption of mood affect the singer? For she missed the vein, the atmosphere, of Strauss's *Traum durch die Dämmerung* of the next group. She sang the *Wiegenlied,* an undistinguished song, with a fine-spun legato, but again exaggerated in the *Ständchen,* and she sadly distorted the end of *Zueignung.* And it was soon time to leave, for Mme Lehmann was losing poise and control through excitement and the fatigue of a long concert, and was spoiling phrases. She will undoubtedly be heard here again, and she will be welcomed and thanked for her appearances. There has been no such singer here, and there are few singers of such distinguished and agreeable presence on the concert stage. She can do almost anything with her voice, but a finer control of her resources is still necessary to Mme Lehmann. She can do anything when this latter condition is fulfilled.

JANUARY 8, 1933

===

The Emperor Jones Reaches the Met

"Instant and sweeping success"

The Emperor Jones, an American opera, American in its dramatic and musical origins, its text, its swiftness and tensity, and all the principal elements of the interpretation, was given its world *première*, with instant and sweeping success, yesterday afternoon in the Metropolitan Opera House.

To this music drama the audience listened, absorbed, deeply moved, from the first tones of the orchestra, from the first savage cries of the concealed chorus, to the final closing of the curtain. Then came the explosion of applause which follows long minutes of accumulating excitement, and a procession, back and forth on the stage, for uncounted recalls, of the composer, Louis Gruenberg; Tullio Serafin, who had prepared and conducted a brilliantly effective performance; Mr. Sanine, stage director; Mr. Mielziner, author of the fantastic scenery and décors; and, above all, for Lawrence Tibbett, whose performance in the title part was a great masterpiece of dramatic interpretation.

The basis of the opera, presented in one act and seven scenes, is the famous drama of Eugene O'Neill. The score, ultra-modern in its material, conceived with a rage of dramatic feeling, is the work of Louis Gruenberg, who is his own highly skilled librettist. It is not easy, in a quick recounting of a first impression, to assay its sheer tonal value. And in that very fact is much of the strength, the inspiration, the verity of the score. As music it was forgotten. As punctuation of the drama, accentuation and intensification of its emotions, it was superbly potent.

Critical analysis of the harmonic schemes, dissection of phrases, developments, and whatnot, are all beside the mark. The music is

176

prodigiously sure, headlong, fantastical, brutal in its approach; yet masterly in contrast of mood and in its major proportions; sheer emanation, as it seems, of the play, and of the glimmerings, the shadows, the hallucinations, and the stench of the jungle.

For the greater part of the seven scenes of the one-act version of the opera presented yesterday the audience follows the main developments of the O'Neill drama. They see Smithers enter the throne room of the Emperor Jones, ex-Pullman-porter, crap-shooter, murderer and fugitive from the law, now ruling the Caribbean tribesmen and soldiers, whom he has made his dupes and cozened and cheated. They listen to the conversation which ends, after Smithers's warning that distant pounding tom-toms herald the Emperor's ruin, with Jones's departure to win through the forest to safety.

The tom-toms are taken direct from the O'Neill drama, but here Mr. Gruenberg's sense of theater avoids a possible monotony or anti-climax. The drumbeat is interrupted on three different occasions by the visions that Jones sees in the forest, and when it is resumed the pace is always faster and louder, till at last drums are thundering from all over the place—and on the very brain of the poor defeated savage.

The audience sees Jones in flight through the jungle; they witness his hallucinations—the Formless Fears; the vision of Jeff, whom he had killed, crap-shooting; the vision of the prison guard that Jones had murdered with a shovel; and that of the old auction block, and the Southern dandies and auctioneer selling the slave to his purchasers; the frantic dispersal of each of the "h'ants" with a pistol shot; the consumption of the precious bullets; and the rapid demoralization of the fugitive, as he casts from him, one by one, his gaudy garments and military trappings, and at last emerges shorn of every garment but the savage's loincloth, and so meets his end—the barbarian, the Emperor, killed with his own silver bullet, dead as any other piece of meat, and thus reclaimed by his ancestors and enemies.

Mr. Tibbett triumphed in a cruelly difficult part, triumphed as actor and singer. Up to the present time, Emperor Jones is his supreme achievement, and it is one worthy of the greatest singer and dramatist and the highest traditions of the musico-dramatic stage.

If this performance and if the opera itself are discussed here in terms of drama, there is only the explanation that nothing in the opera of *The Emperor Jones* can be otherwise discussed, particularly after an initial experience. Least of all can it be particularized from the purely musical standpoint. But we come now to Mr. Tibbett's singing—or what little singing he had to do. His principal, indeed, his only opportunity in this aspect of his art came with the prayer in the forest. It is a passage admirably written for the baritone voice. It lay splendidly in Mr. Tibbett's register. He made the most of it, in the sonority of his song, in his dramatic diction, his subtle contrasts of tone color and gradations of sonority, his noble gestures and facial play. He had previously stirred his audience by dramatic force, excitement, climax. Here he invoked pity.

As for the dramatic appropriateness of this passage—it is matter for argument. The "spiritual" and its text are inserted deliberately by Mr. Gruenberg. Musically, their presence has every justification. The one thing, the thing that would otherwise be lacking in this opera, is the moment of lyrical expansion. Here it is. It is a very brief and fleeting efflorescence of song, if so it can be called, but it is extremely grateful and it provides a second of repose and emotional expansion in a work which otherwise would move too feverishly and precipitately to its end.

Drama and music spring out together, full grown and inseparable. It is, first of all, an opera that commands immediate attention and respect for its unflinching sincerity, imagination, dramatic blood. And it is vividly contemporaneous—a native approach, owing little or anything to precedent and nothing to European standards for its quality. For an opera to be performed at all merely because it is by an American is local self-flattery. For an American composer to have a genuine triumph with an opera is a matter for congratulation. But for an American opera to appear which not only stands on its own feet but represents a treatment of the form that could come only from a new country and a young people fully alive to the present day, is the thing which makes this success of Mr. Gruenberg so gratifying and important to the future.

=====

The *Gambler* Suite and Third Piano Concerto

"One still wonders what on earth Serge Prokofieff
will evolve into."

ONE still wonders what on earth Serge Prokofieff will evolve into,
and wonders the more after listening to him as composer and pianist
at the concert given by the Philharmonic-Symphony Orchestra,
Bruno Walter, conductor, last night in Carnegie Hall. He is a
born virtuoso. He appears to be a temperament and a mind very
symptomatic of this age. He is also a very gifted composer, but of
what category and what future?

Last night Mr. Walter conducted the first New York performance of a suite taken from the music of Prokofieff's opera after
Dostoevsky, *The Gambler*. The opera was sketched in 1916 and
revised ten years later. The suite was made by Mr. Prokofieff in
1932 and was first performed last March in Paris. Later Mr. Walter
performed it at a Gewandhaus concert in Leipzig. The composer
took passages almost verbatim from the opera and found that he
could fit them well together. But he changed the orchestration for
concert purposes.

This orchestration is very brilliant and it accents the dramatic
character of the music. But the composer's explanation of the dramatic meaning of the suite, printed in the program, did not wholly
illuminate us. "Here is the amorous Alexis; here is Pauline,
haughty, enigmatical, at the same time passionate, unhappy; here
is the General, giving himself important airs, but trembling lest
the Grandmother will not give him her money (he has lost his);
and here is the Grandmother, rich, imperious, knowing that they
await her death to inherit her property, nevertheless showing some
tenderness in speech for Pauline. At last the denouement, where
events hurry upon one another, leading to a dramatic end." On
the stage—no doubt. As a musical marginal note to scenes of the
novel—perhaps. In the concert hall we hear music by Prokofieff,
bearing hallmarks of his later style. This music is at times grotesque,

ironic, even sentimental, but principally it is nervous and energetic music, alternating real ideas with other passages that suggest theater, but are not especially convincing in the concert room.

Prokofieff's Third Piano Concerto, which followed the suite and which was conceived at nearly the same time, is nevertheless a much younger score. It has also more melodic juice, and some of the themes are remindful of folk music. The concerto is frankly a virtuoso piece, in a modern vein, and it is aflare, from beginning to end, with the nervous force and the youthful zest of the composer.

Mr. Prokofieff, as solo pianist, played this music with overwhelming brilliancy and fire. He performed with the same certainty and *élan* that he had previously and obviously brought to the composition of the piece. It is not one of his most substantial compositions, and there are defects of style. There is too much piano, going all the time, for the best orchestral effect, and some of the writing is performer's padding. But the sweep and exhilaration of the music exert a tonic stimulus that Prokofieff's music, even when it is not good, is seldom without. Meanwhile the orchestral combinations with the solo instrument are very effective.

Mr. Walter conducted the performances of both suite and concerto with a special sympathy, but, after all, the driving propulsive force was that of the boyish-faced composer at the piano, who swept everything with him and seemed to desire a greater task than he had set himself as outlet for his spirits and his musical energy. Even in the slow movement of the concerto, a theme and variations, Mr. Prokofieff cannot long remain quiet. Slow variations—the fourth is one of the most fanciful pages of the score—are quickly relieved by the rush and excitement of other passages. The finale is a play of rhythms and crashing chords and spinning piano figures that whirl giddily and seem to pull the other instruments into their orbit. The last movement includes a touch of buffoonery, with the harlequinade of the second theme announced by the piano. That is the grimace of the jester, and as a jester Mr. Prokofieff often appears incorrigible.

Mr. Walter brought balm to the ears of the more conservative in the audience and, in fact, gratified everyone by his direct, virile, sincere reading of the Brahms Symphony No. 1. He attempted no tricks for the gallery, being well content to immerse himself in the score and convey the music with a fine masculinity and conviction. The rest could confidently be left to Brahms, and was. The symphony had the long line, the heroic spirit. If some refinements of phrase or finish of detail were not present, their absence threw into relief the great outlines of the music. In the finale Mr. Walter was unusually fortunate, because of his admirably adjusted changes of tempos, which never dragged; his emphasis of dramatic contrast, implicit in the score; and the broad brush strokes which built up the towering climax.

MARCH 2, 1933

Toscanini Introduces Howard Hanson's "Romantic" Symphony

". . . in its perfectly obvious and unconcealed sentimentalisms lie its weakness and its strength."

MR. TOSCANINI's return to the New York Philharmonic-Symphony Orchestra last night in Carnegie Hall was the occasion of a warm demonstration in his honor and of some exceptional orchestral performances. The program contained a novelty in the form of Howard Hanson's "Romantic" Symphony No. 2. Otherwise it traversed familiar ground in the instances of Wagner's "Faust" Overture and Richard Strauss's *Heldenleben*.

Mr. Hanson has almost gone out of his way to write a melodic and rather conventionally formed symphony. He states his belief that the cerebral element is predominant in much modern music, but he believes that music should be the expression of feeling. "I have therefore aimed in this symphony to create a work that was young in spirit, lyrical and romantic in temperament, and simple and direct in expression." In this score are ample and clearly defined melodies, but they are not unmixed with modern dissonance, especially in the first movements. The various parts are connected, or associated in the listener's thought, by certain motives—a motive of three tones in the introduction, which often assumes importance, and other motives carried over from one movement to another.

This is a familiar device, one, in fact, which is almost inevitable in symphonic writing today. When, in these days, connecting themes

181

are not employed, the composer is likely to call his work a suite, and even then he sometimes reminisces, in one movement, about another. But the questions of form and even of melodic intention need not detain us here. The only question is whether Mr. Hanson has written an interesting symphony.

Interesting the symphony is for its new departures of manner, for its inequality of material and the curious incongruity of its elements. At first there is some harmonic strong meat—polyharmony and mixtures of tonalities. But soon we have themes—they could almost be called tunes—of mellifluous and often sentimental hue. And it may be said that in the straightforwardness of this music and its perfectly obvious and unconcealed sentimentalisms lie its weakness and its strength. Is it a reflection upon an ambitious and reasonably sophisticated modern composer to say that one suspects Mr. Hanson is most himself in precisely this simple melodic vein? Certainly not! What he has done, if this suspicion is correct, should be hailed with delight by his admirers, because it is from the moment that an artist dares to be precisely himself that he begins to find his real creative vein. Furthermore, this finding of the rock bottom of creative identity is sure to lead naturally to those logical evolutionary processes which at last bring what is loosely termed "style"—a style, whatever it may be, native to the composer's thought, and the unmistakable garment of it. Therefore, the symphony deserves the welcome it received, whatever its ultimate value may prove to be. The audience gave the work a very friendly reception, and Mr. Toscanini brought Mr. Hanson to the stage to bow his acknowledgments.

The orchestral readings of the two works of Wagner and Strauss were instances in which Mr. Toscanini, evidently in excellent health and spirits, outdid himself in his uncanny capacity to mold every musical phrase into an expression of poignant beauty and to make perfectly clear, in the most complex passages, every strand of the tonal fabric. The introduction of the "Faust" Overture was a beginning in this direction. The opening phrases immediately gripped the attention by their subtlety and the intensity of their expression. This was music unbound and free of the chains of bar-lines and the beat of the metronome, at the same time retaining its form and logic of statement. The thought of the composer was carried so directly and with such apparent spontaneity of utterance to the listener that it seemed as if there were no instruments present as intermediaries. Perhaps the conductor was too prodigal of his genius for song and elaboration of detail; nevertheless, there was deeply comprehending and passionate interpretation of the overture.

In the same way and for the same reason it may be that Strauss's tonal picture of an autobiographical hero was less muscular in its outlines, less bulging and strutting in demeanor than the composer himself designed. But what a glorification and lumination of Strauss's score! When Mr. Toscanini made the orchestra sing the love music and hymn it to the skies, he sang himself, as he often does when conducting, and it is this impulse, this possession by the spirit of song, which makes his orchestra so eloquent. The interpretation was both fiery and noble. Only in the shattering din of the battle music was it impossible to give distinction to a work which has so much of the baldly bourgeois in it. The hero's wife! From this giggling creature (solo violin) or anything like her may we be delivered. The hero's heavy wooing! The hero's complacency and braggadocio! Oh yes, these things are in the music.

But when the love music swells to its climax; when the hero, shouting and brandishing his sword, disperses his enemies, and his theme with its seven-league stride leaps again from the orchestra; and when the hero performs his works of peace, and approaches his own apotheosis—then, indeed, it is something more than a *Pickelhaube* on a beer-drinker who stands before us. It is a being heroic in stature, his gaze lifted to the heavens. Is it for nothing that one of the last quotations which Strauss makes from his own works is the one from the tone poem *Don Quixote*—the ride of the disillusioned knight homeward—and that a final progression, very near the end, one that leads to radiant major chords, is the motive of the sunrise music from *Zarathustra*? For they say that in *Don Quixote* Strauss was laughing at his own disillusions, and he may well have thought of these at the end of his journey, and of Zarathustra's apostrophe to the dawn, when he conceived the hero's ascension.

However all these things may be, Mr. Toscanini's performance was an utter triumph of tonal beauty and brilliancy, and virtuosity not only of technique but of spirit. It was the act of a most profound musician, who seldom touches that which he fails to adorn.

The New Criticism

"A blindfold analyst to whom a theme is a theme
and nothing more"

IN THE current issue of *The Chesterian*, R. W. S. Mendl discusses "The New Criticism"—in this case, of course, the "new criticism," if so it should be called, of music. This new criticism dispenses once and for all with the romantic and subjective type of "criticism." It approaches the subject of music, according to Mr. Mendl, from a more scientific standpoint. The reader is spared the fanciful inventions of the yarn-spinner. "Fairy stories and rhapsodizings about musical compositions have had their day." Let us devoutly hope so. "There is no question that there is a need for something more scientific which shall give us a genuine insight into the workings of a composer's mind, based on an investigation into the facts and not on the romantic imagination of enthusiastic fellow-musicians and music-lovers."

Dilettantes, officious investigators, and interpreters of "the composer's mind" have indeed been hard upon the composer, his compositions, and the public. They have often planted the most superficial and misleading conceptions in the mind of the listener. A Chopin nocturne meant this; Debussy's String Quartet mean that; whereas nothing was meant but exquisite and co-ordinated music. Nor, perhaps, is anything in music more wonderful than the spectacle, or experience, of following the sheer development and foliation of a musical idea.

The idea in the composer's mind is a seed that grows, and grows—artificial as apparently his methods are—with the logic and beauty of growths of nature. The sense of design that is perpetually amazing, indeed incredible, in the forms of plants, seems to manifest itself in the designs of perfect music. But there are more analogies between music and nature than those of design. There is the dynamism and emotional impulse of the hot-blooded organism. For everything is reflected in this art of invisible sound, the least corporeal of human expressions, which seems more than any other one to be the expression of nature and of human experience.

And here, as Mr. Mendl points out, is where the more fanatical of the opponents of "subjective" and "interpretive" criticism seem to lose sight of their objective and become lost in the forest because of the trees. They pursue analytical schemes of interpretation. They trace tonal designs and developments with the passion of the shortsighted detective. They explain them proudly, as if this material evidence was the secret of the composition.

To a certain limited extent these are clues to what the music is undergoing and manifesting from the depths of its inner life, but. they are not that life itself, any more than the surgeon's examination at the operating table is the secret of the organs upon which he is working. Analysis on the part of the critic is essential to the proper accomplishment of his task. It is the same with any worker in art. It is the same with the composer; but the structure of mechanism of music is one thing, its artistic import another. . . .

It seems strange that any individuals seriously interested in and at all sensitive to music as an art should fail to realize the necessity of combining and balancing the elements of form and expression, intellect and imagination, before criticism can be in any sense a living thing. Perhaps, where the critic is concerned, sensitiveness, taste, and imagination are the first and indispensable qualities. They will lead him to the truth, where technical analysis in itself would completely fail. The critic needs imperatively to know as much as he possibly can learn of the composer's methods and tricks of trade, but these are only data, useful mostly for his private information. When he has such data clearly in mind he is at the threshold of his task. . . .

Nothing is further from the norm of the ideal critic than those who, on the basis of the little technical knowledge which is such a dangerous thing—and nowhere more dangerous than in the attempt to estimate an art—would assure us that everything subjective, romantic, personally interpretive of music is false and misleading, while only that is true which examines the cords of a musical structure, strand by strand, motive by motive, movement by movement, in order to comprehend it. Nothing could be further from the truth or more misleading than this. The essence of art is its revelation of beauty and feeling and, perhaps, incorporated in that expression, the impression of certain ideas. The critic is lacking himself in capacity for response—and is therefore hopelessly out of the running—who is not passionate enough and courageous enough to peer as earnestly as he can into the mystery of beauty, and state, as clearly as he may, what he finds and feels there.

If he is sincere and has any measure of talent for his work, he will find an amazing number of different substances—as many different substances as a collection of mineral deposits has for the chemist and geologist. He will find the greatest composers taking a frequently realistic attitude in their writing—as realistic as the orchestral commentary in cantatas of J. S. Bach or the program symphonies of Hector Berlioz. He will listen to the voice of a Beethoven and know that he is talking face to face and shoulder to shoulder with a man as human as Peter Ilyich Tchaikovsky, and with far more control and vision and power. The message of that man, his stormy soul, his adoration of nature, his conflict with the destiny which that nature tries in vain to impose on him, will be the living truth of Beethoven, and not Beethoven's first, second, and subsidiary themes.

Or if the critic be of the temperament which eschews the dramatic and sensuous currents of his art, he may contemplate the same symphony and be enraptured by the harmony, strength, and organic life of its developments, and exclaim in rapture as he would if he stood before the Parthenon, and in such contemplation of form, rhythm, and design find his way to the stars.

The generations that pass will see the symphony in different lights and give it new interpretations, all of which will be true, and every one of them false, according to the nature of the beholder. But the one who will be furthest of all from the secret of the symphony will be a blindfolded analyst to whom a theme is a theme and nothing more.

===

Virgil Thomson's *Four Saints in Three Acts*

"A brilliant audience . . . applauded and cheered itself
hoarse."

A BRILLIANT audience, a most knowing one—an audience, indeed,
that included all our choicest spirits of modern verse, music, and
drama—gathered last night at the Forty-fourth Street Theatre and
applauded and cheered itself hoarse at the end of the first performance in this city of the opera *Four Saints in Three Acts*, the text by
Gertrude Stein and the music by Virgil Thomson.

Harry Moses presented this opera, "by special arrangement with
the Friends and Enemies of Modern Music." To the conventional
acknowledgments of the authorship of text and music should be
added immediately those of the creators of the scenic settings and
costumes, done with the most diverting wit and play of fancy, the
décors in cellophane, by Florine Stettheimer; and the stage business and choreography, which are the felicitous invention of Frederick Ashton. These and others who had contributed to the spectacle assembled at the last before the curtain, before an audience
that was disappointed when the house curtain was lowered in order
to end the celebrations.

In fact, the work was adjudged by the elect a masterpiece, a perfect masterpiece. But this was known in advance, ever since the
Hartford *première* of the opera on February 7. It was known that
the opera was about nothing in particular, hence its charm and its
grave beauty. It was known that the scenery was of cellophane. The
rumors that the Negroes' costumes were also of cellophane, though
disproved at Hartford, had added another prospect of something
new and piquant. And had not one of the greatest of the prophets
of the new era, writing with trembling hand and steam coming from
his shoes, cried out that the originality of this conception was
equaled only by *Pelléas et Mélisande?* And had not Mabel Dodge
Luhan herself proclaimed on a first hearing of Thomson's score
that "this opera should do to the Metropolitan what Picasso did to

Kenyon Cox"? Debussy and the poor old Met were buried last night, buried to shouts of joy and hosannas of acclaim for the new dawn of the lyric drama.

Well, it is about time that there were some suggestions of the new dawn in opera; and, nonsensical exaggeration and literary bravura aside, there are good things, refreshing, unconventional, and amusing things in this opera. The audience had a right to its pleasure, not only the personal right but the artistic one. They saw, in the first place, a stage that was a delight to the eye and a color scheme of admirable audacity and play of fancy, with a gorgeous play of silvers, blues, white, red, and a dark Spanish costume and a pair of superb orange lions; they chuckled to behold the antics and the burlesque, by the Negro dancers, of phases of the classic ballet, for which the saint duly gave thanks—excruciating parodies of things from Spanish fandangos to the evolutions of a Pavlova. And this, and the style of the music, with its inspired foolishness, its intentional and foppish innocuities, were of a unit. It was plain, and would have been plain had the purveyors of the entertainment had no reputation at all, that there had banded together a group of individuals of sophistication and affectation sometimes collegiate in its ineffable smartness—but people of sensibility, artistic knowledge, and prevailing esprit, who had a diverting idea and put it through with delightful audacity.

As for the text of the St. Theresa Stein, you could take it or leave it. But it did suffice for its avowed purpose, to be suitable for musical setting. The words are perfectly wedded to the music, as in no other American opera that had appeared before. And this union has been accomplished with remarkable skill and felicity by the composer.

For Mr. Virgil Thomson, as an opera composer, is several desirable things. He is not a melodist of any particular invention or distinction, at least in this score. He is not, apparently, a musician with very much resource of harmony or workmanship, although it is obvious that his syrupy and dulcet consonances are those of deliberate intention. But he is a composer who is far too intelligent and witty to do a thing heavily or in a clumsy and self-conscious manner; and he knows the voice in a most exceptional degree; and—*mirabile dictu*—an American composer has turned up who knows the laws of prosody and can write recitative magnificently. These are indeed significant straws in the windy waste of American opera.

If the performance was not finished in every detail, it was, under Alexander Smallens's masterly conducting, very spirited and significant in detail. With an inspired perception of their possibilities, Mr. Thomson and his collaborators decided that the cast should consist wholly of Negroes. They believed that Negroes could recite the Stein text without being troubled by self-consciousness because of its apparent senselessness, as white singers, perhaps already inured to operatic and textual traditions, could not do. Whether this comparison was right or not need not detain us. The fact is that there was some superb singing, a number of beautiful voices and highly intelligent interpretation. With only one important exception, the diction was admirably distinct and perfectly co-ordinated with the music.

The double personality of St. Theresa, or the two St. Theresas, was represented with gusto and vocal virtuosity by Beatrice Wayne and Bruce Howard. The beautiful voice, the diction and vocalism of Edward Matthews, the St. Ignatius, served notice of an uncommonly gifted singer and interpreter, as did the extreme unction and the laughable solemnity of his performance. The profound bass of Abner Dorsey, the Compère, was another arresting factor, though his text was not distinct. Mr. Bonner's Chavez deserved more than the recognition it received.

The text asks much of the singers, as the music parodies everything from recitative and aria to ensemble, from Handelian choruses to Gilbert and Sullivan, Negro spirituals, and all sorts of ditties. There are a few quotations—*My country, 'Tis of Thee*, "in which St. Theresa is not interested," and a sailor song, and Stravinsky of *Petrouchka*. Most of the time the music comes near to familiar tunes, then skips away from them, and the listener hunts in his memory. The trio of St. Ignatius and the two Theresas; the take-off of a Spanish serenade, while Ignatius twangs the harp, the vocalises of the two sopranos, while others gather, amazed at their prowess; that solo and chorus, already classic, *"Pigeons on the grass alas,"* with the connotations that the words have for sensitive minds, are among the gentle witticisms of poet and composer.

It is a pity that with his special talents Mr. Thomson's technique as a composer is not more complete. If it were, he would possess a weapon he now lacks—interesting harmony. His orchestration, also, is loosely hung together, usually poorly balanced, and in color uneventful. But, whatever is reckoned for or against him, he has produced music which is in the happiest contrast to the labored or lumpish scores by Americans that have been heard of late in and out of the opera house. There is at least a sense of métier—lightness and clarity of statement, and a feeling for scene. The method may be derivative. It may remind the listener of the kind of thing that can, quickly become tiresome. But let us give praise for an American composer who can laugh, and write a melodic line, and set a very difficult text with absolute virtuosity, and combine his art so fittingly with that of his gifted colleagues of the theater.

MARCH 4, 1934

The American Composer and the American Critic

"We are snobs. . . . We turn Judas."

CERTAIN correspondents accuse us of an inverted chauvinism—whatever that may be—when American compositions are not favorably mentioned. We are snobs who believe that everything European is good and anything American is bad. We turn Judas to our own when a native symphony or opera is given. We praise an American copy of a Paris fad, an exotic operatic compound of Gertrude Stein and Virgil Thomson, and deny more virile spirits recognition.

What should be the attitude of American critics toward American music? Should they foster this infant industry by a policy of warm praise for anything remotely deserving it and a kindly shortsightedness where defects are concerned? Should the American composer, in other words, be given a handicap over his European colleague? Should not the American critic exercise particular care when he approaches a new work of native origin? Harsh words may have a blighting effect upon a real creative talent. And they may prove a boomerang. It may be that posterity will point to that critic as the man whose only claim to fame is that he castigated the masterpiece of an American genius. It's all in the mail. As one of our hopeful young musicians put it recently: "Not even your letters to me will make you immortal!"

So far as the province of critical opinion is concerned, the answers to these observations are simple. Any reviewer's attitude toward any music, whether the reviewer is an American or a Chinese, whether the music comes from Andalusia or Tin Pan Alley, should be fundamentally the same. He listens to the music with a personal curiosity and a professional endeavor to weigh his reactions as carefully as possible before they are printed. He then expresses his conclusions for what they may be worth. That is the be-all and end-all of music criticism.

The popular mistake concerning its purposes and functions is precisely the mistake the commentator would never dream of making—that he is in any sense the divinely appointed judge, assigned by destiny to the momentous task of separating wheat from chaff, sheep from goats, and regulating the progress of the musical art. The critic hears music and registers an opinion. The significance of opinion is determined by the equipment of the critic and the quality of his mind—matters which he is in no position to judge. Criticism is one of the processes which go to the shaping of the musical tendencies of a period. No one but a moron, accidentally seated for a few moments in a reviewer's chair, thinks of his work as anything more than his individual contribution, for whatever it may be worth, to what is going on in his art. He will stand up for what he believes in, and oppose, in argumentative fashion, what he believes to be false or misleading. That is his duty and function. The rest is in the lap of the gods.

As to the verdict of posterity: Do any newspaper commentators really write with the fear that their opinions will be read twenty-five, fifty, and a hundred years hence and be compared with the verdicts of later generations? If so, they have absurd and childish notions. Most opinions printed in a newspaper are for a glance at the breakfast table and then the wastebasket. Some, dealing with a disputatious theme or a sensational event, or the (very rare) appearance of a masterpiece, may very possibly be scanned after the writer of the criticism has been placed beneath the daisies. In the latter exceptional event, the value of his opinion will not rest upon its measure of prophetic accuracy. It will rest upon the strength and significance of the ideas expressed, though they may be contradicted by the march of musical history.

As for the native composer, the American critic has a special and utilitarian task to carry out. Here he can be of practical and legitimate assistance to the cause. Native musical effort should engage a good deal of the American newspaperman's time and work, wherever there is the slightest prospect of encouraging something good and sincere and original by such efforts. If partiality toward subject matter ever has an excuse, it should be shown in favor of native effort in music against well-documented approaches from abroad. Because American music is not only the expression of the critic's community and nation, with which he should be closely identified, but it is the field in which his own motivation should prove fruitful and creative. American music is in need of the right kind of encouragement. It is also in dire need of unprejudiced criticism.

Just what is meant by unprejudiced criticism? What is meant here is criticism that refuses under any circumstance to ballyhoo a native product because it is of native manufacture, or to close an eye to faults which would be promptly attacked if they appeared in a work that was not of local origin or surrounded by local interest. When it is a question of assisting American composers by advance publicity of their offerings, or news of their activities, or discussion of their tendencies, the office of the American commentator is obvious. The composer and the performer, when they have something to give, should be afforded every chance to get their product before the public. Once that is accomplished, the obligation of the official critic is clear. The music must be discussed in detail and with unsparing frankness. Good American music will never be helped by any other policy, and sincere American musicians would not wish it to be.

The writer believes that particular caution should be taken in America to avoid the pitfalls of provincialism to which the European press is so prone. France is the worst example. There is hardly a possibility of finding a reliable evaluation of a new French work in a French newspaper or in many of the periodicals. It is not that good critics are lacking. Paris has them in abundance, brilliant writers, admirably equipped in musical and literary knowledge. But frankness in speaking of native compositions is a luxury reserved in Paris for the composer's enemies and the cliques that are leagued against him. What is the result? The French composers have no means of learning anything about themselves except what they discover by their own perspicacity and their contacts, which may be highly misleading, with their colleagues.

This provincialism is not only in Paris. It is in Europe, in varying degrees. It is rampant in German cities, where a German work so mediocre and provincial that it would not làst a week on the other side of the border is made the subject of pedantic encomiums by the press. There is no good reason why American musical cliques and the American press should adopt any such attitude, and fortunately there is no likelihood of such a thing. If there is one advantage that we have over other countries of the world where musical traditions are in the ascendant, it is in our degree of orientation toward any fixed tradition, and freedom, in our big musical centers, from the domination of the petty provincial influences. Music criticism has a freedom from influence or from special interest of any kind which is the best possible augury for its future on this side of the water, and also is certainly for the best interests of our composers.

Standards of achievements, however, should be insisted upon, and comparisons with outside effort constantly made. The position of the American composer has changed very much for the better in the last twenty-five years. In the opera house he remains at a disadvantage, since there are so few lyric theaters in the land, and the composer, with the exception of special performances got up here and there, must either make the Metropolitan or, operatically speaking, remain in obscurity. In the symphonic field, on the other hand, an increasing number of American scores is heard. Publishers are increasing in number who are willing to put the American creator of big scores into print. The fact is that in this field the pendulum of luck is swinging his way, and all sorts and kinds of composers find their opportunity before they are themselves fitted to take full advantage of it. The same thing applies too often to our performers, and there is no question that our native musicians, as a class, labor under weaknesses they have shown for years—weaknesses due to insufficient training and technique and a startling lack of capacity for self-criticism. So far as this commentator is concerned, he intends to comment freely and frankly upon the actual shortcomings of native composers whenever he believes that he has discovered them, and he is possessed of more than the hope—in fact, he feels an optimistic certainty—that the time is near for some real American achievement in music and some enduring American masterpieces.

===

The Artistic Creed of Ernest Bloch Holds True

"I, for one, do not believe that humanity
has finished its march."

THE forthcoming production by the Schola Cantorum of Ernest
Bloch's setting of the Jewish Sabbath Service will be occasion for
the American public to become acquainted with the latest composition of one of the few composers who have produced music of importance since the appearance of Stravinsky's *Sacre du printemps*.

This latter statement may be warmly disputed by those who continue to believe that Stravinsky the prophet can do no wrong, and
who, through Stravinsky's various tonal adventures since the *Sacre*
in abstract and "neo-classic" and other experimental styles, have
acclaimed each separate composition as the masterwork of a genius.
That none of these works has held the stage as the *Sacre* or the
earlier and more persistently cultivated *Petrouchka*, though they
are more recent than those two scores, does not necessarily prove
anything. Great works by great composers have remained unper-
formed and unsung for longer periods than those of the post-war
Stravinsky. But it might be claimed that the Stravinsky cult is not
so inactive, nor its propaganda so inexpert, as to leave long in the
shade a work with real possibilities of promotion. And comparison
of the Bloch of the "Israel" Symphony or *Schelomo* or the
Viola-and-Piano Suite or the Piano Quintet with the later works of
Stravinsky establishes for Bloch's representative music, so far
known to us, a greater ratio of red corpuscles and a far more propulsive emotional power and originality of thematic invention than
any recent score of Stravinsky can offer.

The comparison between Bloch and the late Stravinsky has been
made with another purpose than that of mere argumentation in
which one may say "I am right" and the other "You are wrong."
There is a difference between the purposes of a Bloch and a Stravinsky which is worthy of consideration here. It is disclosed in

Bloch's own words about his new Service, which aims to be a universal prayer, not for the proponents of any one religion or dogma, but for the peace and salvation of mankind. It is also disclosed in one of the few articles that Bloch has written and published.

The general tendencies and pronouncements of Stravinsky have been in the direction of the "neo-classicism" that he professed in works which invoked Bach (the Piano Concerto), Handel (*Oedipus Rex*), seventeenth-century ballet (*Apollon Musagète*), and, in various compositions, "abstract form." These last compositions were to be devoid of subjective attitude or "romantic" feeling on the part of either composer or interpreter. In the *Symphonies d'instruments à vent* the wind instruments were employed for the reason that they had not the mobility and expressiveness of the strings—that music of a more static nature could be written for them. The interpreter was not to put himself into the music at all, but perform it as a purely objective task of execution, in precise conformance with the signs on the printed page. Away with emotion or romanticism! The essence of music is form; in that is implicit everything music has for humanity!

Stravinsky's new war cry, following the detonating explosion of the *Sacre*, was that of a whole clique—almost of a generation of young composers who developed just after the war. It had comparisons in the buoyant and brilliant atonalism of Hindemith. It found a sympathetic echo, though not a parallel practice, in the atonalism of Schoenberg and his twelve-tone scale. But the Schoenberg thinking and the Schoenberg sincerity of purpose—whatever the value of Schoenberg's work may ultimately prove to be—lie deeper than the practices of the other composers mentioned. His individual creative effort may be less fructile than the youthful and spirited output of Hindemith. It may not have the blandishments of title and of various experimental styles that the later works of Stravinsky afford. It has, however, a deeper conviction and has probably done more than the work of any other European of the period to enlarge the boundaries of musical expression.

Against the anti-romanticists, neo-classicists, expressionists in the musical art, may be placed such figures as Vaughan Williams, a great tonal poet of his race; Jean Sibelius; and Ernest Bloch. Bloch's music has a racial intensity and humanity and a passion and dramatic accent which place him in a lonely position of his own. Sibelius is more introspective and architectonic. But both these men have written primarily with expressive and communicative purpose.

It is worth while to consider Bloch's own words on this subject, words which express an artistic faith that he has always followed and a conviction which is the antithesis of the doctrines of contemporaries. The present issue of the *Revue musicale* quotes from an article which he wrote as early as 1917 for the magazine *The Seven Arts*, which article the composer describes in a few prefatory words as the expression of ideas that have not materially changed in the interval.

Bloch says, among other things, that "thus far the war does not seem to have had any great effect on music and musicians. . . . Before this overwhelming trouble music remains indifferent. . . . This, the most direct of all arts, the art that is best qualified to express life and human passions in their entirety, seems to have remained alien to the great drama."

Elsewhere he continues: "There is something tragic in the degree to which music has gradually divorced itself from life and become an egocentric and an artificial thing. . . . Already, before the war, it had wandered from the source where all art must find its strength and its continual rebirth; it was no longer the expression of our soul and of our mind, of our epoch, with its struggles, its agonies and its aspirations. . . . In all its branches it had become a cold and calculated thing, lifeless and unspirited. Music was no longer the emanation of a race and a people, a spontaneous birth of our life. *It was a music of musicians.*" The italics are ours.

"Both on its higher and lower levels art has broken with life. And this, doubtless, explains why the fearful events now transfiguring mankind have had so little effect upon it."

At the present time, in the composer's belief, "the world of art is divided in two great currents. The lower one is that of the masses; their facile taste is sinking with the love of platitude and the weight of mechanical inventions—phonograph, radio, cinematograph. The other current is that of the 'highbrow.' With perverted taste it looks on art as a luxury, as a purveyor of rare sensations, as a matter of intellectual acrobatics."

To some of our brave young men, atonalists, expressionists, or what you will, the following will appear outmoded stuff of the romantic era: "The two worlds gravitate upon different orbits. But what must be the result? Are we at a period of transition; or are we virtually on the decline? Like all things, art is born, lives and dies. Is its story told? Or is a rebirth coming? I, for one, do not believe that humanity has finished its march. Humanity has merely turned a corner. We are not yet ready to deny the best within ourselves. But, be sure, it will not be formulas, procedures, new theories, that will create the art of tomorrow.

"I believe that some day we shall be weary of this daily miserable struggle, that a little true love will be born in the withered hearts of men. Perhaps, after our hatred, kindled only by a few, there will come one of those cleansing revolutions that will shake the world on its foundations and sweep away the poisonous vapors. Perhaps, then, a new life will rise up and with it something of youth and verdure and joy; while the old limping religions, the gods in whom no one believes, will be swept away with the ruins. . . . A little fraternity, a little love, a little gladness will gleam on the face of the world and catch up the hearts of men in one impulse, in one rhythm. And for these new hearts there will need to be new songs."

The last paragraph, which still rings prophetically, relates specifically to time of war. But it holds true. It may be said, aside from any calculations of the quality and value of the new score, soon to be heard, that it is the spirit back of these words which has given representative works of Bloch their life and significance. And these principles will continue to hold true as long as life and art endure.

FEBRUARY 6, 1935

———

Shostakovich's *Lady Macbeth of Mzensk*

"Lurid, overdrawn, naïve, sensational—
and an immense success"

AN EXTRAORDINARY thing was witnessed last night in the Metropolitan Opera House, when Dmitri Shostakovich's *Lady Macbeth of Mzensk* was performed magnificently, for the first time in New York, by the Cleveland Orchestra, with assisting soloists and the chorus of the Musical Art of Russia, Inc., and Artur Rodzinski, conductor. On this occasion an opera with a musical score flimsily put together, full of reminiscences and obvious and shallow tricks, with almost no originality or creative quality, attached to a libretto of communistic hue, lurid, overdrawn, naïve, and sensational, had an immense success.

It has been many years since such a large and brilliant audience has been in the Metropolitan Opera House. Everybody who was anybody, as the old phrase goes, was there. Expert press-agentry and the success of the performance that Mr. Rodzinski and his forces gave in Cleveland, where the American *première* of the work took place on January 31, would in part explain this interest. But no amount of ballyhoo or partisanship could account for the gales of applause that swept through the house last night and, at one place in the performance, cheers for the opera, the conductor, and the artists.

What would happen with a few repetitions of the work would probably be very different. Its cheapest and most obvious features, which in some cases had little to do with the actual exposition of the drama, won the most frenzied applause, as, for example, the dance that the orchestra completes after the curtain has closed on the antics of drunken peasants who have discovered the fragrant corpse of a murdered husband behind a shed. The stage spectacles that took most were those of burlesque character. There is much burlesque, satirically intended, in the opera. Some of it is cheap and unamusing as well as bestial. But the sight of a group of Russian police behaving like a set of mechanized Keystone Cops amused New York, apparently, almost as much as they would have amused Moscow. And the scene of a wedding feast, with a priest in his cups, a scene in which Mr. Shostakovich conveniently remembers Moussorgsky's tavern of *Boris Godunoff*, a scene admirably enacted, with ironical and uproarious humor, also proved excellent divertissement. And good theater. These scenes livened up the show just as the audience was reaching the point where Mr. Shostakovich's stock of effects and makeshifts were running out. They, with a final scene which, on the whole, is the best in the opera, pulled it through to triumph.

The story of the work is far less significant than the tale which Mr. Shostakovich and A. Preis took as the basis for their text. As it stands now, the opera has nothing whatever to do with Shakespeare's Macbeth or his lady. It is based on a novel of N. S. Leskov, published in 1864, in which a woman of the Mzensk province murders for purposes of ambition and gain. Shostakovich, it appears, was even reproached for selecting the story of such a reactionary as Leskov for his musical setting, and the story of the opera was changed so that Katerina is portrayed as the wife of a rich landowner whose character is distorted by her false and effete surroundings. Shostakovich has told the world that he sympathizes with this character, who is only the victim of her fate when she murders a stepfather, assists her lover in the extinction of her husband, and then drowns a rival. A more appropriate alternative title has been given the work, that of *Katerina Izmailovna*. She is the heroine, abused by a lecherous father-in-law, whom she poisons. She then becomes the willing victim of the clerk Sergei. When she is deported to Siberia with him for the murder of her husband, she kills another woman of the convict train for whom Sergei has deserted and deceived her. The curtain falls upon the miserable boatload of unfortunates disappearing in the shadows, bound for the place of punishment.

The opera moves effectively. A reading of the libretto, translated from a Russian text already toned down from the original for the Russian performances, does not wholly prepare the reader for this. The stage settings are economical and original. The mushroom tops and gilded spires of a church loom in the background. Most of the scenes are those revealed at the beginning—a living room of the Izmailov house on one side and on a higher level the bedroom of Katerina, in which a scene of considerable verisimilitude is enacted with frankness and to the descriptive accompaniment of the orchestra. This drew roars of laughter from the audience. The two other scenes are the smarter one in the police station and the very simple but highly suggestive scene of the embarkation for Siberia. Before each act the story of the act to come was told by Richard Hale, taking the part of narrator. One reflected that there would be no harm if this were a custom for the benefit of such Metropolitan patrons as one who recently presumed that Lohengrin wrote *Meistersinger*. Such mistakes are discountenanced in Russia. Last night the audience knew what was happening, and it helped in the understanding of the performance.

The music has its lyrical and melodious passages. Most lyrical are those for Katerina, which may be the expression of the author's sympathy with her character. There are some vocally effective if not particularly emotional passages for Sergei. Much of the music is satirical, while some of it professes to explain the psychology of the characters. There are ironical waltzes and other dances; there are take-offs of Wagner and Verdi, presumably intentional. What is not intentional is the reminiscences with which the whole score abounds, the imitations concealed under a thin veneer of modernism. For this is not, in the aggregate, new music. This is actually pretty old stuff. It goes as far back as Borodin and Moussorgsky, and as far forward as Stravinsky and especially Prokofieff, who was ironical long before Mr. Shostakovich, and with much more mastery.

As a matter of fact, there are pages—there are quarter-hours—during which one simply wonders at the composer's effrontery and his lack of self-criticism. Pages of this music are puerile in immaturity and naïveté. There are passages of melody, yes. But of what sort and grade? There are opportunities for the chorus, which took superb advantage of them. The orchestration is by turns thin and noisy, and there is a restless whipping up to climaxes. The composer sees to it, however, that there is constant contrast of pace, rhythm, and manner, even if this becomes an artificial diversity of means. Any old thing goes, provided it fits plasibly with the theatrical moment or treads water while action goes forward and the composer gets time to evolve an idea. In the comic scenes a light-opera or jazzy style serves the purpose. Here and there is a special passage. A passacaglia prefaces the scene in Katerina's bedroom. Better music is the concerted piece between her and her husband in the same scene. There is a fugue in the scene of the feast held for the planned wedding of Katerina and Sergei. But there is little real continuity or sequential, therefore structure, in the score. And there are pages of sheerly nothing, in the sense of real music.

Why, then, the success of the evening? First and last, because of the composer's feeling for the theater. Whatever else his piece is not, it is always theater. And it is the writing of a young man sure of himself, even when he has no good right to be. The music seldom fails, whatever its inner lacks, to emphasize, if only by accents of a drum or a glockenspiel, the doings on the stage. In the last scene there is a truer utterance. Katerina's lament arouses some emotion, which is true of very little of the score. The music is simple in this place. The crashing brass chords as the woman realizes her betrayal are effective rhetoric, if no more. The chorus of the exiled, dying away in the distance, stirs the imagination. The stage effect, with changing light, contributed to this.

At this time little can be said of the performance, which, first of all, reflected the highest honor upon Mr. Rodzinski, born, one would say, to conduct opera. The principal singers acquitted themselves in very difficult parts with marked success. The acting was vivid, eloquent, excellent in character parts as in larger roles. It was well to present this formative work of a young composer— Shostakovich is twenty-nine—so sympathetically and so brilliantly. And who knows—someday Mr. Shostakovich may write a real opera!

MARCH 3, 1935

====

Kreisler's Delectable Musical Hoax

"Should the man who has kissed the wrong girl in the dark condemn the practice of kissing?"

THE outcry following *The Times*'s disclosure of Fritz Kreisler's authorship of fourteen compositions which had been published and played for more than a quarter of a century as "arrangements" by him of the works of old masters has involved some curious interpretation of the acts of Mr. Kreisler and his publishers.

It has been implied that the secret was wrung from Mr. Kreisler only through the pitiless perseverance of a musical sleuth who could not be swerved from truth's path. It has been suggested that the disclosure was a trick of publicity to promote interest in the compositions. By some, Mr. Kreisler has been bitterly condemned for attaching the names of composers long vanished to his compositions, thereby deceiving the public, the critics, and his fellow artists.

Let this last reproach pass for the moment. The first two accusations are without foundation. Mr. Kreisler, before this writer stumbled upon the facts of his authorship, and without pressure from anyone, had decided to acknowledge as his own the works hitherto listed as transcriptions. The courteous and co-operative head of the editorial staff of Carl Fischer, Inc., Mr. William Kretschmer, opposed no obstacles to the investigator. He had no reason to do so, for Mr. Kreisler, on the occasion of his last New York recital of 1934, on December 12 last, had ordered that the fourteen compositions hitherto listed as "Classic Manuscripts" should be published as his original works in the catalogue for 1935. In that catalogue they are so listed. Mr. Kreisler's American publishers (the "Classic Manuscripts" were issued originally from the presses of Schott of Mainz) asked only, as a special precaution and courtesy due the composer, that his personal endorsement of the information they had furnished be secured in advance of newspaper publication, and this—a precaution desired equally, of course, by the newspaper representative—was done.

The events which led to the revelation of Mr. Kreisler's authorship were very simple, and may be cited here merely to show how unpremeditated the disclosure was on the part of those who had had the secret in keeping. This writer had been engaged by the Brooklyn Institute of Arts and Sciences to give a lecture recital with Yehudi Menuhin on certain modern aspects of violin music. After many compositions had been considered with a view to illustration, it was decided to begin with what was then known as the Kreisler transcription of the *Praeludium and Allegro* of Pugnani.

It therefore became the business of the lecturer to find out what the differences were between the supposedly original composition and its arrangment by Kreisler. Was Pugnani's score available, either in print or in manuscript, in this country? Intensive search in New York and in the Library of Congress failed to reveal a note of Pugnani which suggested the material of the professed transcription. The investigator then asked the Carl Fischer house for information on the subject. It was promptly given him by word of mouth and in the printed form of the new Fischer catalogue. His inquiry was made easy and simple, as it happened to coincide in point of time with Mr. Kreisler's decision to make known his authorship.

There was no pursuing Mr. Kreisler to his lair and forcing from him an unwilling acknowledgment of his culpability in the matter. Asked by cable if he would verify the information *The Times* had secured, he answered promptly, under date of February 6: "Your statement absolutely correct," and continued with particulars which have since been widely published. His explanation was simple and frank, and it gave his reasons for concealing for some thirty years his creative identity.

The reasons seem to us quite logical, and in no sense such as to reflect discreditably upon Mr. Kreisler. He told us years ago of his pride that by means of these short pieces he had been able materially to enrich the violinist's repertory. It was undoubtedly to the great advantage of the compositions that they did not bear his name as composer. For it is unfortunately true that there is a great deal in a name. Neither the public, the press, nor Mr. Kreisler's colleagues would have taken as kindly to these compositions had they been designated as being merely the creations of a living violinist. It is true that he took in vain the names of old composers. In some cases those composers—Pugnani among them—gained rather than lost in standing thereby. Other names were those of greater composers than Mr. Kreisler. Who has been harmed by the hoax? The public has had occasion to appreciate music which otherwise would probably have gone begging for recogition. Other artists than Mr. Kreisler have waited long years for such attention, withheld until some accident of fate elevated them before the gaze of populations who preferred an appearance to a reality.

Recently, commenting upon this affair, an editorial writer for *The Evening Sun* said: "The practical jokers of the world will regret that the deception did not take the form of ascribing the works to non-existent composers." And there was a musician, years ago, who announced his belief that there had never been a Pugnani at all! He should have been asked, by way of discipline, to conduct the recent laborious search that was pursued through the shelves that preserved Pugnani's musical remains.

One of the most amusing features of this case is the number of statements made by various persons, after the publication of the facts, that they knew it all the time. Some did know. Many who said they knew had played the Kreisler transcriptions and listed them as such. One of these, especially vocal after the discovery, had palmed off in years past the piece of another composer as his own. For years there had been those who adopted the tone of a distinguished musician who said to the writer, about eight weeks ago when the search for the original Pugnani was in process: "You will find, when you have the original, that there is much of Kreisler in it, and little of Pugnani." But, with all the talk, no one produced the evidence.

It must be admitted that in this matter the literary gentlemen, reviewers of music and the like, can be taken to task. The reason why the Kreisler pieces were not investigated sooner is simple. They were in almost all cases compositions in small forms, used between larger compositions or as features of the last group on violin programs. Nobody paid them special attention or deemed the matter momentous enough to sift thoroughly. It is a commentary, and not altogether a flattering one, on the manner in which all sorts of facts which should be promptly questioned are allowed to pass in this field. Outside of a very few leading figures, musicographers the world over are open to criticism for lack of scientific method and accurate classification of data.

Let us admit that Mr. Kreisler has hoaxed us rather handsomely. Has not the principal harm, if any, been done to the feelings of the hoaxed? Nothing has been taken from the reputations of composers of the past, nearly all of them minor figures of certain epochs. No one of them has lost royalties or reputation by a device which has again and again been employed in the history of art, and nowhere more harmlessly than in the present instance.

It seems, in fact, that Mr. Kreisler has produced some rather delectable and unpretentious music. As he himself has remarked, he could have been far more plausible had he intended permanently and seriously to mislead his public. For Mr. Kreisler is a musician as well as a virtuoso, with a real knowledge of the history and the materials of his art. He could have adopted a classical tone considerably less dubious in certain instances than he did, when the name of Kreisler was not the one to conjure with that it is today, and when, at the same time, he did not wish to overload his programs with the name of Kreisler. The manner in which he put out these products is evidence of the lack of guile behind them. In the meantime, the pieces have been greatly enjoyed. Their sale has has apparently not diminished since the exposé. The Fischers have gallantly offered to refund the money of anybody who feels that he was cheated in music that he purchased under the impression that it was a transcription of an old master by Kreisler. The result seems not to have been disastrous. Indeed, there has been something of an extra demand for printings of the old edition as souvenirs of one of the most amusing examples in recent history of the genuine talent of an artist and the ease with which he misled persons who exalt appearances. Mr. Kreisler has added to the gaiety of nations and the violinist's repertory. Shall we begrudge him that? Should the man who has kissed the wrong girl in the dark condemn the practice of kissing?

APRIL 5, 1935

Alban Berg's *Lulu* and the Beethoven Fifth

Beethoven Sounded Almost Abnormal

MR. KOUSSEVITZKY, whose New York programs have of late verged perilously near the conventional, is to be congratulated for having stirred up his audience with new music, gratifying to some and highly vexatious to a large number, from Alban Berg's opera *Lulu*, which was played for the first time in New York by the Boston Symphony Orchestra last night in Carnegie Hall.

It was plain that partisanship had its share in the response to the various items of the program. The mixed reception of Berg's music, strenuously and persistently applauded by a minority, was followed by an ovation after Beethoven's Fifth, which ended the concert. The applause was richly deserved, but the excitement of opposing factions, and not only artistic enthusiasm, was in it. Would that we might have a little more controversy at our orchestral concerts, which of late have fallen into such a rut of routine.

Nothing could have been more strikingly indicative of the way in which the language of music is being technically enriched and extended than the sound of the opening motive of the Beethoven Fifth after the atonalities and the strange and subtle orchestral colors of Berg's composition. It positively took a moment to readjust the ears to Beethoven's style, which seemed not only incongruous but, under the circumstances, almost abnormal in effect!

The question then arises whether this newly organized language says something worth saying. Two seasons ago, when Berg's opera *Wozzeck* was given in Philadelphia, this writer believed emphatically that he had a significant, dramatic, poetical contribution for the world. The score of *Wozzeck* seemed to prove that. Probably, if it were heard again now, it would renew the same impression. The

music of *Lulu* has in a number of places harmonic novelty and fascination. In one movement, the *ostinato*, the wild rushing of the
basses is dramatic. As a whole, this writer considers it poorer music
than *Wozzeck*, less concentrated, less concise, by no means as clear
in objective and achievement as the earlier score; he also considers
that it represents a musical impasse, long since reached by Schoenberg, which now confronts the most gifted of his pupils.

This score is in the now familiar style and method of the atonalists, who profess to revive old forms as elements of the structure of
opera. The music is very skillfully wrought, and nowhere more
amusingly than when tunes of the popular street-ditty kind are
played, with their implicitly banal and old-fashioned harmony, in
one part of the orchestra while about them is thrown a dress of
atonality and counterpoint in the ultra-modern manner.

That is amusing. We learn that in *Lulu* it is not old dance forms
but "song forms" (as aria, duet, recitative) which make the structure of the score. What was plainly to be heard in the vocal solos
of Mme Olga Averino was that Schoenbergian whooping and scoop-
ing, an entirely ugly, unfertile, unvocal, and inexpressive style
which has nothing to do with the functions of the voice or with the
natural unfoldment of melody. It was very hard to sing and so unpleasant to the ear that Mme Averino's achievement went unap-
preciated. As for "vocal forms" as the basis of the score, we cannot
imagine a more unprofitable affectation on the part of a composer.
And what is it all about? To what great end do these mighty utterances lead us? To a climax of a highly cacophonous nature, having
to do with the disembowelment of Lulu by a sadist. To us Mr. Berg
and his ilk are becoming tedious, rather childish, and distasteful.
As for the music per se, it is involved and subtilized to the point
where nearly all has been whittled away except intricacies, while
the first movement is flimsy, boresome and formless. It is easy to
applaud this music and claim an insight into it which outsiders
have not. Why not face the fact that it is an offscouring of a past
period in composition; that Berg, like Schoenberg before him, has
reached a creative end of the path, the result of an emotionally impoverished period.

Isn't it time that we say "enough" to music which bluffs itself
and will bluff us, too, if we allow it to do so? Who wants to be
such a dupe of an artistic deception? From all this straining of the
mountain in its frantic endeavor to produce a mouse or two, the

art of music has derived some new technical procedure calculated to have value when a composer comes along with something inspired and significant to say. Let us render all respect to the patience and ingenuity thus exemplified; to the palpable effort to find a new way out; to the cruel self-torture and frustration of what might, if allowed natural expression, prove a demonstration of a romantic and somewhat Wagnerian lyricism. As it stands, we are looking back at a past that the world is leaving behind as rapidly as it possibly can, and not into the future, when we listen to this elaborate and decaying composition.

The performance, so far as the ear could tell, was a tour de force of conductor and orchestra. Two other performances, of the highest quality, gratified the audience. The first was the playing of Ravel's suite *Tombeau de Couperin*, a wonderful example of métier and style. There is, perhaps, inherent anachronism in this music. It savors less of Couperin's century than of a period further back; in fact, it smacks of the *"moyen age."* That is the quality of it. It has a delicious archaism, rather than the pretty and decorative quality of the French clavecinist. The pieces *Tombeau de Couperin* will outlive most of Ravel's brilliant and scintillating pages.

The closing performance invoked the spirit of the hero Beethoven and rendered again fresh homage to him. The concertgoer sees on the program "Fifth Symphony: Beethoven." He settles settles himself back in his seat to approve the honorable composer of Bonn, so long and well known, so highly esteemed. But with the first savage outcry of the orchestra a figure appears whose mien is terrible, who cannot be overlooked or greeted with mere politeness; to whom one can be neither deaf nor indifferent; who exacts from each of us his utmost response. That is Beethoven, incapable of less than the whole truth, the unlimited defiance, whose truth with himself and the world and posterity was that described by Polonius. It was in this spirit that Mr. Koussevitzky, with inescapable conviction and dramatic fire, stirred the audience and projected the symphony.

Porgy and Bess and the Future of American Opera

Inside the Metropolitan? Outside on Broadway?

WHEN Mr. George Gershwin's "folk opera," *Porgy and Bess,* after
the play of the DuBose Heywards, was given its New York *première,*
the critics had a high time, and Mr. Gershwin a double press. For
critics of both drama and opera had a go at the piece. The results
were amusing, and to some extent surprising. They were surprising by reason of the fact that the dramatic critics, or some of them,
had reservations as to its dramatic fitness!

All that one poor, helpless, and bewildered commentator can do
is to crawl into his own hole—what Mr. Brooks Atkinson so de-
scriptively terms his "cubicle"—and ruminate subjectively—if you
will, ponderously—on what *Porgy and Bess* appears to be when estimated by operatic standards, and on the allied and entirely fresh
subject of what constitutes American opera!

Let's see. Let's go back of *Porgy and Bess* and consider what has
been happening lately in American opera, or efforts thereat. When
this angle of the subject is considered, some interesting points come
into view. In the last five years, for example, a whole lot has been
done by American composers of opera and of dramatic music. Some
works technically belonging in the category of opera have proved
deficient in all that an opera should be, even though they were
pontifically presented to the public in the greatest lyric theater in
the world—that is to say, of course, the Metropolitan Opera House
—with all the trappings and appanages thereof. Other works, not
even aspiring to the title of opera, have come up from nothing in
particular, at least from no background of elaborate operatic
theory or pretense; have bobbed up as dramas that employed music,
or musical shows, or even episodes of vaudeville, and, by George,
these unconscious and unpretending entertainments have had real
elements of opera!

What are these elements? Shall we not differentiate between
strict technical definitions, so often a crutch and umbrella for the

highly informed and fundamentally academic kind of mind, as contrasted with certain living principles whose demonstrations, in some instances, will lie clear outside the bounds established by the pedants and grammarians. Thus: grand opera, or *opera seria*, is opera sung throughout, in costume, with scenery and full orchestra. *Opéra comique, opera buffa, Singspiel*, etc., etc.—see the music histories and dictionaries—is opera of various degrees of ponderability, which includes, cheek by jowl with recitatives, arias, ensemble numbers, and choruses, passages of spoken dialogue.

That is the general definition. If you superimpose upon that the workings of the principle as defined by practice and by durable results through the ages, then it may be claimed that opera, or music drama, whatever else it may or may not be, is drama which employs music as an indispensable agent of expression; drama which, without music, would be incomplete if not entirely impotent. Perhaps we are free and easy with our definitions, but we go so far as to claim that this operatic principle, either in a highly evolved or a very elementary guise, may be found in works as far apart as *Tristan und Isolde* and *The Green Pastures*. Which latter, any specialist will tell you, is no opera at all or anything like one. But we hold to the contrary.

What has been happening in the last five years in America, outside as well as inside the portals of the august homes of lyric drama? Or, if we want to be local and specific, inside the Metropolitan Opera House and outside on Broadway?

First as to the Metropolitan. The Metropolitan, under the regime of a certain very able and broad-minded Italian gentleman, one Giulio Gatti-Casazza, was a hospitable sanctuary if not a completely successful shrine of American opera. Its records are testimony to Mr. Gatti's long, determined, indefatigable search for the gifted American dramatic composer.

Another impresario might have been disheartened at the results of his patient search and experimentation. For years nothing but ineffective or abortive things came from the American musical dramatist. There were utterly untheatrical and ineffective pieces, like the first opera they tried, F. C. Converse's *Pipe of Desire*. There were elaborate and pontifically dead affairs like Horatio Parker's *Mona*. There was the fluent and saccharine Indian opera *Shanewis* of Charles Wakefield Cadman, one of the best of the early crop.

There were operas that the composers did not even know how to score. There were machine-made operas, glibly after the style of Strauss or other European composers. Nothing emerged, nothing stuck, for a long time. But at last two works, strongly contrasted, appeared in successive seasons, works which did set a new level of achievement for the American dramatic composer, did interest the public in one way or another, and did lay some kind of foundation for worth-while future accomplishment in this field. They were— they are, since they have held the Metropolitan stage for three and four successive seasons—Deems Taylor's *Peter Ibbetson,* after the Constance Collier version of Du Maurier's tale, and Louis Gruenberg's *Emperor Jones,* a musical investiture of the celebrated play of Eugene O'Neill.

The first opera pleased by its touching story, its very effective and musically adaptive libretto, and the melodious and flexible nature of Mr. Taylor's score. The second was a much grimmer and dramatically and musically more mature affair. It was stripped bare and to the bone of superfluous operatic accessories, so much so that in spite of continuous music it may still be ranked as a drama with incidental musical reinforcement rather than an opera in the sense of a drama that finds complete fulfillment only through the combination of text, action, and the intensification of mood and climax possible by means of music. Yet there were masterly factors in the Gruenberg score which will always command our admiration. His ultra-modern, atonal idiom proved remarkably fitting to the savage, fantastical, fatalistic theme. He has technique of a modern and most finished order. He is dramatic-blooded and keenly conscious of the theater. If he had supplied just a little more sheer music, we might be taking our hats off today to the great American music drama. As it stands, *Emperor Jones* the opera remains a drama that, lacking the amazing interpretation of Lawrence Tibbett, would have been just as effective, or more so, without the music at all. But here, anyhow, was an American composer of opera of full intellectual and technical stature for his task. Here, also, if only the dramatic and technical standards of *Emperor Jones* could have been maintained by other composers, was an end to amateurishness and weak experimentation in the lyric theater.

But outside the Metropolitan other things were happening as important (or more so) to the future of opera as anything transpiring within. Three such manifestations, all of very recent appearance, come at once to mind. Two of them were definitely and unmistakably opera. They were *Four Saints in Three Acts* and the present *Porgy and Bess*. A third was no opera in form, but it was unforgettably potent through the workings of the operatic principle—the Negro parable, or mystery play with popular music, *The Green Pastures*.

What have these works, if anything, in common? Four of them have this very important feature in common: that they rest upon successful dramas. They are of the American popular theater rather than the great opera house of European traditions. Dramatists, not opera librettists, in every case supplied the material. *Peter Ibbetson*, *Emperor Jones*, *The Green Pastures*, *Porgy and Bess*. The fifth work was a special, modern, highly stylized and sophisticated setting of symbolistic verse, also of allegedly dramatic implication, by Gertrude Stein. This verse Mr. Thomson most amusingly, and with a flirt, as it were, of an agile and flippant tail, wove into an organic fabric of music. And indeed, of all the compositions mentioned, this is nearest to .the complete and unified opera.

It is the opera organic in every one of the elements, all of which are welded into a consistent whole, from the words to the music, from the action to the stage setting. Take it or leave it, the people who put it together knew their business. However, this work is rather a very expert and diverting by-product of the musico-dramatic stage than a thing prophetic of American tendencies in the opera house. More shall be said of Mr. Gershwin's score, and about other interesting operatic up-croppings in our popular theater.

JANUARY 16, 1936

═══

Schnabel Plays Beethoven

"He establishes communication . . . and never by raising the piano's voice."

ARTUR SCHNABEL last night in Carnegie Hall returned to his large New York public when he gave the first of a series of seven programs which will offer all the thirty-two Beethoven piano sonatas, on consecutive Wednesday evenings. Mr. Schnabel's public is not only a substantial but a distinguished one. In the majority it consists of musicians and students and those music-lovers of this city who go to concerts with more than a superficial entertainment in mind. A great many in the audience had scores on their knees, and they followed every note of the interpretations.

Again there was reason to marvel at the perfect proportion, the depth of thought, and the genuineness of feeling that Mr. Schnabel conveyed. His is an art that recognizes at the same time the grand line and the most significant finish of detail. His interpretive purpose is true and unostentatious as his manner on the platform. He appears with utmost simplicity and sits down with equal simplicity to play.

The performance is complete concentration upon the music, which is projected with extraordinary significance. As each sonata of the thirty-two is a different world in itself, so does the treatment of each one vary in accordance with the nature of the music and the period that it represents in the evolution of Beethoven's thought. Neither for eye nor ear are there gymnastics. Everything is done with the minimum of effort and the maximum of result. For the observer, Mr. Schnabel might be any quiet gentleman with a fondness for Beethoven's music who sat down before a circle of intimates to communicate some of his own pleasure.

In the wide spaces of Carnegie Hall he establishes this communication; and never, so to speak, by raising the piano's voice. It is unnecessary for him to do so. The tone carries; the musical thought carries, and this by means of a very finely adjusted scale of values. There is a remarkable degree of difference between chords "mezzo-piano" and "piano," between the dynamic value of each note of a short expressive phrase. There are equally subtle gradations of tempo—witness the last appearance of the theme of the slow movement of the so-called "Pastoral" Sonata—not that the work was so nicknamed on Mr. Schnabel's program.

Some would consider this playing unemotional, and it is true that last night Mr. Schnabel was, by comparison with other performances he has given here, in an uncommonly objective vein. He seemed to say: "This is Beethoven's sonata. So far as I have been able to discover in a lifetime of study, it is precisely as Beethoven wanted it to sound. If you can show me where I can more precisely approximate his purpose I will be greatly obliged for the suggestion. My authority is Beethoven's score, which I have examined in all the existing manuscript and printed versions, of which my own edition states my conclusions. They are as follows . . ."

And forthwith, in succession, the D major Sonata, Opus 28; the late Sonata, perhaps the most mysterious of the whole set, in A flat, Opus 110, ending with the fugue; the First Sonata in F minor, Opus 2, No. 1, of the set that Beethoven published as available for either piano or harpsichord; and finally, the Sonata in G major, Opus 31, No. 1.

Each of these sonatas, as we have observed, had its special style. The tranquillity of the first made a particularly felicitous prelude to the demoniac and mystical rhapsody of the Opus 110, wherein Beethoven dreamed dreams and saw visions. The First Sonata was performed with the fullest realization of its prophetic character, but without forcing this note. For the slow movement was sung with an immaculate cantilena and a legato that it would be hard to conceive as issuing from the harpsichord, yet with a Mozartean grace and simplicity of accent. The finale was more than a premonition of the Beethoven to come, and indeed of the course of the romantic movement in piano music.

The audience was attentive to every note. The occasion was testimony to Mr. Schnabel's established reputation and his power as a musician. There was long applause after each sonata.

FEBRUARY 21, 1936

———

Toscanini and Serkin Play Beethoven

"It demands supreme mastery to give a performance of that simplicity."

IT IS very rarely that the performance of a soloist can match an orchestral interpretation directed by Arturo Toscanini. When a soloist of such capacity arrives, and Mr. Toscanini from his stand on the rostrum discourses great music with him and the audience, it is an occasion to remember. Such an occasion was the concert given by the Philharmonic-Symphony Orchestra, with Mr. Toscanini conducting, and Rudolf Serkin, pianist, taking the solo parts in concertos of Beethoven and Mozart, last night in Carnegie Hall.

Rarely at a Toscanini concert has such enthusiasm after the performance of a concerto been witnessed, and this is mentioned here not merely as a matter of chronicle but because of the testimony it afforded of a public which immediately recognized the significance of an interpretation which had only the qualities of mastery and none of the qualities of sensationalism about it. But Mr. Toscanini, with his complete self-abnegation and his profound and intuitive understanding of music, has through seasons accustomed his audiences to such revelations of masterpieces. His own pleasure in the success of a young colleague was obvious as he applauded him after the performance. It was not only the generous enthusiasm of a great artist. It was more: it was gratitude for aid in rediscovering and worthily conveying the secret of Beethoven.

The first concerto was Beethoven's Fourth. It was preceded by the most appropriate introduction possible under the circumstances: Beethoven's First Symphony, played with a reduced orchestra, and this with a clarity, grace, and modified sonority which constituted a precise observance of the character of the work and its place in musical evolution. For the boldness of the introduction was not that of the later Beethoven, either in volume of sound or manner of utterance. The allegro was not taken too heavily or portentously; its relation to the Haydn style was implicit.

The Mozartean flow of the slow movement, with the delightful formality of its "limitations," was observed by the tempo as well as by phrasing. Too slow a tempo is here the course of too many conductors. It was in the movement misnamed "menuetto"—since it clearly deserves, as much as any corresponding movement in the later Beethoven, the title of "scherzo"—that the horns and hoofs of the demon of the new genius in music showed themselves unmistakably; but, even here, with an ideal beauty of tone and simplicity of statement. It is extremely hard, it demands supreme mastery, to give a performance of that simplicity.

Characteristics of Mr. Serkin's Beethoven performance deserve detailed mention. We have seldom heard a pianist's performance which so admirably combined the most penetrating analysis with artistic enthusiasm and warm feeling. Similarly, the technical performance was clean and precise, but also beautiful and of a poetic coloring. All this was part of a symphonic conception of the score.

Most pianists, realizing the rarely intimate and romantic nature of this concerto (in which Beethoven anticipates Schumann of a later generation, but within the grandeurs of a form of which Schumann was incapable), emphasize its introspective measures, but neglect to convey the full measure of characteristic force and energy which are also present, especially in the first movement. Although it was only once, in the powerful repetition with full chords of the initial motive, that Mr. Serkin allowed himself to utilize the full resources of the modern piano, he played with a prevailing virility and fire which gave the music all its qualities instead of some of them, including the strength and architecture which underlie Beethoven's lyricism.

The slow movement, with the wonderful dialogue of the piano and strings, is one of the things of which a well-advised person hardly attempts to speak. Here it need only be said that its mood and its utterly original beauty were fully conveyed. Nor did the impetuous measures of passage work just before the end of this movement break the spell. They only enhanced it.

The whole performance was so adjusted that one recurring chord, in the last movement, too sharply accented, emerged as disproportionate. No doubt Mr. Serkin, who obviously is a passionate student of Beethoven, would have his reasons for that. The question that it raised only threw into relief the quality of the whole performance. In the first movement Mr. Serkin played the second cadenza—and a magnificent passage it is—that Beethoven composed for this work.

The remainder of the program consisted of Mozart's last piano concerto in B flat, admirably interpreted, but by no means one of Mozart's strongest concertos, and Sir Henry Woods's noisy orchestral transcription of the Bach D minor Organ Toccata and Fugue, which might be appropriate in Queen's Hall, if nowhere else. Need it be said that the audience which assembled last night was carried away, so that applause crashed, long and loud, at every opportunity? None of the scores was of revolutionary import. At the same time, one was aware of a past period of very great music.

Berkshire Symphonic Festival

"The time is ripe in America for such a festival."

THE exceptional musical event of the summer in America was the Berkshire Symphonic Festival given by Serge Koussevitzky and the Boston Symphony Orchestra on August 13, 15, and 16. The public response to this festival was extraordinary. An average of five thousand attended each of the three concerts. The audiences would not be accounted large ones at the Lewisohn Stadium, where fifteen and sixteen thousand have gathered on certain occasions. But if the relative proportions of population be considered, and also the fact that the Berkshire Festival was given on a private estate loaned for the occasion, and far from lanes of cheap transportation, the attendance will be seen to have been tremendous. It bore the most impressive witness, not only to the attractiveness of programs and performances, but also to the appetite of the American public for great interpretations of symphonic music.

The character of the performances given by Dr. Koussevitzky and his men were of a quality to set them wholly apart from any others the writer has heard at summer concerts in America. This was due to three things: to the presence of one of the two or three most distinguished conductors in the world, who gave of his very best; to the qualities of a celebrated symphony orchestra of the same rank, appearing as a unit for the first time outside its concert series of the winter season; and to the determination on the part of all concerned to spare no pains in preparing the kind of performances which usually are reserved for the climaxes of the winter season.

The things which militated against the hundred-per-cent realization of this objective were principally the acoustical problems of open-air performances, and the unaccustomed strain upon players sworn if possible to surmount them. This was shown by preliminary nervousness in the orchestra, by a tendency at first to force tone,

216

and by the unexpectedly poor effect of the opening performance of a Bach chorale-prelude in Schoenberg's scoring. But the orchestra quickly found itself, and there was a great improvement in tonal adjustment as the evening passed. The last item of the first program was the Sibelius Second Symphony, a work thrilling enough under any circumstances, and one which, in the judgment of all present, singularly vindicated itself by the curiously effective and *natural* sounds of Sibelius's orchestration. (It reminded this writer of the excellent remark of Paul Rosenfeld, to the effect that Sibelius's music would survive comparison with nature if it were heard in the open air, while the works of most composers would suffer irreparably from such an environment.) The results of the second concert, following extensive experiments in the reseating of the orchestra made in the interim, were a great improvement over the first. But the sheer sound of Mendelssohn's "Italian" Symphony and of Wagner's prelude to *Lohengrin*, on the third program, gave a surprised and delighted gathering the genuine sensation of symphonic music with all its characteristic resonance and variety of tone color. This was an astonishing achievement, and it pointed to all sorts of possibilities for the future of the festival.

What its future will be is a question that many people are now asking. The fundamental fact established is that America in the summertime can provide an enormous audience for these events, if they maintain present standards and improve the acoustical conditions attending the performances. With that foundation, and with the musical means afforded by the Boston Symphony Orchestra and its enthusiastic conductor, almost anything can be accomplished. As it stands, without further developments, the festival could go along fairly comfortably, provided that Dr. Koussevitzky considered such an undertaking sufficiently interesting to continue in it.

That, however, is unlikely. We miss our guess if Dr. Koussevitzky would be contented with any such *status quo*. He is not only an orchestral leader of singular brilliancy, but a man of imagination who looks to the future. He has had energetic co-operation from Miss Gertrude Robinson Smith, president of the Berkshire Symphony Festival, and her co-workers. The festival can be developed until it is an institution of international significance. It is not likely that its direction will be willing to stand still on the basis of one pre-eminently successful season.

But if the institution is to become permanent and expand, important steps will have to be taken. The festival requires, in such a case, a permanent home. Last season it was given on the Hanna farm, with Henry Hadley conducting an orchestra assembled for the occasion. This season it took place on a fine sweep of land and trees on the estate of Mrs. Margaret Emerson. The estate is for sale and might not be available another season, unless it should be secured in some way by the authorities of the festival. Other magnificent estates in the vicinity would house the festival very charmingly indeed if their owners should be so hospitably inclined. In some way the festival should secure a permanent headquarters.

There is need not only of a permanent place for the festival, but also of an auditorium or theater, as open as possible in good weather but capable of providing shelter from storms. The storms at Berkshire were scheduled providentially this season. They held off before the opening, and one fell with violence between two of the concerts. But this has not always been and certainly would not always be. Furthermore, a symphony orchestra can play like the heavenly harp when the conditions are propitious; it simply cannot guarantee accurate pitch and brilliant tone quality with heavy moisture in the circumambient atmosphere.

At the European festivals, or at some of them, certain open-air performances of an unpretentious nature are given, usually in courtyards of theaters or in great squares where the buildings that rise on each side provide good acoustics. But the great orchestral and operatic performances are given in concert halls and theaters. There is not enough good weather going around, especially in southern Germany and Austria, for any other kind of undertaking to be successful. Only in Hollywood in America is there the dispensation of a climate which remains stable and air which is invariably cool and clear, and the great natural Bowl which so astonishingly carries the orchestral tone. At Ravinia Park, outside of Chicago's center, where they have had in previous years very successful opera and have lately devoted themselves to concerts, there is a covered stage and a covered auditorium, open, if memory serves, at three sides. In hot weather it is very pleasant and cool there, and the music sounds well. An open-air auditorium which provided shelter should readily meet the requirements for a summer music festival. It could have beautiful architecture and be beautifully landscaped. If an auditorium could be constructed which had facilities for opera and symphony, it would give the conditions necessary for a festival of international importance.

It should be added that the time is ripe in America for such a festival to be instituted. The public is ready for it. The resources are here, and returning prosperity will increase them. The nucleus of a very great artistic achievement is available in the form of the Boston Symphony Orchestra and its wholly exceptional leader. Furthermore, if this thing which can be done in the Berkshires is not done there, it soon will be undertaken somewhere else. There is very little doubt that in the next twenty-five years the significant advance in music will be in America. It only remains to be seen what particular places and what particular people will lead.

OCTOBER 17, 1936

Josef Hofmann Plays a Chopin Concerto

And Walton's Modernism Sounds "Old-fashioned"

EUGENE ORMANDY, now permanent conductor of the Philadelphia Orchestra and soon to be heard in that capacity in Carnegie Hall, directed his second Friday concert here [Philadelphia] this after-noon in the Academy of Music, with a program which attracted an immense audience, and which, at least in the instance of certain familiar compositions, evoked cordial applause.

Mr. Ormandy has risen rapidly in late years to the position he now occupies. He had today the benefit of a pre-eminent soloist and a symphony new to Philadelphia and to New York, where he will soon perform the work. The soloist was Josef Hofmann, who made the piano sing the larghetto of Chopin's F minor Piano Concerto with the voice of a nightingale. The symphony was the composition acclaimed in England as a last word in modernism, and is by William Walton, a leader of the young English School. Completed in 1935, it has been in Europe one of the most controversial creations of its decade.

The symphony is not markedly original, facile as it is and bril-

liantly scored. Its derivations are several and in nothing more interesting than the fact that for the first time in a modern symphonic
work we have a composer strongly influenced by and almost imitative of Sibelius. But Mr. Walton imitates, though in no crude
fashion, more than one composer. And he gives us whole pages
weak in structure as well as material, tautological, long-winded,
although the symphony is comparatively a short one. And finally—
be it whispered of an arrant modernist—we think the piece old-
fashioned.

It is not old-fashioned in its outward dress but in its inner spirit
and its lack of a genuinely assertive individuality. It is old-fashioned because of its emulation of modernisms that the world has
already tired of and perceives to be smart sophistry.

When Mr. Walton set the amusing and sophisticated verses of
Edith Sitwell in *Façade* he was wholly in his element. When he
wrote the genial and typically British burlesque of the *Portsmouth
Point* overture he said something rather like Stravinsky, but nevertheless something joyous, scintillant, and racy. When he wrote his
most effective score, *Belshazzar's Feast*, he employed a perfect
arsenal of modern harmonic, contrapuntal, and choral effects like
a confident young master who set out to please the crowd in the
market place, and did so with astonishing ingenuity and vividness
of style.

But in this symphony Mr. Walton repeats himself and others,
and fishes about with this and that allegedly novel device. Some
themes have the whine of woodwind and the fierce accumulated
force of certain effects of brass which are the hallmarks of Sibelius's
style. Persistent basses and reiterations of small ideas occur in a
way that looms portentous, then comes to nothing.

Sibelius is not all. Debussy of *La Mer* is heard, and Hindemith
in the scherzo. Ideas essentially commonplace are treated to a tonal
counterpoint. It is, after all, old-hat.

The first and third movements—the latter the slow movement—
are the most significant, but the thought will not down that in his
heart Mr. Walton had not the symphonic feeling, or even, perhaps,
the conviction that he had in him that which demanded symphonic
utterance. The fact that he finished the last three movements some
time before he completed the finale could be due to a hundred
simple reasons of accident or occupation, but when that final movement is heard it is so unconvincing and labored that it sounds like

an unloved duty and a reluctantly completed job. Nor do the savage final chords, for which see the last movement of Sibelius's Fifth Symphony, give anything like the sensation of massive power conveyed by the latter work.

Mr. Ormandy, who is rather thick-set, quiet in manner, authoritative with the occasional gesture, is of just about the stature of Mr. Hofmann, who played with him. Mr. Ormandy conducted the whole program, including the Walton symphony, which is technically of great difficulty, from memory. It should be said that, so far as a new work which offers no standards of comparison to judge by is concerned, the performance was an excellent one, reflecting high merit upon the leader, to say nothing of the superb orchestra, whose qualities need no description now.

Fortunate also was Mr. Ormandy's conducting of the accompaniment of the concerto, when Mr. Hofmann took every liberty in the world with the music—liberty justified by its rubato style—and was given both support and complete freedom in a manner that must have been inspiring. How beautifully he played! He played the concerto very quietly, with a technique as fine as old lace, without exaggeration, without attempting to scale the modest conception of Chopin to the sonorous dimensions of the modern concert hall.

For precisely that reason the concerto was fully able to take care of itself, with an aristocratic disdain of bulk, weight, or noise. And when Mr. Hofmann played the dolorous song of the slow movement, the one inspired by the beautiful young Constantia Gladowska, it was realized that sometimes calf love, instead of being the ridiculous thing that the hard-boiled would make it, can be the finest and purest emotion of the heart. A sovereign artist communicated this, and the audience recognized his presence.

It seems to us that a Philadelphia Orchestra audience is easily frightened. Some two hundred, it was estimated, walked out between movements of the Walton symphony. After all, why? The fault of the symphony is neither its growl, bark, nor bite, but its essential lack of these things. But they walked out on it, did the two hundred, and that with a distinct air of trepidation, the while that several young matrons whose charming features and attire proclaimed their residence on the right side of the right street held the situation in hand by radiant smiles and twitterings through the worst of the cacophonies. Some would consider this a more polite way of treating a modern composer.

Moriz Rosenthal: One of the Few Remaining Pupils of Franz Liszt

"This is a vanishing race."

MORIZ ROSENTHAL, one of the few remaining pupils of Franz Liszt and one of the greatest names among the pianists of the last fifty years, returned after an absence of some seasons to New York and gave last night, at the age of seventy-four, his first American recital of the present season in Town Hall.

The concert was an impressive occasion. Mr. Rosenthal in former years was accounted, above all other things, a technician, and more than a technician—a heaven-storming virtuoso. A virtuoso he was. A virtuoso, as he showed astonishingly in certain performances of yesterday evening, he still is. But inevitably the time has come when virtuosity is the secondary consideration, and when, no doubt, careful thought must be taken in conserving the sheerly physical resources.

It need not be claimed that he announced the early measures of the Beethoven Sonata, Opus 111, with the muscle which he might have applied to this passage in earlier years. The force was not inherent in the thought. Strength, tempered and conserved, was the vehicle of something that was not physical, but the expression of the poet and the interpreter, to whom the years had brought intimacy with Beethoven's thought that Mr. Rosenthal's youthful period may not have known.

In the course of the exposition and the development of the opening movement, Mr. Rosenthal showed what the years bring to the musician whose entire talents are placed unremittingly at the service of his art. He gave the apparently rhapsodic music the closest and most organic unity. Subtle tonal gradations, cunning accentuations of the phrase, and a climax fully proportioned gave this movement its march and prophetic fire.

But the air and the variations that conclude the sonata was the passage which revealed the pianist at his greatest. There he conveyed the message of Beethoven the mystic and the bearer of un-earthly tidings. That is the movement where the composer, with an incredible simplicity and a sublime naïveté, far from the world, confesses his spirit and hears the "whispers of heavenly death" and the beating of wings. This is not music for the fledgling, or even for the heroes of the keyboard who can outplay an orchestra and who need a fresh piano every evening to resist them. The profound simplicity and noble clarity of the performance, and the elimination of what was merely personal in the playing, brought the listener and Beethoven face to face.

Mr. Rosenthal played a large Chopin group—five of the preludes, the F minor Ballade, three of the mazurkas, a waltz, and the Liszt transcription of the *Chant polonais*. It will be seen that he chose that ballade which is the very apotheosis of Chopin's lyricism. The whole performance was one of sublimated song, and pages in half-tints made the more towering the grand peroration. The mazurkas had the genuine caprice, the unexaggerated rubato which a pianist either does or does not understand, and without which the Chopin of the mazurkas goes uncomprehended. The poignant melancholy, irony, humor of these little masterpieces never become a thrice-told tale, never lose wonder, in the hand of the proper interpreter.

Then Mr. Rosenthal played his Variations on an original theme. It is a piece for the super-virtuoso, and then the audience had an opportunity to gauge the degree of virtuosity that pianists of Rosenthal's background and schooling bring to their performances. There is no question about it: this is a vanishing race. Will the art of pianism ever return to this plenitude of power and of technical resource? It was an astonishing performance, and it brought down the house.

And this seemed to loose all the powers of the performer. He played for a last group two Brahms intermezzos, the Schubert-Liszt *Soirées de Vienne*, and Liszt's *Venezia e Napoli*. The first Brahms Intermezzo was the little-played one in A flat—a silver fantasy, a moonbeam of music, performed with the utmost delicacy. The Schubert-Liszt waltzes reminded us of the craftsmanship and poetry of Liszt's transcription, and also of his admirable choice of Schubert's waltz themes, some of which are decidedly commonplace. Commonplace, in another way, is much of the *Venezia e Napoli*, but Mr. Rosenthal, whose brilliancy and command grew as the performance went on, drove it home in the old style.

He had a very enthusiastic audience, one that bespoke the presence of many faithful followers of days gone by, but also one that showed its unanimous approval and enthusiasm for the occasion. Mr. Rosenthal played encores.

JANUARY 31, 1937

The Mighty Pushkin—the Hundredth Anniversary of His Death

"He has inspired generations."

THE revival of *Coq d'or* this week at the Metropolitan is one of the musical events which signalize in this country the hundredth anniversary of the death of the mighty Pushkin. His fantastical and satirical poem is the subject matter of Rimsky-Korsakoff's last opera.

There is a singular analogy between the position of one of the greatest of poets when he produced this work and that of the composer who set it.

. . . Both men, in their respective situations, and nearing the end of life, were beset by official restraints and suppressions which inhibited creative expression. They were weary and saddened by the shams and obstructions of Lilliputians who surrounded them, which gradually sapped vitality and inspiration.

It is known that the government's interference with the production of his opera irritated Rimsky-Korsakoff and hastened his end. It is perhaps a providential if extremely tragic circumstance that the poet who is root and branch of all Russian literature and music, too, should have met his death, while still young, in the duel with D'Anthès, one hundred years ago last Wednesday.

An invisible net had been spread about the poet who was born to be free. This was seen to by Nicholas I and his court—the net of apparent tolerance, of luxury, security, and social privilege while the Decembrists perished or went to Siberia. The system of the iron hand beneath the courtly glove was applied to the pardoned Pushkin. The obstacles, politely veneered, which confronted him wherever he turned would have frustrated, softened, and eventually ruined him. The supremely creative spirit could go no further. It was as if fate had determined to intervene and prevent a worse than physical disintegration. A bitter commentary, which doubtless emanated from circumstances that inspired revolt, colors the poem of *Coq d'or*, which was censored. Similar circumstances, following Russia's abortive revolution of 1905–6, had to do with the early history of the opera.

But, then, you can no more separate Russian music from Pushkin than you can a tree from its roots. Never was an art more conclusively demonstrative of the connection between the artist and his expression and his soil. No Russian literature of importance since Pushkin is explicable without him, and he is so interwoven with the development of Russian music that the one can hardly be referred to without thought of the constant presence and the inexhaustible potency of the other.

> Near a sea cove an oak is growing;
> Around that oak a golden chain:
> Along that chain Sir Cat-the-Knowing
> Doth ever walk and walk again.
> Goes to the right—a song he chaunteth,
> Goes to the left a tale he tells. . . .
> There I have been; there I drank mead,
> Saw the green oak near sea cove growing
> And sat beneath; Sir Cat-the-Knowing
> Did with his wondrous tales proceed.

The famous prologue to *Russlan and Ludmilla*, which stirred all literary Russia and divided it immediately into two camps, furnished music that was equally historic. Glinka, younger than Pushkin, knew and associated with him (1828) in Petersburg. The day was yet to come when Glinka would awaken from the thralldom of Italian opera and other foreign cultural currents and do for music what Pushkin was already doing in his poetry, but that time was not far off. In 1836 came the opera *A Life for the Czar*, which is the cornerstone of Russian national opera and the true beginning of the Russian school of composition. Its plot was based upon the poem of Pushkin's associate, the older Zhukovsky. Then, in 1842, appeared the opera in which Glinka wholly identified himself with the new movement and in which are found the germs of so much of the later music of the nineteenth-century school—*Russlan and Ludmilla*. Thereafter every prominent composer and song-writer of the century was to dip deep and always deeper for inspiration into the spring of Pushkin's genius. . . .

Primarily for the reason of inadequate and until now incomplete translation, there is the general impression in English-speaking countries that Pushkin's eminence is principally that of a national bard. This, of course, is anything but the case. Pushkin had indeed listened to tales of the fabulous cat. He had heard them from his nurse, Arina Rodionovna, in his childhood. She, indeed, was his friend and comforter as long as she lived, and she joined him in the enforced sojourn in the Caucasus. Besides this, the folklore of Oriental as of Occidental Russia was Pushkin's constant interest.

It was profoundly associated with the nature from which it came, mirrored in the marvelous Caucasian land, experienced there in his actual wanderings with a gypsy tribe which gave rise to a famous poem, and in a thousand other experiences of a life lived with singular intensity. But Pushkin, descendant on the one side of six hundred years of noble ancestors, and on the other of Abraham Gannibil, the Abyssinian, "Peter the Great's nigger" (actually the son of an Ethiopian King captured by the Turks and sold as a slave)—was brilliantly educated, precocious in letters. The early literary influences were Parny, André Chenier, Voltaire, whom he fanatically admired. During the first Caucasian visit he learned English and was imbued with Byronism. In due course he relinquished Byron for Shakespeare, whose influence is manifest in "Boris Godunoff." Dante and Goethe were familiar.

It may be said that what these men did for their national literature Pushkin did for Russia and the Russian tongue, first revealed by him in all its naturalness, variety, and beauty. He fused the idioms of popular and cultivated art in one manifestation, and this as early as *Russlan*, a product of his youthful years and of European as well as native influences.

He was a magnificently schooled technician, a virtuoso in his craft, but never a sophisticate, never less than an adorer of life and a Russian prophet of mankind. No wonder that when he read the first version of *Russlan* to the older Zhukovsky the latter inscribed his portrait, "To a victorious pupil from a defeated master."

Pushkin's universality is rooted in the earth, is Russian in a way and to a degree that the intensive, highly developed, but more exclusive culture of Europe does not know. His humanity and vivid perception of nature, his adoration of life as supreme teacher, underlay the simplicity, vigor, and raciness of his style. . . .

They present him in powerful contrast to a European culture which, for lack of fresh currents, is drying up at the roots. Not the least impressive proof of his significance lies in the utter change of the present Russian Government toward him since the earlier days of the revolution. Then Pushkin was virtually banned. Now he is exalted, as also the sources of racial strength which inspired him— the folklore, customs, melodies of his country.

Were there time and space, Pushkin's universality of mind, and the mingling of racial understanding and intuitive and objective contemplation of mankind could be better defined through allusions to the nature of various poems. So that, from revolutionary fanaticism, as well as the preoccupations and the somewhat supercilious attitude in the past, of European culture toward the Russian, Pushkin rises always higher and more secure in the regard of his country and the world. Has any other poet been identified more completely with the music of his native land? It is nevertheless probable that Pushkin's sun is rising rather than setting. . . .

It is the fact that among musicians only Moussorgsky, in *Boris Godunoff*, and Tchaikovsky, with less dramatic success, have come near the true inwardness of the greater aspects of Pushkin. But he has inspired generations.

Mention of a few compositions inspired by his masterpieces is scarcely an indication of the extent to which his influence has been felt. But consider certain of the more prominent instances.

Glinka sets *Russlan* as the most appropriate possible theme for a leader of the Russian school of opera. Dargomijsky sets *The Stone Guest*, in its exact original text—the story of Don Juan—and also *Russalka*. Tchaikovsky takes *Eugen Onégin, Pique Dame,* and *Mazeppa,* from the poem *Poltava.* Cui and others set *The Fountain of Bakhtchisarai,* and Cui *The Captain's Daughter.* Rimsky-Korsakoff uses *Tsar Saltan, Mozart and Salieri, Coq d'or,* captions his orchestral *Skazka* with the *Russlan* prologue, and sets many of the poems as songs.

Moussorgsky uses many poems for songs, and creates from the text and subject of *Boris Godunoff* his operatic masterpiece. Rachmaninoff's operas *Aleko* and *The Miser Knight* are after Pushkin. Stravinsky sets *Faun and Shepherdess* for voices and instruments, and makes a one-act opera of *Mavra*.

It would be easier, in fact, to mention Russian song-composers who have not used Pushkin texts than to enumerate those, great and small, who have. This refers even to the moderns—the Dukelskys, Gniessins, etc.—as it does to the older men, present and past, the Rachmaninoffs, Gretchaninoffs, Medtners, Tcherepnins, Glazounoffs, and Arenskys.

And why? Because of his ancestral power, the greatness of his soul, the genuineness and vitality of his winged words and their music. Because of his perception of wonder in the innermost things, his capacity to perceive in a flash the eternal significance of a gesture or everyday occurrence. Because he was a master poet and universal spokesman for humanity in terms of his race, his words live and immortally sing.

"This capacity," said Dostoevsky, in his memorable speech at the Pushkin ceremonies of 1880, "the pre-eminent capacity of our nation, he shares with our nation, and by that above all he is our national poet. . . . For what is the power of the spirit of Russian nationality if not its aspiration after the goal of . . . omnihumanity?"

When Pushkin died there was fear of a popular demonstration, so that his remains were carefully removed to the cemetery in the nighttime. To many who hurried on the night of his death to watch before his house, two words—"To Pushkin"—sufficed to shout to the overworked cabmen.

Perhaps Russian music will again realize its soul, lost in political and other confusions, when it returns to the spirit reflected in the manifold aspects of the great poet's genius. Then again, as now, it will be time to say, in salutation and gratitude: "To Pushkin."

Deems Taylor's Suite *Through the Looking Glass*

"Grown-ups can also be as children when
they hear this music."

THE program given by Artur Rodzinski with the Philharmonic-
Symphony Orchestra in Carnegie Hall yesterday afternoon included Weber's poetical overture to *Oberon*, and Deems Taylor's
suite *Through the Looking Glass*.

It was a pleasure to hear this suite again and to realize that,
though it made its first appearance, as scored for chamber orchestra,
in 1921, and its appearance in the full orchestral version heard
yesterday in 1923, the music has not lost its freshness, humor, and
fantasy. Tenderness, wit, and imagination, as might well befit a
tale for children, characterize these pages. But grown-ups can also
be as children when they hear this music. It is unpretentious and
inspired. It makes no effort to storm the heavens or to be anything
but what it is, and it is perfectly appropriate to its subject. It is Mr.
Taylor talking in his happiest and most fanciful vein.

There are no literalisms; everything is fantasy, with a vein of
true sentiment and happy memories.

The gay scherzo movement of "the garden of live flowers" is interwoven with the music of the dream. The absurdity of the Jabber-
wocky music is not forced or overdone. In one place there is an
overlong string of sequences; as a whole the music is admirably proportioned, in ideas, in development and instrumentation.

What a pleasure to hear music which is neither bumptious nor
apologetic, but true to itself, and thus of the stuff that cannot be
false to the art it professes! At the end of the performance Mr. Taylor was repeatedly called to the stage. He had reason to be gratified
with the public response to his music, and still more with the music
itself.

The other performances of the afternoon, those of Sibelius's Second Symphony and of Richard Strauss's *Till Eulenspiegel*, were
proof of how rapidly orchestra and conductor are growing together,

and of the conductor's essential qualities, including those of temperament and of exceptional capacity for leadership. There was an audience of good size and much enthusiasm.

MAY 30, 1937

Unheard Melodies

"The old awareness of the wonder of the world"

A RECENT visitor to the city of Washington, D.C., went there to attend a music festival at which music new and old was presented to an invited public. Some of the new music had unmistakable vitality and physiognomy. Some of it appeared mannered, or altogether lifeless. This is no denigration of modern music, for similar conditions have existed through the centuries. That is to say, there has always been more worthless music than worth-while music composed, although certain centuries have apparently been richer than others in the more desirable product. It was a decidedly worth-while festival. But there is another permanent festival of music held in Washington, D.C. You can find it in the rooms that contain certain Chinese paintings in various mediums and marvelously drawn designs which are centuries old.

Here, for example, is a winter scene of a comparatively late period —the sixteenth century—done in black and white. There are a rhythm and an ecstasy quite beyond words in the thing, and a degree of "atmosphere" which the uninformed might suppose to be attainable only by means of sounded music. But this sings as gloriously as the winter moon and wild freezing winds that blow over bare snow-clad distances. A dead, dry branch, knotting, twisted, on which the few stiff pods and wisps of frozen tendrils remain, sweeps downward in a great, careless, rapturous curve from the top to the bottom of the oblong frame. Mysteriously you are aware that this is the grand, inhuman song of the life of the universe and the cycles of death and resurrection which also is sung by the stars that whirl in the skies.

In the next room, among other wondrous things, are a number

of the long scrolls which unfold whole panoramas, done in the various techniques of different centuries of the later medieval period and what corresponds to the period of the early European Renaissance.

There is a deeper magic in a particular one of these scrolls. It is less romantic, more profound in feeling and in the sheer harmonic quality of the creation. This scroll has all the fundamental qualities which we associate with the purest tonal art. It has the supreme logic and flow of what a musician of today often calls "line," as well as rhythm, perfection of formal balance, and a complete unity of, we had nearly said, all sonorous elements.

There are a poetry and serenity, a deep content, a simple acceptance of the earth and its all-pervading mystery, which are more static than the noise of today, yet communicative of an intensity of emotion that only the fundamentally contemplative spirit can know. Here are spacious halls and courts of a great palace, a courtyard, a pool, steps that mount again from the courtyard, etc.—a succession of pleasant vistas, in some of which guests are perceived seated on a roof, while in the background trees are visible—in a word, a design. The visual effect of the great scroll, which must be ten or twelve feet long, is of the pleasant sights that a guest at the palace would see as he traversed its halls and courtyards. But the singularly atmospheric effect of something created by means of a multiplicity of the finest and cleanest lines has the glamour of a dream.

Looking upon it, one realizes again the strange paradox: that time passes quicker than thought, yet always we are in the unchanging center of time; that life is everlasting and all-inclusive; that we who live were there, are there, and always will be there, in that special center created by art. That nothing on the scroll was placed there either hurriedly or in a spirit of idle experiment. The scroll must have grown under its creator's hands as naturally as the great tree that puts a ring around its trunk with each year that passes. Strange to say, the completely formal design has in it the life and the very breath of nature. And why not? Is it not the perfect and timely result of the fertility of the properly functioning mind?

One doubts little that the man who did this exquisite and unalterable drawing adored and completely lived in his task. He must have risen and looked upon the dawn, and turned with a sigh of delight to his work. As inch after inch, and foot after foot, of the scroll was covered, he must almost grudgingly have reflected that there were only so many feet left for him to fill with the beauty that intoxicated him.

It is also easy to believe that the light grew dim too quickly for him, and that, as he turned from his work and looked upon the world enveloped in the shadows and the changing hues of the twilight hour, he exulted; that his own day's labor and thought had prepared him to wonder anew at it all, and rise again and, with the same instinct and the same passion, continue from the place where he had stopped with his great and consuming task.

Certainly every stroke was done with the utmost deliberation, preciseness, and care; with a concentration that saw the end in the beginning; with an inspiration that grew and accumulated as the days passed and the work neared completion. In this work there could hardly have been a thought of anything but the all-absorbing fascination of the mystery invoked and unfolded, as the design materialized, from the very depths of the soul.

The time has passed, probably, when a modern artist can find the environment and the spirit which so naturally created this art and brought it to surpassing perfection. It must be the problem of the modern musician, in his turn, to achieve this isolation and this absorption in the creation of beauty, without any other reward. What reward, indeed, would be commensurate with the successful execution of such a task? There is no equivalent joy. It is for the creative musicians of the modern community to recapture, not the old technique, but the old awareness of the wonder of the world, and reverence for it, and absorption in its service. For this profound consciousness and nameless rapture lie at the core of great art.

AUGUST 18, 1937

———

On the Passing of George Gershwin

"The immense virtues of his defects"

No OTHER American composer had such a funeral service as that held last Thursday for George Gershwin. Not a MacDowell, not a Chadwick, not a Stephen Foster or Dan Emmett or John Philip

Sousa received such parting honors. Authors, editors, playwrights, and critics; national figures of the stage, the screen, the radio, the ballet; celebrated musicians, from Paul Whiteman to Walter Damrosch, composers as well as executants, gathered to say hail and farewell. This was eloquent of the place Gershwin held in the public esteem.

His immense success was due to his own great and indisputable talent and also to the period in American music. Some could read in this success and in the popular support of Gershwin a significant sign of the times. Popularly speaking, at least, Gershwin was the musical man of the hour. His rise to fortune was a Horatio Alger epic of Grand Street. As a boy he lived, played, fought, rose via the coop of a song-plugger in a music shop to the rank and fortune of the most widely known American composer. In that capacity, at the height of his reputation, he was busily producing, at one and the same time, light operas and orchestral works bid for by famous symphonic organizations. He was a public figure on two sides of the water, and all the concomitants of spectacular success were his.

He also benefited by the fact that metropolitan society was changing its ways, as, indeed, our ideas and manners were changing, the while that the conditions of urban life replaced the prevalently agricultural environment of the American of the former century. The day that saw a singing waiter make millions in music and eventually wed the daughter of a millionaire saw also the metamorphosis of the boy of immigrant parentage into a cosmopolite who was sought by managers, interviewers, photographers, impresarios—yes, and young women of Park Avenue who leaned and languished over the piano as George played. All this, and much more, happened to him, in the Babylonic epoch when everybody was so gay and everything so flush and amusing. He relished it, too, in an unbelievably naïve and simple way!

Gershwin had precisely the gift to delight and entertain. He was a born melodist, with a native instinct for exotic harmonic effects and the rhythmical ingenuity that usually pertain to musicians of his experience and kind. His way of playing the piano was maddeningly his own. He could never write down his accompaniments as he played them, although the edition of selected songs which appeared some six years ago had affixed to them a series of laughably appropriate embroideries on the melody for the keyed instrument. How original, felicitous, and piquant were the best of the songs! How he could hit off a verse, preferably by his brother Ira! *Swanee*; *Stairway to Paradise*; *Sentimental Oriental Gentlemen Are We*; *Virginia*; *Lady, Be Good*—these were inimitable miniatures. It need not be claimed that George had studied the laws of prosody with a scholar's passion. No. But he had the feeling of words, as the vaudevillian values them, and his musical style was the one tonal investiture for Ira's texts.

There is no need now to expatiate upon the details of the *Rhapsody in Blue*, but its consequences were many. One of them, which may not have worked out for the composer's best good, was that well-meaning critics and musical friends talked earnestly with George, and found him more than willing to attempt serious, even symphonic composition. He had shown that he could write a theme susceptible of symphonic treatment, granting that he could summon the necessary technique and structural power—a thing that he was not completely able to do. At the same time, he had shown dazzling possibilities in a new and original treatment of the outworn form of the piano concerto.

It is said that when Gershwin accepted the order of Damrosch and the New York Symphony to write a concerto in three movements he went out and bought a textbook to find out what a concerto was. He made an astonishingly good attempt at the big form. It is a technical growth, but not a creative evolution. Essentially, Gershwin sang one song. It is of the city, the music hall, the mechanical age. Granted poetry in the Concerto's slow movement: it is the peace of the twilight outside the stage door. The doorkeeper puffs his cigar in the hot summer evening, he sees blue and yellow electric lights, hears the echoes of the street and the hum of the approaching elevated. It is city music, topical music, free of introspection or problems, written in a gay, thoughtless decade. It is sensuous, amorous, and of a racy idiom, but it unfolds no broader horizon.

The best of the other orchestral works was undoubtedly *An American in Paris*, with the exhilarating hilarity of the "walking themes," and the unity of the impression augmented by amusing and personally devised instrumentation. The composition gets no further than the earlier works; it reveals no new artistic or emotional ground. Gershwin strove in certain compositions toward the higher realms of composition. He looked into the promised land, and pointed a way—one way—that a greater musician might follow.

As it was, he displayed the immense virtues of his defects as a craftsman, his lack of musical background, his youthful ignorance of symphonic usage and tradition, and the environment which fortunately was not that of a standardized institution of musical learning, following with comfortable routine the century-old traditions of other lands and peoples than ours. Gershwin was free of that. He talked, musically speaking, the language that his countrymen and generation knew.

This, admittedly, was a dialect used by the less cultured of the populace, but it was a patois that everyone understood, and one upon which a creative artist could genuinely build. Gershwin used the idiom in his own way. Others, such as Henry F. Gilbert and John Alden Carpenter, had approached the same issue through the medium of grander forms and complicated style. They were not widely understood. Gershwin was far enough from the bottom and near enough to the top to foreshadow an art that will spring from the people and sublimate their expression, but in a way that reflects the individuality of the thinker and artist.

No doubt Gershwin was materially aided in his career by the intense desire of his countrymen to see something of that sort happen in the development of an American music. It is also to be remembered that at least until the turn of the century few Americans took the study or cultivation of good music seriously. The man in the street passed Carnegie Hall distrustfully. A chap that composed was likely to be a "highbrow" or sissified, or both. The general popular acceptance, and indeed astonishing enthusiasm, for great music by Bach and Wagner and Debussy and Strauss, to say nothing of a Bloch or Sibelius or Stravinsky, is a very recent thing. It was only in Gershwin's generation that the American people as a whole took with ardor to good music. He came on the scene just at the time to be a connecting link between the "serious" and "popular" composers of America. It was a highly desirable development.

And here is a point for consideration: the process, too often imitative, with our schooled composers, of foreign models, versus another process, which is one of normal growth through creative energy and power of assimilation, on the part of our most gifted composers of light music. The conservatory student kneels before Mozart, Beethoven, Brahms, Wagner, Schumann, or Strauss, and it will be hard indeed for him to proceed in his work independently of these models.

But the man in Tin Pan Alley, of meager technical knowledge at best, writes the melody that comes into his head, writes to please. While he is doing that there comes into his ear a chord he has heard in a work by a classic master, and he finds he can profitably incorporate that progression in one of his songs. He does not imitate, he absorbs. The chances are all for the composer who grows upward rather than for the gentleman who condescendingly holds out a hand to people outside his circle, and who seems to fear anything savoring of common expressions. But they are good for native art. Doubtless the author of the *Rhapsody in Blue* was overrated, just as he and his ilk had in preceding days been grossly and snobbishly undervalued. It may be soberly said that the *Rhapsody in Blue* has had a strong and lasting influence for the good upon American composers.

They do tell the very amusing story, which can perfectly well be true, of Gershwin's asking Stravinsky to teach him composition, whereat Stravinsky is supposed to have asked blandly: "What is your income per year?" When Gershwin, somewhat embarrassed, said he supposed it was in the neighborhood of $100,000 per annum, Stravinsky said: "Then I think you'd better teach me composition!" We shall certainly expose ourselves to contumely when we say that we would prefer one of the representative Gershwin songs to many of the later compositions of Igor Stravinsky. This despite the fact that Stravinsky almost invariably succeeds in putting down on paper what he wants there, thus carrying out to the last tone his musical conception. Gershwin could not do this, perhaps could not even harbor a conception that would require vast skill to realize. It remains that, as Debussy said, there is one music, which may inhabit a waltz or a symphony. Gershwin was *en rapport* much of the time, and in his own way, with that magic. Sometimes he conveyed it in a way that made him a pioneer of importance. This writer finds his expression limited, emotionally, imaginatively, stylistically. It is fundamentally popular music, jazz music, and music which has intrigued the whole world. This writer has had jazz scraped and blared into his face in Tiflis. It is a music of a new color, and it has given to the art new energy. Its elementary structures of jazz, its banalities, its effects in any amount you please, do not stultify its vitality and its wide appeal. It gained a new consideration with Gershwin, and Gershwin, in turn, contributed individual genius to the form. When the tumult and shouting are over —and already they are subsiding—he will have a secure place in the American tonal art.

Songs That the Legion Sang

"The songs of those who knew neither hate nor fear"

WE WERE not present when the virile representatives of the American Legion fired pistols in Macy's department store. No one assaulted us with a squirt gun. The cannon, the crackers, the whistles, yells, ditties, and marches sounded fiercely, but at a merciful distance outside the office doors. Though why the door of this department had to be passed by a posse playing upon whee-jees, with a bass drummer and a leader interpreting Chopin's Funeral March upon a fife, is incomprehensible. Perhaps it was intended as a ceremony for the Unknown Musician and a preview of the hereafter of a music reporter.

The reunion of the American Legion in New York had memories for those who embarked from these ports to make the world safe for piracy, and for those who watched them go. One of the most stirring of the parades was the procession of sons of the war veterans, a whole new generation sprung up since 1918, marching with a magnificent snap to music that had been heard "over there." And, of course, the occasion revived the American songs of the World War.

That war generated much music and verse. An army always sings; modern warfare found the song as efficacious as ever to promote morale. It would be hard to make detailed classification of the variety of American songs, composed here or invented on the spot for the occasion. There were fighting songs, marching songs, mother songs, ribald ditties—prime favorites—and travesties fitted to famous tunes expressive of heroic sentiment.

The many unprintable adventures and recommendations of *Mademoiselle from Armentières* gave vast satisfaction through the length and breadth of the line. It was probably the lively rhythm of the song and the Rabelaisian jocosities of the verses that commended it. *Madelon* was of the same genre.

One of the best songs was certainly George Cohan's *Over There*, a racy exhilarating tune, like so many of the songs that Cohan produced, music and verse, and imbued with the spirit of his day. The appeal of the song was in the energy and simplicity of its idea. The motive had irresistible dramatic suggestion, and the rhythmical pounding of emphasis on the words of the last line, "And we *won't come back* till it's over, over there," says something, when sung by he-men, that isn't forgotten. It is of such simple and real stuff that a war song is made.

Cohan companioned this song with *Good-bye Broadway, Hello France*, which was of a less dramatic and a gayer sort. It made a fine marching song, and so, as it proved, did *Keep the Home Fires Burning*. Geoffrey O'Hara's *K-K-K-Katy* went over big, and had many textual variations, such as "C-C-C-Cootie."

The favorite sentimental song was the *Long, Long Trail*, and sentimental airs were much liked. The mother song, dwelling upon the significance of each of the letters, *M-O-T-H-E-R*, was often intoned—sometimes, it is to be feared, with the effect enhanced by beverages, as when, on a certain occasion back of the lines, it was performed very earnestly in several different dialects by Americans, Canadians, British, Irish, and Scotch. Then an Irish sergeant reached forward and crashed a beer bottle upon the head of an Englishman who happened to be within range. A perfectly grand free-for-all ensued.

There were all sorts of comic songs, and topical ones, such as *I've Got My Captain Working for Me Now*. The English liked *Over There* almost as much as they did *Tipperary*. The Canadian song of Captain Gitz-Rice, *Keep Your Head Down, Fritzie Boy*, composed after the Battle of Ypres in 1915, came somewhat belatedly to the fore. Here and now, down in the street as we write, sounds one of the grand old-timers that has served for so many occasions great and small, *Hail, Hail, the Gang's All Here*.

Well over a hundred songs went into the repertory of the soldiers, aside from the far greater variety furnished by the Y.M.C.A. entertainments. But this must be said, when you come right down to it:

nothing invented during wartime surpassed or equaled such magnificent creations of the American past as Dan Emmett's *Dixie* and the best of the marches of John Philip Sousa.

Individuals will vote differently for favorite airs. For this writer nothing America has produced in the line of popular song has equaled for characteristic and original expression the wild, laughing, debonair *Dixie* of our old American minstrel. For this is one of the most glorious and reckless tunes in the world. It has the laughter of haughty young men, and something of the skirl of a bagpipe, and the unmistakable accent of the free-born. It would illustrate well the subtle distinction drawn by the psychologist who said that an Englishman entered a house as if he owned it and an American as if he didn't care who owned it. What a miracle is this glorious tune, and what must it have meant to our men overseas!

And you shall rank only a little lower Mr. Sousa. In certain of his strains he struck an incomparably popular and vital note. He said the national thing in a certain way that no one else ever achieved, and that could be said only of this nation. What other country since the eighties has put such powder into its marches? It is true that all sorts of things enter into a Sousa march. There is national braggadocio of the imperialistic era: Uncle Sam in his striped hat, goatee, and trousers, out to lick the world, by gum. The introductory flourish of *The Stars and Stripes* always makes us think of that. But what follows says something else again, and says the brave and gallant thing with a lift that would put heart into a sheep and fire housewives to deeds of derring-do. And there's the tune of the trio, the serene, long-sustained, deep-breathing melody that John Philip once told us had come to him as he was sailing homeward to America and, looking up from the boat deck, saw the flag of the United States streaming nobly against a turbulent sky.

But we are not here to apostrophize the literature of American national song or provide notes upon the many marches of Sousa. These questions are apropos: How do the songs that the American soldiers sang in the World War impress us today? How many of them will stand, after the occasion that produced them has passed, as living music? Will any of them rank with the earlier compositions to which reference has been made?

It is hardly likely that they will. Nothing evolved in the last war period matches the great national songs of the earlier days. The reason for this may be the pure accident that no genius appeared, as a Rouget de Lisle, to compose a *Marseillaise*, greatest of all war songs, in the passage of a night. And there may be another reason which often has operated in music. This is, that music, which comes, in its greatest manifestations, from a source so deep in the individual as to rest in the subconscious, appears often in history to have been the latest of all the arts to mirror the emotions or experiences through which a nation has passed. This, at least, is a theory supported by the evidence of the "romantic" school of composition of the nineteenth century, which evolved after results of revolution in thought and society had manifested themselves in literature and other arts; and by the birth of music drama, and the modernism of Monteverdi, constituting one of the last of the fruits of the dying Renaissance.

Did the war last long enough for it to engrave itself upon the profoundest consciousness of our people? Probably it did not, save for those who knew the ultimates of sacrifice and suffering at the front. Their majority, sweeping triumphantly forward, was not to know a single crushing reverse, or the despair of others, to whom defeat and annihilation must have appeared at certain times inevitable.

Our war songs, sometimes melancholy in a sentimental way and once or twice, in the verses, tragic and grimly realistic, are as a class the songs of those who knew neither fear nor hate, and to whom, with all its horrors and catastrophes, the journey overseas meant a gallant and honorable adventure. They are football songs. They would go splendidly during a game. They are expressions of buoyant, confident youth, of the irrepressible spirit of a young and singularly fortunate nation which began in an adversity that our forefathers knew and that we do not know and cannot wholly comprehend. The boys overseas had the stuff in them, and showed it immortally, to endure any hardship, take any position, and fight with invincible energy and the generosity of those who have not yet had bitterness wedged into their very souls. How young and glorious in their spirit they were, and how young, untwisted by cruelty or terror, they remain! It's in the songs. We can be thankful that their spirit did not alter, and has not changed.

On Misreading Meanings into Sibelius

*"A composer born in Finland who goes to Italy had better
be careful. If he doesn't, he'll find that he has
composed Il Trovatore."*

A voice, gently admonitory, raises itself from the pages of a recent
program book of the Boston Symphony Orchestra, warning readers
that the conclusions of "early commentators" who found the Second Symphony of Jean Sibelius expressive of northern nature,
legend, revolution, and whatnot of the same sort, should be taken
with a grain of salt. How does anybody know that Sibelius was
thinking of these things when he wrote the Second Symphony? As a
matter of fact, he probably wasn't. How do we know that he probably wasn't? Because, as it transpires, a considerable part of the
Second Symphony was written by Sibelius, not when he was roving
the wilds of Karelia, but when he was sojourning, in the spring, in
sunny Italy.

This shows how careful northern composers should be when they
write symphonies. A composer born in Finland who goes to Italy
had better be careful. If he doesn't, he'll find that he has composed
Il Trovatore. The men who discuss his symphonies had better go
slow, too, or they will find that just when they thought Sibelius's
orchestra was muttering of war and Northern Lights it was really
depicting moonlight pouring down upon the Villa d'Este. And anybody with any sense would know that Sibelius wouldn't write like
Sibelius if he were in the land of the Villa d'Este. His style would
then become that of Monteverdi. It's lucky that he missed Naples,
else we might have had hymns with guitar accompaniment to *dolce
far niente.*

What music criticism needs, in the above and similar connec-
tions, is debunking. Why should music be construed to mean anything? What have a composer's race, past, environment, or individual temperament to do with his creations? Every thoughtful and
educated person knows that great art is international, and great

241

music—just music. Sibelius has no more to do with Finland and the north than Tchaikovsky's "Pathetic" Symphony, with its alleged Slavisms and wails of despair, has to do with the nation that begot Dostoevsky, or Beethoven's Fifth with that composer's ethical or temperamental reactions to his epoch. The Fifth Symphony is simply music, and it is a pity that Schindler's legend of fate knocking at the door was ever promulgated. These people who find "meanings," scenes, dramas in music!

What is music, then? Music is a wonderful arrangement of tones in certain positions and patterns which, for reasons we have not successfully analyzed, gives us a certain esthetic pleasure—that is, if we are really cultivated people. We then derive from it, as the Greek philosopher said, a gentlemanlike joy. This orderly and symmetrical arrangement of the tones takes our minds off the real and urgent problems of existence and lifts us above the human equation and the fairy story in art. But Beethoven knew better, and this knowledge is what gives his music universality. Wagner knew it, too, and likewise the youthful Sibelius.

We—the editorial we—that is to say, in this case, good old Downes —should be glad to know these things and to stand corrected, for "we" were among the erroneous "early commentators." What is worse, we are unregenerate. While we are not yet limping, purblind, or of a hoary gray hue, we persist in discovering the elemental northern and magnificently ancestral thing in Sibelius's compositions, at least in the early symphonies and symphonic poems. These appear to us inalienable and unmistakable characteristics of the music. Nor can we easily believe that persons normally responsive to music, with any degree of imagination—a faculty still applicable to that art—and with even a little blood in their veins, can fail to find something of that spirit in the scores.

Whatever its form, music emanates from sources inseparable from the individual and the things deepest and truest in his personality. One or another aspect of the personality may be uppermost at the moment of creation and find expression in a manner that seems incongruous with various factors of the moment. Schubert, nearing his end penniless and in need, shouts his praise to the skies. Beethoven, in the terrible years of the Heiligenstadt Will, creates one of his most joyous works. It is none the less a true emanation of himself, a moment of triumph snatched from the very jaws of tragedy.

Proof and not ᴄontradiction of this principle is supplied by Sibelius's frequent denial of the intention of northern nature-painting in his scores. He says that he writes simply the music that comes to him, and perfects it as well as he may in putting it on paper. That is what every composer does. It is not the business, and in many cases it is not in the power, of the composer to explain himself, although it should be said here that when composers such as Schumann, Berlioz, Wagner, Debussy have explained themselves they have not done so in terms of abstract art, but in very vivid word pictures of dramatic or poetic conceptions. When the composer, like a Beethoven, is not given to self-analysis by explication, it may well be the province and usefulness of outsiders to do him and his music this genuine service.

Sibelius, his birth and background being, what they are, would have written the music he has written whether it had been composed in Florence or at Niagara Falls. If he had been born in America of Finnish ancestry and lived his life here, he would have produced some other kind of music. As the years have passed, his scores have become far less those of a musical landscapist and romantic revolutionist in his art, and there are good and logical explanations of this. One is that prior to the composition of the Fourth Symphony he drastically changed his conditions of living, getting out of Helsingfors and its many companionships, living a much quieter and more introspective existence than in earlier years, and becoming, as a consequence, always more alone and individual in his music. This was in marked contrast to the period of the Second Symphony, completed at a time of feverish nationalism, when Finland was under Russian rule, and he was one of a young band of artists and writers whose emotions were of a sort—granted the presence of a young composer of genius—to result in a Second Symphony.

There are people, of the paler or academic cast of mind, who persist in attempting to make one rule for everything in music; who would, if they could, put not only limitations but blinders on the art, and fit it to their own limited vision and experience. It is just as ridiculous and unperceptive to close the eyes to patent characteristics of certain compositions and their sources in race and personality as it is to make up silly legends about other works with which officious and impossible tales have obviously no connection. To read events, for example, as many people have, into Beethoven's

Seventh Symphony is as impertinent and beside the mark as it would
be to deny an implicit meaning to symphonies Six or Nine (in the
finale) by the same composer.

To which may be added the following: that the ultimate significance of an art work is determined not only by what its creator intended, or by that of which he was conscious when he produced it,
but also by the meanings and the values discovered in it by many
individuals and generations.

JANUARY 2, 1938

An Evaluation of Maurice Ravel *

"Is his art the fruition or the last vestige of a defeated
and vanishing culture?"

THE art of Maurice Ravel is artificial, sophisticated, brilliant to a
degree, gallant and heroic. He could live only in his art, for his
physique was delicate and miniature. No doubt he had keen senses.
But his life on the personal emotional side seems to have been extremely solitary and sterile. He never married. One cannot imagine
him as having human issue.

Of most composers there are amatory legends of one sort or another. But even Paris credited Ravel with a singular aloofness in
this as in all other fields of the emotions. He lived a bachelor existence, in the country, on a hillside at Montfort l'Amaury, some
forty miles out of the capital. There, where he cultivated strange
plants and, in almost monastic seclusion, fondled Siamese cats, he
was bullied by a devoted housekeeper. In Paris, Ravel was a man
of the cultivated world, acquainted and on equal terms with its
denizens. How many, if anyone, knew him?

By immense industry and sheer mastery of his medium, Ravel
gradually won his distinguished position in French music. He was
a very hard worker and an extremely fastidious one. He never wrote
music badly or thoughtlessly. He never repeated himself as a composer, and he never covered up a clumsy passage by glittering instrumentation. But he could, and often did, make out of the slight-

* Ravel died in France on December 28, 1937, five days before the publication
of this article.—ED.

est material patterns and colors of tone which, if they had not the substance, certainly had the perfection and the harmonious proportions of a masterpiece. It is a question whether any modern composer—Strauss, Respighi, Stravinsky, Sibelius—had Ravel's knowledge of instrumentation.

He was born an artist, but not one with a powerful creative gift, nor was he ever the man to lead a cause or project a new kind of music. These things were not for him. He had to make something significant out of small and insignificant material, and he did so. He was thus a great artist, very distinguished.

The surface of a composition by Ravel was sure to be modern for its decade. But at heart he was a French classic. He was classic in his basic formalism, his faultless taste, his clarity and symmetry of arrangement and economy of means. Take the score of *Daphnis et Chloë*, one of the most brilliant and exciting, for sheer rhythmical and orchestral effect, in the literature of present-day music. At the bottom it is eighteenth- or seventeenth-century—an echo of the old French courts, with their masques and ballets. One could say that if either Lully or Rameau had had this period's means of composition at command, they would have composed in Ravel's manner. And Ravel is true to them. *Daphnis et Chloë*, in its prettiness, its courtliness, its brilliant wit and amiable sensuality, is of the *"ancien régime"*—part and parcel of it.

For we must not confuse evolutions of technique and style with those of feeling. Rather gallantly, Ravel belongs to the ranks of the Bourbons who learned and forgot nothing. To the roughness and impertinence of the modern world he opposed complete urbanity and faultless elegance. When he was here in 1928, already an elderly man, he was skipping about, looking into everything. Jazz was, of course, one preoccupation. Other European composers had gone into it, but there might be some earth as yet unturned in which Ravel would be able to dig for something fresh for his music. He was to be found in Harlem, at rehearsals of Paul Whiteman's orchestra, and in every odd corner of the city he could contrive to visit. How, with his excessively delicate nerves and stomach, did he keep pace with American travel, hospitality, homage? He survived, imperturbably. He said once: "In art nothing is left to chance." The same thing was true of Ravel's living.

Often it has been said that the French are a nation of critics; in his music Ravel was superbly critical and selective. He had a hard time in emerging from Debussy's shadow, and there is no need to pretend that he owed nothing to that genius. On the contrary, Ravel seized eagerly and with the keenest appreciation on that which was useful to him in Debussy. But not as an imitator. He was selecting, as he also selected from his predecessors, Fauré, Chabrier, Satie, and, above all, where orchestration was concerned, Rimsky-Korsakoff.

It is not surprising, when Ravel's piano piece *Jeux d'eau* appeared in 1901, if Debussyites, and, as Philip Hale suggested, Debussy himself, rubbed their eyes and wondered where they had hatched this chicklet! And there was not only the *Jeux d'eau*, with its aqueous tints and vaporous overtones, but also the earlier piece, the Habañera, which Ravel had produced in 1898. In 1903 Debussy, who had borrowed Ravel's piece and lost it, produced the set that included *Soirée dans Grenade*. Ravel, who had written his piece first, was accused of plagiarism.

If there were doubts of his originality and creative sincerity, they should have been dispelled by the time the String Quartet appeared in 1905, and the Sonatine and the other piano pieces, *Miroirs*, which came two years later. The quartet had not forgotten the Debussyan ninth and other characteristic harmonic devices, but it plainly followed different and more classic lines than the work in the same form by Debussy. It is to be seen, always more clearly, how utterly Debussy was the subjective poet and Ravel the scene-painter, the satirist, and the connoisseur; how Ravel constantly sharpens his pencil, while Debussy, though probably influenced by Ravel in *Ibéria*, becomes always the more an impressionist. Ravel had neither so much feeling nor such richness of nature as his older colleague. Indeed, there can be the suspicion that, contrary to Debussy, who in his special and sensuous way went out to meet life's offerings, Ravel avoided these encounters, with special artistic precautions.

His most virile and strongly colored compositions are those inspired by some aspect or other of Spain. The *Alborado del Gracioso* of the *Miroirs* is an early instance. The *Spanish Rhapsody*, which incorporated the earlier Habañera in its pages, is more masterful and complete in its scope. It has also imagination and carefully concealed feeling. The macabre shadows that accompany Castilian landscapes under the moon are in the opening *Prélude à la nuit*. It is mysterious music; its sensuousness is bitter, and the gibbering cadenzas of clarinets and bassoons say something else again from what is said by the magical orchestra, in a similar situation, in Debussy's *Ibéria*, which came later. The *Spanish Rhapsody* is a haunted piece, in the Prelude and Habañera. The Malagueña and the Finale—*At the Fair*—also a subject that gave Debussy his last movement for *Ibéria*—are most brilliantly and savagely colored. The instrumental dialogue in the last movement would make you think of Carmen and Escamillo before the bull ring, a passage that might well merit, in its African flavor, the epithets of Nietzsche—happiness short, sudden, and without forgiveness. This is an entire departure from Debussy, whose knowledge of Spain was anyhow imaginary, while for Ravel it was the country well known to the man born in Ciboure, in the Pyrenees, almost on the border.

Ravel, however, was more than a landscape-painter. He was never more poetical than in his *Tombeau de Couperin*, first composed as a set of piano pieces, later orchestrated, with its re-creation by modern means of the spirit of an old period. *La Valse*, a post-war satire on themes of Straussian swing and flavor, may be called a savage caricature, a pronouncement, as Mr. Gilman admirably remarked, as perturbing as a mobilization order, or a Victory Ball like the one described by the English poet.

Then there is the orchestral version, a profoundly creative act, undertaken at the behest of Serge Koussevitzky, of the piano *Tableaux d'une exposition* of Moussorgsky. The marvel of the work is its utterly barbaric, Russian, and Moussorgskian character; a score, in this writer's belief, for which Moussorgsky, who knew little or nothing of orchestration, would have gone down on his knees in gratitude. And an unkind fate indeed it was which left it to Rimsky-Korsakoff to orchestrate *Boris Godunoff*! Ravel was born many years too late to do that job for Moussorgsky, whom, strangely, he understood by intuition.

Is the art of Ravel the fruition or the last vestige or mere mirage of a defeated and vanishing culture? We do not have to decide that; the future will save us the trouble. At least in pages left behind him Ravel proves the existence of his realm and his absolute sovereignty in it. His accomplishment is as immaterial as a victory can be and retain relationship with human existence. It is the sheer triumph of mind and will over the injustice of nature—a thing which, of course, is true of all art that rises from the consciousness of man. But it is particularly striking and admirable to behold on the part of an epigone of an ancient society.

===

Toscanini Conducts the Verdi Requiem

"A tone drama of the judgment day"

ARTURO TOSCANINI's performance of the Verdi Requiem, with the chorus of the Schola Cantorum and a quartet of excellent singers and one great one, took place last night in Carnegie Hall. Superlatives are not only dangerous but wearisome. Yet it must be said that this was very nearly the perfect performance, and that the imperfections were passing details for which the leader was not responsible. The effect was overwhelming.

The performance was given for the benefit of the unemployed musicians of the New York Local, 802, American Federation of Musicians, and Verdi Rest Home for aged and destitute musicians in Milan. The performance found the conductor, not unnaturally, in a serious if not despondent mood. As soon as possible he ended the applause of the audience that rose when he appeared on the stage. Afterward he would not return to the platform to acknowledge the persistent demonstration. The soloists respected the leader's wishes, and followed him off the stage. But the audience felt otherwise. It was reluctant to leave the hall without another sight of the master who wrought a surpassing achievement and stood at the right hand of Verdi as he did so. He had accomplished a revelation.

This was done with a wonderful balance of passion and inexorable logic. All know that the Verdi Requiem is not a Teutonic reverie of death and resurrection, but a tone drama of the judgment day, a fresco with designs of fire. There is supplication, terror, resignation, faith, all in terms of the impulsiveness and forthrightness of the Italian nature. There is not pretense or artistic attitude. The composer is as one confounded by the thoughts of the dread visitant and the experience which levels the mightiest with the humble. He flings forth his music with an instinctive and unblemished sincerity. And so with Mr. Toscanini. His performance was so completely, unqualifiedly, and without conditions—Verdi.

Everything in this interpretation seemed inspired and inevitable. And every act was one of incorruptible musicianship. It is customary, for example, to let the singers run with the tempo of the great unison outcries of the *Dies irae*. Mr. Toscanini held back the passage, so that every one of the whirling descending tones had its full weight and terror.

Some of the tempos, as of the *Sanctus*, were very fast, and ideal for the music's purpose. The rapid, softly sounded figures in the movement named seemed to fill the air with light and the whisperings of cherubim and seraphim. In the *Recordare*, because of the strict tempo and the beautiful singing of the florid passage for soprano and alto on the word *donum*, the passage became not an operatic cadenza but an exquisite tonal flowering of the phrase from which the ornamentation sprang.

There were a thousand illuminating details, such as the slow grace notes in the *Lachrymosa*. These details fell inevitably into place; they enhanced the effect of the whole, for the interpreter's mind was fixed upon the composer's vision and the grand lines of the composition.

The mystical and shadowy mood of the opening, with the orchestra covering the voices, was illuminated by a shaft of light, with the sudden fortissimo on the word *eleison*. The contemplative nature of this movement was interrupted terrifyingly by the great G minor chords and the thunderous drum, in a way never to be forgotten, of the chant of God's wrath. The chorus, admirably trained by Hugh Ross, was the remarkable vehicle of the conductor's wishes.

The Schola has done this work before, and eloquently, with Mr. Toscanini. Last night it established a new record for itself, as regarded clean intonation, even in unaccompanied passages, technical finish, and, above all, feeling. The double chorus of the *Sanctus* and the concluding contrapuntal chorus were particular instances of virtuosity. There were many others.

Of the soloists the one that towered was Zinka Milanov. She not only brought a great voice and vocal art to the test, but she had the great spirit of the music as none other present. Her voice served her well, in passages of legato song, in dramatic outbursts, in sustained high tones, such as the B flat of the last movement, and in the trembling supplication and fervor of the *Libera me*. This was great singing.

Charles Kullman, the tenor, did admirable things. Then there was the rich-voiced and emotional Bruna Castagna, the contralto. Nicola Moscona, the bass, from the Metropolitan, substituted at ten days' notice for Ezio Pinza, who had originally intended to sing. Mr. Moscona gave a highly creditable performance.

For the *Tuba mirum* Mr. Toscanini used ten trumpets. Six he concealed, seated at opposite ends in the back row of the chorus and above most of the performers. Four others were in front of him in the orchestra. The echoing calls and the gradual increase of the sound made a passage that fired the imagination. And who will forget the *Rex tremendae* in unison with the trombones?

The quartet, individually of excellence, did not display a good blend of voice qualities or accurate intonation in an *a cappella* passage—a pardonable lapse. As the composition progressed last night and each movement became clearer in its relation to the others, the conductor seemed to accumulate power. The final section is in effect a synthesis of everything. Performing it, Mr. Toscanini gathered up the whole design, mightily crowning and summarizing the qualities of the "Manzoni" Requiem.

MARCH 26, 1938

——

On the Hundredth Anniversary of Moussorgsky's Birth

"He towers always higher as the years pass by."

It is almost exactly the one hundredth anniversary of the birth of the Russian immortal who is still far from being appreciated at his full value—Modest Petrovich Moussorgsky. He was born March 21, 1839, at Karevo in the Government of Pskof. He was without doubt the most original and the most completely Russian composer, in idiom and national consciousness, that his country has produced. His genius, ill-nourished and incompletely expressed, was nevertheless so fearless and powerful that it became one of the great shaping forces of modern music.

The question could be raised, and often is raised, whether Moussorgsky's nationalism was so pronounced as to have an exclusive effect, thus depriving him of the wide comprehension and international significance which pertain, for example, to Tchaikovsky. There is also the fact of the greater productive range of Tchaikovsky, Tchaikovsky's gradual mastery of symphonic means of expression, which Moussorgsky never attained, and the comparatively small amount of music that Moussorgsky left behind him.

It is in spite, and not because, of Moussorgsky's deficiencies in these directions that he towers always higher as the years pass by. He was much longer than Tchaikovsky in attaining any degree of technical mastery. He never attained the self-organization which Tchaikovsky, fully as neurotic a type, nevertheless, and surprisingly, did attain. But here Tchaikovsky had the enormous advantage over his colleague—whom Tchaikovsky never understood—in the enlightened and munificent friendship of Mme von Meck. Tchaikovsky would, in all probability, have vanished from the creative scene early in his career had it not been for his patroness, who saved him from want and made possible concentrated creative effort. Moussorgsky's fortunes, on the other hand, declined, always faster and more wretchedly, toward the end of his career. This fact and his creative isolation from even the colleagues most sympathetic to his aims no doubt had much to do with his alcoholic relapses, the disorganization of his genius, the sudden, trivial, tragic end.

As for Moussorgsky's profound and embracing humanity, his unerring dramatic instinct and endless power of invention, and essential grandeur of spirit—the opera of *Boris Godunoff* is sufficient proof. It is the one great opera which has crossed the Russian border and gained a great and enduring position in the world's repertory of music drama, and it has been a mine of ideas for composers of many nationalities who have succeeded Moussorgsky. But it is very typical of him, his social conceptions, his quality as a musician, that his greatest and most completely personal expressions occur in his songs. They are unique, without any exact parallel in song literature. They are longer in reaching appreciation by artists and public than the songs of other masters, principally by reason of their unconventionality, which is still conspicuous, and, above all, by the difficulty of securing adequate translations, particularly where English is concerned.

These songs are a *Comédie humaine* of lyrical, realistic, and superbly imaginative expression. If all the Moussorgsky songs are examined, imperfect or even insignificant ones, especially in his earlier period, will be found. But his craftsmanship in this genre developed with conspicuous and astonishing rapidity. Thrown back upon the most direct of all means of musical expression by his nature, his lack of superfluous virtuosity, and also his few opportunities of performance, Moussorgsky delved deeper and deeper toward the truth of melody and of harmonic investiture, toward the truth of language and the truth of the human heart.

In his last songs he is a consummate master. There is always the habit, in the human mind, of developing a certain opinion, or conception, and holding on to that conception, as originally formed, a long time after the justification of it has disappeared. It is time that Moussorgsky were critically examined through fresh spectacles. When that is done, the technical mastery with which his ideas are realized will be apparent.

In speaking of his supremacy as a song-writer, the reference is not merely to the melodic, the rhythmic, the harmonic originality of Moussorgsky's procedure—and in the best songs he is equally remarkable in each one of these directions—but to a deeper thing, which is the union of the tone with the innermost color, nuance, inflection of the text. He unites the two things which are equally indispensable to a master composer of songs—endless and unfailing invention and, as the supreme guidance for his genius, the meanings and the very aroma of the poem itself. Indeed, in a certain sense Moussorgsky was not a musician but a poet, dramatist, humanitarian. His aim was always *verismo*; all musical and other means were directed uncompromisingly to the expressive end.

That is a pitfall which has on occasion ruined a composer's effort, or affected it disadvantageously, as, for example, so great a master of song as Hugo Wolf was more than once disadvantageously affected by this consideration. Sometimes Moussorgsky, in turn, is hypnotized by a realistic or literary conception and becomes a second-rank musician. But that is rare. He is saved by the power and authenticity of his musical inspiration, and he is reinforced—indeed, protected—by an armor, mightier than perhaps he always knew, of the probity of the Russian folk spirit which permeated all his art. Russian folk music is woven into every inch of Moussorgsky's creative fabric. There is no halfway process about this, either. It is the sound and musical instinct of his people which always affects him. He speaks with their voice, and he is incorruptible. He was eternally concerned and absorbed in the human lot, but the prating of "internationalism" as the necessity of an art which has universality would have found him entirely cold. He comprehended as a seer, but he spoke in music his native speech, heightened and strengthened by the individual powers of his mind and spirit.

He suffered a creative tragedy singularly related to the course, at the time, of his nation. He had a reservoir of enormous potencies, a nature of a sincerity and an emotional force which spared neither himself nor anything nor anyone about him. He was shattered and broken by reactionary forces in art and in social directions that opposed him. He is one of the spirits of whom it was said by somebody that "one forsook, and one denied, and the lonely man of destiny went on his way." In his last years Moussorgsky was uncompanioned, and at a time when he was in greatest need of the comprehension that even Stassoff was unable to extend. It is now evident that as Moussorgsky became always clearer-sighted and more uncompromising in his quest of the truth, the lesser ones, even the most faithful and well-meaning, dropped away. The great and unfortunate master continued as best he might, to the end of despair and disintegration. His achievement proves as veracious as it is indestructible. There may be later occasion in these columns for indulgence in the discussion of various aspects of Moussorgsky's genius which cannot now be undertaken. Here it is only passingly possible to commemorate one who will never need commemoration.

APRIL 13, 1938

═══

On the Passing of Chaliapin

"He had an infinite capacity for life."

To THE millions who saw and heard him in the capitals of the world, to the multitude in all walks of life who had known the man as well as the artist, the death of Feodor Chaliapin comes with special poignancy and sense of loss.

There was neither man nor artist like him. As a "singing actor" he was pre-eminent, and veritably the creator of a school of vocal interpretation. He was so great a dramatic interpreter that the exceptional qualities of the voice itself, and the superb art with which it was employed, were sometimes forgotten. For he could have triumphed by his voice and his song alone. He is a historic personality. He had physical stature and he conveyed the sense of an elemental power. To these characteristics he added exceptional native sensibility and imagination, and a human understanding which reflected itself in every phase of his art.

The richness of his nature was exemplified by the Shakespearean variety of his characterizations in opera, and also in the qualities of Chaliapin the man. For he was an inimitable companion, a person of great native shrewdness and originality; a marvelous mimic and raconteur; a *bon vivant*, with a fabulous appetite and appreciation of good wines and other forms of pleasant living.

He had, in fact, an infinite capacity for life. Moreover, he had come up from what Gorky called "the lower depths." He never forgot the realities and the tragedies of the insulted and injured, whose lives and lot he knew. He had at the zenith of his career and his fortunes the homage of the great world. He remembered and he learned. He drew upon this profound knowledge for his great, realistic, human art. No triumph or acclaim robbed him of "the common touch."

When Chaliapin attained his artistic majority, the then "neo-Russian" school of composition had come to fruition, and he was the interpreter born to express the national and dramatic tendencies of that school. The classic style and the European tradition were not for him. If he had undergone long instruction in a conservatory, he never would have developed such a genuinely popular and individual art. His work was hewn from his nature and experience. It was his response to life, which he had found so difficult, dangerous, and fascinating in its myriad phases. He sang in his own way. He often subordinated purely musical considerations to laws of dramatic portrayal. It may, in fact, be said that he amalgamated the music drama and the art of the modern theater.

Sometimes music per se suffered as a consequence. He would tear a rhythmic pattern or a melodic line to pieces for the sake of emotional emphasis. Sometimes his imagination, which he translated in highly realistic fashion, took form in such shapes as the dirty, fawning, avaricious Basilio, in *The Barber of Seville*. No wonder that this, with other Chaliapin interpretations, roused the indignation of the classicists among the music critics. His Mefistofele in Boïto's opera was one of the butts of hostile reviewers when he first visited New York, and was not appreciated by a generation poorly disposed toward his methods, while Chaliapin's Devil in Gounod's *Faust* was found out of key with the traditions of that opera.

His most famous role was his Boris Godunoff in Moussorgsky's opera, an imperishable creation that will long remain as the supreme model for interpreters of this part. It was a picture of a dark power and a savage intensity of feeling that had no parallel on the operatic stage, yet it was only one of Chaliapin's great dramatic portraits. Another was his craven and sensual Leporello in *Don Giovanni*. Another, and one of the last roles he sang in America at the Metropolitan, was that of Massenet's Don Quichotte, a figure of such pathos and spirituality that one forgot the cheapness and futility of the music as he watched with blurring eyes the scene of the death of Cervantes's hero.

Whatever character Chaliapin undertook became a dramatic masterpiece. He carried his gift for characterization into the concert hall. A Chaliapin song recital was first of all a wonderfully suggestive dramatic recitation. In a moment he could limn the figure and tell the story of a lifetime. His humor was as infectious and original as his tragedy was overpowering. His voice was capable of innumerable shades of color and meaning, and his facial expression, without the operatic make-up which was in itself an act of genius, explained everything that he was singing in his own language.

Chaliapin came after the romantic period represented in Russian art by Pushkin and Glinka. He was of the epoch of Moussorgsky, and of the art movement that had its roots in the Russian spirit, adopting as its slogan the motto "Back to the people." The generation of the Russia that disappeared with the revolution honored and nourished his genius. There was in him much of the spaciousness and the opulence of his land, and of the essential humanity and democracy of Russia's people. He was so great that, while as an artist he only "interpreted," actually he created representations of life and beauty that will remain as lasting works of art in the memories of the generations whom he inspired.

Mayor La Guardia Pontificates about Tempo

"And we thought this was a country of free speech!"

MUSIC criticism often centers upon a conductor's tempo. A tempo is too fast or a tempo is too slow, and ink is shed about it. Lately the super-critics have been at work upon this theme. What does a mere critic, a mere biological entity lifting his quavering voice in the surrounding infinity of time, dream by daring to question a conductor's tempo? And anyhow, what of it? What's in a tempo?

There is our own Mayor [La Guardia], a doughty champion of art if ever there was one. You catch him off duty at the Wagner cycles at the Metropolitan. If you get the right sleuth, he will lead to His Honor's lurking-place at the symphony concerts in Carnegie Hall. Our Mayor has ideas about tempo, and about critics, too. He let them be known in a recent manifesto delivered from the stage of the Federal Music Theatre.

"I think a critic might say that a composition is played too slow or too fast to suit him, or too fast in comparison with someone else's rendition, but I do not think he has a right to say that a piece is played too fast or too slow. That is a matter for the conductor. If we establish a rigid tempo, we might as well put a metronome up in front of the orchestra."

And we thought this was a country of free speech!

There is so much that is perfectly right in the Mayor's remarks that it is hard to refute him. A metronome in front of an orchestra would be a disaster, though perhaps no worse a one than the incredible distortions of tempo that conductors have produced in the name of their individual conceptions of the music. The tempo is a matter for a conductor, and then, again, it isn't. The composer, also, has some rights in the case. The conductor's problem is the tempo, as orchestral leaders who have lost sleep and beat their heads against the wall in trying to discover the precise pace needed to reveal the true quality of a composition will testify. But the tempo isn't exactly the conductor's possession. The music cannot be deprived of

its right to a particular tempo with any fortunate results for either
the art or the bungling interpreter.

This is a moment when the critic often speaks up, and we maintain stoutly that the critic has all sorts of rights that the hi-jackers
of the critics want to deny him. By heaven, he shall speak, and he
will! "Let the public be the judge," was another of the Mayor's
remarks. Well, who can help that, and who wants to? Not us; not,
we are sure, the Mayor. The public is invariably, in the last resort,
the judge, with time as the ultimate arbiter where questions of lasting importance are concerned. Only, the public itself is rather in
the habit of calling in the experts—men with at least a measure of
knowledge of and perspective on the subject in hand—before clamp-
ing down upon its own conclusions. On the whole, it's a good idea.

In the first place, the critic has documentary evidence for his
opinions. A composer indicates a tempo in his score, more or less
precisely—with increasing care and precision, as a matter of fact, as
the centuries roll by. This is in part due to modern mechanical invention. Not only can the composer provide the general directions
for a tempo as being fast, or moderately fast, or rather slow, or very
slow: he has now, and has had for a long time, that instrument
which accurately ticks off time units and by means of which he may
indicate by simply comprehensible formulas the precise rate at
which he wants his music to move. We mean the metronome, and
the metronomic indications of tempo found in most modern scores.
Critics have some reliable data on this subject. There can be differences more tangible than those of temperament or purely personal opinion upon it. There are definite bases for judgment and
comparison of tempos, though not so definite as to constitute any
final court of appeal.

But here is the strange thing: that so many casual listeners or
readers about music apparently fail to realize the overwhelming
importance of the question of tempo. You would think that a critic's
fuss about a tempo was a mere bit of academism; that it didn't matter particularly one way or the other; that if the music sounded well
enough to make a good harmonious noise and gratify the ears of
those who didn't even know it, the mere detail of a tempo could be
safely left to the dunces of the dictionaries.

Whereas, of course, the tempo is the very life and soul of the
music, being almost its entire secret. Find the right tempo and, if
you are musical at all, you can hardly miss the true import and the

essential beauty of the composition. "The whole duty of a conductor," says Wagner in the essay on conducting, "is comprised in
his ability always to indicate the right tempo. His choice of tempi
will show whether he understands the piece or not." And he adds
the inevitable corollary: "With good players, again, the true tempo
induces correct phrasing and expression, and conversely, with a
conductor, the idea of appropriate phrasing and expression will
induce the conception of the true tempo."

In other words, the two things, the pace and the expressive elements of the music, are inseparable. Wagner heard Habaneck conduct Beethoven's symphonies with the orchestra of the Conservatoire in Paris, performances then unequaled in Germany. Wagner
observed that the orchestra "sang" the symphony, and that "the
possibility of its being well sung implies that the true tempo has
been found"; and that "our conductors frequently fail to find the
true tempo because they are ignorant of singing." The word
melos, of classic derivation, was used by Wagner to imply the
melodic core of the music—its really essential being—and he avers
again: "The right comprehension of the Melos is the sole guide to
the right tempo; these two qualities are inseparable, and the one
implies and qualifies the other."

In other words, there are right tempos and there are wrong
tempos, and the decision as to the right tempo is almost the final
one, where the power of the interpretation is concerned.

But let it not be supposed that the truth of a tempo is a matter
that can be arbitrarily determined. It is a truth, but a truth no more
absolute than any other; one never to be conclusively stated by
critic or conductor either; a center if you like, but one about which
there is an eternal and bewildering play of relativities. Tempo
changes with generations as with men. In Bach's time slow tempos
were not as slow, and fast tempos not as fast as they are today. Instruments didn't permit of so much variety in tempo. Everything
moved more deliberately, but there is no doubt that dance movements which are for us jolly, sturdy, and rather contented had the
effect at the time of delirious speed, and communicated the wild
reactions of a modern presto. Did Habaneck, whom Wagner so admired, take the scherzo of Beethoven's Seventh Symphony at the
rate our orchestras and conductors take it today? Unlikely. A conductor's tempo, unconsciously, will be different on different days
in different hours. So will an orchestra's. A tempo fully fast enough

when the orchestra is rested at a morning rehearsal may be a trifle slow to get the same musical communication at the concert the following afternoon. Nikisch, one of the greatest of conductors, was fully aware of this and of the manner in which the physical and the immaterial interpenetrate in an interpretation by artists. He said that his first horn, who responded to a brisk beat with a full and brilliant tone at one time, could accomplish the same effect only with a slower beat at another. And Nikisch spoke of his need, when there was to be glorious music-making, of getting into rapport, via tempo, not only with composer but orchestra; of making the orchestra "breathe" with the music, of feeling and evoking the "respiration" of the orchestra—matters fundamentally of tempo. Then what of the composition? The same masterpiece can have different meanings, which are largely dependent upon, or bound up with, the chosen tempo. The tempo, at least, must appear to have its own integrated, irrefutable logic. That logic may be a different logic at the hands of different interpreters.

Concede all this, yet consider how irritating it would be to hear a Sousa march played a third too fast, and then ask yourself whether tempo matters throughout an opera of Wagner, or the Fourth Symphony of Sibelius, or *L'Après-midi d'un faune* of Debussy. There is no end to the problem, especially if the conductor be himself a man of introspection, supersensitiveness, imagination. The music must have its true pulse, its winged flight, its points of repose, its inevitability in denouement. The tempo must be the common denominator between the composer, the conductor, the orchestra, the audience that listens.

The moment has come to call the music into being, therefore to re-create it. Maybe at the very last second, by a sudden impulse, the conductor will alter his beat by an infinitesimal fraction and the thing that wasn't right, that seemed as though it never would or could be right, solves, and the music soars and triumphs. The audience applauds. It would perhaps have applauded anyway. What will the critics say tomorrow? It doesn't matter. Nothing matters, because he knows now, deep in his soul, that for once *he found the tempo*. No power in hell below or heaven above can take that from him. Once truth unveiled her face. The beat came from his heart. The stars swung to his baton. He's lived for an hour, when it was given him to know what music means.

There's no way out of it. If we really love music, and think in its terms, we'll be eternally fussing about tempo.

AUGUST 21, 1938

===

On Barring Applause

"What have I done? I thought I had made some music.
Are they mad?"

AT THE last but one of the Boston Symphony performances at the Berkshire Symphonic Festival a situation arose which is frequent today at orchestra concerts, but nonetheless deplorable for that. We mean the ridiculous banning and absence of applause between the movements of symphonies.

This modern form of snobbery has gained widespread support in late seasons. A symphonic movement may be never so brilliant and exciting; it may come to an end with a finality that concludes a mood as well as a musical development in a most emphatic and unmistakable manner: the audience is *not* to applaud.

It is not to applaud, although it is perfectly clear that the movement has come to an end, with no indication, explicit or implicit, that the following movement may have relation to what has been heard, either in thematic substance or expressive intention. Therefore the conductor does not turn to bow. The audience rustles for a moment uncomfortably, twists about, cranes its collective neck, whispers, or whatnot, to fill in a gap and relieve a tension which is felt by everybody and has no business to be there.

The musical hiatus would normally be filled by the applause. The audience would have had the opportunity to release the emotion and enthusiasm that the music engendered, which was precisely what the composer intended, and by which the performers as well as listeners would have benefited. Then, with the relief and the relaxation afforded by those normal processes, the listeners would have composed themselves anew and the orchestra addressed itself with renewed mind to its task. But no! This would not be the proper way for an audience highly educated in symphonies, and in dead earnest to absorb some more culture of the same sort, to behave.

The symphony was Tchaikovsky's *"Pathétique."* Its third movement is one of the wildest and most fantastical in the literature of the art. From the mysterious opening till the end the great and terrible march gathers momentum and power, until it concludes with the earth-shaking descent, with roaring brass and pounding drums, to the final chord in the low registers of the instruments.

On this particular occasion Dr. Koussevitzky was not able completely to stifle the applause. Few conductors can, in this place. Part of the audience broke loose, but almost as quickly subsided. The conductor made a gesture of command, paused and mopped his face, collected himself for a moment, then began the last movement of the symphony.

Now that movement is a dirge, slow, somber, elegiac, music of a momental resignation and despair. The dirge came to an end, dying away till the softest of pianissimos of basses and cellos had faded into complete silence. No one wanted to applaud then, and no one should have. But it was the end of the symphony, therefore time to applaud. The audience, still under the spell of Tchaikovsky's matchless threnody, was silent for some seconds, then began to demonstrate.

The manner in which the applause gathered strength was no doubt satisfactory to the conductor. Some may have considered it an instance of the effect of his exceptional interpretive powers. But applause at the end of the *Symphonie "pathétique"* can constitute shallowness and vandalism, while applause after the march movement is the normal, sincere, unaffected response to the work. Why should a conductor thus get directly between the audience and the music, as if it were his music and not theirs, and his the responsibility of dictating an audience's response?

Let not these remarks be constituted as a criticism of Dr. Koussevitzky's personal actions or motives toward his art. There is before the public no more zealous interpreter or champion of music. It is against the meretricious custom that protest is made. Today all the conductors do it—Toscanini, Stokowski, Klemperer, and the small fish as well as the leviathans of the baton likewise. But what nonsense!

How anti-musical it is! Snobbism *in excelsis!* An unnatural and sterile exhibition in the name of high art! The movement that should arouse frantic excitement is hearkened to as if it were the funeral of a statesman, where everyone should wear black and walk with muffled tread. The great dirge, one of the noblest and most poignant of lamentations, is thus vulgarized and desecrated where an audience, if it really meant what it did, would depart in silence, deep in thought.

On the other hand, there are symphonies which have musical as well as emotional connection between movements, where there is no pardon for applause. The pains Mendelssohn used at the end of the first movement of the Violin Concerto to prevent the interruption of applause by the sustained tone which connects it with the following movement is well known and observed by discriminating violinists.

It is an elementary device. Symphonists of the romantic or modern period go much farther. The cyclic symphonic form relates separate movements by recurrent themes; or it telescopes two movements into one, like Franck in the middle movement of his Symphony in D minor; or it connects movements by musical bridgework.

There is a subtler connection than that between the slow movement and scherzo of Schumann's "Spring" Symphony, which Dr. Koussevitzky performed at his last Berkshire concert. The first movement is brilliant and complete in itself. The slow movement ends otherwise. Its apparent conclusion comes with a half-cadence, giving the intentional effect of incompleteness, as it ceases with the dominant chord of the key in which the next movement is to begin, suspended, as it were, in the air. This is one of the loveliest places in the symphony—the tender reverie, the unanswered question that finds its only possible completion in the square-toed vigor of the ensuing scherzo, which thus furnishes the real reply. At this point there is a pause, indicated by the composer, in the score, which by Dr. Koussevitzky was fittingly observed. But we maintain that the composer's intention was not followed at all after the first movement, so gay, so buoyant and lyrical, and ablaze with the glory and the shouting trumpets of spring. The last exuberant chord crashed from the orchestra. Again the audience broke out, but was even more quickly snubbed than at the previous Tchaikovsky performance. A warning gesture from the leader; a frightened relapse into silence, and more furtive whispering and glancing about till the

violins took up the song of the slow movement. Both movements of
the Schumann symphony were thus treated in the same undiscriminating manner, so that a measure of the delicate and intimate effect
that Schumann wanted in the middle but not at the beginning of
his score was lost, as well as a measure of the contrast of mood that
he wished to emphasize.

It is not good. It does not speak well for the genuineness and
thoughtfulness of many who profess to love music and desire to
serve it. Does anyone really think that Haydn, when he composed
a symphony, for Esterházy or for Salomon in London, didn't intend
his audience to applaud? Quite obviously he did. Quite obviously
most of eighteenth- and nineteenth-century music was created with
an eye, or a deep instinct, for time value and the reactions we call
applause. Music is composed for people. People are not assembled
merely to observe a musical ritual. But a conductor rules otherwise. So the audience behaves like the well-trained flunkey that it
is in the interpreter's presence. But if Beethoven were there he
might be dismayed. He might think that his music did not contain
the freedom and the overflowing wine of life that he thought he
had poured into its measures. And think of poor Mozart! He used
to exult when he hit it off with an audience or a friend. He had
not false pride. He liked to give people beauty and joy. How de-
pressed that child of heaven would be if he had the "Jupiter" Symphony played and watched the careful, attentive, yet sepulchral be-
havior of those who listened. He would have said: "What have I
done? I thought I had made some music. Are they mad, or have I
no genius?"

There are situations where no applause should be permitted, and
most conductors know what they are. But why should not a little
common sense, a little choice, a little ordinarily good taste be substituted for the pretentious decorum with which it is ordained that
all of us should behave, taking off not only our hat but our shoes
in the Presence which seems to frighten us so much—that of Art?

Toscanini Introduces a Young American
on an NBC Symphony Program

"Mr. Barber had reason for thankfulness."

THE audience assembled last night for the Toscanini concert of the NBC Symphony Orchestra felt the same eagerness and listened and applauded with the same intensity which is customary in this series of events. There was the same almost laughable silence and solemnity as the orchestra ceased tuning and the gathering waited for seconds for the conductor to step silently through the door that opens on the stage. And there was the same highly privileged sensation of listening to performances which had almost the clarity and purity of chamber music, and, finally, of hearing some interesting new works.

Two works by Samuel Barber, the young American composer, twenty-eight years old, were performed for the first time anywhere. They are an *Adagio for Strings* and an *Essay for Orchestra*. It goes without saying that Toscanini conducted these scores as if his reputation rested upon the results. He does that with whatever he undertakes.

Mr. Barber had reason for thankfulness for a *première* under such leadership. And the music proved eminently worth playing. The *Adagio* for the strings, particularly, is the work of a young musician of true talent, rapidly increasing skill, and, one would infer, capacity for self-criticism. It is not pretentious music. Its author does not pose and posture in his score. He writes with a definite purpose, a clear objective, and a sense of structure.

A long line, in the *Adagio*, is well sustained. There is an arch of melody and form. The composition is most simple at the climaxes, when it develops that the simplest chord, or figure, is the one most significant. That is because we have here honest music, by a musician not striving for pretentious effect, not behaving as a writer would who, having a clear, short, popular word handy for his purpose, got the dictionary and fished out a long one.

This is the product of a musically creative nature, and an earnest student who leaves nothing undone to achieve something as perfect in mass and detail as his craftsmanship permits. A young man who has so genuine a talent and purpose should go far.

The *Essay for Orchestra*, modestly named, is well integrated, with clear instrumentation, and with development of the ideas that unifies the music in spite of changes of tempo and marked contrasts of orchestration. The *Adagio* impressed this chronicler, at the first hearing, as the better composition of the two, but it would be premature to put this down as a definite conclusion, and it is a matter of secondary importance. Of the first importance is the fact of a composer who is attempting no more than he can do, and doing that genuinely, and well.

The program opened with a pleasant suite, *The Flute of San Souci*. Admirably performed, the music entertained.

The audience was fascinated by Debussy's *Ibéria*, by the performance as well as by the extraordinary music. When Mr. Toscanini interprets Debussy he does so very cleanly, with the finest taste and the most scrupulous observance of artistic detail. No particle of beauty escapes him, and Debussy, though an impressionist, can stand microscopic examination. Analyze his apparently vaporous art, with all its sonorous color and illusion, and you find underneath the glamorous surface the most definite lines, the utmost economy and cunning in the technical manipulation of material.

It is probable that Mr. Toscanini, with his Latin feeling for form, loves to discover this structure in Debussy and to proclaim it. Proclaim it he does, always in memorable fashion. Nevertheless, in doing so he loses, for one listener, some of the poetry and exuberant life of the music. The wonders of the scoring of this work are almost unending. We know of little else in any period of composition when so much that is important, though unobtrusive, happens in five minutes. In some ways this is the most carefully fabricated of all the Debussy compositions, but this is not to be known to the listener. It is what the music says, and not how it is made, that counts. On this occasion the music appeared to us not only microscopic, but episodic. Colors stood out against each other, rather than mingling; it was the same with many of the interlacing rhythms. They were carefully unlaced, and we doubt that the composer meant them to be. Great playing? Yes. Orchestral virtuosity and warm and passionate inflections of each fragment of song imbedded in the score—yes. But not the completely revealing Debussy interpretation.

The concert ended with the Dvořák *New World Symphony*. Coupling its appearance on the Toscanini programs with that of the Tchaikovsky *Pathétique* on the Saturday preceding, it looks as though Mr. Toscanini were meeting to some extent the popular taste, which includes both these works among its favorites.

As for the virtuoso performance, the *New World Symphony* last night was rubbed bright and clean. Indeed, there were places to which the conductor gave an almost suspicious newness. With force, brilliancy, and beautiful mezzotints of sound in the slow movement, the symphony made its wonted appeal. Whether it is "New World" or not may be posed as a question for academic argument. Or whether it is purely the musical expression of a homesick Czech written here out of nostalgia for the homeland is a matter that also can be begged.

In the lovely symphony, as usual, Toscanini promptly found some hitherto unnoticed details of instrumentation. For the rest, he followed his convictions as usual. He performed the symphony, as nearly as one person can, as it was written. In this unusual guise the work was welcomed back to the repertory with open arms.

NOVEMBER 20, 1938

═══

Copland on a Boston Program with Beethoven and Brahms

"It is a brilliant adventure."

THE place that Serge Koussevitzky and the Boston Orchestra hold in the esteem of the New York public was shown again yesterday afternoon by the audience which packed Carnegie Hall and testified after each performance its enthusiasm. As is customary at these concerts, there was no soloist. None is required. In fact, in most cases at these concerts a soloist would be an intrusion. For the orchestra, when Koussevitzky and his men make music, is itself the supreme soloist.

A novelty by Aaron Copland, *El Salón México*, was performed for the first time in this city on this occasion. The music was suggested to Mr. Copland in the course of a visit that he made to Mexico six years ago. He heard the players and watched the dancers in a popular resort in Mexico City, and he has transcribed his impression.

In a program note Mr. Copland is careful to state that he has not attempted to portray the Mexico of ancient civilization or modern revolution. Neither is this a tone picture of the Mexican land. It is Mexican in the same sense, presumably, that a Frenchman's music would be American if he had gone to the Casino in Harlem and later composed about it on the basis of what he heard there, or, rather, the sort of music that he heard there. For Mr. Copland does not take his themes from a sketchbook wherein they were noted down as he listened. He has taken them from two Mexican collections of popular melodies, as Chabrier wove his *España* from known folk melodies of Spain.

This music is ingeniously orchestrated, with the aid of certain percussion instruments which are exotic and with suggestive effects which bestow color and twang. The harmonization does not seek for strangeness, yet avoids the conventional and pursues a course dictated by the nature of the themes.

It is a brilliant adventure in a certain idiom. There is always the danger, where many themes are employed and especially when they are dance themes of a clearly defined length and rhythmical physiognomy, of a composition that will be patchwork. This danger is met competently by the composer because the motives are made to cohere and, in the process of development, to accumulate—at least technically. The work was very well received. After Dr. Koussevitzky had brought Mr. Copland to the stage, the latter returned by himself to acknowledge the welcome of the audience.

With the exception of this work—and, for the writer, rather regrettably—the program was confined to classics of an order eminently safe and sane. This is not to slight the beauty and delight of Beethoven's Second Symphony and Brahms's Fourth. But most of the orchestral programs given in the city follow the beaten track, whereas in former seasons one could always look to the orchestra from Boston to let us know what many contemporaneous composers were doing and, in a majority of cases, to produce some worthwhile novelties. No doubt for some in the audience the present type of Koussevitzky program is comforting. Yet we are supposed to be a public curious and receptive to new ideas.

The performance of the Second Symphony was ravishing for its finish and for the beautiful blend of the sonorities. Though early Beethoven, it is a perfect masterpiece, and it was received with an enthusiasm that belied its years. For it is as fresh today as the day it was born. However, the performance tended overmuch to the discreet. Doubtless Dr. Koussevitzky views this early symphony of Beethoven as pure classicism—as Beethoven still the dutiful heir of Haydn and Mozart. The conductor evidently intended to keep it to that scale of sonorous values.

But there is much in this score which is revolutionary, of an explosive force, and a jocosity particularly Beethoven's. It was in the last movement, principally, that this quality found expression yesterday. As a whole, we heard a Beethoven who was somewhat on his good manners. There is impoliteness in the Second Symphony.

One might say that the whole era of the classic symphony was synthesized in the concert which began with Beethoven's Second and ended with the autumnal music which Brahms composed only a few months before his death, and which will endure as one of the supreme monuments of the tonal art.

JANUARY 15, 1939

The NBC Symphony Performs Shostakovich, Franck, and Strauss

"Nor was the symphony of the youthful Shostakovich the least arresting of the works."

THE audience of the air which listened last night to the concert given by Arturo Toscanini and the NBC Symphony Orchestra in Radio City had reason to be impressed not only by the program and its superlative interpretations but also—granted, of course, the adequate means of reception—by the beauty and richness of tone quality that were captured and conveyed. If it had been necessary, it could be said that this concert alone would suffice to prove that the days when a broadcast of a symphony was an appeal to the imagination rather than to the ear are over. The program permitted the emphasis of this achievement because of the very individual orchestral schemes of the works that were performed.

Then there were the various creative qualities of the music. The program consisted of Dmitri Shostakovich's First Symphony, two movements from César Franck's symphonic poem *Psyché*, and the dance of Salome from Richard Strauss's opera of that name. Nor was the symphony of the youthful Shostakovich the least arresting of the works played.

It is a score that really appears to owe its central inspiration to the revolutionary Russia that Shostakovich's boyhood knew. This is not because the symphony has a "program" or "story," or anything of that sort. It is an expression, we would say, of words, perhaps of visions, that the composer would never own to or explain.

It is a grim, sardonic score. Some of its pages are profoundly melancholy, not sentimental but tragic and without pity. Most of it is stark and hard in color—iron twilights and metallic brilliancies which suddenly flare from the orchestra.

The form and methods of development are of the purely classical kind. They diverge from the beaten path. There is very little waste material, though the symphony is long. It is not the work of a matured master. It has its melodramatic places and sometimes the suspicion of an attitude. For all that, the composer has something unmistakably of his own and his time to say. The tragic broodings of the orchestra, even more than his climaxes, prove it.

The more did this sardonic and fantastical music emphasize the wholly different and far more tender spirit of César Franck. It could be said of him that he was a mystic not only in religion but also when he thought of love. The music of *Psyché* is of an ineffable sensuousness and a rapturous flight possible only to this composer. His technical devices are now well known and perfectly apparent. His idiom is familiar to all who know symphonic music. Yet his expression is inimitable and irreplaceable, and none could either imitate or caricature so pure a soul. All this was conveyed with sheer inspiration and mastery by Mr. Toscanini.

By the side of it, Strauss's music was theatrical, dramatic, in its way sensual, cyclonic if you say so, but how far beneath Franck! That the dance made a very effective climax of the concert would go without saying. It displayed the power of the conductor and the technical resources of the orchestra, which it sets off like a firecracker.

But, after all, the final triumph of an interpreter is when he equals the sincerity and the genius of a great composer. Mr. Toscanini was perhaps greatest last night when he conversed with Franck.

FEBRUARY 25, 1939

The Literati and Cognoscenti Discover Charles Ives

"If snobbism was present, it was not the fault of a
ruggedly individual composer."

A CONCERT of Charles Ives's music was given last night in Town Hall by John Kirkpatrick, pianist, and Minna Hager, mezzo-soprano. The hall was packed. Literati and cognoscenti were present in larger numbers than had been witnessed since the last Town Hall concert of the League of Composers.

This knowing audience had turned out largely because of the special publicity which had followed Mr. Kirkpatrick's courageous introduction of Mr. Ives's "Concord" Sonata in the same concert hall on January 20.

If snobbism was present, it was not the fault of a ruggedly individual composer. Articles acclaiming the sonata itself and other articles recounting the strange and interesting career of the man of business and insurance who had been all his life creating highly modern scores had prepared the public for a sensation. Therefore, many people who, before it had received critical approval, would have passed by the "Concord" Sonata without the flicker of an eyelash were now present, audibly and visually to be counted among those who really understood and appreciated the singular music of Mr. Ives.

And it is singular music, music of singular ingredients and a singular point of view, music of a composer incorrigibly himself in his purpose and feeling, if not invariably free from other musical influences or able fully to express visions which obsess him. Consider the "Concord" Sonata. The titles of this sonata, written between 1911 and 1915, in four movements, are *Emerson, Hawthorne, The Alcotts,* and *Thoreau.* The sonata is described by the composer as "an attempt to present one person's impression of the spirit of transcendentalism that is associated in the minds of many with Concord, Mass., of over half a century ago."

Emerson is here conceived as "America's deepest explorer of the spiritual immensities," and this movement introduces a version of the fate theme of Beethoven's Fifth Symphony—the theme not in minor but major, emblematic of "the Godliness of spiritual courage and helpfulness." The "translation of this motive places the motive above the relentlessness of fate knocking at the door" and "toward the spiritual message of Emerson's revelations."

The motive haunts the first movement and reappears in other movements of the sonata, thus binding them together. It appears to gather force with repetitions and with various rhythmic or harmonic alterations.

Hawthorne is the Hawthorne of the "half child-like, half fairy-like phantasmal realms." This in fact is a fanciful scherzo of various moods. *The Alcotts* is the picture of "spiritual sturdiness" lying at the root of that New England town with its arching elms. *Thoreau* is the Thoreau of the Indian summers, the days and nights by Walden, the harp of the winds, the end of the day and the return of the "shadow-thought" that he dimly perceived in the morning mist; and Thoreau's "liberty in Nature, a part of herself."

This is mood-painting—transcendent moods, and sometimes common, sometimes "transcendental" figures of musical speech. The sonata is lengthy in the treatment and development of ideas, but it is not easy to be brief with so many thoughts, nor is it easy, on a first hearing of the sonata on the writer's part, to come to a definite conclusion about such music.

Some of its characteristics are evident. One very fine one is the influence of New England hymns and the tunes that the band played in the village square. The whole thing a creation spun out of a man's home memories and consciousness—not a fabric of tone to fit a model outside of himself. An American composer thus dares be himself.

The sonata is filled with interesting ideas. Its structural form will be clearer with later hearings. The stuff of a fearless man and artist is in it. Whether the expression is always felicitous, whether the work would gain by elisions and condensation is a question that also must wait. The passages which strike one the quickest are those when the musician's fancy lovingly lingers over the melodies of his childhood, and a homely and tender idea of his own wraps itself about the old tune, varies and transforms it according to the expressive need of the passage.

Something of the same origin of inspiration is encountered in the songs, of which there were two groups sung by Miss Hager, and of which a number, in response to applause that was enthusiastic throughout the evening, were repeated. The homelier the song, say we, on the average, the better. *Autumn*: the composer thinks of the autumn, her work done, the empty fields, the declining sun, the Peace of God, and his melody is very close to a church chant. *Down East* brings irresistibly the memory of *Nearer, My God, to Thee*, the Sunday morning, the chores done, the melodeon and the historic song.

Perhaps the best of all the songs is the dramatic, satirical, fantastic setting of Lindsay's verse *General William Booth Enters into Heaven*. With the songs of a lighter or more humorous character we are not so much struck. The humor is sometimes a little self-conscious and in some cases after patterns of other songs by well-known composers.

Yet none of the songs heard last night is complaisant or merely conventional. They represent a composer who thinks his own way and is not to be stirred from his course. As a consequence of this, he stands forth today an artist in his own rank and one to whom last night the public rendered homage.

Paderewski, at Seventy-eight, Embarks on His
Twentieth American Tour

*"It is not easy for one reviewer of this concert to give a
complete account of it as a musical occasion."*

ONE of the most impressive musical events this city has seen in
many years, one that stirred the pulse and tightened the throats of
those who were present, both as spectators and listeners, was the
appearance of Ignace Jan Paderewski yesterday afternoon in Studio
8-H in Radio City, when he opened his twentieth American concert tour before a visible audience of a few hundred and a radio
audience estimated at fifty million, which listened from near and
far over the continents and the oceans of the world.

The occasion had a tenseness, before Mr. Paderewski's appearance on the stage, not easy to describe.

When the man who has made history as artist, statesman, and
humanitarian, also as the possessor of one of the most glamorous
personalities before the public, stepped at last upon the stage, the
audience rose at once, applauding. It was not the racket caused by
some sensational development so much, it seemed, as the expression of the most earnest admiration and, indeed, reverence of those
present. It was known that Paderewski, in his seventy-ninth year,
had emerged only recently from a serious indisposition which must
have temporarily affected his strength, and that he was facing a
particularly strenuous test with the gallantry and high purpose of
the heart of oak that he possesses. The supposition was strengthened
by the deliberation with which the figure in the familiar black
frock coat and white Windsor tie moved to the piano, and the impression he gave, despite his kingly way, of a man husbanding every
possible physical resource for the task that lay ahead. And there
was that in the circumstance and the bearing of the man that spoke
of crisis and courage.

It is not easy for one reviewer of this concert to give a complete
account of it as a musical occasion. The reason for this is that two

273

audiences were listening, perhaps with very different reception of the sound. It is to be said here, however, that on one fundamental point, according to reports from the invisible audience reaching us as we write, both sets of hearers are agreed. It is the beauty of the tone that prevailed throughout the recital.

Mr. Paderewski struck a few chords, as an improviser might sweep his harp, and was soon engrossed in the first movement of the "Moonlight" Sonata. We had not heard him play this music with such tonal beauty and such poetical effect. He did not exaggerate emotion, but let the music speak for itself. Those who have heard him play the same piece in the screen drama *Moonlight Sonata,* which has been seen and heard over this continent, were no doubt interested to see that he took the movement a little faster yesterday than he did in the sound picture. The music lost nothing by this, but rather gained a certain unearthly quality. This remark, it should quickly be added, is not made with thought of the sentimental title of the sonata, simply styled by Beethoven *"sonata quasi fantasia"* and having nothing whatever to do with a moonlight scene. We experienced the evocation of beauty by a consummate artist at the full maturity of his thought and artistic experience.

The scherzo was played very lightly, and without as much dramatic contrast as some interpreters give it. The stormy finale achieved its effect by carefully adjusted proportions—in a word, by thought and imagination, not by speed or brawn. The scale of sonorous values was relatively discreet throughout the concert.

Mr. Paderewski, with but the shortest pause, went on, interpolating a piece not announced in the printed program—the Schubert A flat Impromptu, Opus 142. He played this exquisite music with true and adorable simplicity, sometimes adopting the pedal rather than a clinging finger touch to connect tones, and not always with impeccable execution of rapid passages of figuration. But the thought and the sound in which its expression was couched were utterly those of poor, tender, wistful, dreaming Schubert. It may be added to this that only the very great can be so simple.

With the performance of the Liszt transcriptions of two Chopin songs, the *Chant polonais* and the *Maiden's Wish,* there was more tasteful treatment of musical ornaments. These were delicate values. What would Paderewski do with one of the grandest and most dramatic of all piano compositions, the lordly A flat Polonaise?

He evoked the vision of the polonaise, not as the young man who once played a similar piece to Chopin and broke a string, but probably far more in the manner in which the supersensitive and physically unrobust Chopin would play that piece and fire his hearer not the less for the physical restraints of his performance. The first sweep of the chromatic fourths, executed with a remarkable facility, established the mood and ushered in the great swinging theme. The thunderous octave passage for the left hand arrived, and it was sorely taxing, but it mounted to its climax, of which the repetition was followed by the strange introspections and effects as of "ancestral voices prophesying war," when the polonaise again gathered momentum and swept to the end. The audience applauded so stormily that Mr. Paderewski, willy-nilly, had repeatedly to rise and bow from his chair. The thrill of the performance was the thrill of the music presented with extraordinary logic of design and artistic suggestion, but also it was the thrill of the deed of a most gallant knight who right worthily had done his *devoir*.

The program as announced on the flexible white cloth came to an end with the beautiful and nostalgic piece of Paderewski—the B major melody from the set which bears the touching and appropriate title *Chants du voyageur*. This piece was written in days when Paderewski was interested in the piano only as a vehicle for his creations as a composer. It was played with the rarest poignancy, lyricism, and gradations of tone. There was a pause of silence as the last chord vibrated through the auditorium, and then the audience would not have enough.

The program stated that "if time permits, Mr. Paderewski will play encores." There was a rustle of approval as the audience recognized the first measures of his Minuet, with the coda that consists of a fanciful embellishment of the main theme.

When he rose, two small children in Polish national costume came on the stage with flowers. Somewhat bewildered, after their hero had taken each of them deferentially by the hand, they were led off the stage. In response to the persistent acclaim Mr. Paderewski, as a second encore, repeated the Minuet, and the occasion was over.

The audience dispersed slowly. There were present all sorts of music-lovers, friends, and old, so-to-speak, comrades-in-arms, who had come to listen and render respect to great art and enduring fidelities. There were members of a younger generation whose uncommon seriousness indicated that they, too, had realized the presence of something greater than themselves or the daily round; something, perhaps, holding a promise to a bewildered world that humanity which gave birth to a spirit such as Paderewski's will not let the things for which he has fought his unyielding battles—liberty and justice, honor and beauty—perish from the earth.

MAY 14, 1939

Villa-Lobos as a Nationalist Composer

*"I didn't come to study with you. I came to show you
what I have done."*

MORE than one observer of modern society has asked what is to become of the creative power of matured civilizations when the freshness of racial energy and outlook upon life has gone from them. Hardening arteries of national consciousness have more to do with present European complications and explosions than we may realize.

In past centuries recurrent processes of emergence, rise to power, and decline and fall of peoples gave place, usually by violent means, to the influx of new blood. In the process some communities matured much faster than others; some even reached, comparatively quickly, stages of decay and an exhaustion of the will to live and look forward. When this occurred national expression in art deteriorated. What of today?

As civilization becomes world-wide and international, which no human power will be able to prevent, there will be always fewer sources of fresh racial power to draw upon. What then will be the process of the creative rehabilitation of nations? We may gratefully leave the answer to profounder thinkers, with the comforting conviction that better ways will be found than those of the various exterminations of a crude past. This matter has, nevertheless, to do with certain aspects of the very interesting series of national programs of symphonic music which have been given, and indeed are still in progress, as features of the music program of the New York World's Fair.

The symphonic programs have shown the greatest originality in production by nations which are the least sophisticated and modernized today and which have the strongest percentage of the primitive to be drawn on for inspiration by their cultured composers. This is not to imply an absence of a high civilization in centers of great nations in all parts of the world. It is simply the fact that certain nations, according to their history and environment, have direct contacts with—indeed, are permeated by—a wealth of the most advanced aspects of modern intellectual thought, while others, such as Brazil, have as natural possessions an immense hinterland of race as well as territory—a source of color, energy, forces which can be very productive of emotion and beauty. This material may be treasure beyond calculation for the native composer.

A case in point is that of the Brazilian Villa-Lobos. His whole course as a composer, and the extraordinary plenteousness and inequality of his creations, are strikingly indicative of ancestry, environment, and powerful individual genius. He is not only enormously creative, he is still naïve, a thing which is of exceptional importance in the creative field. When the artist can never lose his self-consciousness, when he cannot completely abandon self-examination because of an obsessing wonder before the fathomless miracle of the life that envelops him, his product is likely, if not certain, to become vitiated. Some of the music of Villa-Lobos is as primitive as Caliban. At the same time, he has not escaped, and did not wish to escape, the marvel of the European tonal art, so that Bach is to him a great and perhaps partly incomprehensible god, whom he worships and to whom he offers his own form of homage in his incredible *Bachiana* suites.

He is also especially aware of the principal strains of Brazilian folk music—those which arise from Portuguese, Indian, and native Brazilian sources. All these elements are discovered in the curious and arresting quality of his music.

He is a composer whom it is desirable to have the opportunity of studying thoroughly—a thing not now possible, for the number of his works is legion, and a great number of them are still unpublished. Even the four compositions variously scored for orchestra, orchestra and solo voice, and orchestra and chorus, which Mr. Burle

Marx placed upon the Brazilian programs, provide astonishing variety, naïveté, and originality of manifestation. What shall one say of these?

Chôros No. 8 is a great symphonic poem, savage and exotic, for full modern orchestra, with two pianos and Brazilian instruments of percussion that can be heard today wherever native musicians congregate. It is one of the most difficult scores to perform that we have seen in recent years. It is full to overflowing of ideas, most of them in dance rhythms. It is so gorgeous, wild, and rhythmically involved in its scoring that in places too many ideas cover each other up. And there are superfluities.

One cannot come to an opinion of this score at a first hearing—whether it is music only partly articulate in itself, or whether repeated hearings would make its whole course crystal clear to the sympathetic listener. A first impression is of something tremendous and only partially explicit; and of harmonies very harsh in places, put down with a frankness and conviction that make one think of some aspect of tumultuous, oppressive, mysterious nature. One could call this almost a *Sacre du printemps* of the Amazon forest! The piece astonished and, not unnaturally, perplexed some and annoyed others who heard it. It is one of the scores which will not subside in the memory, and which leave behind them an intense wish for further acquaintance. Yet it is probable that this is not a one-hundred-per-cent clear and complete expression on the part of the composer.

Now, on the same program was a soprano aria from the Fifth *Bachiana* Suite. Villa-Lobos, in a printed preface to these *Bachiana*, remarks that Bach is the most universal of geniuses; that his music reflects all life; that all life, in itself, can find a reflection in Bach's conception of music. Therefore, in his *Bachiana* suites, Villa-Lobos has looked to Bach as to an all-father. He has found it possible to express his own relation and that of the art of his people to this great master, this tonal mirror of the universe, by compositions which shall synthesize folk melody and his own musical thought in an individual and stylized expression.

And so with the "aria" from *Bachiana* No. 5, which Miss Bidú Sayão sang. It is an air quite beautifully chiseled, in its first part, after the character of the classic Bach line, with a contrasting section quite far from Bach, being passionate in mood and manner, and set to a text of the most lyric and extravagant sort. The semiclassical curve of the first part of the aria is accompanied pizzicato by the lower strings, making one think of a guitar. The principal melody, first intoned on a vowel and at last hummed in a reminiscent and introspective way, had a beauty of its own, and of an unexpected kind.

Further on the same program was another *Bachiana* movement. Its name? *The Little Train,* or *Tiny Train.* Or let us say the Toonerville trolley—run by steam—which carries berry-pickers and other hillmen, and pants and jangles from town to town, its whistle resounding o'er height and valley, in the province of São Paulo. This piece was written irrespectively of the suite into which, when it had been orchestrated, it was inserted. In the suite it is called a "toccata"—as good an excuse as any for its inclusion in a group of allegedly "Bachian" pieces. The toccata figure is supplied, of course, by the rhythm of the imaginary wheels of the train—as it is supplied, in a much more sophisticated and also masterly way, in the chef-d'oeuvre of Honegger, *Pacific 231,* which concluded the Swiss program, given under Messrs. Gans and Schelling on a later evening, in Carnegie Hall, also as part of the Fair music season. *The Little Train,* for all its simplicity and naïveté, is laughably clear, natural, felicitous in tonal device. Villa-Lobos actually wrote it in an hour, bumping over the rails, and played it that evening, with his wife, a cellist, in the original form for cello and piano. *Hommage à* Bach!

We come to his *Chôros* No. 10, for full chorus and orchestra. It is a perfect beauty, and fascinating in its color, native eloquence, and evocative power. It is sung, in large part, over an Indian chant of the savage and roughly rhythmical sort. The text discourses of the aching heart, the burning sun, the cross of suffering. It implores the singing birds to intercede with God for that heart, and in the orchestra is such a warm and ecstatic trilling and piping as nobody else ever thought of in terms of instruments. It is, and is not, imitation. It is rather an impression inseparable from the thought and the word. The instrumental combination includes high wind instruments, as, of course, flageolet tones of the cellos, and related devices. It vividly communicates the sensation of something tropical, natural, impassioned, and ten thousand miles from a modern or urban civilization. So, one would say, a savage would sing, with all his heart, with no difficulty in finding a melody or accompanying device to convey his response to the natural world about him and his complete unconsciousness in communing with its god. To this fundamental naïveté and spontaneousness in the present instances may be added an admirable technical address, and a form consummately adapted to the expressive purpose.

Mr. Marx tells us that when Villa-Lobos went to Paris he was perhaps arrogantly, but rather refreshingly independent of certain supercilious musicians of that city. They, it appears, assumed that he had come to the French capital to learn composition. "But," he said, "I didn't come to study with you. I came to show you what I have done." He has had that attitude, it seems, for better or worse. The policy has its virtues and its dangers, but it is certainly superior to, and reveals far more creative integrity than, that of many a gifted composer overawed by French traditions and esthetic who took to imitating Parisian models of composition and lost his own creative birthright in the process. Here, whatever he does, is a composer of genius, integrated in his spirit, fearless, with that to say which is his own, and hence significant of natural art.

NOVEMBER 24, 1939

Koussevitzky Conducts an All-American Program

Piston—Foote—R. Thompson—Harris

Dr. Koussevitzky and the Boston Symphony Orchestra gave a program consisting entirely of American music at the opening concert of their New York season last night in Carnegie Hall.

To the best of the writer's recollection, this is the first time that a leading orchestra of the country has devoted two of its subscription concerts exclusively to symphonic works by native composers. Dr. Koussevitzky believes that Americans have produced enough music and to spare that is worthy of such exploitation. He himself has been exceptionally curious as to the product, and encouraging to American creative musicians, from the time of his arrival in this country fifteen years ago.

In fact, the entire program of yesterday evening consisted of works that the Boston Symphony Orchestra had already played at various concerts, although on the previous occasions they had been interspersed with European scores. These two programs of American music—that of last night and that which will be played tomorrow afternoon—represent a selection from one hundred and twenty-six compositions by forty-seven American composers which Dr. Koussevitzky has performed during his tenure of office at the head of the Boston Symphony.

It is a pleasure to record, before statements of personal opinions of the music heard last night, that Carnegie Hall was packed for this occasion with a very brilliant and representative audience, and that each performance was long and vigorously applauded. How much of this applause proceeded from the sympathy of the audience for the native sons, and how much was induced by playing so finished in technique and so glorious in its euphony and richness of color that much poorer music would have sounded with deceptive magnificence, could be matters for debate. In any event, the occasion constituted a public welcome and an artistic triumph for the courageous step taken in the composition of the program.

This program consisted of Arthur Foote's E major Suite for string orchestra; Walter Piston's Concertino for piano and orchestra, with Jesús Sanromá as soloist; Roy Harris's Third Symphony; and Randall Thompson's Second Symphony. The music was full of interesting and suggestive contrasts. Each work was unlike the others, in technique, style, approach, and development of subject matter. And each was well written, and some put down with sheer virtuosity—above all, in this respect, the Concertino of Mr. Piston.

This might not have been the case twenty-five years ago in this country. Certainly, at that time, no program which presented one American composer no longer living and three in their creative prime would have demonstrated such craftsmanship and thorough acquaintance with the modern devices of the art. There were some pages, in different places, not as strong as others. But in no case was there technical ineptitude or amateurish orchestration. This program alone would have demonstrated that the day is past when any American composer need be told that he doesn't know his business.

This is important: not only for the present, but even more important for the future, because it means that at last our composers have sharpened their weapons and learned how to use their tools.

However, the leading question is yet to be considered. Admitted all the highly creditable facts just cited, what had the composers to say?

The Foote suite is charming, not highly original; in the first movement, redolent of Schumann; in the second, the pizzicato, inescapably reminiscent of a certain familiar symphonic movement of Tchaikovsky, yet entertaining, written with sincerity, refinement, and grace in the style of an earlier day; and, in the case of the final fugue—certainly the best of the three movements—constructed with genuine skill and created with musical passion. It is music. It grows and accumulates and sweeps to a climax—the work of a true maker of beautiful sounds who long since won the high respect bestowed upon him in his lifetime and now accorded his memory.

Came the exhilarating technique and the nervous flight of Mr. Piston's highly modern concertino. It is a work remarkably made, reminding one in some pages of Hindemith. It is not all polytonal counterpoint either. The middle part has a Hindemithian shadow, a dark and brooding quality, with much color, some melodic substance, but little actual invention.

Then the fast movement returns and there is an electrical conclusion. The thing is that this music remains dry, juiceless, in a sense academic; for you do not have to be somnolent to be academic, or even old-fashioned. This very expert music of Mr. Piston often ticks, and one feels a mild curiosity to take apart the clockwork. But the curiosity is only mild. There is more music, in this writer's belief, in other scores of Mr. Piston. The orchestral performance was of the finest; the piano part was played with soundest musicianship and fingers of quicksilver by Mr. Sanromá. As virtuoso and musician he would have deserved anywhere the homage he received.

Mr. Harris's symphony is a striking advance, according to last night's impression, over his previous work in the same form, and, indeed, over his other instrumental compositions that we have heard. It is much clearer, stripped to simplicities, shaped with great care. The opening is striking in the breadth, the fashioning, and the spacious intervals of the main theme, not in itself distinguished or fascinating but projected with a fine starkness, yet suppleness of line, against a meager tonal background. Some might say that the heroic bare hills and plains of parts of America could have inspired that. Others might discover in it more direct relationship to plainchant, of which Mr. Harris has made an earnest study in recent years. This introduction, however, demands much to complete it, and that "much" is not wholly forthcoming.

There is a lighter passage of some length, with persistent waving figures for the strings, and short singing phrases put over them. But, while the sonorous effect is pleasing, the passage does not impress the listener as being more than a bridge for connecting two pieces. A passage that comes considerably later, an ostinato over a drum beat, is the most immediately effective passage in the symphony. The final part falls short because it does not really get anywhere. A short and explosive motto theme hurls out from brass instruments; it twists and turns about, in and on itself. Can one say that here, either, is a genuine musical fruition?

For us there is the spectacle of a highly encouraging advance over Mr. Harris's earlier symphony; of a work, written in one movement, but which, essentially, seemed almost to drop apart into an introduction and a three-section structure, which seems divided in parts none too well fitted together. Or, on paper, they may fit. But the eye is not the ear.

Mr. Thompson's symphony is commendable for its unaffected and spontaneous ease of manner, its real melodic content, its lack of portentousness. There is much in it that is Negroid, as for instance the opening theme: the "blues" song of the middle movement, so short, as though it feared to attempt development. One must admit that the scherzo is mostly a rhythmic figure which keeps repeating while the listener says: "Good boy; but, now that you've got the preliminaries out of the way, what's your theme?" That theme does not materialize. It may be remarked that this would not be the first scherzo to hurry along without any real theme except a certain rhythmic profile.

The best movement is surely the finale, the glorification of the singing theme, its alternation with other matter, and the peroration, which delighted the audience. It is a symphony which is slight of material, slight in other dimensions, but melodic, expressive, attempting no more than its nature justifies, expressing high spirits, sentimentality, zest. The ideas are mostly short-breathed. Sequences, as also in another way by Mr. Harris, are overworked, etc. But a symphony by a real musician, palpably an American, with an entertaining style.

The concert was rewarding, and not only to the composers, most of them present and called in turn to the platform to acknowledge the applause.

Stravinsky, Sanromá, and Koussevitzky Score a Sensation

"Prince of Fiddlesticks!"

THE sensation of the concert given by Dr. Serge Koussevitzky and the Boston Symphony Orchestra yesterday afternoon in Carnegie Hall was the performance, with Jesús Sanromá as soloist, of Stravinsky's *Capriccio* for piano and orchestra. This took place in the presence of the composer, who, immensely acclaimed, first bowed from a box and then came on the stage with the conductor and the pianist. Mr. Stravinsky had reason for self-congratulation, as the audience had occasion to rejoice in an electrical accomplishment.

In fact, and in friendship, one is moved to urge Mr. Stravinsky always to allow Dr. Koussevitzky to conduct his music. It can make an immense difference! What the orchestra, the conductor, the pianist did with the composition yesterday was hardly short of the uncanny, in both technical and interpretive aspects. In fact, the performance had such sensitiveness and zest, such humor and nuance and thrust, that it took on a completely creative character. In no small measure the performance was the music, and this is said without desire to be invidious, since the Capriccio is certainly one of the most spontaneous and witty compositions of Stravinsky's later period.

It was first performed here by the same artists as yesterday, on February 7, 1931. To the loss of this writer, the date conflicted with that of the *première* of an American opera, Deems Taylor's *Peter Ibbetson,* which took place that afternoon, and so the music went, for the time, unknown to him.

It makes a very amusing piece. In explaining the composition Mr. Stravinsky raised his eyeballs to the skies, literally speaking, and murmured that in writing the piece he found his thoughts dominated by "that prince of music, Carl Maria von Weber, whose genius admirably lent itself to this manner. Alas! no one thought of calling him a prince in his lifetime." One is tempted to exclaim "Prince of Fiddlesticks!" and to remark that we know Weber only by such a petty title as composer of *Freischütz*. Mr. Stravinsky might just as well, and quite possibly would, just as seriously, with tongue in cheek, have said that he was going in for Gounod, Bizet, or Verdi. He would have written just the same music in these cases. An influence far more obvious in the score is that of Maurice Ravel, especially in the slow movement. And as certain peppery, sardonic dissonances crackle from the orchestra one thinks of a word picture, by a colleague, of Stravinsky and Ravel seated side by side before a piano, Ravel playing some queer chords, Stravinsky pushing him aside to play still queerer ones. This concerto is like that—waggish, impudent, sophisticated, and extremely diverting.

You asked yourself, as this playful chicanery flew back and forth from conductor to orchestra and soloist, and from instrument to instrument, how they could do it. By what consummate skill or inspired tomfoolery can modern musicians so amazingly disport and complement each other? The rabbit leaps into the hat, and—the hat is empty. A sudden and terrifying hubbub—the bewildered listener turns around—there's nothing there except some insouciant little double notes, very sweet, very shy, being tossed off as innocently as nobody's business by Mr. Sanromá. He isn't even looking your way, but flourishing his paws and blandly regarding the conductor, with whom he is playing catch!

It was a sort of lively conversation between a group of very clever people with passwords of their own, only half intelligible to fascinated onlookers, all of it so quick, so mercurial, that everyone else was fat-witted by comparison.

It may be said that in music of this sort Koussevitzky, the orchestra, Sanromá are really unique. Very much of the secret of this species of composition will be lost when they have scattered or ceased to co-operate.

As for Mr. Sanromá, he has grown, by an industry and talent as remarkable as his modesty, from a student of a few years ago to a modern pianist whose performance yesterday could be equaled by a very few and outrivaled by no one. It is also to be said that as he has matured, so also has his tone become more many-colored and more mellow. His strength yesterday was equal to everything that the score and the orchestra required, yet not a tone was forced. He played the music joyously and with the confidence of complete mastery. Every rhythmical problem—and there are some rhythms which in themselves would justify the word "capriccio"—found him

on the spot, on the split second, sure as a cat that lands on its feet
however you throw him into the air. And what a good time he had
of it!

It was all sportive and diverting beyond compare. It is no wonder
that after this *jeu d'esprit* the audience went wild; that the three
fellow creators, the composer, the conductor, the pianist, had to
come back again and again in response to the applause.

It was a rare concert, the more refreshing after the curiously dull
one of the preceding Thursday. The symphony was Mozart's, the
one in C major which Köchel numbers 338. Less celebrated, far
less pretentious than such a work as the "Jupiter" in the same key,
it is a glowing, singing, pulsing little masterpiece, and was played
in the tradition, with abounding vitality and luminousness of tone.

The concert ended with Brahms's Second Symphony, a work in
which Koussevitzky has always been fortunate, but in which he outdid himself for breadth, poetry, virility of spirit. In fact, a lesser
performance, great though the music is, would have paled before
the snap and glitter of the Stravinsky reading. This was a notable
climax.

A Great New Violetta, A Great Old Germont

New Meanings in *La Traviata*

THE performance of two artists, one a newcomer this season and
the other a veteran who returned to the company after an absence
of years, and a performance of exceptional animation and gusto
produced the best-interpreted *Traviata* that has been offered the
public in many seasons last night in the Metropolitan Opera House.
The artists were Jarmila Novotna and Giuseppe de Luca.

Miss Novotna, the Czechoslovak soprano, had shown her intelligence, refinement, and sincerity in earlier appearances and other
parts. But *Traviata* is thus far, and unmistakably, her crowning
achievement. She sings the virtuoso passages with a security and

brilliance ample for all practical purposes. What is much more important is the fact that she conceives the music, from first note to the last, dramatically, and portrays the character with an aristocratic sensibility and simplicity which, at last, bestow upon the role its full meaning and power.

Here is an admirable actress, who never exaggerates or misses an expressive detail. Her appearance on the stage is eminently representative of the heroine of the tale. Miss Novotna is a beautiful figure on the stage, whose passion or agony never means loss of dignity or betrayal of the greatness of sorrow. No measure of the text, sung with the purest and most admirable Italian, lost its effect or failed to carry over the footlights. The word and the tone were indissoluble; the phrasing was that of the finest musician. Pathos was never overdone; by contrast, the *élan* of her attack when she began the *"Sempre libera"* made the pulse beat quicken, yet never lost the mood of the desperate gaiety of the condemned.

Very often the Violetta, or "Traviata," is estimated by her first act and her last—the first affording her a sustained air with a bravura wind-up, and the last act being so charged with feeling that the most uninspired singer can hardly neutralize the impression of the scene and the music. But the second act, on this occasion, was what it should be, an increase in dramatic tension over the first; and we fail to remember a soprano who has done as much with it. To hear the *"Così alla misera"* sung, for nearly a total exception, "piano," almost as the aside of a woman who faced the eternal parting, and with a pathos that wrung the heart, and then the wild outcry of the stricken spirit, was to have a new understanding of the character in the drama and the genius of Verdi. In fact, there were for many listeners new meanings in this masterpiece of an opera which the public has so obstinately cherished for nearly a hundred years while so-called intellectuals showed their pedantry and blindness by decrying it.

In every page there is genius. At the beginning of the third act one marveled anew at the means by which a simple dance rhythm and an almost banal melodic twist are made completely to convey the frightful agitation and premonition of evil which oppress Violetta as she surveys, while her heart breaks, the whole festive scene. Here is less to do and perhaps more difficulty in doing it than in the more obvious drama of the earlier passages. However, no one we had seen in the part approached the tragical dignity and the frozen terror with which the "frail one" perceived the presence of Alfredo. But one could go on narrating details of the plot, music, and of this interpretation and we would still be far from the musical and emotional sum of it. Miss Novotna is a great Violetta.

The second sensation of the evening came when Guiseppe de Luca, the veteran baritone and master of noble cantilena, who had left the Metropolitan when Gatti-Casazza retired in 1935 and had since remained away from America, stepped from the wings in the second act in his role of Germont *père*. It was not surprising that, on receiving the thunderous tribute of the audience, it was hard for Mr. de Luca to control his features or summon the breath to sing. The emotional situation very probably intensified his performance. And when he did open his mouth the first five notes made the pulses beat because of the art and the beauty of the song. The quality of the legato, the perfection of the style, the sentiment which ennobled the melodic phrase, struck the whole audience. Probably many were not able to analyze their sensation, which lay in the artist's vocal skill and his lofty conception of a melody which verges so perilously upon the sentimental but was made on this occasion a wholly acceptable expression of genuine humanity. Or was it that the atmosphere of the moment made this expression acceptable as it would not have been at some other time? But no! It was again Verdi's lyricism, Verdi's supreme knowledge of the human heart and his miraculous power of conveying that by means of the simplest tune, of which we were made newly aware. Then there were the dignity of the figure, the perfection of the acting.

Thus a young singing actress of radiant beauty and interpretive resource, and a veteran of many years of mastery gave the whole opera of *Traviata* an ordinarily unsuspected measure of meaning.

There is no need at this time to expatiate upon other highly creditable features of this performance, which have been discussed on earlier occasions. Mr. Charles Kullman's youth and warm and manly voice, his straightforward if not particularly subtle treatment of his part, may not have been most sensitively in accord with the composer's style, but here again were youth, conviction, and warm impulse. And there was the orchestra, once or twice ragged in attack, but directed by Mr. Panizza with much authority, expertness, and sense of theater. An immense audience was very demonstrative.

Italian Overtures and German

Answer to a Letter from Mario Castelnuovo-Tedesco

In an interesting and suggestive communication, Mr. Mario Castel-nuovo-Tedesco takes courteous exception to statements made by this writer concerning the Italian operatic overture, of which it was said that "the methods of the symphonist are not those native to the Italian genius, while they are at the very basis of German symphonic composition."

The statement struck Mr. Castelnuovo-Tedesco as "a little excessive and unjust, because there are different methods of symphonic conception, and fundamentally not only each country but each composer has his own methods."

Mr. Castelnuovo-Tedesco, not only a composer but a scholar of high repute, of course concedes that "for almost two centuries Italians, too much absorbed in opera, rarely devoted themselves to symphonic music." And it is true that we had in mind, too exclusively, the nineteenth-century overture in Italy. But here also is an exception, and an important one: Cherubini, of whom our correspondent tellingly reminds us. Cherubini's overtures have a pronouncedly organic as well as dramatic nature, and, perhaps for practical reasons, have survived operas for which they were written. Then there is the king of Italian operatic overtures—Rossini's to *William Tell*.

This, as Rossini's countryman remarks, is a "tone poem" as well as an overture, and another of the works in that form which has far outdistanced in its hold on the public the music drama to which it was the introduction. It is, however, in part landscape music, and, while dramatic, does not go very far under the surface. It is cast in sections, rather than in terms of continuous musical thought. Nor has it the close-woven texture we had in mind in mentioning the fundamentally symphonic nature of the nineteenth-century German overture.

The *William Tell* overture is a masterpiece. It has some superb thematic material, and a noble form. But it is in sections which balance and complement each other, while they do not represent that germinal growth and interlacing of elements which, as we see it, is the quality of the essentially symphonic style. And this applies to other Rossini overtures, which are usually original, melodically significant, with dramatic accent, but less frequently of a piece in invention, or cumulative in development, or entirely free of contemporary convention—bold as Rossini could be for a composer of his early environment. Nor did he, in any other place, approach the architecture or substance of the orchestral prelude to *William Tell*.

Do his lesser overtures "bear the undeniable imprint of symphonic creation," as stated by Mr. Castelnuovo-Tedesco? Is there only a difference of racial or individual approach between these scores and those of the German composers, from Beethoven to Wagner, which Mr. Castelnuovo-Tedesco has himself described as pertaining to "the heroic period of the overture"?

It is a period not only of spirit, but of a development of the form which is unmistakably the heritage of German music from Bach onward; having its roots, one would say, not only in a contrapuntal technique elaborated far beyond the practices of any other nation of the nineteenth century, but also in a technique impregnated with imaginative conceptions which make the orchestra the true protagonist of the drama.

That is the quality which is specifically German and which makes not only of an overture but of a whole drama a symphonic poem, as witness *Tristan and Isolde*. In fact, in this case the visible is wholly subordinate to the invisible drama expressed by sound alone and enacted in a realm of the consciousness of which it could almost be said that it was remote from the physical world.

This is so much the case that the German operatic procedure is often the worst sort of theater. Thus the *Leonore* No. 3, which precedes *William Tell* by roughly a quarter of a century, is the spiritual drama of *Fidelio* flung upon the music paper with an intensity, a momentousness and epic power only fragmentarily displayed in the opera that follows. It is when Beethoven is freed from his stage and his sovereign spirit is released and made omnipotent through his instruments that we feel overpoweringly the pulse of his heart and sense the vision which in the rescue of Florestan, and the liberation of the prisoners, saw symbolized the freedom of mankind.

The *Freischütz* overture, completely national and romantic in tone, is, with all its simplicity, romanticism, and folk spirit, almost a philosophical summary of the drama. And all the Wagner overtures proceed in this royal line. So, even, do the operas, at least from *Rheingold* onward. The music is impregnated not only with feeling but with introspective thought, finding expression by means of the symphonic orchestra, with an effect that far transcends anything on the stage. This development with Wagner is beheld as early as the *Rienzi* overture, not nearly as distinguished in invention as that of *William Tell* but in the dramatic as in the structural sense more organic.

Wagner, moreover, is a long time in catching up in his stage music with his symphonic introductions. How infinitely superior to all that follows and eloquent of the whole idea of the *Flying Dutchman* is the overture thereof! With *Tannhäuser* something else emerges, and while there are many who will prefer to experience this music drama by means of the emotional synopsis that the overture offers, it cannot be said that ensuing pages provide nothing that is additional. Tannhäuser's narrative of the last act, Elizabeth's scenes in the preceding one, are cases in point of indispensable music. We come nearer here to real dramatic episode and progress and what might be called the genuinely "personal note" on the stage than in any other of the Wagner operas.

But what is there in *Lohengrin* so important as its prelude, unique in all music, which alone would have given Wagner a firm seat among the immortals? He says there what he can say nowhere else, says it with a beauty and mysticism beyond compare, and by fugal procedure!

The *Ring* is a different matter, because there everything is interwoven into a vast symphony in four movements, the first an odd two hours, the others an odd four hours in length, with themes carried over from movement to movement, and opening with the symphonic introduction to Father Rhine. *Tristan* is, for all purposes, a static drama and a symphonic revelation of the spirit, a tone poem in which voices have obbligato parts.

Nearest, of course, to the original ideal of opera—poetical speech heightened and intensified by the power of music—comes *Meistersinger*. Here is a wonderful blend of symphonic expression with the spontaneous impulse and varied musical speech of the characters, but who will deny the predominance of the symphonic element and

its essential Germanism, and what is to compare, in its co-ordination and sublimation of all musico-elements, with that prelude, so-
called, which introduces the opera and is one of the seven wonders
of the musical world? There, in this introductory tone poem, is all
of it—the Meistersingers, and their guildsman's self-respect and
complacency and pride; and the love of Walther and Eva, for which
Wagner finds as specific a symphonic expression as he found for
the mature and terrible passion of Tristan and Isolde—expressions
different from each other as the night from the day; and the pedantry that opposes Walther's genius; and the triumph of youth and
inspiration over all conventions and officialdom; and Sachs's wisdom, love, and humanity; and the acclaim of the folk, as the genius,
which they have recognized and rewarded, raises them to fresh
levels of wisdom and joy.

Let this be added: that by every original tenet of opera as drawn
up by the Florentines of the seventeenth century and as exemplified
by the very nature of true music drama, the German procedure is
all wrong. It is blind, self-centered, arbitrary, and opaque, as compared with the glorious clarity, the flexibility, the spontaneousness,
and the noble and harmonious forms of the operatic Italians. By
song and by a dramatic instinct in which only the French approach
them, they have accomplished, with a logic and beauty and miraculous apprehension, what the symphonic school could never achieve.

First of all, they triumph in basing their musical art on that of
the instrument which is eloquent beyond all others, and nearest the
core of music—the human voice. In a school of lyric dramatic expression, of all German composers only Mozart—if he is to be called
a German—in his position of benevolent neutrality between the
thinking and practices of two races, was capable of comprehending
and apotheosizing these tendencies in his art.

For from Pergolesi onward the Italians conceived of a musical
theater that has no parallel for dramatic eloquence and truth, and
clarity and beauty of expression. The spontaneous, unfettered communication of feeling; the melodic simplicity and eloquence which
pierce straight to the heart of an emotion or situation; the musical
forms which may apotheosize a whole dramatic development in a
few movements of perfectly co-ordinated harmony and rhythm; and
the grand architecture which often constitutes a great symphony
of voices and of vocal development—all these are theirs and lie
at the very root of true operatic writing. This basic principle is only

to be contraverted by the instrumental and symphonic creations of the nation on the other side of the Alps.

Nor does this generalization exclude the operatic masterpieces of the French composers, from the Italian-Frenchman Lully right up to Bizet or Charpentier, or even the *Pelléas* of Debussy, for which see the early operas of Monteverdi and the Florentines. It is an old saw, but a perfectly true one, that the Latins in music drama place the statue where it belongs—not in the orchestra but on the stage —and that they admirably detest that which is not direct, passionate, and lucid, or what is unbalanced and inharmonious in form.

When we examine the pages of an *Otello* or a *Falstaff*—the tragic in one case, the comic and humanitarian in the other—we come across such expressions and such admirable theater, and such a master's treatment of orchestral resources delegated to their place in relation to the stage, as neither Wagner nor any other composer of his school ever dreamed of. Here are Italian "symphonies" of an incomparable sort. But one does not have to cite either of these mountain peaks of music drama, or attempt to minimize or exaggerate the qualities of any nation's art, in order merely to honor another's.

NOVEMBER 24, 1940

Schoenberg Himself Conducts *Pierrot lunaire*

Composer as Interpreter

A REMARKABLE performance of his *Pierrot lunaire* was conducted by Arnold Schoenberg at the concert of the New Friends of Music in Town Hall.

For the record, be it noted that *Pierrot lunaire* was performed for the first time anywhere, not in Leipzig, but in Berlin. The first New York performance was given by the International Composer's Guild in 1923. The work was given two subsequent performances by the League of Composers, in 1925 and in 1933, when it received a stage performance under the direction of Leopold Stokowski.

To this writer's knowledge, there has been no parallel in excel-·lence to Mr. Schoenberg's reading of his music.

That performance demonstrated several principles. The first was the importance, indeed the utter indispensability, to music, of adequate interpretation. Adequate interpretation, as a few seasons' experience in listening to concerts will convince anyone, is extremely rare.

Competent performance is not the same thing. There are quite a number of competent performances, even of performances deserving of that vastly overworked adjective "brilliant," yet performances that do not reveal the essence of the music.

The revelation of that essence is wholly in the power of the interpreter, whose importance in the presentation cannot be minimized. That of the mere executant, or a famous executant's "personality," is often overestimated, which is quite another matter. The composer is more important than anybody else in the musical field. There is no question about that. But the printed music on the page is not the composer, or any more than an approximation of his idea.

Someone says he will be perfectly satisfied if the performer will simply follow intelligently and respectfully the composer's directions for the music's interpretation. What he means is that if only the composer's voice is heard in the performance, instead of the musical ideas of an officious interpreter which are not really those of the composer, he will be satisfied.

But the fact is that the music is not really released from the page—"re-created," after all, is a perfectly accurate and just description —unless it is brought to life by the intuition and re-creative power of an interpreter who reads far back of the signs on the printed page to the actual thought of the composer. Then you have the re-creation of music, the only condition under which music can fully reveal itself and communicate its innermost secret to the sensitive listener.

This is rarely accomplished even by a composer when he presents his own music. There are two reasons for this. One is purely practical. It is simply that a composer does not know the effective method of making the performers carry out his precise intentions. He hasn't the technique needed to do it. He may be, in practice, a distinctly poor interpreter of his own works. The second reason is that the composer is too subjective in his mental processes to realize from the point of view of the objective listener the precise character of the sounds he secures in performance.

There have been, of course, and there are, composers who are notable exceptions to this rule. Sometimes a composer triumphs, without a conductor's technique, because of the clarity of his thought, which he communicates by a form of telepathy rather than visible indication to the players. We shall never forget a rare opportunity of hearing Sibelius conduct his own music, at a quasi-private musical occasion back in 1914. He cast a spell that no other conductor has ever bestowed upon the works he then interpreted.

What Mr. Schoenberg could do if he conducted his compositions for full symphony orchestra is not known hereabout. But if—and why not?—he can do with a full orchestra what he did with five chamber-music players and a soprano at the New Friends of Music concert, then he is one of the few composer-conductors who are indispensable for the complete understanding of their music. If conductors of our great symphony orchestras have come no nearer Schoenberg's real intentions they came at previous hearings in this city of *Pierrot lunaire*, then we have never heard the major Schoenberg scores. We could give a great deal, in the light of the recent revelation, to hear, for example, the enigmatic Variations, Opus 29, clarified by their composer.

Then comes a question dealing more exclusively with the composer's achievement, although it results from the musical effect of Schoenberg's performance. *Pierrot lunaire* is a relatively old Schoenberg score, not nearly as radical in content as his more recent creations. It could be called convention itself by the side of the orchestral variations to which reference has been made. Its vitality lies in the fact that it is an unconditional expression of Schoenberg's nature at the time the music was written. When its secret is revealed as it was at the New Friends Concert, the listener is plunged deep into a particular world of sensibility, in which everything but its truth disappears. How *Pierrot* will appear to the next generation or century may not be known now. But its genuineness and present validity were memorably established. How the composition was made, or what of, was seen more clearly than ever to be the business of the composer. The question of technical procedure is largely superfluous, despite the special form, the novelty of the tonal texture, and the use of the song-speech. These are but means to an end. What if the musical framework of the eighth poem, *Nacht*, is a passacaglia? Or if, in the *Parodie*, a doubly inverted canon at the half-bar is developed between voice and piccolo, and clarinet and viola, or a double canon, "cancrizans," is written with such devilish ingenuity that from the latter half of the tenth bar the music runs backward to the beginning? What about it? Could not Mr. Schoenberg have accomplished the same expressive result in a much simpler way? It is quite possible, even likely. But he did it in the way described, and it turns out, under his revealing generalship, to be expressive and organic music.

Water moves very fast under the musical bridges. The use of dissonance, in which field Schoenberg has made his own discoveries, has not stopped or stood still. The very striking fact of *Pierrot lunaire* is that, despite all developments since it was written, it sounds today strikingly modern, where other compositions just as drastic in their temporary effect are being forgotten. That is a result proceeding fundamentally from the integrity and scruple of Mr. Schoenberg as man and artist.

NOVEMBER 20, 1941

===

The Philharmonic Scores with *Show Boat*

"Distinguished listeners were humming. . . ."

THE audience which packed Carnegie Hall last night at the concert given by Artur Rodzinski, conductor, and the New York Philharmonic-Symphony Orchestra listened to the piece which culminated the program with a degree of excitement and an obvious joy in the music which testified more strongly than any words could to the nature of its experience.

The music that created this pleasurable emotion was not Beethoven's First Symphony, or Paul Hindemith's ultra-modern "symphony" *Mathis der Mahler* after the painting of Grünewald, or even the exquisite music that the youthful Mendelssohn composed for Shakespeare's *Midsummer Night's Dream*. No! The piece that created that commotion was the composition of an American musician who had long since won a lasting place in the hearts of his countrymen with a creation which is an enduring "classic" and masterpiece of its kind in its popular field. No one could hear that music, those glorious tunes, without an answering grin, or surreptitious tap of the heel, or even leap of the heart. For the composer was Jerome Kern, and the music, in a new orchestral version created by him on the invitation of Dr. Rodzinski, was based upon the score of *Show Boat*.

When it was agreed last spring that at least one composition by an American composer should figure on each of the Philharmonic-Symphony programs of this season in New York, Dr. Rodzinski, with a quality of appreciation and a degree of imagination that become him well, thought immediately of Mr. Kern as one of the most representative popular American composers of this period. He considers *Show Boat* a very typically American masterpiece, in its field. Dr. Rodzinski also asked himself why, if waltzes by Johann Strauss are considered legitimate entertainment at a symphony concert, the fascinating melodic invention of a leading American who long since had gained a permanent place in his particular domain should not have at least the same rating and the same opportunity for a hearing. The result was the "scenario," as Mr. Kern entitles it, on themes from *Show Boat*.

They—the themes—were enormously successful with the audience. It need not be claimed that they are combined in what one could call a truly symphonic style, or developed, either, after the symphonic manner of acknowledged masters of orchestral composition. There is a simplicity and directness of procedure in this "scenario" as sincere, simple, direct as Mr. Kern himself, and so remote from the standpoint of the sophisticated symphonic craftsman as to be rather deliciously naïve.

But the melodies themselves! The audience sat intent from the opening, which is like that of the overture to the operetta and leads after reference to several themes into the first announcement of *Old Man River*, to the end. The tunes come in a succession which generally follows the course of the opera. One was impressed with the instantaneous flash of understanding and fellow feeling, as you might say, which traversed the atmosphere from the audience to the stage.

For this is music, of course, in the popular vein but, in its most representative pages, as native as Mark Twain or Edna Ferber's novel. Some melodies are not as good as others. Some fall into operetta routine. At least half a dozen are irresistible and unforgettable. Distinguished listeners were humming them as they went home.

There are those who sniff at music of this kind, given this kind of reception. The writer is not of them. It is a native idiom, and it is excellent melodic invention. It smacks, with sheer direct inspiration and without any pose, of an American period and an American scene —if you like, of an American romanticism. It is infinitely farther toward a native form than the vast majority of our cerebral and imitative American symphonies.

And that is the explanation of its reception. With the last chord the applause almost impinged upon the sound of the orchestra, and Dr. Rodzinski, turning to bow, quickly dived into the wings to get Mr. Kern. He appeared and was given an ovation, repeatedly called back to the stage, applauded, cheered, welcomed as only an artist is welcomed for whom the public of his country feels the affection and esteem that this sincere and modest man of native genius has long since earned in this land!

Saying which, let us consider this score for a moment from the symphonic standpoint. It is not symphonic at all in the sense of development and interweaving of the musical ideas. This lack of the customary symphonic procedure is deliberate with Mr. Kern and probably well advised. He has written for the popular lyric stage. He does not exaggerate his own powers or technical resource in the symphonic field. He thought it would be better, safer, and more characteristic of his own methods of expression if he used what he called a melodic "scenario" of his operatic score.

This score is actually a potpourri, a selection, rather too generous and extended for its own good, of themes from the show. Too many themes are employed. Five or six less of them, with some pruning of connecting passages—which, in instances, are none too adroit or effective without the accompanying stage spectacle—would make the piece more concise, pull it together, and centralize its architecture. It might be well if *Old Man River* were held in reserve for a more lengthy final peroration and many other passages shortened or cut out.

Per contra, one place that wasn't long enough for our personal wishes was the comparatively brief mention given *Why Do I Love You* and the omission of its dance variation, as in the opera score. But that is personal. The orchestration has excellent passages; the presence of "saxes" and various percussive auxiliaries, including sets of bells, would be all right if there was not rather too much attempt to make every kind of effect that one can with these various instruments and work it in before the end is reached. In a word, it is over-orchestrated, and the melodic continuity is not of the best. Here is the nucleus of a better piece, and one that would be more effective than what was heard last night, greatly as it pleased, and much reason as Mr. Kern has to be gratified with his reception.

Mr. Kern has detained us in the accounting as engagingly as his music did at the concert. There were other notable matters more in the symphonic tradition. Discoursing the works of modern and classic masters, Dr. Rodzinski gave further proof of his conspicuous and constantly developing resources as an orchestra leader. He achieved admirable clarity, classic line, grace and animation in the early Beethoven symphony, and this with remarkable control and economy of effort.

He gave a reading of special virility and authority, albeit a reading tending occasionally to coarseness and overemphasis, of Hindemith's singular score, which did not impress this listener as strongly last night as it has on earlier occasions.

A very interesting matter was the effect of the *Midsummer Night's Dream* music, played with uncommon fancy, brilliancy, and poetical imagination. For a reservation, there could have been some clearer and better balances in certain pages of the overture—a detail amid the manifold beauties of a memorable performance. And how miraculously today, as on the day that Mendelssohn's overture to *A Midsummer Night's Dream* was first heard, more than a century ago, does this music evoke Shakespeare's fantasy, and merit the adjective which in itself is accolade: "Shakespearean"!

For once the sylvan fantasy of the nocturne did not move on leaden feet—was not played too slowly, or with mortal weight or sentimentality. The admirable player of the horn solo was designated by Dr. Rodzinski, and given special applause. The scherzo was equally spirited, and finished, and fanciful. Throughout the evening the orchestra performed, not with invariable perfection, but with a fine discipline, rhythm, and versatility of style. By and large, the best orchestral performance, as yet, of the season, at the hands of an exceptionally gifted, poised, and authoritative conductor.

PART III

The Magic Flute—150 Years After

"One strange mélange of nonsense and genius"

IT IS one hundred and fifty years, almost to a day, since Mozart's death (December 5, 1791) and a few months more than that since the *première* of his last opera, *The Magic Flute* (September 30, 1791), which the Metropolitan presents, for the first time on its stage in English, next Thursday evening. That is the opera, *singspiel*, farce, symbolic music drama, theatrical piece that mingles burlesque, fairy tale, and Masonic symbolism in one strange mélange of nonsense and genius, and it is the last miracle that Mozart wrought for the lyric theater.

The piece was done at the instigation of a comedian and barnstormer who concocted a libretto made up of odds and ends by himself and others of the unworthy, who kept Mozart under his eye while he was composing under customary pressure in a little summerhouse by the theater where the piece was given, and occasionally feasted with the composer to keep him amused while the work was being created. Text and situations were so devised by Schikaneder that he himself appeared in a comic part that provided many of the gags and the fattest songs for his use. The "book" was turned out episode by episode, Mozart composing the while, with constant changes of material and of direction, as a million such pieces have been turned out in theaters of a sort the world over, for tomorrow night's opening and, for all anybody knows, next month's wastebasket.

It will be remembered that Schikaneder made comparatively little of Mozart's participation in this task. For "The book of the opera, adorned with two copper engravings, showing Herr Schikaneder in the part of Papageno, engraved after the actual costume, may be had at the box office of 30 kreuzer," and "Herr Gayl, the theater painter, and Herr Nessthaler as decorator, flatter themselves to have worked with all possible zeal according to the prescribed plan of the piece"; and it develops, in a note under the listing of the cast, that "The music is by Herr Wolfgang Amade Mozart, Kapellmeister and Imperial Royal Chamber Musician in Ordinary," and that "Herr Mozart will, in deference to a gracious and honorable public, and from friendship for the author of the piece, conduct the orchestra in person today."

This Herr Mozart did, between a million distractions—the having of a new baby by Constanze, pressure of debts, the piteous letters for just another little loan from friend Puchberg—and, we may be certain, without any particular thought of the fate of his composition. He was writing a score for the entertainment of Schikaneder's public. Of its ultimate significance in the history of opera, and indeed of German music drama, he had no slightest thought. At one of the early performances he called the turn on Schikaneder by surreptitiously playing the bells when the comedian sang the bird man's song, "*A maiden or a little wife.*" Mozart stuck in an arpeggio which took Schikaneder by surprise, so that he paused and burst into laughter. But Mozart made no sound when the passage returned, and now the disconcerted Schikaneder, befooled in the sight of his public and mightily annoyed, shouted at the silent accompanying instrument "Shut up!" to the audience's immense enjoyment.

All this was of a piece with the spirit of the occasion and with a libretto which, despite irrelevance and absurdities, has much of the folk element and a popular romanticism which fascinated Goethe and caused him to begin a dramatic sequel to *The Magic Flute*. With all its discrepancies the opera has vital things in it—libretto as well as music—that well from popular sources and confer the vigor and racy originality that works arising from such sources may well possess. It is one more of the protean manifestations of Mozart's genius in its beauty, its health and universality. That genius stands in an extraordinary relation to us of today. For this is the time, after the great romantic upheaval of music in the nineteenth century, and in the period of another world upheaval of such a tragic nature and extent that no man can know what the future may be, that Mozart emerges with an unexpected power which astonishingly affects contemporary feeling. This art reveals and clarifies, transporting us, not away from life, but to its ultimate meaning. Seldom if ever since his death has Mozart appeared so popular and potent for the good of humanity. Works by the majority of great masters endlessly divide musical opinion. Mozart's conquest is without violence, and he comes always the more completely into his own.

A further proof of this is that we see him differently and, at least in America, more comprehendingly than he was ever seen before. On the personal side, much of the sentimental and hypocritical nonsense tolerated about him in all times has been dispersed. Mozart is no longer the "glorious boy." He was a complete man; a sensuous and impressionable being, responsive to all of life's challenges, full-blooded, yet exquisitely sentient and of an intuitive understanding that went much deeper than conscious reason and, indeed, could only find adequate expression in music. Would a different sort of person, an ignoramus or a pure fool, have been able to leave behind him works with the Shakespearean gamut of the Mozart music-dramas? Obviously not, and fortunate we are that the cobwebs are being brushed away from this aspect of Mozart the man and artist.

And perhaps we also understand better than we did Mozart's essential classicism and what a genuine classicism means. It does not mean the pseudo-classicism that some modern composers have preached and affected. It does not mean avoidance of emotion for the sake of being formally balanced. It does not mean that small forms and niggardly content are the proper antidote for the extravagances of the romantics. It means that the form crystallizes the emotion which created it. Mozart's genius is a vast inundating sea which fills every channel from the smallest to the widest, and reflects every phase of the life of the universe. And it is never the art of a weakling or one who dreads the world. Every age has found in this music its fulfillment, and the present age, more complex than any previous one and with a greater multiplicity of problems, turns instinctively to Mozart and finds in him a strangely healing consummation. And the wisdom of it companions its simplicity. In the last analysis, it may mean even more for us than the mighty intellectualism of a Bach.

Mozart has been written about endlessly, and will be so written about as long as there is music, not because men are short of ideas, but precisely as the sunrise and the glory of the tides and sky and forests and sea will always occupy the thoughts of the race. Like those phenomena, he will remain an enduring and fascinating mystery. Wholly appropriate—indeed, one would be tempted to say, inevitable with him—was the manner of his departure from life's stage. Some of his biographers think that even in the heyday of his short youth Mozart was mystically aware that his would be an early end, and that this sentience is ominously present in certain of his scores. This may easily be fancy, or special interpretation. But what seems the perfect conclusion of his career is the very event that is so often and so keenly lamented—that Mozart, the man, the face and the form that men knew, completely disappeared; that no one knows where he lies; that the mortal coil, shuffled off, was cast with other human leavings into an unknown grave. The seen, said Whitman, is proved by the unseen. Mozart's music is the supreme, the ultimate transmutation.

FEBRUARY 3, 1942

―

The "Neo-Classicism" of the Bright Boys

Is it "just plain fake classicism"?

WE RISE to ask a plain question: What is the actual meaning, and what are the representative illustrations, in contemporary music, of the word "neo-classic"?

This word in late years has given flow to gallons of ink and fountains of esthetical rhetoric. It has served as a handy argument for bright boys whose music none of the unintelligent could possibly understand. They weren't trying to write music, they explained, in an emotional way; they were trying to create musical forms, rhythmic and melodic designs, which had nothing to do with personal feeling or its communication. They were just being "neo-classic."

Well, we know one thing. We know that in order to be a "neo-classic" composer, and therefore in the swim, it is imperative not to be a "romantic." This last is the outer darkness, the final degree of innocuous desuetude. But here again is a term for definition. What is a "romanticist" in music?

To be a romantic composer, one gathers, is to tell your own story in tones, in your own way, according to your personal feelings in the matter and your own expressive idiosyncrasies. To be a classic composer you do not do this. In the first place, your approach is structural. You do not write from personal motives. You are impersonal, objective; you use rhythm, counterpoint, and abstract tonal designs rather than the terms of subjective, impassioned utterance. Thus you avoid the excesses of romanticism and serve the ideal of a pure, transparent, classic art. From feverish intensities, grandiloquent rhetoric, tonal splendor, you shall abstain if you know what is good for you. Remember always: you are not expressing feeling or extramusical ideas. You are expressing music, which has nothing to express but itself. So back to your fugues and passacaglias.

It is, however, hard to accept these and similar definitions at their face value. They do not seem quite to fit the *Jupiter* or the *Eroica*, or the harmonic counterpoint of Bach, or the serenity of Palestrina, the dramatic passion of Gluck, or the emotional vigor of Handel, or the humanity of Mozart, or even the modern classicism, as it has been called, of good old Johannes Brahms. Or was he classicist? Or neoclassicist? And if not, what?

Sometimes, in moments of doubt, one wonders if the exponents of "neo-classicism" don't really mean "pseudo-classicism," or just plain fake classicism, or the superficial imitation, in most unfortunate style, of the shell instead of the substance of the works of past masters. And then one looks at the musical examples advanced. There are the works, for example, of Stravinsky's late period, sterile, feeble, melodically commonplace creations, pieces which imitate this and that master, which emulate the styles of various periods and express none of them, and one wonders. Then there are the little, short, gentlemanly pieces of well-bred composers whose whole avowed object it is not to be exciting, or portentous, or serious, or anything but witty, plausible, and sophisticated in their sources. They are applauded for their sanity, their lightness of touch, their insistence, in every note they write, that there is nothing in the world worth being serious about. It is like the precious little minnows which leap and flash in the pools, where there are no terrible depths or storms or monsters, assuring themselves that if they are smaller they certainly are smarter than the big fellows outside. No doubt this sort of thing is reassuring, especially to those who, with the Greeks, feel that music should communicate a gentleman-like joy. . . .

By what reasoning do we create a "new" period in music by simply applying a new-sounding word to it? Every bit of living art that appears is "neo" for its day, and "post" for its yesterday. The real distinction lies much deeper. Thus, we apply sadly overworked words to art which is "classic" as contrasted with art which is "romantic." The classic art has a quality of objectivity. It pays the most vigilant attention to balance and proportion of parts, to the structural relations of all the elements of the work, to its architectural purposes, finding in the process the complete transfiguring realization of the idea. Whereas romantic art, fundamentally of a subjective and egocentric inspiration, entails the accommodation of the form to the idea's demands.

Even these familiar, generic terms are none too clear as to boundaries, because no classic masterpiece has yet been perfected without profound feeling on the part of the one who conceived it, and no romantic, however red-hot his inspiration, ever produced a passionate expression which existed without a form—not a traditional form, nevertheless a form of unquestionable logic and power, forged by the artist's imagination and craftsmanship to the point where it fittingly embodies the artist's concept and reveals new horizons of beauty.

All know that the pendulum sways, as the ages pass, from one of these creative principles to the other; hence, in every epoch there are the before-the-event and after-the-event tendencies expressed by leading creative spirits of the day. So that "neo" this and that is a term of such superficiality and ephemeralness that it is little more at any time than a platitude.

MARCH 28, 1942

Bach, Brandenburg & Busch

"The most entertaining compositions in existence"

ADOLPH BUSCH seems to have been one of the few musicians to have realized that the sure way to fill a modern concert hall is to announce the six "Brandenburg" Concertos of J. S. Bach and leave the rest to the public. It is only curious that this did not become a seasonal practice years ago.

A previous occasion in Town Hall gave us "Brandenburg" Concertos Nos. 1, 3, and 6. Last night an audience which packed the place applauded thunderously the playing of Mr. Busch and his colleagues in Nos. 2, 5, and 4. At the end of the concert the audience stood for minutes to cheer.

One is tempted to say that these "Brandenburg" Concertos are among the most entertaining compositions in existence—these six masterpieces through which Bach immortalized the princeling to whom they were humbly dedicated and by whom the gift was apparently ignored, and which, in 1734, were sold in a lot at a valuation of twenty-four groschen.

Moreover, the popular savor of this music is manifest. True, it must be played with a sure virtuosity on the part of the soloists, including the player of the high trumpet, who "highly" distinguished himself last night. The performances were of an exhilarating mastery. It is hard to imagine interpretation more thoroughly in the character of the music.

The procedure of the first concert of this series was repeated: the orchestra played without a conductor, and with a concertmaster in the person of Mr. Busch. Some of the soloists, or those who formed the "concertino" group, stood, but the trumpeter, Mr. Vacchiano, sat behind his music sheet while he performed deeds of derring-do with a prevailing virtuosity and spirit that communicated a breathless excitement. Would he, could he, keep it going, way up there in the stratosphere? Since he was human, Mr. Vacchiano was not absolutely flawless in his performance, but what he did accomplish with the pealing, silvery tones of his instrument was one of the features of the evening to remember.

At the piano Mr. Serkin was a host in himself, whether playing the solo cadenza in the Fifth Concerto or suppling harmonic parts and strengthening voices in the traditional way of the eighteenth century. Nor must Mr. Serkin's "continuo" for *The Star-Spangled Banner* go unmentioned. His harmonization of certain measures is new and good—indeed, refreshing to the ear.

The players of solo instruments were excellent in their tasks—John Wummer, the admirable flutist; Joseph Marx in his tasteful oboe solo; Mildred Hunt, the second flutist in the performance of the Fourth Concerto, which ended the program. The wind-up of the concerto, with Mr. Busch as a demon fiddler, will be forgotten by no one present—the great chords flung out like the crack of a whip, the exultant strength and virtuosity of the whole ensemble. No! It is not astonishing that when the "Brandenburg" Concertos are played in this way an audience packs the hall, and breaks into applause, as an audience should, between movements, and at the last stands up and cheers.

MAY 31, 1942

═══

Homage to a Predecessor, Richard Aldrich

He is trying to find out, not who is right, but what is right.

Concert Life in New York is a substantial volume of music criticism by Richard Aldrich, selected from the multitude written by him in the twenty years from the season of 1902–3 onward when he was most active as reviewer of events of the concert and opera stage for *The New York Times*. One lays down this book with a singular sense of emolument, and gratification that its material has been conserved in book form. For when Richard Aldrich ceased writing for *The Times* something precious and irreplaceable went with him. This was a reflex of his own nature, the texture of a mind rarely attuned to high values, his noiseless devotion to the art that he loved, and his selfless endeavor to bring something of its beauty and significance to his readers.

The book would have its special importance on the historical side alone. Any twenty years of New York's musical life, accurately and appreciatively chronicled, would have fascination and value. But in the first quarter of this century New York became the musical center of the world. Nowhere else was to be met in the course of a season so many commanding personalities, interpretive and creative, of the period.

Aldrich's observations begin in the years that saw the maturity of Paderewski, Ysaÿe, Nikisch, Richard Strauss, Debussy, Puccini, and a surrounding galaxy of composers when they were dominant figures in the creative sphere. It continues with the coming of age of Josef Hofmann, Fritz Kreisler, Elman, Heifetz, Casals, Caruso, Chaliapin, Toscanini. It describes the *premières* of operas as various as *Salome,*

Elektra, Madama Butterfly, The Love of Three Kings, and the *Love for Three Oranges.* The survey includes, of course, the earlier figures of the American school of composition—the MacDowells, Chadwicks, Parkers, Loefflers—and ensuing developments, and the advent of the Schoenbergs, Stravinskys, Prokofieffs from overseas.

From this the substance and richness of the record will be clear, but criticism is something more than the factual, descriptive, or even judicial. It is interpretation, in this instance interpretations of matters that lie under as well as upon the surface of an art. The task of the American critic of Aldrich's generation was one of particular difficulty and responsibility. For this was a period of rapid change and of far-reaching consequence. The changes were not only artistic and technical but social and psychological. To the conservatives of the period that included the cataclysm of ideas as well as the cataclysm of government of the First World War, the very ground was shifting under their feet. And in music, as in other fields, the radicals, with much racket, were acclaiming as permanent a great deal which has already proved to have been momentary and superficial in the changing complexion of the modern composer's expression. In this situation a critic of preconceived ideas, insensible to new developments and incapable of responding to them, would have been totally at a loss. And in the same situation an observer by temperament unstable or disinclined to assess soberly the sensation of the moment would have been swept, without compass or anchor, from his moorings.

Aldrich, with the background and perspective of a genuine culture, with a native modesty, tranquillity, and independence all his own, listened, reflected, went into the sanctum which was not only that of his desk but of his spirit, and, searching his soul, put down without fear or conceit what he found there. And what he found, so far as we of today, two decades later, can discern, astonishingly holds water.

How did he do it? His attitude has been described. What was his method? Aldrich accomplished what he did, fundamentally, by the sheer honesty and passion for the truth that was in his soul. His other attributes: the knowledge and perspective he was always seeking to broaden; his journalist's training and technique, which were those of a master of his task; his capacity for orientation and his abhorrence of partisanship—these qualities, indispensable too, were in the second place. His profound sense of obligation to his art, to his employer, and to his reader—these and the fineness and graciousness of his mind inform every line he wrote and honor him past the telling.

He never attends a performance with the intention to prove a point. He is trying to find out, not who is right, but what is right. He pursues the inquiries with the rarest intellectual courage, without dogma, without browbeating, with an earnestness which scorns the coining of a phrase as it does the wasting of space upon malefaction or incompetency in performance. Things that are manifestly outside serious consideration are quickly disposed of and dropped with some distaste from the end of a pair of tongs ("it would be a mournful task to enumerate the defects of his playing"), and so to worth-while matters. He is concerned with every aspect of technique, style, or interpretation which is pertinent to main issues of music. He is neither impressed by an international reputation nor condescending in the presence of one yet to be made. In fact, he watches his younger artists and notes carefully their progress or weakness in successive seasons as if they were his chicks.

Matters of a more enduring nature, since they enter more deeply into the musical evolutions of a period, are the critic's estimates of new works by contemporary composers. It is fortunate that the contents of this book are not confined, as we believe was originally intended, to concert performances alone, because, in that case, we would have missed the historic reviews of such works as Strauss's *Salome* and *Elektra* and Debussy's *Pelléas et Mélisande*. For us of today these works are water under the bridge. But they will probably loom larger rather than smaller in the perspective of tomorrow, and it is important to know the impression that they produced when they were first given and how they were received by a rarely unbiased and extremely observant commentator.

And so, at the height of a sensation greater and more alarming to minds of the old school than anything we can realize today—perhaps the latest parallel to it was the racket when Stravinsky's *Sacre* was given for the first time in Paris—we have Aldrich very quietly proclaiming that, for all the possible noisomeness of a subject that was almost taboo in America in 1907—certainly taboo where the pastor of Pierpont Morgan's church and, by consequence, the direction of the Metropolitan were concerned—for all the fuss and scandal, the opera [*Salome*] that was withdrawn for more than twenty years after that *première* was in its kind a masterpiece of "a force, of a faculty, if not productive of beauty and of uplifting influence, then certainly wonderfully powerful in execution, of inexorable logic, of marvelous technical skill in the treatment of all the resources that the evolution of music has slowly accumulated, and of endless fecundity in the invention of new ones. . . . Strauss has been able to build up a superb fabric—dazzling, thrilling, overpowering, often beautiful, but, at all events, wonderfully expressive of what he aimed to express."

In the next years when idolators of the German school of composition can see nothing but diaphanous triviality in *Pelléas et Mélisande*, he says of the text that "it is fascinating; and its fascination is now, and is likely long to be, inseparable from the music through which Debussy has heightened and deepened its significance"; of his harmonic progressions, "that they are so far from being justified by the grammarian that they cannot even be convicted by him. Yet they have their own justification with their strange eloquence. The beauty of this harmonic flow is inexplicable, but is irresistible"—and much more that it would be a pleasure to quote from if endless space permitted.

He recognized, similarly, the intense dramatic power of Strauss's *Elektra*, criticized its neuroticism less than he did the excessive details of the score, and noted the grandeur of Mazarin's impersonation —utterly unapproachable and unforgettable by all of us who heard it. He described the "bric-a-brac novelty" of Puccini's *Madama Butterfly* and did not overestimate it; he rejoiced in the recrudescence of certain beautiful and poetical qualities of Italian art, which had been temporarily pushed out of sight by Puccini's fellow realists, in Montemezzi's *Love of Three Kings*; and he roundly excoriated Prokofieff's *Love for Three Oranges*. . . .

The book is worth the reading and re-reading which it will receive. The title is as unassuming as its writer would have wished, and so is its accessory material. There is a short biography, almost too brief and simple, by Richard C. Aldrich, the son, and a foreword by Otto Kinkeldey.

Rachmaninoff: The Passing of a Great and Modest Master

"I begin my tour tomorrow in Lynn. It will be r-r-rotten."

THE tragical disappearance from our musical life of Sergei Rachmaninoff, who died last week in his seventieth year, is a most poignant loss. This is due not only to his extraordinary personality—which, once encountered either in a room or from a listener's seat in a great concert hall, was singularly felt and never forgotten—but to the sincerity and greatness of his spirit. It is due also, in this writer's belief, to the genuineness and the qualities of greatness in his music. As is well known, that music was no particularly modern expression. This was not Rachmaninoff's position as a creative artist. As far as style, method, technique were concerned, it could have been written in Russia of a hundred years ago.

Like most of the important Russian composers of the older generation and the pre-revolutionary period, he came of the upper landholding class, or "little nobility." This meant, in the first place, an immense love of the soil, and acquaintance at first hand with it and with the people. Tolstoy came of the same breed, as did so many other Russian artists, humanitarians, and even, as we know, revolutionary thinkers. It is not forgotten. Most of these people could not change or sympathize with the future. But the cosmopolitanism was symbolized in a great many Russian country homes of the older order, whose masters often worked with their men in the fields and came back to living rooms which had the scores of the world and magazines of art and literature.

In principle this applies to Rachmaninoff, and it is clearly revealed in his art. In practice he leans overmuch, perhaps, to German method, but the sensuous curve of his themes, the lordly sweep of certain movements of the symphonies and concertos, the color and the flavor of romantic introspection which so often characterize his works, are of the land and the period. It is the music of a true artist, a true representative of his nation who had its life intensely at heart, and a composer of richly gifted invention. Defects of this music, such as its tendency to over-ornamentation, in weak pages to sentimentality and at times an acceptance, too easy, of familiar formulas, are well known. In the main, one is and has been impressed again and again by the way this art holds up at a time when whole epochs and harmonic and stylistic advances have apparently passed it by. For one thing, it is much more spacious and has far more of grand line and of generous and emotional utterance than the more highly intellectualized and emotionally much skimpier music of composers of later tendencies. Above all, there remains its reality and genuineness of inspiration.

When Rachmaninoff came to America for the second time in 1917, uprooted by the Bolshevist revolution, he was a man and an artist without a country. "There is no Russia," was his growl in response to a question about his opinion of the political developments there, and he made no bones of this attitude, even when the stock of the Soviet Republics began to rise and when it would have been easier and more diplomatic to have changed his tune. Without doubt, this cyclonic catastrophe altered his course, if it did not stop it completely, as a creative artist. Yet it was the same man who passionately supported Russia and her cause in the present crisis and who gave large amounts of his earnings to her war needs. The fact is mentioned only for the reason that it bears so characteristically upon the strength and integrity of his position as a composer. That is, he never swerved to right or left in his artistic progress.

He went his own way. Among his great assets were his inherent sense of proportion and the habits of hard, methodical work which he learned early in his life when he was subjected, especially by his first great piano teacher, Svereff, at Moscow, to severe discipline. It was much needed by a youth who had been considerably spoiled in his boyhood and a man who knew what it was to battle enemies of doubt, melancholy, and self-examination. These were certainly sides of a typically Russian spirit of a former period. They were more than balanced and compensated by habits Rachmaninoff formed of the most practical and systematic methods of work and the acquirement of the ability to make decisions and enforce them.

Always he had to fight a house divided within him, just because of the number of his gifts, and his nature too intelligent, too complex and burdened with the spectacle of human futilities ever to be, under any condition, wholly happy. Nevertheless, he took a straight and powerful line and carried forward. He did this with a dignity and inherently aristocratic self-containment and power, which always emanated from him and constituted the fundamental cause of the fascination which his sparse and saturnine figure always had for the most unreflective public. He was also capable of what many never suspected: of uproarious humor. "But," he once said to us, "when I took my desk in the Imperial Opera House, as long as I was there, they never saw me smile!" And laughed as he said it.

He never gestured to the gallery or resorted to any species of theatrical play. In the first place, he didn't have to. No virtuoso ever dominated his audience by such purely musical means. Yet Rachmaninoff was far from a full-fledged pianist when he first came to America in 1909. He was then a composer-pianist who utilized the solo instrument principally to present his ideas. In 1917 he had to win such a position, and he did so, as a first and indispensable step, by the hardest and most grueling labor. Of course, no young student who complains of "nervousness" and all the rest of it apparently realizes that no great artist is without this foe, and it was one of Rachmaninoff's most formidable opponents. One early fall day he sat at his piano in trousers and undershirt, and asked his visitor to wait just a few minutes in the adjoining room. They were spent in one-hand practice of certain piano figures which culminated in a mordent, which would not go. He came out in a little while, heaved the sigh of an Atlas, sank moodily into a chair. "I begin my tour tomorrow in Lynn. It will be r-r-rotten."

It is a pity that America had so few opportunities of hearing him conduct—at least, his own music. It is said that he dreaded the necessity of absorbing himself in attaining the length and breadth of the symphonic repertory, which he would have to do if he accepted such a post as that offered him by the Boston Symphony—an extremely logical conclusion.

It is very significant to look at his position today as a composer. To take one prominent illustration among many that could be offered: the respective fates, in the compositional field, of Scriabin and Rachmaninoff. Incredible, to those who were hypnotized, as we ourselves have been on earlier occasions, by the special harmonic and other qualities of Scriabin, who certainly appeared as an innovator of possible epochal importance at the turn of the century and the decades immediately following—incredible that, *mirabile dictu*, Rachmaninoff is today the stronger. How long his music will endure after his going, which perhaps is the only fair condition of comparison, we may not prognosticate. Without any doubt, it will pass. In all probability the presence and the activities of its composer over a wide area have promoted its interests. And yet such scores as the Second Symphony, the work, you might almost say, of a Russian Mendelssohn; the *Isle of the Dead*; the two last piano concertos; more than one of the piano preludes, more mature in style in the opus numbers of the later years than the irresponsible one in C sharp minor, which Rachmaninoff composed when he was twenty, and sold, it is said, for as many dollars to a publisher; and a large number of his songs, which are undervalued; and his church music, which is very beautiful though Tchaikovskian, will probably for long years be with us. Today there is a certain artistic reaction in his favor. We are becoming, temporarily if no longer, aware that it is not idiom or style that makes a composition important, but things which are harder to establish or analyze, things having in the first place to do with inner probity and invention, and secondly with the artist's determination to become a past master of the tools of his trade. Rachmaninoff was never anything but impregnably himself, and in himself was greatness.

JUNE 6, 1943

═══

Oklahoma!

"The thing has style."

LIKE everyone else who has gone there, this writer found *Oklahoma!* a delightful show. First because of a number of especially good tunes by Richard Rodgers and excellent lyrics by Oscar Hammerstein 2nd, and tasteful and suggestive décor on Americanesque motives, and, above all, because of the dancing that is so original and so expressive of genuine things that lie deep in the people and the soil.

And the thing has style. The music is not folk music, but that of a Broadway composer writing in popular vein, freely, skillfully, and with taste and a fortunate relinquishment of the jazzeries of previous fashion. It is to an older, homelier, more truly ancestral source that Mr. Rodgers has gone for melodic elements of his score.

No more is the dancing folk dancing. But it has the folk sub-structure and is wonderfully interpretive of a phase of national temperament and tradition—a new burgeoning from an old root, and never merely realistic or photographic. This also applies to Russell Bennett's instrumentation of Rodgers' material. It is an orchestration valuable principally, not for its treatment of sonorities and its carrying power in the theater, but for its imaginative suggestion, underlying situation and text. Listen to the instruments when the wretched Jud speaks of his loneliness and need and of the howling of the mice in the doors.

Else the piece would not make such an impression, and the décor, the times, the dances, and the sentimental period pieces of a by-gone era and bygone conventions of the nineties weld not together as they do. The result is something which not only interests but moves the beholder.

One watches with the unequaled delight that is felt when the intuitive artist reveals that which was previously inarticulate in a form of new beauty and meaning. The reference is particularly to Miss de Mille's dance designs, to the lovely gawkiness of the girls and the sweep of the step of the men, and the riotous energy and exuberance and fancy of the whole business. This was prefigured in the dances Miss de Mille arranged for Aaron Copland's ballet *Rodeo*, but in *Oklahoma!* the conception goes farther and deeper.

Furthermore, the ballet is in itself a completely conventionalized design, whereas these dances emanate from the music and the situations and do not merely stylize but interpret them.

The dances of the girls seem like the dreams of Cinderellas of the ranch and farm come true—those of the generations deprived and suppressed by the old religion and hard work and flat plains and arid soil. They dance eagerly and wildly, quaintly and with ecstasy. An intense freed thing takes wing as the chains drop from them, and the very stiffness and constraint and inarticulateness of gesture that elsewhere would be obstacles stand transmuted of the soul.

The songs, as matter of fact, serve as a springboard for the dance numbers and the singing that usually goes with them. It is all of a piece—or most of it. It is true, at the same time, that there are inherent incongruities in this show, inconsistencies of procedure so curious that at the present time this observer is still fishing about in his mind to see if he can produce a completely logical explanation of its great and deserved success.

Oklahoma! is a lot of different things. Some have compared it favorably to *Show Boat*. That comparison with another work in which Mr. Hammerstein 2nd was strongly involved falls to the ground immediately. It falls if only because *Show Boat* has a real and great story, whereas the libretto of *Oklahoma!* is a hash, however expert or felicitous in the sum of it, of a drama which in its original form was much stronger as story and theater than this offering. Then there are those who dislike, and with some reason, the other raw and Freudian interpolation, as the present book makes it appear, of the figure of the sinister and lascivious Jud. When he is killed we don't mind so much, for it is so patently a device to get him out of the way and bring an end to the story. But the character is somewhat out of drawing for what is, after all, a "musical" and a comedy, the which implies a certain pleasant frame of mind and accepted convention. But Jud implies weakness in the story, resulting in the need of something to sharpen the situations and provide movement. Enter the Freudian farm hand. This commentator asks what is perhaps an extremely amateurish question where good Broadway showmanship is concerned: namely, whether it would reduce Jud more to scale if he sang his remarkable song of tormented loneliness and desire first by himself and in solitude, before the rollicking hero appeared, and then they sang the parody of his imaginary funeral together. Wouldn't this further accent the egregious egocentricity of this unpleasant character, so admirably portrayed by Mr. da Silva? We just ask *en passant*. The question doesn't have to be answered by anybody, not even by the most devoted correspondent.

As for the basis of the show, it is old-fashioned musical comedy, with modernizations and unconventional details, such as the absence of the opening chorus and walkaround, with the immediate introduction of the best hit of the whole score, which is a peach and is already known to the thousands who have attended *Oklahoma!* and the numberless thousands who will do so in weeks and months to come. Doubtless they, like ourselves, have formed the habit, on arising and looking out on a fine day, or roaring in the bathtub on a dull one, of chanting: "Oh, what a beautiful morning! Oh, what a beautiful day!" A song positively therapeutic to body and soul.

But, again, it is the sum of the piece, and not its component details, that counts, and indicates a direction that American opera of native cast might take in the period before us.

For, look you: real national opera has always begun somewhere in the vicinity of the position now occupied by *Oklahoma!* The grand opera was the classical thing, ceremonious, weighty, more or less international in idiom. But when *La Serva padrona* of Pergolesi and a thousand other little pieces of its kind were produced in Italy —little comedies, patter pieces, diversions of a patois sort with conversation as well as singing, in the eighteenth century—then a living opera, expressive of people and not courts or churches or social ceremony, came into being. This kind of opera has knocked the stiltedness of grand opera silly, time and again. When it came to a Paris dominated by the Lully-Rameau repertory that was then outliving its time, it created a complete revolution, and the war of words and pens twixt the "Bouffonistes" and their opponents was on. This stimulated, in turn, the French *opéra comique,* which sprang from similar sources. It went in succeeding years all the way from Rousseau's *Devin du village* to Bizet's *Carmen* in its scope and subject matter.

The Beggar's Opera, a selection of popular verse, dance, and ditty, demolished Handel, who followed outmoded grand-opera models, as opera composer. German opera throve on Mozart's singspiel *The Magic Flute,* and on other works by him and by others which followed this genre. The complete affirmation of the German spirit was the singspiel, the folk opera, of Weber, the immortal *Freischütz.* And Singspiel, spoken text, and comedic situation persist even in Beethoven's tragic and great (though manifestly imperfect) music drama, *Fidelio.*

American composers today have repeatedly essayed grand opera without a single significant success. It is in the field of musical comedy and operetta that we have so far done best and in which, by the evidence before us, we can expect to advance and are most racy. Jerome Kern's *Show Boat* remains our best. Gershwin's *Porgy and Bess* survives by its melodies and not by the dramatic appositeness of the score. His comedy *Of Thee I Sing* is much finer and better integrated and more reflective of period and environment. *Oklahoma!* is not topical and has, as we have noted, many of the characteristics of a period piece. But there is in it something special of the nation and its earlier adventure. Under the comedic mask and the convention of spurs, revolvers, and ten-gallon hats we recognize an ancestral memory, echo of an experience that went deep, a part of the adventure that has made us ourselves.

Oklahoma! succeeds, in the first place, because of what it is, essentially a very good and entertaining musical show—a first requisite. But it looks ahead to something more important and urgent today— to a compellingly native art of the lyric theater.

JANUARY 21, 1944

Hindemith & Hubermann

"Nothing like frankness between friends"

THE program and the performances given by Dr. Rodzinski and the Philharmonic-Symphony Orchestra last night in Carnegie Hall were uncommonly interesting and provocative.

There was a novelty, a Symphonic Metamorphosis on themes of Carl Maria von Weber, by Paul Hindemith, and it was one of the most entertaining scores that he has thus far given us, a real *jeu d'esprit* by a great master of his medium in a singularly happy mood.

There was a performance of the Brahms Violin Concerto with Bronislaw Hubermann as soloist, and Mr. Hubermann, with some stridency of tone and roughness of style, played in a great spirit, with a splendid grasp of the music's essence and a virile spirit that inspired his audience.

The orchestra was in excellent form. Witness the playing of the oboe solo of the slow movement of the concerto; the virtuoso brilliancy and glow of the performance of Hindemith's music; the noble and mellow tones of the trombones in the music from Wagner's *Meistersinger* which concluded the occasion!

As for what Mr. Hindemith, who was present, has done with the themes of Weber, he must take the full responsibility. He has remarked that since these are by no means the best of Weber's themes, he has felt the freer to treat them as he pleases! Nothing like frankness between friends, and the wonderful Carl Maria is safe in his grave! We confess that we have no knowledge of the themes used for "homage to Weber" in the peculiar manner of Hindemith.

But we must also confess to finding the music diverting and delightful. Its wit and its mastery alike intrigue us, and suggest a fresh if not a new departure by this composer.

Sometimes the Hindemith counterpoint has been as busy and energetic as the works of an automobile, and as meaningless. Sometimes it has been thick and overstuffed in its style. This Metamorphosis employs counterpoint as a matter only incidental to the gay development of the ideas, and there is sunshine in every nook and cranny of the transparent, debonair score.

It is music, one would say, that has gained by human contacts. It is without pompousness or dead weight. The *chinoiserie* of the second movement, based upon Oriental motives that Weber shaped for incidental music to Schiller's *Turandot,* is patent and intentional absurdity, with waggish nonsense of percussion instruments, from summoning bells to thuds of drums and clucks of xylophones.

For quite a while there is no fugue, but of course Hindemith has to come to a fugue before he has gone too far without one, and the fugal business in this movement does not cease to be diverting. His andante is in singing style, with broad developments and proper contrast to the other movements. His final march has a humor and a gusto which do not come as an anticlimax after all the capital fooling and perspicacious music-making which has preceded. How delightfully is learning carried in these pages!

An inspiring concert. Vigorous music, full-bloodedly played. Some might prefer more polish, maybe more of Olympian balance and suavity in the playing of the noble, rugged music of Brahms. We would rather hear the dramatic fire of Mr. Hubermann, feel the exaltation of his sentiment, hear him scratch in his excitement or ask more than one stringed instrument can readily give in the course of some grand pronouncement. Here, too, was superb coordination of the orchestra and solo parts, when soloist and conductor completed each other's ideas, united in the service of the composer. Mr. Rodzinski's tempos in the *Meistersinger* excerpts were brisk, but his reading was structural as well as vivid in color, and suggestive of Wagner's theater.

===

Young Mr. Schuman's Third Symphony . . .
Mature Mr. Menuhin's Mendelssohn

"The fine effrontery of fresh power"

A PROGRAM of exceptional significance for its values and contrasts in the most flexible and brilliant playing that the orchestra, returning to its former excellences under Dr. Rodzinski, has done since he took charge, and the presence of Yehudi Menuhin as soloist in the performance of the Mendelssohn Violin Concerto, distinguished the concert of the Philharmonic in Carnegie Hall last night.

The brilliant and audacious Third Symphony of William Schuman was pointed up by the introductory presentation of the Handel *Water Music*—in this instance the Harty arrangement of six from the twenty-odd pieces that Handel wrote to the eminent satisfaction of the British King. The fanfares that echo from choir to choir of the orchestra in its opening movement tested each division in a way that emphasized its virtuosity and tonal excellence. The playing of the Air, which is as gracious and mellow as old wine, revealed anew the suppleness, the beauty and expressive intensity of the strings. And this sunny music, so virile and melodic withal, was the perfect foil to what ensued.

For young Mr. Schuman's Third Symphony, obsequious as it may appear toward the contrapuntal forms of Handel's day, uses these forms after an organic concept of his own, and does so in a way that mocks them by the modernity, the rhythmic energy and dissonant bite of the music. Presumably Handel would have turned in his grave if he had heard this. Or would he? He, too, might have confessed to a great delight in the exuberant vitality and boldness of this writing; its plenitude, if not excess, of ideas in the treatment of this material; and the imagination that fills the old bottles with the elixir of young blood and the fine effrontery of fresh power.

The symphony should not have waited for so long a period to be heard a second time in this city since its introduction by Koussevitzky three seasons ago. The score may be too luxuriant in number of its ideas and their fructification. It may not be written in the manner that Mr. Schuman will favor later in his career. All this is secondary, if not beside the mark. He has written a very brilliant and arresting symphony, in ways he may or may not follow in later years, and this with the conviction, exhilaration, and laughter, too, of his age. We will have opportunity of knowing it better.

And here is a coincidence: the next music on the program consisted of two pieces composed in emulation of Handel's contemporary, J. S. Bach, by Villa-Lobos of Brazil. One smiles at the device, which, however, begets some admirably invented music. The Fifth *Bachianas Brasileiras* gives to a solo cello, while the others play a pizzicato like a Spanish serenade, a Bach-like air which the soprano sings in unison with the solo instrument. The second part, in total contrast, is an outcry of disappointed love, and wholly contrasted in its agitation. The first part returns—an admirable form and inspired method. Here the audience delights in the gift, and in the fresh voice of Dorothy Kirsten, soprano, as in the music.

The humorous piece *The Little Train of the Caipira* is also from a *Bachiana*—this time No. 2. The train chugs up over the mountains carrying the berry-pickers. It is, one gathers, a sort of Toonerville Trolley, bumping along, climbing slower or faster, and with a vast clanking and hooting of its machinery, as it goes on its undiscouraged way. This piece is amusement, the other one is much more, and both attest to the prodigality and unevenness of Villa-Lobos's genius.

The Menuhin who played the Mendelssohn Concerto is now the matured artist, no longer the student of genius emerging from a certain master's superintendence. Poise and elasticity, stability and lyricism, an authority that never deserted him, an ease which comes only with authority, throughout characterized his playing. It is true that the concerto has, on some other occasions we can mention, burned with a more incandescent flame, and that the slow movement, while it was in no sense breathless or without serenity, was played as fast as its nature would reasonably permit, and with some loss of *Innigkeit*. In the finale there were some ragged edges between player and orchestra; the *élan* of the interpreter more than recompensed for this, and the end caused the inevitable demonstration, continuing as reviewers left the hall.

MacDowell's Absence from the Hall of Fame

"Pretty narrow and academic"

ELECTIONS for names of Americans to be added to New York University's Hall of Fame on University Heights have taken place every five years since this gallery was founded at the beginning of the century. There stand, in commemoration, seventy-three bronze busts of American men and women who have greatly served their nation and the world.

No name is, of course, ripe for addition to the list until its bearer has been dead twenty-five years, the smallest interval in which any historical figure could be estimated with an approach to perspective in the choice.

The names that represent art are in enormous preponderance. American poets and writers include Emerson, Longfellow, Hawthorne, Lowell, Holmes, Poe, Harriet Beecher Stowe, James Fenimore Cooper, William Cullen Bryant, Mark Twain, Washington Irving, Walt Whitman—this list does not pretend to be complete. Among actors there are Charlotte Cushman and Edwin Booth. There are two painters, James McNeill Whistler and Gilbert Stuart, and the sculptor Saint-Gaudens. There is one composer, Stephen Foster—and at the luncheon which the National Federation of Music Clubs tendered Mrs. Edward MacDowell, widow of the composer, last Tuesday in this city, the question was properly raised as to why in this American Hall of Fame there was as yet no recognition of America's first great tone poet.

It is to be remembered, of course, that America's musical development has been more tardy than her progress in all others of the fine arts. No doubt there is in the minds of the committee which makes the selection of names to be added to the Hall of Fame the thought that the nominee should have a position of lasting influence and importance in the life of the nation as a whole. Nevertheless, it appears that in their selection the point of view has been pretty narrow and academic and, even where the writers are concerned, not characterized by a very wide range of vision.

As for MacDowell himself, had he been modestly present on such a board to advocate choice of membership—which never, in his opinion, would have included himself—he would have protested that not only music but all the fine arts must be seen as forming a most vital and significant part of the spiritual development of the nation, and would have insisted that not only a greater proportion of musicians but of painters, architects, playwrights, and sculptors should be there enshrined. Clearly the selection, from the cultural standpoint, is narrow and somewhat antiquated. With regard to musicians—world-famous executants as well as composers—it is poorly balanced and incomplete.

The choice of Stephen Foster as a beginning in music is indisputable. His finest songs are warp and woof of the life of the nation, and they will endure. This is really folk music, despite the known authorship of Foster's melody and verse—folk art, which the American people have taken to themselves as their own. MacDowell stands in a wholly different position in the domain of individual expression in a highly developed aspect of his art. Of that art, in America, he is an immortal forerunner.

The question is not how many of his works endure, or whether his tendencies are followed. Nor does the unarguable fact that in some day to come we will have composers whose works will outlive them longer than MacDowell's best pages have already outlived him. MacDowell stands, as the years pass, as the man who marks the beginning of the epoch of serious American musical composition in a way to cast the highest credit upon his creative position in it.

This is not because he lacked important and productive contemporaries, such as Parker and Chadwick, who preceded and outlived him. MacDowell was the poet and seer of them all, the most sensitive and original spirit that American music has yet produced, the one whose imagination projected farther in the realm of the seen and the unseen than that of any of his fellows.

He studied extensively in Europe and was inevitably influenced by Raff of Germany—as, without any direct contact, his musical sensibility was strongly responsive to the expression of Grieg. He was by descent a Celt, and this had much to do, no doubt, with his susceptibility to Grieg's northern imagery and harmonic novelty. But at no time did MacDowell, creatively speaking, rest on these men. He was a seeker, in fact, after farther things.

In pages of his sonatas there hover great shapes and the lightnings of mighty dreams. The music is prescient with them. In the best pages of the concertos and orchestral scores there is the dawning power of structure and epic design. So far as he went, he succeeded most fully in the smaller lyric forms, where his technical and architectural resources are fully adequate to his needs and where his play of imagination is the least weighted and most fancy-free.

But that was a relative weakness, subject to correction, could he have continued. His place is unquestioned, despite the passing of his era and style, the development here of modern musical technique and of composers' opportunities. His was the nature and expression of the complete artist—of the reaches of his spirit, and his perception of nature and the beauty and tragedy of human destiny, revealed to him by his "familiars" of forest, sky, and sea.

MacDowell had not completed himself when he died. What he might have become, had it not been for the fearful and premature catastrophe of his end, we cannot know. How far he would have completed his creative span, or how far he could hope to go in a country where music was not as yet a widely and highly cultivated art, is a matter merely for fruitless speculation. But the achievements and the unlimited implications of his art, his inexorably individual utterance, and his historic primacy in his field make him a foremost figure who cannot be rejected in any recognition of our national music.

NOVEMBER 26, 1944

No New Operas at the Met

"Not by Mr. Johnson's choice but by necessity"

No NEW operas are scheduled for production by the Metropolitan Opera Association, whose season opens tomorrow night. The opera for the opening is Gounod's *Faust*. Why not *Aïda* and be done with it? Well, *Aïda*—a magnificent masterpiece—might be better than *Faust*, but *Aïda* comes on Thursday, not Monday.

The other operas of the first week are likewise old, though fascinatingly individual. The oldest of them is *Don Giovanni*, which saw the light of day in 1787. The latest is Puccini's *Bohème* of 1896. What remains the most modern-sounding of the lot, and a gigantic creation, is Wagner's *Walküre*, for the Saturday matinee; and for the evening—the good old never-failing *Traviata*.

Let us look farther back over the past five seasons of the Metropolitan. What is the most modern score, and what is the earliest one in date of composition, to have been mounted in this theater? The earliest is Pergolesi's *La Serva padrona,* that historic *opera buffa* composed in 1733 and revived on Broadway's lyric stage in the 1942–3 season. We could count in J. S. Bach's cantata *Phoebus and Pan,* given as a short comic opera under Beecham's direction, and by his choice, in the preceding season. But that is not really an opera, and it had no success, for the simplest and most logical reasons. Pergolesi remains the earliest composer to be displayed in the last five years of Metropolitan activities, with Gluck of *Orfeo* (1762) and *Alceste* (1768) the next nearest to us.

Who are the latest composers that recent Metropolitan audiences have heard? There is young Mr. Menotti, whose *Island God* was given in the season of 1941–2. But that was a flash in the pan. What are the operas, latest composed, which have gained position?

The palm must go to Richard Strauss's *Rosenkavalier*, if the number of performances in consecutive seasons is the criterion. There is one other opera which has repeatedly returned to the Metropolitan boards, always with an approving reception by the public. We mean Italo Montemezzi's *L'Amore dei Tre Re* of 1913. Also should be mentioned Puccini's *Gianni Schicchi* of 1918, a short opera, the third of Puccini's triptych composed in that year. It is usually presented apart from its original two companions and in conjunction with some other and more substantial work. *Gianni Schicchi* is like the handy bachelor who can be counted on at short notice to fill in at the dinner table. But it has not the substance or the standing of *Rosenkavalier*, or its degree of permanency.

Thus the character of the Metropolitan repertory of the last five seasons, seasons which have increasingly gained the support of the public. It was not by Mr. Johnson's choice but by necessity that he kept to these operas. He had to give opera and balance his budget. These were the works he could count on to fill the theater.

There was no reserve cash for experimental production, as there had been during Gatti-Casazza's regime. In the years of his direction the Metropolitan was a decidedly progressive institution, although thoughtless and poorly informed criticism failed to take notice of that fact. Every season Mr. Gatti-Casazza mounted a number of new operas of various schools and origins, including, virtually every season, a new American opera or ballet, which he mounted to give native composers opportunities. At the same time he kept his audiences in touch with European developments. How many of the new works produced, usually in a sumptuous and expert manner, by Mr. Gatti found public support and a place in the repertory? Exactly not one!

Is it, then, that no great new operas, or operas capable of commanding a public and paying their way, have appeared in the last quarter-century? That is pretty nearly the truth, though it in no way implies that new works should not be given quick production and sympathetic hearing.

The public is assured that if the coming Metropolitan season proves as successful as the last, and the scale of expenses versus intake can be properly balanced, the organization will resume the production of novelties the following season. It is essential that this should be, and incumbent upon a modern lyric theater to see that it be done; though the Metropolitan would not lose audiences without such additional entertainment.

Why is this? Is it simply because the public is not curious about new music, or cautious and hesitant about welcoming anything that is fresh and original in this art? Suppose that a *Bohème* were composed today, or a *Don Giovanni*, or a *Walküre*. Would these works have to wait decades for public approval? History does not say so.

Always, of course, with a new style of composition, or a new treatment of the musico-dramatic problem, there have been reactionaries, impervious to new ideas, and puzzled and dismayed, if not antagonized, by novelty. But the new quickly muscled in and made its own position. This applies to Wagner but little less than it does to Puccini or Gounod. *Faust* was alarming for its novelty at its *première* in 1859, but fifty-seven performances of the opera were given in that one season. As for Wagner, as Ernest Newman remarks in his superb biography which is appearing volume by volume from the presses of Alfred Knopf, the "quaint legend" of his unpopularity as a composer is one of the choice historical fallacies. *Tannhäuser* was first produced in Dresden in 1845. Wagner was exiled from Germany in 1849. But in 1852, when he was still an exile, *Tannhäuser* was given fourteen performances in the city of Schwerin alone. What would be said of an opera which attained that many a season at the Metropolitan?

Suppose we stop berating the public for its blindness to new forms and ask ourselves why the operas that do inhabit the repertory fill the house season after season. There must be reasons.

There are reasons. They reside in their melodic eloquence and their strength and balance of structure—whether of ancient or modern type.

The dramatic and musical forms of the Gounod *Faust* are remarkably welded together. The second act, especially, is a musical and structural masterpiece. The writing for the voice is as masterly as is the melodic texture. Gounod's orchestra, a little light, a little plushy for modern taste, is nevertheless an epitome of taste, skill, richness of instrumentation. Above all, there are emotional moments which stir you by their inspiration and sincerity. There are sentimentalities, theatricalisms, and banal places. The significant thing, as Oscar Thompson once remarked of works of genius, is that their defects, however freely acknowledged, don't matter enough to destroy them.

It is not good that we should have to rely upon the successful operas, perhaps fifty to sixty in all, that make the present international repertory. One wishes this repertory were more inclusive. But that will come. In the meantime we can profit as listeners by a fresh approach to familiar works and recognition of their unique qualities.

JANUARY 11, 1945

Bartók's Concerto for Orchestra

"An emergence from pessimism"

DR. KOUSSEVITZKY, on occasion, is a bold but by no means tactless program-maker. He introduced a new Concerto for Orchestra in the modern vein by Béla Bartók at the concert of the Boston Symphony

Orchestra last night in Carnegie Hall. He prefaced this more or less problematic score by the folklike simplicities of the little prelude with which Moussorgsky prefaced the opening scene of his opera *Khovanchina*, and he followed it with the familiar and justly popular epic of Brahms, the C minor Symphony.

The Concerto, given its *première* in Boston last December 1, was written for the Koussevitzky Foundation, established in memory of Natalie Koussevitzky. Cushioned between Moussorgsky and Brahms, it had a very cordial reception.

This was due in the first place to the fact that the score is by no means the nut to crack that other of Bartók's late works have offered. It is a wide departure from its author's harsher and more cerebral style. There might even be the suspicion, with an artist of less sincerity than this one, that he had adopted a simpler and more melodic manner with the intention of an appeal to a wider public.

But that would not be Mr. Bartók's motive. Nor would the emotional sequence of this music, and the care with which it has evidently been fashioned, support such an assumption. What is evident is the courage, which this composer never has lacked, with which he is striking out, in his late years, in new directions. The style is less involved and ingrowing than we have thought much of Bartók's late music to be, and it escapes in a large measure the pale cast of isolated thought which has brooded over so many of his pages.

In sum, as he himself has stated, it is an emergence from the pessimism which might pardonably have engulfed him, as it has so many leading artists of today, especially those of European schools. And of all things courage is the most praiseworthy.

The score is called a "concerto," meaning a work cast in the eighteenth- rather than the nineteenth-century mold, with, of course, contemporaneous idioms. This is not a piece for soloist and orchestra. It is a series of movements in terms of instrumental parts that form an ensemble. There are also elements of the classic symphony in the structure. Only two of its parts have musical relation to each other. Each is individually complete and different in form from the others; all are subjective in feeling.

The important point is the character of the music. It begins with a somber prelude, the theme in the low strings, several times repeated, with a sort of miragelike reflection of itself in harmonies of the upper strings. Mr. Bartók says that the second movement, scherzo-like, is a jest—though one would say a bitter one—and the third a lamentation. There are references in the fourth movement to the first, and then, as a brilliant and entertaining contrast, a joyous, whirling finale in Hungarian style. Often there is the suggestion of dance rhythms and of the singsong of folk strains—a "happy" and resolute ending.

Is this a temporary divagation from the road Bartók so consistently has traveled? Is the tendency more than skin deep, or its fruits of lasting value? The audience showed that it enjoyed the music, taking to it more readily than anything Bartók has recently written. Dr. Koussevitzky did him a notable service by his performance, which was of extraordinary spirit and virtuosity. There were places where the whole string choir had to be so many Heifetzes; when the whole orchestra, singly and en masse, did feats of derring-do. Repeatedly Dr. Koussevitzky led Mr. Bartók from the wings, and finally left him alone on the stage with the applauding audience. After the Brahms symphony there was also a demonstration.

FEBRUARY 18, 1945

—

The Magnificently Disciplined Form
of Tchaikovsky's *"Pathétique"*

". . . this antiquated nonsense" demolished

WE CONSTANTLY hear about the necessity of an open mind in listening to new music. Does it occur to many that an open mind is also a necessity with old music? There is at least an equal distrust of ideas in the one field as in the other, and old music as well as new, is in constant need of re-examination.

This was borne particularly upon us at the concert of the Boston Symphony Orchestra last Wednesday night when Koussevitzky gave another of the many performances of the Tchaikovsky *Symphonie "pathétique"* which he has given in this city. Be sure that the Doctor, in the course of a very personal interpretation, spared no emotional value, no stroke of rhetoric, no detail of the scoring with its sable magnificence. He was freer with his fluctuations of tempo than ever—in some places, we thought, unnecessarily so. The pros and cons of that matter are already forgotten in the face of an interpretation which, as a whole, was of overwhelming emotion and tonal splendor. But this emphasis of the rhapsodic element in the music also drove home the very attribute which it has been the long-accepted convention to deny Tchaikovsky. We mean the wholly exceptional power and originality of his form.

This, as the writer took occasion to remark in comment the morning after the performance, is no matter of opinion. It is plainly to be perceived in the documentary evidence of the score. What has no doubt confused pedantic minds, or those so immersed in the German conception of symphonic form that they have been wholly dominated by such tradition, is the fact that the form here discovered is not that of Mozart or Beethoven, but Tchaikovsky. As for the symphony's emotional content, it is so genuinely Russian that the same type of mind and of criticism which for long years found Russia's greatest moralist and psychologist in letters—Feodor Dostoevsky—merely a bad example of a morbid and undisciplined soul, also finds Tchaikovsky "hysterical," "uncontrolled," weak and deficient in structure. It is not to be wondered at that this antiquated nonsense has been repeated ad infinitum by generations of people satisfied to repeat the sayings of others and prone to be embarrassed by Tchaikovsky's intense humanity and directness of speech. And then there is the tendency, latent in all of us, to find reasons, not for logical conclusions, but for what we want to believe. The partisanship of European culture toward any manifestation outside its own ways of thought and esthetic is particularly manifest in the instance of this Russian, and its criticism is parroted by the majority of our academicians and smart intellectuals here. To the cultivated Continental mind the conception that there could be wider and freer horizons than those perceived by its own artists is mythical. However, that illumination will come—in fact, is on its way today. For the world is irresistibly growing larger, and in its new perspective various composers will stand in different relations to each other than in the past. This may even prove true of Tchaikovsky. Let us consider for a moment certain of his technical problems.

Throughout his creative development, so abruptly and tragically terminated, Tchaikovsky had great difficulty with form. Of this difficulty he was humbly and distressfully aware. One reason for this was the luxuriance of his ideas, so difficult to control and co-ordinate, particularly with a man of his intensely emotional nature. Another was the fact that such an original genius as his could not accept classic form as he found it. Tchaikovsky was ever seeking that form which should be the logical germination of his individual ideas. As with Beethoven before him—Beethoven, who was less radical in his innovations—if the mold did not fit the idea, then the mold must be recast in such a way as fully to release and render effective the idea's dynamism. In all of Tchaikovsky's symphonies he is fighting for this clarification and formal logic. In the Sixth he has almost completely achieved it, with the result that the passage of time reveals the *Symphonie "pathétique"* as exceptional among all modern works of its class for its sweep of line and the astonishing originality of its development.

The work is genuinely symphonic, in a manner which utilizes the methods of composition not only of Beethoven, but of Liszt; and which, within its inborn lyricism and profoundly racial character, embodies the quality of synthesis of which the Russian mind has so signally proved itself capable. The relation of the movements, as well as their internal structure, is also symphonic, though they fall neither into the mold of Viennese classicism or that cyclic form which stemmed from Liszt and was adopted by so many of Tchaikovsky's contemporaries in Russia—not one of whom, from Rimsky-Korsakoff to Moussorgsky, was capable of Tchaikovsky's architecture. None of the accepted formulas is relied upon for this achievement.

When we come to the interior structure, one remarkable idea after another confronts us. The movement nearest symphonic precedent is the first, although it is the one movement with anything of padding or of the tentative and experimental. There are new sequences in the statement of the themes, in their proportions in relation to each other, and in special processes of development. The spectral introduction of the first theme, which takes form like some tragic ghost in a land of shadows; the transition which is the inevitable consequence of the mood, from the slow tempo of the introduction to tempos of the movement proper; the succession of episodes interspersed with the rich development; the return, in one of the greatest orchestral climaxes, to the reprise where, for dramatic as well as structural reasons, the first theme is eliminated; and finally the contrast of color when the second theme reappears—these represent not only inspiration, but sheer technical virtuosity.

The 5-4 movement is the movement in which the problem of that irregular rhythm is solved more felicitously than in any other composition that we know. The orchestration of the whole symphony is so masterly that it would be folly to begin particularizing with the famous drum beat and its reinforcements while over it the strings wail their tragedy.

The scherzo is replaced by the terrible march with its scheme of a triple against a duple rhythm. The way in which the triplets first dominate the scene, the gradual emergence of the duple rhythm of the march, the absorption of the triplet figure by that march, ever expanding, growing irresistibly in its power—not only an immortal master but a colossal nation speaks here, and this under an iron control. If Hitler's men had known this symphony they might well have hesitated as that music unfolded. It has a parallel in the extent of Russia's battle line, the tread of her hosts, the accumulated fury of her people.

What of the unique finale? No formalist would have more ably contrasted its two themes than Tchaikovsky. Who else would have followed the battle-drunk processional with the final elegy which is a lament for nothing less than humanity and its end? That too is Russian, as his compassion, in which the supercilious find only self-pity, is equally of Tchaikovsky and his nation. What might we not have expected of the man who at fifty-three created the "Pathetic" Symphony?

NOVEMBER 4, 1945

―――

Should Critics Get Mad?

"All the world is mad but thee and me, John. . . ."

SHOULD a critic get mad when he hears a piece of music to which he feels acute objection? Mad, not merely as a matter of stimulating esthetic discussion, but just plain carnally mad at what he—mistakenly or otherwise—deems to be a violation of artistic principle? And to what extent should he betray that fact in his writings?

This is more than an academic proposition, as would be shown by perusal of the letters of several correspondents who take this writer to task for what they variously consider to be his "temperamental," "prejudiced," "destructive" commentary upon Mahler's First Symphony, performed here under Mr. Rodzinski.

We pass over the question of the point at which an opinion becomes a prejudice, though it is an important one. There are many who call their own opinions "opinions," but consider other opinions, which disagree with theirs, "prejudices." But that is all right, and very human. "All the world is mad but thee and me, John, and even thee——" Nobody is free from either opinion or prejudice. But in what degree is it appropriate for an officially appointed critic of artistic events not only to state reasons and conclusions but, emotionally speaking, to show his hand?

People take questions of art with different degrees of seriousness. Only a few of them are serious about it at all. To the casual bystander, as the crowds pour out of the exits after the concert, the vehemence of the ensuing arguments seems out of line with the values of the subject, and even rather ridiculous. What, in heaven's name, is all this verbal shooting about? These musicians! These critics!

Suppose Conductor X did manhandle the score of Composer Y? What if Mr. Avant-garde can be proved to have written in consecutive thirteenths instead of consecutive fifths in his symphonic poem about the love-life of spiders according to Fabre? What of it? Isn't music something that gentlemen can discuss with courtesy and equanimity? The other night two of them almost came to blows over the question of Toscanini's tempos in the middle of the second movement of Beethoven's Seventh Symphony. It appears that these people have convictions, even passions, about music. Is that normal? Is it advisable? Or is it merely ill-breeding? Can such heat be countenanced in such a rarefied realm?

Some people draw a very flattering portrait of critical omniscience functioning in an atmosphere of Olympian calm. The critic is to judge, not feel. In his pontifical robes, unmoved and untroubled by the emotional vacillations of circumambient society, he is calmly to adjust his spectacles, examine the evidence, and, with authority incontrovertible, separate the sheep from the goats, while delivering the verdict that settles the business. This, as we say, is a highly complimentary conception, although we have yet to discover the reviewer who would feel that he could measure up to it. What is implied by this fanciful picture is no doubt the idea that the critic, at all times and under all circumstances, should maintain the "impersonal" and "judicial" attitude.

There is another school of thought. Its tenets were neatly outlined by George Bernard Shaw when he said that unless a mother was good and mad when she spanked her child she was a hypocrite, a sadist, and a bad parent. Hit, if you will, he implied, but be honest about it. The children will respect you not less but more, in Mr. Shaw's judgment. And, by the same token, a blow that causes pain, delivered with deliberate self-righteousness, or following some abstract theory of judgment, is a horrible cruelty, productive of evil. It is the full-blooded mother who knows darned well why she is mad, and what she intends to do about it, who is likely to have an improving effect upon the offspring. It is an idea, and there may be something in it.

Certainly there is an immense difference between the motivations. Moral pretense is one thing, and genuine moral indignation another; or even other kinds of indignation, misjudged as they may be, and unwisely unveiled, provided that at least they be heartfelt, and proceed not from self-love, conceit, or another ignoble motive.

The rest is beyond the power of man to decide. But an honest mistake, if it be such, is far more of a contribution to the ultimate formation of enlightened public opinion than an insincere and pussyfooting attempt at balancing of pros and cons and the cautious refraining from any precipitating conclusion. We see this pussyfooting all around us today. And it is not confined to Mr. Milquetoast's ideas about music. It was admirably said recently by a celebrated historian that the most fruitful centuries for mankind were those in which there had been the most danger and the least stabilization. The analogy is perhaps a distant one, but it may be added that similar periods when criticism was not of a pattern, and its primary objectives were not amiability or even good manners but those of acute reasoning and passionate conviction, were the ones in which ideas made the greatest progress.

The trouble with most of our musical criticism, and our music, too, is its lukewarmness. Where is the precipitating issue? Where are the dynamic forces? What composer today is worth a desperate defense or opposition? As soon as one appears—as he will—there will be a resurgence of critical energy and uncompromising opinion—good fighting, not, pray God, on the battlefields, but in the fruitful arenas of ideas, concepts, cultures. It goes without saying that present company has nothing to do with these vistas. We are talking of the shape of great things to come. When that day arrives, be assured that there will be stout-hearted and keen-penned critics who, on good occasion, will lose their tempers.

FEBRUARY 14, 1946

The Finest Russian Symphony in Twenty-five Years: Prokofieff's Fifth

Forms, Not Formulas

WITH a fine courtesy to his audience and to the art of modern music, Dr. Koussevitzky repeated Prokofieff's Fifth Symphony, which he had introduced here earlier in the season, at the concert given by the Boston Symphony Orchestra last night in Carnegie Hall. The symphony is certainly one of the most interesting, and probably the best, that has come from Russia in the last quarter-century. It is unquestionably the richest and most mature symphonic score that the composer has produced. There are new spiritual horizons in the serenity of the opening movement and wonderful developments that come later.

The symphony is considerably less dissonant than other representative works of Prokofieff—for example, the Sixth and Seventh Piano Sonatas, which are harsher, grimmer, and more warlike. The Fifth Symphony, composed in 1944, impresses us as being another story. The opening theme, which recurs in the introduction to the finale, is an index to the loftiness of the whole conception. It is quite possibly extravagant, after what was for the writer a first hearing, to say that the slow movement, very emotional and grandly planned, reminded him of passages—one would almost say "processes"—in certain slow movements of Beethoven.

But we forget, and are due for a sharp reminder from that advanced school of thought which busily informs the public today that no really distinguished music has any definite emotional implications, when we claim that this very element, plus the strength of the form, make the Fifth Symphony superior to other of Prokofieff's scores. His emotion is deeper and more genuine. His harmonic scheme and his key relationship are more transparent. His forms are classic.

When the progression of the musical thought leads naturally and inevitably to it, there is as much dissonance, and no more, as the logic of masterly part-writing requires. But that is not new. It is as old as Mozart and older. The "forms," we have said, are classic. This does not mean that they are slavish copies of formulas. The opening movement—in case that matters a hoot—is in the age-old "sonata" form—and is splendid music.

The scherzo, which is very exciting and picturesque along immediately recognizable lines, varies the ancient procedure in a striking way—as, for example, in successive transformations of the main idea of the movement instead of a mere repetition of phrases and sections, as in the Mozart-Haydn model. There is also an extra theme in the first part of this movement, etc., etc., etc. No doubt our "absolute musicians" and our apostles of "pure music" would be pleased to read more of this kind of thing as a commentary upon this art work. We suspect, however, that the ordinarily intelligent reader would finally collapse if it were long continued.

The slow movement, an unusual blend of passacaglia and free development, is important for its melodic and emotional content, its wealth of ideas, its variety and resource and yet fundamental unity in their treatment—again real pulsing music that never once descends from its emotional heights and never once flags in the continuity and strength of its inspiration.

The finale has the fine introduction that brings back the Olympian mood of the opening, with the theme itself. Then comes the rondo movement, a variant of the old practice. A main theme near in character to the initial motive alternates with various dance motives and fragments of joyous song which are flung into the pot as the movement sweeps along to its climax. Then a trombone—if memory serves us where the instrumentation is concerned—shouts a variant of the earlier theme in counter rhythm to all the whirling dance figures. It is a finale by a composer who has no hesitation whatsoever in speaking in popular musical parlance, who here writes holiday music for a rejoicing people—and how!

The performance was one of supreme virtuosity and much more: it seemed to pierce to the innermost possibilities of the score as it is written. The remainder of the program requires no particular comment here. The Beethoven "Pastoral" Symphony is a chef d'oeuvre of this conductor and orchestra, and a never-ending delight for its music. The "Coriolanus" Overture fittingly introduced the occasion.

APRIL 14, 1946

The Tardy Recognition of Charles Ives

"Sturdy, luxurious, savorous, and thorny"

WHEN a nation is settling its land, breaking its earth, absorbing constant immigration and the turbulent forces that come with it, it is not surprising if single personalities of exceptional capacities are unrecognized or ridden over roughshod in the scramble by contemporaries too busy themselves to pause and recognize a particular individual's value to the new civilization.

It is just the same in music. In America we are only now establishing our boundaries, only now beginning to assess the achievements of our pioneers, and only now, where our creative artists are concerned, getting really rooted in our soil.

On this soil there start up all sorts of different growths, some of them delicate and some of them hardy, some indigenous but most of them seeds wafted from afar, all mingling together in fantastic combinations and gradually, in the terms of our spring gardeners, accumulating a mulch from which always stronger growths will develop. And in America, today, we find one of the deepest-rooted of these growths—the one which is the most sturdy, luxurious, savorous, and thorny, too—in the music of Charles Ives.

The singularly individual quality of his art is attested by recent events which have emphasized the nature of his product and certain co-related facts of his career. In the first place, Charles Ives is seventy-one years old. But last week at the concert of American music by living composers which the New York Little Symphony gave in Carnegie Chamber Music Hall, it was his Third Symphony, then given its world *première*, which far surpassed everything else on the program for virility, originality, and essential modernity. The reviewers were unanimous upon this point, as they were upon that of the racy and national quality of the music. And the symphony, then heard for the first time anywhere, had lain around in a Connecticut barn and adjacent places for forty years!

That sort of thing has happened before when Ives music was played. One afternoon in 1927, grumbling at the number of concerts that had to be covered, this reviewer lurched into Town Hall, and as quickly as he sat down sat up, electrified. For the orchestra, under Eugene Goossens, at a Pro Musica concert, was playing music of vigor, raciness, and audacity as unheralded as they were astounding. The score was concerned with the composer's recollection of a New England village on a Fourth of July before the turn of the century, with the commotion, the brass bands, the hymns to Old Glory, and the rest of it; things he had known as a boy, and which memory had transmuted into astonishingly imaginative vigor. It was a movement—two of them were played—from the Fourth Symphony of Charles Ives, then unknown to us by so much as his name, though he already had passed his fiftieth year.

It is well to say here that, having heard such original music only once—a performance never since repeated in this city—we may have overestimated its unmistakable vitality and novelty of expression. But the impression was so strong, and has been so indelible, that, coupling it with other fragmentary manifestations of Mr. Ives's quality as musician, one believes in the presence of a significant creative spirit.

A third episode may now be recounted which has its regrettable connotations.

Some six years ago certain leading members of the Monte Carlo Ballet, Russian dancers and musicians, were seeking new American music as a subject for choreographic interpretation. They asked the writer for some suggestions in this direction. He gathered together a few American scores that he thought might interest them, including one by Ives. It was the only score that the group took seriously. They clustered around the piano, where Nicholas Slonimsky, one of the two musicians we knew in the entire nation who could play from an Ives score, was officiating. Whether Charles Ives would have been disappointed by their conclusions is not here to be conjectured. Choreographic "interpretations" visited upon helpless symphonies today are legion and, more often than not, sheer misrepresentation of the music. The Russians concluded that, in view of the difficulty of the score, it could not be readily converted into a ballet. But the aside of one of them while the discussion was going on was striking. He said to us in whisper: "Too bad—Stravinsky."

For answer we simply pointed to the date on the music page. It was 1901, in which year Stravinsky was still wet behind the ears, having composed not a single one of his important works. Schoenberg had written *Verklärte Nacht* by that time, a work which Ives could not possibly have heard. Hindemith had yet to gain a public. The voices, in a word, of the leading modernists of that decade were unknown in America. (And certainly no one in this country, at the time, would have taken Ives's audacities seriously.) When we indicated the date on the score to our Russian friend, he said: "Still too bad; too late."

That is to say that, although Charles Ives had anticipated in the work under examination the polyrhythms and the polyharmonies of the author of *Sacre du printemps* by a round dozen of years—indeed, by almost two dozen years before American audiences heard that very controversial work—musical progress apparently had passed him by. As a matter of fact, this is not so. For the resemblances to Stravinsky were superficial, consisting principally in certain technical formulas in which the American had preceded him and all his fellows. This was not true of the substance of the music, which is as American, as personal and racial as Stravinsky never has been since the *Sacre*. What was true was the very advanced musical thinking of Charles Ives, so clearly shown in a composition that had been penned more than thirty-five years previous. That is what happened to a man who, whatever the comparative merits of various of his works may prove to be, is by all signs and tokens one of the most independent and progressive of American composers of this epoch.

True, a few of Ives's songs have been sung, a little of his chamber music played. And last season John Kirkpatrick played his "Concord" Piano Sonata, a work to which much and favorable attention was given in the reviews next morning. The writer did not fully assimilate this sonata at first hearing, and is not as sure of its ultimate value as some of his colleagues were at the time. There were pages that he found loose in structure, sometimes redundant, and a space,

as it seemed to him in places, between the conception of the composer and the sometimes naïve expression.

Conductors, shown Ives's scores, almost to a man turn from them,
first of all with the complaint that the music is not only extremely
difficult but in places impracticable. It may be so, but in these days
of superabundant virtuosity it seems strange that all of them have
stopped there; that apparently none has attempted to consult Ives
about problems of performance of his works—even in the years when
he was not partly invalided, as he is today, and when he, an excellent
musician himself, could surely have done much to elucidate difficulties, or even to aid the conductor by some appropriate simplification.

And, furthermore: the Third Symphony did not offer such insuperable difficulties, even to a minor orchestra whose director had
the courage to play it. Had any other conductor but Lou Harrison,
who appeared as guest leader with Joseph Barone, the enterprising
director of the Little Symphony, even seen, or tried to read, that
score? Suppose Stravinsky, Schoenberg, et al had offered such scores
for examination. Would they have remained unexamined, unper-
formed? It is very unlikely.

It would be a pleasure here to speak at length of the man and artist himself, of the singular idealism and independence of his thinking and his attitude toward the fundamental questions of human
existence. It is to be hoped that it will not be necessary for Charles
Ives to die for his representative music—included in some eleven
volumes of chamber music and six of orchestral scores in the Library
of Congress, the Fleischer Collection, and the American Music Center—to gain a hearing.

OCTOBER 13, 1946

Myra Hess Returns from the Wars

"All imaginable intimacy and inner feeling"

THE audience which inundated Town Hall and overflowed upon
the stage yesterday afternoon to greet Myra Hess, the pianist, who
made her first appearance here in recital since the war, was almost to

have been taken for granted in its numbers, its friendship, and its enthusiasm for the qualities of the artist. Miss Hess's musical ministrations in London during the catastrophe, her complete disregard of danger or fatigue or any claims whatever upon her gifts and her strength where it was so badly needed, can never be forgotten.

Add to this her exceptional qualities as a musician! From the standpoint of performance alone, she has been too long away. The audience rose when Miss Hess appeared, remaining in the hall to the last note of a long and demanding program, to listen absorbed, to applaud, and to cheer. The affection as well as the admiration evinced must have been precious to the woman and the artist.

In a few fine words spoken from the stage during the intermission Miss Hess said that she had been overpraised for her London concerts; that they had been a privilege which only increased her obligation to the brave people who endured every trial and privation and held on for mankind and civilization. The continuation of the concerts through the fearful years would not have been possible, she continued, if it had not been for a multitude of American friends who, from the time the London National Gallery opened its doors for music on October 10, 1939, until even after hostilities had ceased, had steadily sent substantial funds required for the performances to be maintained. Miss Hess added her belief that this mutual effort of men in a work of culture so necessary to bring the two nations together would remain an enduring bond.

The paraphrase is ours, and it would not be easy to match the simplicity and the warmth of her words. Nor is it even possible to give more than an indication of the effect, for example, of the mystical sonata, Opus 110, of Beethoven, as she played it yesterday with all imaginable intimacy and inner feeling—music in which Beethoven broods in his loneliness and his prayer and hears the rustle of wings. It is scarcely the occasion to compare the details of this interpretation.

Enough that the tone quality, as well as the inflection of phrase and co-ordination of thought, conveyed the musical essence, and that in no pages was Miss Hess more eloquent than in those of supplication and pathos which occur between the two great fugal developments of the final part. This was not a virtuoso imposing a dominant personality upon an audience, but a true and modest musician who was saying, in her own way: "These are some of the pages of Beethoven that I most deeply revere. I hope that I can persuade you to feel

them with me." And the audience came very truly into rapport with
Beethoven.

Miss Hess began with one of the gayest and most charming of the
Bach suites, the French Suite, the fifth, in G major. It contains the
popular gavotte, for one thing, but that is one thing only. Every
movement is a delight, and there are tucked away, in odd corners,
some of Bach's bold dissonances, as in the bourrée, and in the loure
one of the most gracious melodies he ever wrote for the keyed instrument.

Bach was followed by Beethoven of the early and seldom played
F major Variations. They are charming in the old style, which was
remarkably communicated. It was true that the program in itself
was unwieldy, with too much sameness of key. Between Beethoven
and Brahms we had F major, A flat major, F minor—no excess of
tone color here. And one can point to a considerable measure of
romantic fusion and to passages which sounded intensely dramatic
in Brahms' day but are somewhat clichés now.

There is the stock romantic pattern of so many German compositions and novels of the time—the Spielhagen thing, *From Darkness
to Light*. The Faust idea is ever present. One knows that after the
poetic song and the Faustian soliloquies, there will be a six-four
chord, a tonal apotheosis referring to themes already heard, and
ascension music in the major key.

But Miss Hess loves this music, feels it deeply, re-creates it with
its original freshness and nobility of spirit. And perhaps nothing is
more necessary than for an artist to accomplish that, and drive it
home. To make us both feel and believe that these are the things
which are true. The audience remained for long, and Miss Hess
played many encores.

The Telephone and The Medium by Menotti

"No other American composer has shown the inborn
talent . . ."

An amusing and felicitous little *opera buffa, The Telephone,* by
Gian-Carlo Menotti, received its *première* last night in the Heck-
scher Theatre and was coupled with *The Medium,* by the same composer, in a double bill. *The Medium,* first heard here in May of last
year, has had some effective revisions, and introduced a superb new
contralto, Marie Powers. The half-hour *opera buffa* has two singers,
who were Marilyn Cotlow, soprano, and Paul Kwartin, baritone. It
is really gay, and done dexterously with a light touch. Also, it is easy
to perform and, with a twelve-piece orchestra, easy to produce. This
is not intended as an advertisement for Mr. Menotti's latest opera—
his fifth—but is intended to emphasize his practical sense of the
theater and his way, on occasion, of writing melodically and wittily
for it.

The piece, to boot, is up-to-date. It could be a scene in any American home, although not always is there to be found a heroine quite
as light-headed as the lady whose interests are divided between her
suitor and her telephone. The timid young man wishes to propose.
He is constantly interrupted by the telephone. His train goes in
an hour. Despairing of ever getting a chance to speak his mind, he
rushes out to another telephone. From there he proposes, and a duet
on two sides of a wall, like the quartet in the last act of *Rigoletto,*
ends happily ever after, the swain taking down his inamorata's number, which ends with the vocally satisfying figure 0.

A short, gay overture leads to the rising of the curtain, and the
lyrical conversation proceeds. The young man's broken phrases are
interrupted by the first ring of the telephone. Into the instrument
the lady sings arias of several kinds, coloratura, dramatic, and sentimental, to texts which are of the most frivolous sort. The young man
has an instant of aria, too, as the girl leaves the stage for a moment.

They have a duet which is a take-off of the Bellini operatic style, with a vapid arpeggio accompaniment. The finale comes quickly and is not too extended. It is good theater throughout and lively, tuneful music. Probably it would rank as the shortest *opera buffa*, or opera of any other specific kind, in existence. Obviously it is a work for a brief entertainment by itself or to be done in combination with a companion piece to fill out a program.

That piece last night was the melodrama *The Medium*. Its first act has been tightened up and given more concentration. It is well introduced with the incantory motive flung out by the orchestra, and is set forth on a stage that is suggestively macabre, filled with the junk of a cheap medium's parlor where the credulous are mulcted of their money. This act has not the musical substance or, naturally, the dramatic climax of the second act, when the medium, terrified at a touch on her throat during a séance, shoots the mute who is her assistant, while her daughter cries for aid.

But whether this scene is better than that one; whether Mr. Menotti is utilizing ideas of his own or idioms which he has absorbed from Puccini, Ravel, Rimsky-Korsakoff, and other composers, we have here the quality of opera. It is dramatic music, emphatic in action as well as feeling, and in essence song, which is what opera must be. No other American composer has shown the inborn talent that Mr. Menotti, Italian by descent, unquestionably possesses for the lyric theater.

The Medium was also the occasion of the introduction here of a wholly exceptional singer. She is the contralto Marie Powers, who took the part of the medium. Miss Powers has a magnificent voice, with all sorts of colors in it, and dramatic brilliancy into the bargain. She is a great actress. The frowsy medium had something formidable and sinister about her; evil hung over her; she was coarse and drab and terrifying. Her high tones pealed out with a breath-taking impact. The voice was now full and incisive, now sensuous and moving in the extreme, and now it was filed down to a whisper, or a pale, eerie color. Miss Powers will not long be an unknown quantity to our musical public.

The remainder of the cast included the dancer Leo Coleman, whose Mute is an unforgettable figure in his facial expression of intense emotion showing inarticulately through a mask, and his amazing pantomime. The fine voice of Evelyn Keller was again heard as Monica, and a trio which, as last year, included Beverley Dame and

Virginia Bealer, to whom Paul Kwartin was added, made the ensemble. Leon Barzin was the very able conductor of the performance.

Toscanini Reaches Eighty

"Tradition is quite possibly the last bad performance."

ARTURO TOSCANINI has his eightieth birthday next Tuesday, March 25. He is allergic to birthday celebrations, but he will hardly escape them on this occasion. His honors have inevitably multiplied in the sixty-one years of his career as conductor, since the historic occasion when in Rio de Janeiro he stepped from the cellist's desk in the orchestra, took the baton and led from memory and without rehearsal an electrical performance of *Aïda*, and found himself established in his career.

Since then the art of music—or should we say the externals of the art of music?—has changed very much. The art of conducting has changed, too. The tastes of audiences have changed. Reputations have been made and unmade by the dozens in that highly competitive field in which Toscanini continues to function triumphantly as a sovereign interpreter and high priest of his craft. Why is this so, and how has it been done?

It has not been done by any swerving from a chosen path as an artist, or by obeisance to passing fads or powerful influences of the hour. It has not been achieved by assiduously seeking advantage or playing politics or pretending to a position in the vanguard of those who would fear to do otherwise than to echo sedulously the *dernier cri* of the ineffably smart. Toscanini's progress has not rested upon variables. It is due to the quality of his genius, to incessant study and lacerating self-criticism, and to passionate integrity in the service of his art. There has been an unswerving progress toward a central ideal. These things are not subject to change or favor. In proportion to their attainment they constitute an artist's power.

But the facts of Toscanini's achievement have a logic to be found

not merely in his genius but in his methods of work. He has not astonished the world merely because of a fabulous endowment. Toscanini studies and thinks with a thoroughness and conscience worthy
of the greatest scholar. He has the powerful and independent mind
of a man who has learned the hard way, who had the innate capacity
and faced the imperative necessity to take nothing at second hand
and to think for himself. Objectivity is his watchword, but musical
interpretation, as he once admitted, has to be more than that. Yes!
Toscanini approaches a score with the most reverent and impersonal
attitude in the world. His examination of the music is not photographic, but microscopic. He is passionately the advocate of revealing exactly what is indicated on the music page, not of reading into
it things which are not there. But he cannot help having the percep-
tions and the expressive powers of a man of genius.

He was engaged to conduct a Verdi opera, and an appointment
was made for him to go through the score with the composer. Boïto
arranged the meeting. He said: "Don't get nervous and you will find
Verdi all right." Toscanini was very nervous. A passage in the score
puzzled and disturbed him. He felt that the tempo should be pronouncedly broader at a certain place, but there was no indication of
this in the music. Toscanini fought with the problem through days
and a sleepless night before the meeting with Verdi. They sat down
together at the piano. They came to the passage in question. Trying
not to do so, Toscanini went considerably slower, and Verdi, with
the first sign of approval he had yet given, clapped him on the shoulder and said: "Bravo!"

Immensely relieved, Toscanini said: "But, maestro, you don't
know what that place was for me. You see, you gave no indication of
a retard——" Verdi said: "And can you imagine what some asses of
conductors would make if I *had* marked a retard?"

When Toscanini told this story, he was reminded that it was in
contradiction of his own gospel of obedience to the letter of the
music. He admitted it. The final decision for the performance must
rest, fortunately or otherwise, upon the taste, the intuition, the conscience of the interpreter.

"And so," said this most scrupulously objective of musical
scholars to us, "with 'the tradition.' What is to be considered as
'the tradition'? 'The tradition' is quite possibly the last bad performance!"

There are too many things to tell about Toscanini to get into a

349

Sunday leader. The sheer facts of his knowledge, his memory, his insistence upon technical thoroughness and finish, and his practical knowledge of the orchestral instruments and all their capacities are amazing, and to a future generation may well appear cause to feel incredulous. But there is a further fact which must have been experienced to be fully understood by any save the fortunate listeners, a fact not easily communicated in words or, perhaps, successfully improvised in any mechanical record, imperfect and incomplete to the subtleties of a performance as these records remain today. We mean Toscanini's power at the height of his inspiration to reach to the very spiritual springs of music and to infuse the performer under his direction with the same almost mystical power. How often have we seen and felt that power stream from him and transform routine musicians into prophets and seers of tone!

His accomplishment and the distance he has traveled as an artist since he entered the Parma Conservatory at the age of nine is a thing plainly to be seen and is very impressive. He began with opera, in Italy, in a land and a period when there was little symphonic music, and still less of adequate symphonic performance, for him to know. From the beginning he was reaching out insatiably for more knowledge, absorbing scores with a rapidity, a hunger, and a mental retention of their contents not easy to believe. If he did this with incredible quickness, he never did it unthoroughly. Toscanini, it is to be remembered, not only knows, but has thought through, interpretively as technically, every slightest detail in the hundreds of operatic and symphonic works in his repertory.

Since the 1920s, and prior to 1926 when he came to conduct the Philharmonic-Symphony for eleven seasons, later becoming conductor of the symphony orchestra that the National Broadcasting Company assembled for him, he has turned increasingly to symphonic music. It has been a remarkable—indeed, speaking from the artistic side, a spectacular—achievement. For symphony is not opera. Yet music is music, and here, as in the opera house, Toscanini had his profound native musicianship, the same artistic rectitude, the same exceptional balance of lyrical fervor and incandescence and classic Italian sense of form which always had distinguished him. These, of course, were not his first adventures in the symphonic field, but they may be called the turning-point in his course from opera to symphony. In the course of this evolution he had become more and more of a classicist.

Perhaps his philosophy—which comes from experience, as real philosophy does, and not from theories into which it has vainly been sought to make experience fit—was expressed as well as it could be when he said to a friend: "I played the first Stravinsky, and first Sibelius, even certain of the first Wagner operas to be heard in Italy. I produced the first *Salome*, the first *Pelléas et Mélisande* there. I worked and I fought with all my power for the new music, which is what a young artist, above all others, should do. Now let the young men take up this fight. I want to understand Bach and Haydn and Beethoven a little better before I die."

In a former period when the coinage was not so reliable as it is today, it was the custom, when a coin was offered, to fling it on the counter to see if it was real metal—if it would vibrate and ring on contact with another substance. The coin of Toscanini has never been adulterated or its resonance clouded. At every contact it rings clear.

OCTOBER 2, 1947

═══

Debut of the Little Orchestra Society

"Without posture or pose, without gestures"

A WHOLLY delightful concert, which in the quality and spirit of the performances and the character of its program sounded a refreshingly new note in the musical life of the city, was given by the Little Orchestra Society, which then inaugurated its career, last night in Town Hall.

This society intends to devote itself to unfamiliar music, new and old, which requires anywhere from eight to forty players in performance. It introduced a new score by David Diamond, consisting of a suite of incidental music for Shakespeare's *Romeo and Juliet*, a score which proved very much worth while. It began the program with a virtually unknown *sinfonia concertante* of Haydn, and ended with an equally unfamiliar symphony of Johann Christian Bach. It presented a distinguished soloist who played his very best, which is saying a great deal. We mean Claudio Arrau, who in turn got out of the rut of conventional solo pieces by reviving the *Concert Piece* of Weber, which is a beauty when so interpreted, and the Andante Spianato and Polonaise of Chopin. There was other modern music than Mr. Diamond's in the instance of two pieces of an early octet by Shostakovich, also interesting, also admirably performed.

The orchestra has been wisely selected; it is an aggregation of exceptionally accomplished musicians. The conductor, Thomas K. Scherman, proved, for a single concert at least, a find. He is not unknown here, but in a first program which showed complete aspects of his art Mr. Scherman distinguished himself by his musicianship, his taste as well as his authority, and by the modesty with which he attended strictly to his business, without posture or pose, without gestures meant for either the gallery or the photographer, or both. Mr. Scherman simply conducted as a man who obviously knew his business well, and gloried in his task.

The Haydn *sinfonia concertante* is exhilarating music, wonderfully written, throughout. It is also of more than ordinary significance in the roster of Haydn's multitudinous works. For it represents a unique example of transition from the early eighteenth-century "concerto grosso," essentially an ensemble piece, and the modern concerto in which the orchestra becomes increasingly the background for the prowess of the solo player.

This piece is a real symphony, with all the classic proportions of the form. It is also a "concerto grosso" with four solo parts instead of one, the whole woven together in a shape which could materialize only just at the time that it was written. The four solo instruments, a first violin and cello, an oboe and a solo bassoon, are combined, singly and severally, in all sorts of ingenious ways. The big ensemble now supports, now absorbs them. There are places where a suspended chord marks the place for a cadenza and the orchestra stops to make occasion for solo display. Here the cadenza is performed not by one instrument but by four. In turn and together they display their skill. The players were excellent, and of course from the orchestra's ranks—the first violinist a young woman with a fine tone, spirit, and style, the first cellist a finished virtuoso, and the same true, in principal, of the wind-players, all welded in an expert ensemble. After their disquisitions the orchestra strikes in again and finishes the tale.

There was also exceptional enthusiasm—in which this writer, for one, concurred—after the world *première* of Mr. Diamond's music. Mr. Diamond has something to say that is his own, and his own way of saying it. He does not follow any musical dogma, ancient or of today. He uses those expressive means which fulfill his needs, writing with feeling that never becomes cheap or sentimental, making no attempt to reflect realistic developments in his orchestra. Instead he speaks through the instruments as one deeply imbued with the spirit of the drama, so that in his prelude the listener may hear, if he chooses, the strife of the two houses, or in the music to the balcony scene the apostrophe to the dawn and to the moment that cannot linger.

In the last movement, the death of Romeo and Juliet, one feels that Mr. Diamond is familiar with the grave and reticent music that Fauré wrote for the death of Mélisande in Maeterlinck's drama. Here is not quite the originality of other pages, but always there are feeling, refinement, invention, and sincerity. Here are pages by a young composer who has surely a future before him.

Mr. Arrau's performance deserves more than can here be said about it. He entered equally into the spirit of Weber and of the Chopin whose Andante and Polonaise are virtually of the same period, if not style. Both he played with exquisiteness, gallantry, address. He sang sentimental airs on the keyboard with unsurpassable elegance, and his bravura was dashing. He so understood the two pieces, quite different from each other, though pertaining to the same age, that he transported his listeners back with him to that age, and to the particular beauty which it secreted. And withal —superb piano-playing!

In the pieces of Shostakovich there was clear the presence of a talent new when they were written, and perhaps more genuinely expressed than in the long and inflated symphonies of Shostakovich's recent creation.

Johann Christian Bach ended the concert in a way that would have been a final fillip of wit and animation if the program had not been too long by half an hour.

=====

A Work of Art: Marc Blitzstein's
The Cradle Will Rock

"... does all the things that it should not do ..."

MARC BLITZSTEIN's musical show *The Cradle Will Rock* was given an electrifying performance last night, under Leonard Bernstein's direction, at the City Center of Music and Drama. We understand that on this occasion the work was presented for the first time completely, with orchestra, chorus, and cast, as the composer conceived it.

It was done with masterly stagecraft, with astonishingly gifted singing actors, and Mr. Bernstein, the only one on the stage in formal evening attire, as a part of the show as well as conductor of the orchestra.

The house was packed and the audience went wild. This is not surprising, for several reasons. One is probably that the text found a special response in the feelings of the majority of those present. But there was a stronger reason than that for this success. It lay in the superb performance, and in the fact that *The Cradle Will Rock*, so presented, has qualities of genius.

This is shown in the first place by the fact that *The Cradle Will Rock* does all the things that it should not do and emerges from the crucible as triumphant art. For art it is, with a technique and form of its own, with popular, realistic expressive purpose.

It does not matter whether the beholder believes in Herbert Hoover or Joseph Stalin. The fact that the piece exalts unionism as the salvation of the world, satirizes capitalism and the host of its alleged "stooges" of polite society, refers sardonically to war profits and "war to end war," in a series of little sharp satirical songs and "parlando" and savage choruses, to a plot which has no plot, to a flimsy of musical idioms from those of Moussorgsky to boogie-woogie, doesn't matter.

It is couched in a patois of slang and slogans, a form that is apparently formless, and—it catches fire, it blazes, it amuses, moves, and grips the listener, until with the really masterly if unconventional structure of the finale—the screaming trumpets in the orchestra, drum beats, the sounds of fifes and of voices chorusing from far and near—the listener wants to beat his palms and shout as the curtain falls.

There are plenty of purists, academicians, and arbiters of elegance who will ask if you call that thing music, or opera, or, for heaven's sake, art. For this writer the answer to all three inquiries is emphatically yes. What kind of art, opera, or music, is the second question, not the first. The work is its own vindication.

In fact, we prefer this score, with its complete freshness of feeling, its bitter sincerity and instinct for popular dramatic expression and projection of the text, to later and more carefully planned creations of Mr. Blitzstein, such as his "Airborne" Symphony. The earlier work heard last night was evidently written headlong, with intense feeling and instinct which could not be cramped or deflected, for the musical theater. There it stands. Regardless of theory, point of view, or propaganda, it strikes home over the footlights. It has genius.

One cannot summarize the excellence of the cast in a short space, which is a pity. The street moll of Estelle Loring was admirable in all things save a degree of distinctness in enunciation. Robert Chisholm's Reverend Salvation, sonorous in song, and of an inimitable unction, was a feat of characterization. It was Shirley Booth, Mrs. Mister, who brought down the house, as well as she might, with her simperings, her insufferable affectations, her art of diction, and her rhythm in song and in movement.

Sadie and Gus Pollack—Marie Leidol and Walter Scheff; David Thomas's druggist, with his slouch and his fatalism; Jack Albertson and Chandler Cowles, as the Yasha and Dauber boys, sycophants par excellence; Muriel Smith's rich voice and thrillingly dramatic delivery of her air—these, and numerous others, and, finally, the Larry of Howard da Silva, easily dominating the scene and invoking the storm. The chorus was first-class. The tempo of the drama was unflagging. Mr. Bernstein was master of ceremonies, dramatic and musical, and he did not fall short in a single instance. At the end, to uproarious acclaim, Marc Blitzstein appeared to share the applause with his collaborators.

═══

New York *Première* of *Peter Grimes*

"Skillful and intellectual . . . artificial and exterior . . .
the façade of an opera"

THE opera *Peter Grimes*, music by Benjamin Britten to the libretto
of Montagu Slater, had its New York *première* last night in the
Metropolitan Opera House. It was well received by a big audience.

Peter Grimes was composed on commission by the Koussevitzky
Music Foundation, and given for the first time in America by the
students of the Berkshire Music Center, August 6, 1946. When the
score was finished in 1944, Mr. Britten said to Dr. Koussevitzky,
who had created the Foundation which bears his name in memory
of his first wife: "This opera is yours." Dr. Koussevitzky replied:
"No. This opera belongs to the world," and thereupon agreed that
it should have its world *première* at Sadler's Wells Theatre in London before it could be given in this country. In that theater twelve
performances were given in 1945 and twelve more the next year.
Since then *Peter Grimes* has had many performances in leading
opera houses of Europe.

This is testimony the more to the strength of the work, since it
is obviously conceived for a smaller theater than the Metropolitan or
any other operatic stage of similar dimensions. Had it been heard
last night in a theater of intimate character, much that could not be
understood either by words or stage business might have been clear.
But this did not prevent the warm welcome of Mr. Britten's score.

We say "score" because a musical composition skillfully put together, with effective instrumentation and an interesting rhythmical and contrapuntal scheme, would seem to be the main reason
for the considerable degree of acclaim that has met this work. Its
story is a grim one, and in itself potential of powerful drama. But
the libretto is foggy and, in the main, both undramatic and untheatrical.

This story is told in rhythmed and high-falutin' verse—verse of
a symbolic, pseudo-philosophic, and undramatic sort, in which

there is little emotional reality. The theme is a man against nature and fate and the opinion of his community. If there were a moral to the tale, it would be "There but for the grace of God——" But the tale is not told in terms genuinely of the lyric theater.

Peter Grimes is a solitary person, an introvert, bitter, lonely, and frustrated. He wants to acquire wealth by his fishing, make himself a man of mark in the community, and, having so vindicated himself, marry Ellen Orford. Grimes has lost several overworked and half-starved apprentices at sea. As the curtain rises, he is under investigation for the death of the last of these. He is advised in the future to have men helpers, not boys of whom he can take advantage. But he secures another apprentice from the poorhouse.

This one, too, meets his death by an accident, as angry villagers arrive at Grimes's hut to discover the actual circumstances there; and Grimes goes mad, sees before him the faces of the unfortunates whom his ambition had brought to their end; is advised by his friend Balstrode to go out to sea in his own ship and sink.

In the bright dawn, the village folk are again at their nets and other customary occupations. Some boat is rumored to have sunk at sea. Peter Grimes, a momentary pin-point on the horizon, has disappeared, and life resumes its customary sway.

There are various accessory characters, some comic relief, occasional ribaldry of tosspots at the inn, a quarrel in the middle of a storm. The action is, for the most part, lugged in to give some semblance of real dramatic life to the picture. The one real character is Grimes. The motivations of the characters are neither seen nor felt; nor are they provided by the actual nature of the music. The composer thinks of his chorus as Moussorgsky uses his chorus in *Boris Godunoff*. Grimes is one man, against the people. Nature herself he defies, and the fine noises of the orchestra depicting wind and storm are among the most graphic pages. Mr. Britten knows his Berg, and builds much of his score upon the foundation of old forms—fugues, canonic imitations, and all that, and a passacaglia on a theme associated with Grimes for one of the best of his orchestral interludes which bind scenes together.

But one does not hear, in a single individual part, the song which naturally and inevitably characterizes the person and the moment. Not that characterization is forgotten by the composer, or that he fails carefully to ticket each personality and some of the symbolic forces of his drama with motives! This is skillfully and intellectu-

357

ally done. For all that, it is artificial and exterior. The melodic outburst of unmistakable feeling and genuineness, revealing character
and emotion in a flash, is not there.

So the opera, for us, is only the façade of an opera. The choruses
are oratorio choruses, not operatic. Like oratorio, they are appropriate for the concerted expression of collective feeling, to verse of
general sentiments, philosophies, etc. The orchestration is one of
the strongest features of a virtuoso score.

But in essence this is instrumental, not lyrical, music—music
thought throughout as if for instruments. It cannot be very grateful to the singers, while often in the principal parts, especially
that of Grimes, it is difficult to sing. The worst feature of the performance was the very poor and indistinct English. Why? We echo
the question. Why is it that with much clamor for opera in English,
with an opera that particularly requires distinct enunciation and
diction of the best, with American singers singing in their own
tongue, the English language suffers as no other language does on
the Metropolitan stage?

As for the performance, or the few particulars about it that can
be recounted now, we do not feel that Frederick Jagel was equal as
singer or actor, or type, to the part of Grimes.

Regina Resnik had a dead part to begin with. Her vocalism was
not of the best, but no one could have done very much with the
straw figure of Ellen, or found anything very convincing to deliver
in her music. John Brownlee's Balstrode was a competent job. The
smaller parts were taken care of properly, with Jerome Hines's
Swallow one of the most outstanding. Emil Cooper conducted vigorously and in masterful fashion. The scenery was a little cluttered,
but not without imagination. The stage was certainly cluttered
with too many people, too much of the time. But the chorus, which
has to be big, was brilliantly effective in a hard job.

═══

Horowitz Twenty Years Later

"The piano was as potent as another orchestra."

A HISTORIC performance of the Tchaikovsky B Flat Minor Piano Concerto was given yesterday afternoon at the Philharmonic-Symphony Concert in Carnegie Hall. Bruno Walter conducted and Vladimir Horowitz gave an overwhelming performance of the work with which he had signalized his American début with the same orchestra twenty years ago.

It is no wonder that the audience made a demonstration; that it broke in between the first and second movements with applause that would not be stilled and that, at the end, there was pandemonium in the Hall, for this was piano playing of a quality that we do not believe would be matched by any other virtuoso before the public today. Familiar as the music was, it was given an unsurpassable breadth, grandeur and fire. The brilliance, indeed, the leonine treatment of the dramatic passages was no more compelling than the lyricism and emotional impulse with which the lilting passages were sung on the keyboard.

The power of all this and the technical prowess were unlimited. The piano, even in its own right and in its own way, was as potent as another orchestra. In bravura, in symphonic rivalry with the orchestra, in declamatory passages, such as those of the superb cadenza of the first movement, the soloist had prodigal richness of color and dynamics at hand.

Such was the grip of the form and the authority of announcement that the end of the work was sensed in the very opening phrases. The complete effect was the most fervent testimony to the evolution of a master pianist's art through twenty years.

Mr. Horowitz might look back through those twenty years to his opening night with the Philharmonic-Symphony in Carnegie Hall with some degree of amusement as well as gratification. For his American début, though it definitely placed him as one of the most brilliant stars then rising in the musical firmament, was not carried through under the easiest conditions.

It happened that the conductor at that concert, Sir Thomas Beecham, was making his début with the Philharmonic-Symphony on the same evening as Horowitz. Either the conductor was nervous himself, or did not understand, or else was unsympathetic to the pianist's conception of the concerto. For he signaled the violins to sing in after the preparatory chords of the piano at a tempo faster than Horowitz had set, with an effect calculated to be demoralizing throughout the movement. It was only in the finale that Horowitz was able to reach an adjustment with the orchestra, and to save the day by the fire and élan with which he closed his performance—an anxious time, indeed a crisis, for a young artist of 23.

But the summation of Horowitz' progress since he first appeared in America received a memorable demonstration yesterday afternoon. His art has always been characterized by a most conscientious musicianship and respect for the letter as well as the spirit of the music interpreted.

But in recent seasons he has shown a new freedom, a new release from any restraint imposed by the excessive conscientiousness of a servant of music. His performances now have the sweep and color, the spontaneous and emotional intensity that made his performance of the Tchaikovsky Concerto yesterday such a thrilling experience.

Here is modern virtuosity and romantic passion, meticulous musicianship and the grand manner. This is the freedom that results from years of self-criticism and searching of the artistic conscience. And the realization that the master of an art must first learn to obey before he can command. This is Horowitz at the height of his power, and we venture to say that his progress in the future is likely to put his development of the last twenty years in the light of an apprenticeship.

The other orchestral works of the afternoon, which have been reviewed previously in *The Times,* were the *Prometheus* Overture of Beethoven and Daniel Gregory Mason's *Second Symphony.* They were warmly received.

Vaughan Williams' Symphony No. 6 at Tanglewood

"Over-luxuriance is magnificently absent."

IF THE eleventh Berkshire Festival, which has been one of exceptional brilliancy, had done nothing but present the American *première* of Vaughan Williams' Sixth Symphony this evening, it would have placed the nation in its debt.

For this is one of the most powerful and deeply felt symphonic writings to have appeared since the turn of the century. The sincerity of the expression blazes in every page. The virility and driving energy of it are companioned by pages of tenderness and mysticism.

Had this music only reflected the realizations and mellow understandings of an introspective spirit and an artist now in his seventy-sixth year, it would have been more than enough. But we have here a score of astonishing strength and of the most passionate emotion. It is drama, inner drama, wrought from suffering and realization, and compassion, and experience. And it is great music.

The symphony was begun in wartime, and it cannot be a misleading interpretation which concludes that the greatest tragedy humanity has suffered in centuries is the origin of its thought. That thought, one would say, has bitten deep into the composer's consciousness. What he has felt, what he has lived beyond verbal power to relate or describe in words, has got into his measures.

Every measure is an emotional imperative. The form is free, the ideas are inevitable. The discursiveness which has marked some of Vaughan Williams' earlier scores—it might be better to say the over-luxuriance of his ideas—is here magnificently absent. The symphony is the last word in concision. Not a measure could be spared. All that had to be put down, and nothing else, is there. There are duly contrasted themes. They are thoughts, not melodies stated merely for purposes of balance and design. All is order and logic, but the logic and emotion and idea to which form adjusts itself. The succession of key is unorthodox.

Whatever may have been the travail involved in the creation of this piece, the listener gets the impression of something that is poured molten hot from the man who produced it, and this under such compulsion that he had to put on paper, with no artifice at all, what it was impossible not to say. It opens with a cry of anguish, and proceeds in a furious and sardonic spirit. Then a theme shines through, of an ecclesiastic character, lofty and tender withal. It first glows in the strings, then is strengthened with brass and ascends, against sweeps of the harp, to a near-apotheosis, only to be ended by the agonized cry that introduced the movement.

As remarked, form is purely the vehicle of emotion. The second movement, with a mournful, chromatic sort of figure, begins like some passacaglia, but instead flowers out into music of a gripping intensity. Three short notes which have been an integral part of this theme are later broadened and flung out by the trumpets, over roaring drums, and reiterated through the rest of the movement like an insistent summons, as if this composer, like Beethoven in his time, were saying: "Thus fate knocks at the door."

All the movements follow each other, as they are intended, without a pause. The scherzo, built on an ascending series of fourths and of a driving energy, is again a torrent fury, an embristling part, somewhat modal and in the folk vein, which, however, does not stay the headlong course of the movement.

And then what? The finale is the shortest, the most unconventional, and perhaps the most poignant part of the whole work. It is a mystical dialogue called in the score *Epilogue*, and it is the music of another world. Remembrances of previous themes, foreshortened, occur. For that matter, all the movements have close-knit relationships. But here it is as though the realities and agonies of the life that is seen had dropped away, and only the essence of faith and of sorrowing wisdom had remained.

Much of this movement is for strings, sometimes subdivided, and in the upper registers. Woodwinds enter in the course of it, solo fragments of an oboe's song are heard. It is solitude, prayer, music so intimate, so unspectacular, unsymphonic if you like, that one knows Vaughan Williams would not have written it if it had not been as inevitable with him as the rest of the work.

The symphony uses an immense orchestra as a palette from which the most delicate as well as the most imposing effects may be gained. A third of that orchestra suffices for this reverie, this self-communing, which finally lapses into silence. For concert purposes, for salvos of applause, a movement utterly worthless. It is a final word, spoken in the silence of the soul.

It is a wonderful thing to see the moment arrive. Toward the end of the most sincere and unassuming artist's career, when every emotion is purged of dross, when the unutterable meaning of life and death begin to reveal each other side by side, "the seen proved by the unseen, and the unseen proved by the seen," and all the expressive resources of a creative career at hand for the consummative deed.

The performance we believe to be one of the finest that Dr. Koussevitzky has ever given. He conducted the work as though his life, and the lives of his listeners, depended upon the music being understood: conducted with command of the orchestra, and an imperious will that left no player immune from the music's needs.

The other two features of the program were an admirable performance of Prokofieff's music to his ballet *Romeo and Juliet,* and rich, beautiful music it is; and finally Richard Strauss's *Don Quixote,* with Gregor Piatigorsky as the cello soloist. It is a score which amazingly withstands the passage of the years, which indeed contains some of the greatest pages that Strauss wrote. And Mr. Piatigorsky, especially in such passages as the conclusion, when the knight of the sorrowful countenance, in all humility and understanding, gives up the ghost, has the tone and the expression that fully and movingly reveal the pathos of the work.

NOVEMBER 17, 1948

Première of Shostakovich No. 9 on an All-Russian Program

He Should Have Laid Down His Pen More Often

INTERNATIONAL politics did not force a musical embargo last night in Carnegie Hall, when Eugene Ormandy and the Philadelphia Orchestra presented a brilliant program exclusively of Russian music.

So Russian that it was not easy to detect the presence in Tchaikovsky's C major Suite of the Mozart flavoring which learned authorities assure us is there! But this suite is delightful and simple music, regardless of the composer's intent to honor the Austrian master in its measures, and the performance was a triumph for the strings.

The other compositions were Shostakovich's Ninth Symphony and the Khatchaturian Piano Concerto, with William Kapell as soloist.

We were struck by the remark of the program annotator that Shostakovich, having completed nine whole symphonies within twenty years, and just before he was forty, could afford to lay down his pen with a sigh of relief. We don't see it. If Shostakovich had laid down his pen often enough to have written half as many as nine symphonies in twenty years, we think he would have produced some better symphonies.

The symphonies of his which have held the stage here are the First, the Fifth, to a lesser degree the Sixth, to a much lesser degree the bombastic and gesticulatory Seventh and the unduly extended Eighth, and the Ninth heard last night, the least familiar of the lot. In all these symphonies there are great moments. In the Ninth, the distinguishing movement is the second—the lyrical movement—which has the melodic persuasiveness and the poetic melancholy which ring tender and true.

In fact, it is often with Shostakovich that the slow movements, in which his native lyricism is given sufficient play, become the most convincing manifestation of his genius. The rest of the symphony heard last night, if one excepts also the striking largo passages with the bassoon solos that come before the end, is convincing enough in places, but in greater part trivial to the point of banality. We have a feeling that slower and more thoughtful symphonic production would have prevented these incongruities.

We enjoyed Mr. Kapell's playing of a concerto that we like very much. True, it is not necessary to beat a piano till the strings not only jangle but rattle, as this pianist did quite unnecessarily in several places. And it is reasonable to believe that if Rimsky-Korsakoff had orchestrated this concerto he would have gotten as much or more from the instruments in the way of clear, rich, vivid sonorities with many fewer notes than Khatchaturian does. An orchestrator who knew his business could take out a few shovelfuls of notes and get as much and better color by the process. But so true is it that the originative idea carries its own logic that as a whole the concerto is effective, original, sumptuous in color, and truly exciting.

It is descended of Borodin and Rimsky, too—Oriental music by an Oriental, in this case an Armenian to whom it is natural to write in this way. He has a modern composer's technique at command, and he knows what to do. The writing is wholly organic. The piano cadenzas are not merely passages of display; they are rhapsodies in the Eastern spirit. The music carries the frequent suggestion of intervals smaller than the half-tone, and of exotic scale forms which, as a matter of fact, are frequently present. The slow movement, especially, fascinates us.

Mr. Kapell plays this concerto very brilliantly indeed. He also sings on the keyboard when he chooses. His rhythm is electric. He gives the piece its full measure of color, bravura, and panache. A good piece. A good show. A rousing finale. Masterly projection of overture, symphony, and concerto by Mr. Ormandy and his splendid orchestra.

DECEMBER 10, 1948

Dello Joio, Haydn, and Bruckner at the Philharmonic

"Now I shall prove how jolly American I am."

NORMAN DELLO JOIO's Variations, Chaconne and Finale were played for the first time at a Philharmonic-Symphony concert under Bruno Walter's baton last night in Carnegie Hall. Two main facts consequent upon this ceremony may be cited quickly: 1. The composition is the best work that we have heard of Mr. dello Joio's; in it his writing is freer, much more lucid, more released in the flow of the ideas and genuinely creative. 2. The work pleased the audience, which applauded it at a length and with a heartiness which caused the composer to come to the stage.

One can make the customary remarks about "influences" apparent in this music, and cite one or two of them. But this is certainly not a determinative fact about a composition when it comes from a young man still in his formative stage. Does the music have a genuine impulsion? Does it say something in a convincing way? After this come questions of taste and style involved. And we affirm, to the best of our knowledge and belief, that Mr. dello Joio has written with marked conviction and clarity, and with a sense of beauty.

His work is in three movements, all of them being really different concepts of the variation device. All the forms and developments cluster about the central idea that the oboe announces at the beginning. Only in one of these movements is the result disappointing: in the finale. There it feels as if the composer had said to himself: "Now I have shown what I can do in old forms and sometimes in the old archaic style. Now I shall prove how jolly American and up-to-date I am"—and forthwith American rhythms, jazz suggestions, a liveliness which is brilliant but a little flippant and a little hollow appear by the side of nobler preceding pages. But again: Mr. dello Joio is a young man formulating his ideas and his style; last night he communicated emotion and beauty.

Mr. Walter had opened his program with the delicious Haydn symphony numbered 86 in the Breitkopf and Härtel catalogue, one of the set composed for Paris and given its *première* at a "Concert de la loge Olympique." This is one of the most captivating of all the symphonies of the incomparable master, who, as usual, is so unconventional in so many of its pages and so freshly experimental in his spirit. The second movement, bearing the title "Capriccio," is simply a gem of romantic feeling. The adjective is overworked, but it is the natural one to use of this music by the great classic master of the symphony.

The minuetto is no court dance. It is heavy-footed—indeed, we think that Mr. Walter made it unnecessarily heavy-footed—in its first and last sections, but the naïve *ländler* dance of the middle part, so simple, so *gemütlich*, is simply enchanting. The finale is one succession of jests, including a glissando slide at the end of one of the most amusing of themes that caused one listener to ask himself, confessedly in ignorance of the original scoring, if this was exactly Haydn's writing notation. It is a question which cannot be answered at this time of writing. The detail aside, the symphony is the gayest possible music, and one of Haydn's most captivating adventures in composition, which is saying a great deal.

The concert, stretching to undue length, ended with a wonderful performance of one of the most enjoyable of all the Bruckner symphonies, the Fourth, the "Romantic"—again the term. How romantic it is! To Wagner is attributed the blame, if blame it is, for the caption Bruckner applied some years after he had completed it: "A citadel of the Middle Ages. Daybreak. Reveille is sounded from the tower. Knights on proud chargers leap forth. The magic of nature surrounds them.

It is a perfectly good-index to the nature of the music, whoever proposed it. The opening is of a ravishing beauty, with the horn call that is answered and at once extended by the orchestra. The answering second theme has the inimitable Bruckner contour, with the broad triplet involved. There is very little flagging or groping in this movement, as usually there is in movements of Bruckner symphonies. And there is continuity of thought between the glamorous opening movement and the one, no less beautiful, which follows. For the opening phrase of the cellos, with the initial interval of the fifth, seems to branch right out from the horn theme that opened the work.

The chorale theme that ensues is, again, one of Bruckner's finest. How nobly and poignantly, a little later on, did the violas intone their significant phrases! With what gusto, what elevation, does old Anton sit down and proceed to write music. When interrupted in composition, he could be magnificently disagreeable. But he feared the critic Hanslick as he feared death, and so pressed a thaler upon Hans Richter "for a mug of beer," as thanks for conducting this symphony. It is not as pretentious or weighty as the mighty Eighth and the elegiac Ninth, but it is more spontaneous and of a better level of inspiration than the grander but patchier scores which came later.

The scherzo with the hunting calls is certainly nature and the vibrant forest echoing to the sounds of life. And, quite as with Haydn, there is a trio that is a pearl, for the middle part. Only in the finale, as in practically every finale he wrote, does Bruckner fall into his regular pits of repetition, non sequiturs, and sequences that repeat patterns and tread water in hopes of the timely arrival of a new and good idea to relieve the situation.

As a whole, the effect of the symphony was engrossing. It must be accredited to Mr. Walter as well as the composer. Mr. Walter is no modernist in his leanings or sympathies, or in the body of his repertory. We do not think it is either his need or his place to be so.

We are fortunate in having in him the artist who re-creates the expressions of a Bruckner or a Mahler—if you like—not only as the composer imagined them, but, so to speak, in the spirit in which the audiences of Bruckner and of Mahler listened to their works. For this is the evocation, not only of a specific score, but of a period. We hear this music with a color, accent, and atmosphere which is its complete rejuvenation and revelation of its innermost meaning. Perhaps the time is too near when father will say to son: "You heard the Bruckner 'Romantic'? You don't know what it is. I heard it conducted by Bruno Walter."

DECEMBER 12, 1948

The Retort Courteous to Arnold Schoenberg

"The 'goût' of only one single 'chacun'"

A CERTAIN Mahler controversy, which the writer seems to have started, has instigated, among other correspondence, the comment of one of the most distinguished masters of modern composition—Arnold Schoenberg. Here is Mr. Schoenberg's comment:

DEAR MR. DOWNES:

You end your review on Mitropoulos's performance of Mahler's Seventh Symphony with the words: "Chacun à son goût."

This seems to me a great mistake, because if once, for instance, all of you "chacun's" who are so proud of your personal "goût" would vote for or against a work, one could perhaps make an advance poll, predicting the result of this voting. This true opinion of the majority might decide the destiny of the work of a master, right or wrong; it would include, at least, instead of the "goût" of only one single "chacun," various opinions; and everybody would understand that in the average which it presents there are included positives and negatives, pros and cons of various grades.

Unfortunately you are so few in whose hands the destiny

of a work is laid and your authority has been bestowed upon you by people who are too modest to do this job themselves. They deem that you understand much more of music than they. But they do not expect that you are so much at variance with other, and even important, musicians, who possess greater authority, based upon their personal achievements, upon studies and upon being recognized by a multitude of even greater authorities.

If I, who would not dare always to depend upon my personal gusto, if I would look around for support of my judgment, I would in first line think of Richard Strauss, who spoke once to me about Mahler with great appreciation and with a respect derived only from his own self-respect. "Only one who deserves respect himself is capable of respecting another man," I have once written. But nothing can surpass the enthusiasm of Anton von Webern, Alban Berg, Franz Schmidt, and many other Viennese composers about Mahler's symphonies. And why do you forget Mitropoulos's enthusiasm?

One who is able to study a score need not depend upon his personal taste. He would see all these strokes of genius which never are to be found in lesser masters. He would discover them on every page of this work, in every measure, in every succession of tones and harmonies.

But all of you have the habit of criticizing a work only when it is performed, and then after one single hearing you pronounce your sentence of life and death, regardless of all experience your trade has gone through when history turned to the absolute contrary of your judgment.

I assume you have, two or more decades ago, written in an unfriendly manner about Mahler and now you are afraid to deviate from your primary judgment. Why? You are not so old that you should not dare changing your mind. I am at least ten to twenty years older than you. I can assure you that I am still ready to change my opinions, to learn something new, to accept the contrary and to digest it, the contrary of all I have believed in my whole life—if it is capable of convincing me. If it is truly great, it is capable.

No courageous man would hesitate to do this.

I ascribe your favorable review of my Five Orchestra Pieces to a same resistance against a revision of your former attitude toward a composition. I assume, similarly to the case of Mahler, that you have two or more decades ago already written about these pieces, but in a favorable manner—as it was the tendency among young men at that time. Tell me: Why should an honorable man be afraid of changing his mind at the time of greater maturity? Must he remain forever the slave of his time of immaturity?

I am afraid many people, who read both these reviews about Mahler and me, will say: One who writes as unfoundedly about Mahler will certainly also be wrong about Schoenberg. Accordingly, I must either be ashamed to please you, or it will cease to be favorable to me.

As I have said before: If you would study the orchestra score you could not overlook the beauty of this writing. Such beauty is only given to men who deserve it because of all their other merits. You should not call me a mystic—though I am proud to be one—because this statement is based on experience. I have seen so many scores, and I could tell at one glance how good the composition is.

Even the piano score of Mahler's symphony would have revealed much of its beauty. . . .

ARNOLD SCHOENBERG

And this is our reply:

DEAR MR. SCHOENBERG:

I have read with interest and appreciation your letter concerning my review of Mitropoulos's recent performance of Mahler's Seventh Symphony. You say some interesting things which it is a pleasure to read. I must add, however, in frankness, that some of your remarks appear to me to be illogical.

I entirely disagree with you that my sentiment of "Chacun à son goût" is "a great mistake." It simply means that in reviewing a work I expressed my convinced opinion, but that everyone else who listens is entirely entitled to his own opinions and tastes in the matter. It also means that, while I am frank to say, as I did say and as I completely believe, that this symphony of Mahler's is detestably bad music, others who think as you do, for example, have an equal right to their conclusions. I think this is the very essence of fair critical practice. I do not consider myself a high priest of art; I do not pretend that my values of any music are conclusive. I do not even claim that I can tell at a single glance at a score whether the music is good or bad, whether it will perish quickly or last onward into infinity.

I must ask you a question. Do you really mean seriously to claim to me that composers, even the greatest composers, are as a rule fair or unbiased critics of other composers' works? Frankly, I can hardly credit you with such an unhistorical

370

statement. Do you think, for example, that a composer who states that Beethoven's Seventh Symphony makes him ripe for the madhouse is in the least intelligent or fair in this, his written judgment? The name of this "critic" was Carl Maria von Weber. Do you take seriously what Schumann wrote of Wagner's *Tannhäuser,* or what Berlioz said on the same subject, or what Debussy said of Beethoven, that he was a bore? These instances could be multiplied indefinitely. I am afraid that the greatest names in the history of musical composition do not connote either balance or perspective of musical judgment. For a final illustration of this obvious fact, let me quote you what an editorial board of five of the greatest composers in Russia said when they were asked by Koussevitzky, as a publisher, whether he should publish Stravinsky's *Petrouchka.* The score was unanimously rejected by these high and mighty gentlemen as being "not music."

And then, Mr. Schoenberg, you really hurt my feelings. Apparently you think that I do not read scores. I hope you don't infer also that I am incapable of this. I can even tell you the score of Mahler's Seventh Symphony has been in my library for years, while as for piano arrangements of his music, I have gone through half of his Fifth Symphony on two pianos and gotten up from the instrument, being really unable to stomach any farther such vulgar music.

Now as to inconsistencies. My dear master, I assure you that so far as I am concerned you are intensely wrong. Why do you assume that I have written in an unfriendly manner about Mahler and am now afraid to depart from a primary judgment? Why?

In the first place, you are uninformed on the subject. I have found things to praise and to enjoy, for example, in Mahler's *Lied von der Erde,* which I formerly liked a good deal more than I do now because its self-pity and sentimentalism are rather unpleasant to me. I enjoy pages of his First Symphony. I have gone "completely overboard" upon the first half of his Eighth, etc.

You seem to think, because I wrote well of your Five Pieces this season, that I have done so because I wrote well of them years ago. I can tell you frankly that I do not try to remember what I have written in the past about music that I listen to in the present. But I think I do remember that I cursed your Five Pieces to high heaven* and I expected that I would dis-

---

* See the review of these Five Pieces, published December 19, 1914, on page 46.—Ed.

like them the other night. To my surprise, I found that I liked them, and realized on hearing them this time how much effect their principles had had upon modern music.

I am afraid I must unhappily come to the conclusion that I think very badly of the Mahler Seventh Symphony and you think very well of it, and that this is merely another case of critics and their readers disagreeing; as, thank God, they will always disagree and in the expression of their convictions greatly contribute to the development of an art.

JANUARY 9, 1949

———

The Metropolitan Puts On a Superb *Figaro*

No Apologies Needed, for Once

IF THE Metropolitan Opera Association had given more performances this season and in late seasons of the admirable quality of the representation of *Le Nozze di Figaro* given yesterday afternoon, the apologia for the shortcomings of its offerings, delivered before the last act by George A. Sloan, chairman of the board of directors, would not have been necessary.

For the Metropolitan showed on this occasion what it can do with an opera when it really tries. The entertainment was a delight throughout, a triumph of co-ordinated direction, distinction of singing and acting, and stylization, too. The aristocratic quality of Mozart, as well as his Shakespearean capacity for character-drawing and emotional revelation, was maintained from beginning to end.

The keynote was struck immediately by Mr. Busch's gay and exciting reading of the overture, which, as Mozart remarked when he conducted at the *première*, should go very fast—one would say as fast as an orchestra can play it. And there was not a lapse of comedy spirit or of movement, wit, sentiment of the libretto, from the prelude to the fall of the final curtain.

It was a pleasure to attend this event. It is an exceptional pleasure to report it. Because, for once, the reporter has not the task of taking out a pair of imaginary scales and dutifully computing the good, bad, and indifferent features of a musical exhibition. He could revel in the effect of the genius of the opera and the exhilaration of its interpretation, and be happy.

The new Figaro, and a very good one, was Mr. Italo Tajo. He was inclined to overact. Against this, and far overweighing it, was the stimulating and individual figure that he made in the cast. If one missed in this Figaro the implicit subservience, craft, cajolery of a servant who secretly despised his master; if he thought to heighten comedy by skipping too much about the stage, or so hurrying his recitative, as in the second act, that it became querulous rather than lively—these were defects of predominating merits of temperament, capacity to weld and project tone and text, and an individuality that was a motivating element in the performance.

For this reason, in part, and because of the unifying spirit of a finely perceptive occasion, everything brisked up. Miss Bidú Sayão, charming, finished, completely the mistress of her role, can be praised for many things: not merely for her skill as a technician, but for her wit and taste; not merely because she is a musician, but much more than that—a true artist.

Mr. John Brownlee's Count, never more fiery, virile, and accomplished in vocalization, was opposite Miss Eleanor Steber, who achieved nobly the dignity and pathos of the Countess, lonely and, under her mask of manners, a poignant figure. A larger voice would be no handicap in the spaces of the Metropolitan, but Miss Steber showed what can be done by not forcing, by relying upon nuance and the beauty of the sustained melodic line rather than upon mere bigness of tone.

To continue in these gladsome tones, we thought Mme Novotna, who has graced Cherubino's part ere this, unusually fortunate in both her airs, widely contrasted in character, as also in the nuance of her comedy and her facial play.

One speaks of the most important personalities in the drama in these ways, but what was more finished or masterly on the stage than Alessio de Paolis's cackling Basilio? Who did as much with the text, or achieved such sly and masterly innuendo? Salvatore Baccaloni's Bartolo was, of course, a comedy. Claramae Turner's byplay with him was first-class. This Marcellina had more voice and considerably more effectiveness than others who have figured in the role at the Metropolitan.

Lorenzo Alvary's Antonio is a gardener of Middle European opera houses and not of a Latin tradition, but none the less amusing. Miss Anne Bollinger made a creditable first appearance on the stage as Barbarina.

At the basis of this fine performance were Mr. Graf's stage management, better, in our opinion, than on any previous presentation of the same work, and Mr. Busch's insight, spirit, and mastery at all times of the score.

MARCH 20, 1949

Roussel, Satie, and Debussy as a Preface to Brahms

"Everyone rejoiced in the kick and the strength
and the clarity."

THE Boston Symphony concert which Dr. Koussevitzky conducted yesterday afternoon in Carnegie Hall advanced familiar yet surprising things—familiar because of their familiarity, surprising because of the unexpected things that Dr. Koussevitzky did with certain of them, ending with a sweepingly dramatic performance of the finale of the Brahms C minor Symphony.

One of the most brilliant moments came with the opening F major Suite of Albert Roussel. How splendidly this fine, solid, vigorous music stands up with the years! It was composed in 1926, at Dr. Koussevitzky's invitation, for the Boston Symphony Orchestra, and is dedicated to him. The music really has no age, because it is so vital, so straightforward and genuine in the writing, that it belongs to no definite artistic "trend"—unless a general one toward classicism—and to the pretensions of no group or clique of composers. It is just superbly well-made music, wholly exceptional, perhaps, in the normality and health of its spirit.

It has a splendid swing and stride, a fine harmonic tension, which sounded good yesterday, sounds good today, and will sound splendidly tomorrow. The dissonance is not discord, it is the strong balanced pull of intervals which have both centrifugal and centripetal relations to each other. They hold the balance of the middle between the compulsions of the opposites. Fine, biting harmony, good two-fisted counterpoint, vital rhythms, clear lines, and in the finale a folk element and abounding vivacity and humor.

And mind: this is not music of the grandiose or of the titanic masters of the art. It is just the work of a first-class sincere musician who appears to have sought no glory, excepting in doing a thorough job for himself. And everyone rejoiced in the kick and the strength and clarity of his art.

It was an ideal arrangement to follow this open-air writing of Roussel with the more original and far more visionary music of the young Erik Satie—the two *Gymnopédies*, two of the piano pieces of Satie that Debussy, with the piercing perception of the born genius, recognized as the dream, only partially expressed, of a fellow artist; recognized the gem for what it was and through his own masterly art gave the precious stone exquisite setting. Dream-play one of these pieces, so bare in color, so chaste in line in the original piano version. Then listen and sense the perfume of Debussy's orchestration, which reveals all of the sensuousness, the nostalgia, the vision of an antique and severe yet tender beauty that Satie could project in skeleton form but could not by himself fully realize. From this meeting of the greater musician and the lesser one emerges the perfect beauty.

Hearing these *Gymnopédies* in an early performance in Boston back in the first decade of the century, and wondering in those our salad days who this strangely gifted composer might be, we asked our good friend Clement Lenom, then oboist of the Boston Symphony, to trace Satie to his lair during his summer visit to Paris. And he found him and recounted to us the rather indescribable personality of a fantastic funny man. What was funny? Mr. Lenom couldn't quite tell us by word of mouth. But he brought back with him proof sheets of the *Gymnopédies*, then some twenty years old, in their original form, and a letter.

The letter described ironically, jocularly, perhaps sadly, too, certain disappointments of the composer's life—perhaps, even, the disappointment of life with him. It ended by remarking with humble pride that Messrs. Debussy and Ravel had done Erik Satie the honor to find something suggestive in his ideas, and that if Satie had failed, it was perhaps because he was a dreamer—dreamers being, nevertheless, unfortunately too rare. The sovereign artist Debussy brings the dream to realization in his orchestration of the *Gymnopédies*. And Dr. Koussevitzky penetrated as deeply to its essence.

The Boston Symphony's performance of *La Mer*—that is to say, Dr. Koussevitzky's particularly intuitive and subtly conceived projection of the music—is now one of the traditions of the orchestra he has been perfecting for twenty-five years. The opening impressed one anew by its mystery and its echoes as faint as those heard in a seashell at dawn. Coloring was of extraordinary fineness, of course, but the curious thing was this: that the music had less of sweep and more of the episodic than is customary with this singularly versatile and unpredictable interpreter, and that the outstanding achievements of the concert were its first two items and that old tried-and-true battle-horse of all conductors in the world, the Brahms First Symphony.

One might differ with a detail of the opening movement, or with another detail farther on. These are minuscule, and, in any event, matters partially of opinion. The slow movement was read with an eloquence and depth of conviction that stand out in the recollection of many performances. The over-all conception was so fresh and impressive in its communication, so great in spirit and dramatically delivered, that hardened concertgoers were astonished at their own reaction. The last movement, exciting as it is likely to be, had a singular cohesiveness, fire, and inevitability. There is a dangerous wealth of material and elaborateness of design in it. Yesterday it was all white-hot, as when the horn passage from the introduction of the last movement returned, amid the tumult; as when the chorale of that introduction, returning, was flung, as if in flaming letters, against the sky.

JULY 17, 1949

════

A New Edition of the Mozart Symphonies

"How dangerously entertaining is this Mozart!"

ONE is in receipt of the Broude Brothers edition of forty-one of the fifty-odd symphonies Mozart is known to have written, though some of them never reached publication. This edition was begun some three years ago and completed last year. Compliments are in order for the handiness of the format, the fine printing and artistic quality of the business. But that is secondary to the fact of the engrossing interest of the music and its reminder to conductors and public that Mozart is not only the inspired creator of the "Paris," "Linz," "Haffner," "Prague," and a half-dozen other great symphonies, including the last gigantic three. There are many other Mozart symphonies, few of which, even those of the boyhood period, are without fascination and significance.

This is the case even in the earlier works fashioned so clearly upon the Christian Bach model, and the ones which palpably follow the older-fashioned Italian overture style. There are perhaps half a dozen in the lot which are important for historical rather than for distinctly creative reasons. But there are at least thirty that would brighten any program, that should be a godsend to small orchestras and musical organizations of serious aims but limited resources who are seeking for beautiful and entertaining music.

And how dangerously entertaining is this Mozart! He cannot for the life of him be dull, or heavy either. He may take a conventional formula or musical figure as his point of departure. From the moment when his genius, once called into play by the task in hand, has become involved, you are confronted with music of such spirit and glow and creative resource that you are hopelessly enmeshed in it, and captive to its spell. Don't begin to read these symphonies if there is an immediate job to be done. For one symphony leads to another, and the material is so alluring, and so laden with ideas and contrasts, that hours have passed and the confounded job—waiting!

Here, in fact, is the whole perspective of Mozart's astonishing development as a symphonist. It is not the less arresting or important for the reason that some of the symphonies, though signed by Mozart, are not his, or that every variety of symphonic effort according to canons of the period is there. We have the opera overtures, the "overture-symphonies," the overtures to Mozart's early operas such as *Il Re Pastore, Ascanio in Alba, Sogno di Scipione,* etc., made into symphonies by adding to the two-part overture form a third lively movement for a finale. But Mozart used the symphony in D major numbered by Köchel 45, with some changes, as the overture to *La Finta Giardiniera.* Until 1778, till he was twenty-two, Mozart used the three-movement symphonic form—one possible exception to this rule will be mentioned. He probably did not use clarinets in his orchestra at all till he came to the brilliant "Haffner" music, inspired by a rather grand wedding. He was always chary of the clarinet, but he used over twenty different instrumental schemes of instrumentation for his symphonies. In three of his symphonies he uses four horns, but he rarely goes far with this latter instrument. Sometimes he omitted kettle drums. In the symphony Köchel 318, intended originally as a three-part opera overture, he has an unusual array—all the winds save clarinets, with two trumpets, four horns, and strings, and this is one of the eight symphonies when he makes special use of the violas, dividing them for purposes of color.

The first five symphonies are of Mozart's childhood. Yet the first, permeated with Christian Bach and also Schobert, has a prevailing *esprit* and a freshness which are not negligible, and is an entertaining if conventional piece. St. Foix believes that the second symphony in this edition (K. 17) is not by Mozart at all, but quite possibly— "perhaps"—one of Leopold Mozart's compositions which he had given Wolfgang to study and copy. He has two strong arguments for the symphony being of at least other than Mozartean authorship. One is its form of four movements. It was many years before Mozart came definitely to the stage of the four-movement, in place of the three-movement, symphony. Then there is the fact that clarinets are used. Mozart never used them—unless this one is accepted as proof that he did so—in his earlier period. One remembers how chary he was of them even in the time of the "Haffner" score and in the last great G minor Symphony. He used them first in the "Paris" Symphony in 1778, when he had an uncommonly large and proficient orchestra at his disposal, and scored grandly for the occasion.

The origin of the third symphony (K. 18) is more surprising, and more completely proved. It is simply that the author of K. 18 has copied note for note a symphony by Abel. Mozart, in studying and copying this work, was learning his trade, while the real influence from which he gained a great deal, that of Christian Bach, remained paramount in all the early symphonies.

You might say that even with the fifth symphony of this series (K. 22) Mozart leaves the ground. The symphony was written at The Hague in 1765, when Mozart was nine. He uses chromaticism in the slow movement in a newly individual and moving manner. In the finale, which is in buffo spirit, Alfred Einstein finds the quality of *Figaro*. One could pass each symphony in review, but that pleasure is not for this column today. One gets a thrill out of such a passage as the slow movement in No. 19 (K. 132) for the sheer feeling and ineffable grace of this music. The feeling runs deep, the movement is of ineffable pathos. No. 26 (K. 184) is certainly an "overture-symphony." The brilliant and quite elaborate fast movement suddenly shifts, in a theatrical transition, to a mood of sadness and suspense—witness the close on chords of the dominant of the key. Then comes the middle movement in C minor, with the walking bass and the replies, above it in dialogue, of strings with strings, and then strings with woodwinds. It is an unforgettable movement, and the replies of first and second violins and later of other instruments to each other haunt the memory.

The G minor, No. 25 of this set and 183 in Köchel's catalogue, is a work tragic in mood, like the G minor Symphony of 1788, and the two works have other resemblances. Both are of highly emotional and dramatic texture.

Then comes No. 29, the one in A major of this set. Done in Salzburg in 1774, it is a beauty and shows the study of the string quartet. The buffo spirit is present. In the slow movement the violas are ingeniously employed. The minuet is in a vigorous dotted rhythm which is coupled with a finale in the gigue rhythm and tempo of 6-8, a reminder of Handelian ideas of an earlier day.

The "Paris" Symphony was done for Le Gros, director of the Concerts Spirituels. Its scoring was uncommonly heavy—"for ten instruments," including the clarinets. It is an imposing symphony, though a majority of Mozart scholars find it to be more worldly and less emotional than simpler pages.

From this work on we get little but masterpieces, of many different kinds, stylistically, expressively, by the master which Mozart has become.

Each symphony from now on requires a study for its proper measure of comprehension. And Mozart's development is that of a supreme genius. He had the impressionability of wit, but the extreme sensitiveness of the mental palate is balanced by the quality of selectivity and the artist's intuition which always guarded Mozart. As he went on he usually cut his cloth, creatively speaking, to the measure, so that at times he seems to change his symphonic approach —to grow almost accidentally. It was not so. All that happened made Mozart greater and more productive. We can look at this music and almost watch him advance before our eyes. And perhaps wonder if there is not one test of genius: this infinite capacity for growth, for unlimited development.

On the Passing of Richard Strauss

"The vision of the tone poet that he was remains with us."

THE phenomenon of Richard Strauss is one of the most curious of modern music. It is indeed almost unique in the history of the art. For example: it has long been acknowledged that Richard Strauss had outlived his creative period at least a quarter of a century before he died last week. If he had been a second-rank composer, who made a quick early success only to have the public discover the superficiality of his appeal and forget him, his career would be explicable.

But Strauss, after having proved in his youth to be a gifted, facile composer in classic forms, of solid technique and conventional direction, suddenly exploded as the revolutionist of his day. He was attacked as viciously and shortsightedly as most exponents of new ideas are attacked when they appear; he triumphed sensationally over fierce and well-organized opposition; he became an acknowledged master with the world at his feet; and then, as suddenly as he had risen from the ranks of mediocrity, completely abdicated the position he had won, and ceased to be a force of any importance whatever in the progress of his art.

So Strauss, as a creative artist, had outlived his time completely. But he was in the bad habit of writing notes, a habit which he could not readily relinquish; wherefore the succession, one after the other, of works each one more routine than the other, or inconsequentially experimental with worn-out formulas of the classic pretension. It was not that Strauss lacked sincerity or the most workmanlike methods of production. He simply and obviously had nothing more to say, although anything that he wrote would be printed and performed (with the exception of the last years of Nazi Germany) as soon as the ink was dry on the pages.

But the striking thing, despite this creative retreat, is the enduring vitality and the indubitable significance of the tone poems which shook the world when they first appeared in the late eighties and nineties, and which are today indispensable and irremovable from

the repertory. The same thing can be said, though with certain quali-
fications, of at least two of the operas, *Salome* and *Elektra*. The composer who didn't know when to stop is nevertheless in an impervious
position because of the vitality, imaginative sweep, and shaking sincerity of his earlier creations.

Other composers, in the technical and stylistic sense, have in different ways outlived their times. The great Bach was looked upon as
both academic and out of fashion by the time that homophony and
the *"style galant"* had come into music. He continued to create in the
difficult outmoded contrapuntal way—indeed, in the last effort, the
monumental *Art of Fugue* (of which the plates were sold for their
weight in copper), with increasing abstruseness. But the immeasur-
able Bach grew to the last moment in stature, composing titanically
to the very end. He could easily wait for the ages to vindicate him.
Rossini—of lesser stature, of course, but a great genius—was sensible.
With thirty years of life remaining, he stopped all important composing. Strauss had less judgment.

Or was he the helpless, only semi-conscious victim of a modern
disease that he shared with such an opera composer as Puccini, with
Debussy, with Stravinsky, and many others of lesser stature in various lands: a tendency to grow old in spirit and essentially uncreative
before the natural time? Apparently there is an inner decay, a reces-
sion from within, a sort of dry rot of the creative spirit.

This, of course, is a speculative analysis to be entertained and rejected according to the individual viewpoint. But there is something
else which we can ascertain about Strauss, which is evident, and of
great importance. He comes into his own as a musician only through
the impact of extra-musical ideas. He is not for a single moment a
"pure" musician, if such creatures can actually exist. We see him
going through his sprouts as a young composer and writing agreeably, yes, promisingly, in classic forms, such as the Serenade for wind
instruments which Bülow performed at Meiningen, where he engaged Strauss as assistant conductor. There Strauss came into contact with Alexander Ritter. This Ritter, at the time a member of the
Meiningen orchestra, was a man of exceptional culture and intellectual range, and a passionate adherent of the Liszt-Wagner school.
He conducted, composed, read widely, and more than dabbled in
literature and philosophy. The influence of Ritter upon him, said
Strauss, was that of a storm wind. It was Ritter (the son of Wagner's
famous friend and patroness Julie Ritter, and husband of a cousin

of Wagner) who directed Strauss's thinking decisively in the direction of music as an art of the most intimate associations with other arts and with philosophic ideas considered by many to be outside the composer's domain.

The change was cyclonic. Everything important that Strauss composed sprang from this stimulus. Of course he was promptly charged with realism, literalism, sensationalism, with supporting bad music by good titles and picturesque "programs," and so forth. The answer is in the music itself which these influences inspired. No one could deny its vitality, the power of its themes, the variety of idioms evoked by the association of music with ideas. They had given a new fertilizing force to a modern and most kinetic art. The first five tone poems, all pouring out of Strauss's white-hot crucible within ten years from 1887 to 1897 inclusive, swept the public and professionals, too, off their feet, and established a new dynamic in the tonal art—and this, mind you, before the turn of the century. No two of these first five tone poems were in the least alike. *Don Juan, Death and Transfiguration, Till Eulenspiegel, Thus Spake Zarathustra, Don Quixote* appeared with breath-taking effect, in quick succession. Perhaps *Eulenspiegel* is the most perfect and distinguished of them all. But all are commanding features of the repertory, and the youngest of these, *Don Quixote*, has passed its fiftieth birthday. The later *Heldenleben* and *Sinfonia Domestica* make plump, healthy, superbly organized but increasingly vulgar music.

In the later period Strauss inevitably passed to the stage. One can ask if *Don Quixote*, in some respects his most remarkable tone poem, is not so much symphonic music as it is a series of orchestral tableaux for the ears. The time was approaching for the visual to combine with the aural drama in this art. *Salome* is really a symphonic poem with stage setting and voices added to the instruments of the orchestra. The development is symphonic. The treatment is both realistic and thematic. The stage incidents are as swift as those of Italian realistic opera. The highest point in this direction is reached in *Elektra*, and *Elektra* is a genuine music drama of nightmarish intensity, neuroticism, sternness, and grandeur. Then comes the brilliant execution and the rococo comedy and nostalgic sentiment of a much lesser and more popular work, *The Knight of the Rose*, and finally the stylistic adventure, so brilliantly accomplished, of *Ariadne auf Naxos*. And then a decadence to such real atrocities of bad taste as the "opera" *Intermezzo*, the "Alpine" Symphony, and succeeding works, which it is just as well to admit do not and never will require detailed discussion.

The vision of the tone poet that he was remains with us, revealing stars that shine eternally in the heavens.

DECEMBER 1, 1949

Twenty-five Years after Puccini's Death

"The man or woman who hears all that without a thrill
is unhappily impervious to the right things."

IT MAY well be asked why no opera has appeared in the quarter-century since Giacomo Puccini died, November 29, 1924, to equal any one of his best or second-best works for the lyric stage?

In fact, no opera has appeared in that space of time, at least on this side of the water, which has made for itself any firm place in the repertory.

Meanwhile, the popularity of Puccini's best dramatic creations has not waned, nor have these works become less effective on the stage than they were a half-century ago.

The Metropolitan has in the last ten days performed all four of Puccini's most representative scores, and the earliest of them—*Manon Lescaut*, vintage of 1893—mounted after an absence of nineteen years from the Metropolitan repertory, proved to have a freshness and theatrical power which particularly impressed the audience.

The remarkable fact about this is that *Manon Lescaut* is neither a work of Puccini's creative maturity nor nearly as close to the period and flavor of the original Prévost story as the *Manon* of Massenet, which preceded the Puccini score by seven years. Massenet's *Manon* is undoubtedly the composer's masterpiece and one of the gems of nineteenth-century French opera. But Puccini appears not to have been at all frightened to attack the same subject and, inevitably, provoke comparisons by his procedure. *Manon Lescaut* was his first successful opera, as it was the first work in which he showed his hand as a dramatic composer.

383

He must have felt in his bones, despite the failure of his first two creations for the stage, that his feet were now on the ground, that he had something important of his own to say which would take care of the consequences. The results prove how right his instinct was, in spite of defects and inequalities in the score that astonished the musical world before the turn of the century. For today Massenet's *Manon*, with all its sensuousness, Gallic charm, taste, and appropriations of style, sounds like a work of a past period, while *Manon Lescaut* is as indubitably a creation of this one.

This in spite of immaturities. The characters of Puccini are less real than those of Massenet. Puccini's figures are images of the theater for him to hang music upon, rather than individual human beings. They stand for emotional and theatrical effects, rather than living them. You cannot imagine the lovelorn Des Grieux singing to Manon of his dream of their bliss together, or imploring a beneficent providence to tear her memory from his heart as he prepares himself for holy orders, or the soft-hearted but weak-tempered Manon singing farewell to their little table.

Des Grieux's anguished appeal to the captain to let him depart with the exiled Manon in the transport ship for America is most blatant and strident theatricalism. And smashing climax. Massenet's seductive Manon is made for love and folly. Puccini's figure is a hard proposition, alluring, adventurous, but well aware of practical values and the advantage of jewelry. She can blaze, too, and glitter, to Puccini's hot and materialistic music, but we do not think of her as being tender or really pitiful, while Massenet makes that illusion possible.

He is sentimental, at the least. Puccini is writing melodrama. But how he drives home the outstanding situations! The embarkation scene, with Manon and the other unfortunates led to their doom, and Des Grieux howling his supplication to be her companion in her misery, and the orchestra blaring forth the music of redemption as he and Manon are seen sunk in each other's arms as the curtain falls, is as good a piece of theater as opera affords us.

Puccini never forgot the aged Verdi's counsel not to confuse the symphonic and the operatic styles. He was too good an Italian to do that, anyhow. At the same time, he developed a skill and resource in orchestration that no other of his Italian contemporaries achieved.

By the time that Puccini arrived at *La Bohème*, which followed *Manon Lescaut* by three years, something else had happened which worked a special miracle. For in creating the music for this series of exquisite vignettes, Puccini had become the true poet and lyricist, which he never became in an equal degree in any other of his scores.

He loves, and remembers that he, too, once dwelt in Arcady. This is beauty and romance, in the picturesque setting of the life of Murger's Bohemians. It is the work which will live the longest of all his creations. Neither fashion nor any other change of artistic expression will put it out of date. *Tosca*, the descendant of *Manon Lescaut*, and the best raw-head-and-bloody-bones stunt that the operatic stage knows, eventually will go. *Madama Butterfly*, the effective aftermath, in its first act, of *Bohème*, will at last bite the dust.

When Mimi appears in the doorway of the old studio, and the strings whisper her motive with a glow of color that seems to suffuse the whole orchestra; when the poet makes the rafters ring with his song of youth and romance; and when the orchestra begins for a moment to develop that song, and the voices of the pair, departing for the Café Momus, echo from backstage as from some haven away and safe from the ravages of the *"vie quotidienne"*—the man or woman who hears all that without a thrill is unlucky, and unhappily impervious to the right things.

The scene of Mimi's death is perhaps the finest moment of all. It suddenly makes all the pathetic little human figures seem extremely small and simple and helpless, almost like the mournful figures of some sad puppet show. The orchestra in turn has become smaller and extremely simple and wistful in its reminiscences. They say that Puccini himself wept as he penned the final measures—the nine simple chords that accompany the passing of Mimi. It is the epitome of his art. Tears, too, have their value for the artist.

FEBRUARY 24, 1950

Bernstein Offers His Own Symphony

"Expression . . . of today's 'anxiety'?"

THE rising tide of American music, or certain swirls and eddies of that coursing current, was strikingly in evidence at the concert that Leonard Bernstein conducted as guest leader with the New York

Philharmonic-Symphony Orchestra last night in Carnegie Hall. And think not that this was a negative or amphibious or somnolent occasion.

It is true that Harold Shapero's Adagietto from his Symphony for Classical Orchestra was long enough in itself for a symphony, and far too long for its gracious melodic ideas to escape the tautological. But there always is something new, with contrast. Then there was Aaron Copland's *Outdoor Overture*, which is lively and so determinedly outdoor that any Boy Scout from Forty-second Street would know; and there was the climactic event, the New York concert *première* of Mr. Bernstein's own *Age of Anxiety* Symphony, which received an ovation.

This symphony, inspired by the poem of like title by W. H. Auden, will be heard as the tonal investiture of Mr. Bernstein's ballet of the same name, which is to have its stage performance next week by the New York City Ballet Company.

The score ought to go most successfully with the stage spectacle. For it is wholly exterior in its style, ingeniously constructed, effectively orchestrated, and a triumph of superficiality. That is a pretty good recipe for a ballet score, and this one is uncommonly constructed. There are thematic continuity, interrelation of theme, and dramatic continuity.

The workmanship is very smart and eclectic. Here is a composer who knows his modern scores thoroughly, and is prominently indebted to Stravinsky. Schoenberg is represented, in definition at least, but the essence of its style is Stravinskian neo-classicism. There is much modern battledoring and shuttlecocking of motives, heard in augmentation, diminution, inversion, stretto, and all that sort of thing. There are two sets of variations connected with the moods and processes of Auden's poem.

From this long and psychological poem of frustration and search for a faith, Mr. Bernstein has selected certain principal episodes. These deal with "four lonely characters," a girl and three men, who are first seen in a Third Avenue bar, seeking orientation in alcohol, engaged in a "symposium on the stage of man." The first seven variations are *The Seven Ages*. The second seven are *The Seven Stages*, in which the four "try every means, going singly and in pairs, exchanging partners, and always missing the objective."

These three subdivisions are part one of the score. Part two begins with a *Dirge*, as the four sit together in a cab bound for a nightcap in the girl's apartment. The *Masque* is the episode in which the four, still arguing, indulge in the escapism of dancing, more drinks, and more abstruse conversation. "Thus the protagonist is free again to examine what is left beneath the emptiness." In the *Epilogue* "what is left turns out to be faith. . . . The trumpet intrudes its statement of 'something pure' upon the dying piano . . . the strings begin to build, with the rest of the orchestra, to the positive statement of the newly organized faith."

This is enough, perhaps, to suggest in barest outline Mr. Bernstein's expressive methods. The form of the variations is unusual. For each new variation takes up an incidental feature of the preceding one, like a conversation in which a reply is made to a remark just made. The solo piano is said to represent the individual artist's reactions to the theme under discussion.

In the *Masque* part there is some lively jazz which will not be amiss in the coming ballet, and was not amiss last night. The music of faith, or the prayer therefor, at the end, is a sort of tinsel, bourgeois evocation of some distant plush paradise. Naturally it made a deep impression. Lukas Foss played the solo piano part very brilliantly. This part should serve well, for example, as a special background for a figurante in the ballet. If this is so, if the piano demarcates pantomime, well and good. As emotional commentary of a musical sort, it is counterpoint, not emotion. But perhaps we seek here for the wrong thing. One must be careful in calling for emotion today in music, or he may earn the horrible name of a romanticist.

In saying these things, be it understood, we do not necessarily question Mr. Bernstein's sincerity, still less his long-acknowledged brilliancy and skill as a musician, either with the pen or with the baton. But just what is sincerity? Is not the glitter of this score, its restlessness, its unease, its obvious artificiality, precisely the sincere expression, by a young musician of today, of today's "anxiety"? Just the same, we predict that the life of this music will consist in its association with the ballet, and not as music per se in the concert hall.

What, by the way, is going to happen to Mr. Shapero? What will he, as a creative artist, evolve into? He has studied, by all the fates and destinies, with Nadia Boulanger, Paul Hindemith, Ernst Křenek, Nicolas Slonimsky, Igor Stravinsky, Walter Piston, and Aaron Copland. He has emerged alive from the process; he has even mended his rather wicked ultra-modern little ways as harmonist and contrapuntalist in the work heard last night. Is he evolving, like the man in Gilbert and Sullivan, into a little Conservative?

The concert ended with a hoopla performance by Mr. Bernstein of Beethoven's Eighth Symphony, a gem of a masterpiece, youthful in spirit, unique in its flavor, but wholly unnecessary to conduct as if the conductor were a prizefighter or a rooter for a football game. This does not conduce to the finest kind of symphonic performance.

JUNE 21, 1950

The Stadium Bows In As Spalding Bows Out

"I expect to remain a musician for the rest of my life."

THE opening concert of the Lewisohn Stadium season took place last night. The occasion had been scheduled for the previous evening, but rain had interfered. The weather was none too propitious, especially for stringed instruments, last night. But an audience estimated at between eleven and twelve thousand assembled, in spite of an overcast sky. And the artistic accomplishments of the occasion were exceptional.

Efrem Kurtz, conductor for the opening week of the Stadium series, directed the Philharmonic-Symphony Orchestra in a program of Wagner, Tchaikovsky, and Beethoven. Albert Spalding, who now chooses to retire from a virtuoso's activities, made the last concert appearance of his distinguished career. He chose for this farewell to the concert platform the incomparable violin concerto of Beethoven, and his performance, as he warmed to his task and became absorbed in the noble music, became always more eloquent, more nobly in the tradition, more completely representative of the special talents and the uncompromising ideals of the musician and the performer.

Mr. Spalding has been before the public for forty-five years. His delivery of the music gave us the true measure of sincerity, his inalienable perception of beauty, unfaltering ideals.

"I have been a musician all my life," he said in a statement to the press. "I expect to remain a musician for the rest of my life." His performance said as much.

It included elaborate and most musicianly cadenzas which were his own. These were not intrusions thrust for the purpose of virtuoso display in the midst of a master's tonal structure; they were further expositions of the composer's thought, utilizing every resource of the violin in the process.

As an encore Mr. Spalding played the first movement of his unaccompanied violin sonata, showing here the skill in polyphonic composition and performance he previously had shown in the cadenzas of the Beethoven concerto.

The occasion was a fortunate one. Mr. Kurtz began with the superb ceremonial music to the third act of *Lohengrin*. He followed this with Tchaikovsky's Fifth Symphony. Presenting a work that everyone plays, Mr. Kurtz did not abuse the opportunities the score can afford a conductor for sensational effects. He gave the music every intensity; he did not exaggerate or sentimentalize.

So the first movement had a classic contour, in spite of its intense emotionalism. In the slow movement he gave the solo horn and other players of solo passages good leeway to shape the phrases for themselves and feel secure in their delivery of this glamorous and romantic music. And, for a rarity, the finale was given its complete measure of grandeur and breadth—a movement which in places approaches the quality of Beethoven. Nothing was hurried or scrambled, yet the mood was wildly dramatic.

There were incidental concomitants of this concert which profited the audience, including the new cyclorama, the completed stage and the new surrounding building for orchestra, instruments, and music, the curtained stage, the improved acoustics. Even the airplane situation is improved. Mr. Kurtz played the long symphony without a single interrupting roar. Lights on the roof of the stage are now so placed as to warn passing planes to give this spot as wide a berth as possible as they pass overhead. Mr. Spalding had such interruptions, though they were few, and they seemed only to determine him to play with more poise and authority.

It could be said that this was an uncommonly auspicious opening of the 1950 Stadium season.

A Memorial to Kurt Weill

"He had a hot heart."

ONE of the most important programs of the present season of the Stadium concerts is scheduled for tomorrow evening—the memorial program of works by the late Kurt Weill. This program, sadly enough, had been arranged by Weill himself before his death on the third of last April, and it embraces, so far as a single concert may, a number of his most significant achievements.

It is sheer necessity of practical program-making that there cannot be included in this concert passages from *Street Scene*, the setting of Elmer Rice's drama, which Weill thought of as an opera of city life as contrasted with *Down in the Valley*, a kind of rustic pendant of American existence.

It is significant that all three of the greater works of Weill's most mature period are of a tragical import, and that he found a way to make these subjects appealing and affecting to the famous "man in the street," who is supposed to avoid an opera in any form like the plague, just as Broadway producers fear the word "opera," applied to anything they undertake to present, as they fear the kiss of death. Weill's sovereign accomplishment was the extent to which he bridged the gap between formal and pretentious grand opera of European tradition and a type of popular opera, corresponding nearest, perhaps, to the German *"Singspiel,"* which speaks to all classes and sorts of American people in a musical language that they welcome and understand.

It is true that Weill aimed straight at popular success and that he was quick, before and after he came to America with Max Reinhardt and *The Eternal Road* in 1935, to direct his efforts toward the end of popular entertainment. He eschewed the highly intellectualized style of his early days in Germany, where he had been the very modern-minded and brilliant technician graduated from study with Humperdinck and Busoni. For practical as well as artistic reasons, he sought deliberately to find a medium of expression which should retain seriousness of purpose and at the same time reach the ears of the mass of his fellow beings. Whether this very purpose prevented Weill from attaining the highest position as a composer that he could have reached is a question· for the speculative to answer. But one does not think so. One thinks of Weill as born to do exactly what he did, and to work steadily and successfully toward a modern art of the musical theater.

Weill was too realistic, too shrewd, observant, and desirous of gaining the public ear to do otherwise, and this is not said in disparagement. He had a hot heart, was passionately democratic. He stood unchangeably for the things in which he believed, and was a rock of strength to the wife, the parents, and the friends whom he loved. He had also lived dangerously and fought furiously, by means of his art, against the deadly, cankerous evils which menaced Germany and indeed all modern society in the period prior to the Second World War.

He allied himself early with that very gifted and mordant writer of the epoch to which we refer, the young Bertolt Brecht, and it was in collaboration with Brecht that he produced his first big success abroad. This was the *Dreigroschenoper*, an adaptation, modernwise, of the famous *Beggar's Opera* of England of the eighteenth century. Weill's wife, now his widow, who was Lotte Lenya, made her great success as one of the principals of the show, in which the authors attacked hypocrisies and cruelties of their day more bitterly and undisguisedly than Gay and Pepusch attacked old-style opera and political abuses of their period in 1728.

Weill was to know personal danger and hardship in the years that led to Hitler's ascendancy in Germany, where he was quite logically marked as one of the artists and Jews most dangerous to the Nazi ideas. Riots broke out at first performances of his operas as Germany came always nearer to her crime and her fall, and Weill escaped from Berlin by the very skin of his teeth a few hours before the police came to his house to capture him.

This was the man who came to America—"an America," he said to us once with a smile, "of which I wrote so critically in the days when I had not an idea of what the nation and the people really were"—where he found freedom and safety and opportunity to develop further as an artists and to make his fortune.

He came to our popular musical theater with the rarest sort of equipment. He was a brilliant master of composition and of every practical exigency of the theater. He was probably the only composer for Broadway who knew how to orchestrate and who composed with an authority and dexterity entirely unmatched in this field. Weill had a strong, if not most distinguished, melodic gift. He was fascinated, as this writer well knows, by American popular song and folk song of all sorts, at the same time that he knew perfectly his Schoenberg and his Puccini. He has created sheer tunes which have become almost classics of their kind, and he has written for the stage with a technique and imagination and heart which make him one of the central figures in the development of an American form of opera.

OCTOBER 29, 1950

Aaron Copland on His Fiftieth Birthday

"If a young man at the age of twenty-three can write
a symphony like that, in five years he will be ready
to commit murder."

ON THE fourteenth of November, Aaron Copland, a leading American composer of his generation, will celebrate his fiftieth birthday. The celebrations in order on that day and on adjacent dates will be more than merely social observations.

On the fourteenth the Chicago Symphony Orchestra will play Copland's Third Symphony under the direction of Rafael Kubelik. This evening at the Chamber Music Festival of the twenty-fifth anniversary of the Coolidge Foundation in Washington there will be given the first performance of the new piano quartet commissioned of Copland by the foundation, and tomorrow night, coupled with Stravinsky's *Apollon Musagète,* Copland's ballet *Appalachian Spring,* a foundation commission of six years ago, will be given stage presentation.

On the fifth of November the League of Composers will tender Mr. Copland a "retrospective program" which will afford a partial view of his development as a creative musician, and will include the first New York performance of the quartet to be heard today in

Washington. And on November 24 Eugene Ormandy and the Philadelphia Orchestra will play in Philadelphia Copland's new clarinet concerto, and will repeat this work on the twenty-eighth in this city.

It is an imposing list of performances. Few living composers could expect such wide representation of their product within such a short time in a birthday year. This indicates two important circumstances: Copland's brilliant advance as a composer within the period of twenty-five years since he returned to this country from his studies in Paris, and the development, within the same period, of what could be roughly designated as a distinctive school of modern American composition to which he himself has contributed significantly as composer, teacher, and propagandist.

A rounded perspective of Copland's development as a composer is not yet possible. Opinions as to his ultimate rank in our national music will never be unanimous. But certain characteristics of his style are significant of the nature of his talent and the influences of the period under which his expression has evolved. This is the art of a thoroughly modern-minded musician, an intellectual and a sophisticate, with a wit, a sense of beauty, and a feeling for design that are his own. It is also the expression of an urban composer, grown up in the crowded city and in the period in which America has changed from an agricultural to a predominantly industrial civilization. Copland's sense of style is that of the American who is of his country, his time, his environment, at the same time that he is spiritually a man of the world, in touch with all the currents of thought from overseas and the sophistications of the European schools of composition. He is neither naïve nor local in his frequent and skillful employment of American folk themes for appropriate expressive purposes.

It is music that reminds us again that America has never had and can never have an age of musical innocence, or witness a national school rising from accretions of folk melody and folklore through centuries, and the maturing therefrom of a specifically national art. We in America have never had a decade in which we were free of foreign influences or could find that much time to be alone with our own musical soul.

Until the time of the First World War the German influence had been paramount with the majority of our educated composers. The political repercussions of that upheaval replaced the German influence with that of the French. Symbolically speaking, where our students of composition were concerned, Rheinberger of Munich gave place to Nadia Boulanger of Paris. It was in this period that Copland became the first full-fledged American pupil of Boulanger and the first of the group which has been wittily described as the "Boulangerie," whose artistic godfathers were Satie and Stravinsky.

Too many of the young Americans who became Boulanger's pupils did so with technical background insufficient to profit fully by her tutelage. Copland had here an advantage over his colleagues, in the circumstance of a thorough course of exacting technical training under Rubin Goldmark, a conservative to the backbone but a master technician, preliminary to similar studies under Vidal before he went to Boulanger.

It is believable that his earlier academic instruction at the hands of musical reactionaries had made him impatient of those teachers. We believe, however, that it was precisely Copland's good fortune that his solid early training had equipped him to face and absorb new modern influences without confusion to his thinking or style. By the time of the second great musical invasion of World War II, Copland was developed and mature enough to hold his own against any possible alien influences, and to continue to develop in an individual way that was characteristic of his gifts.

He has composed in various forms and styles unmistakably of this period, including scores for the ballet and for the films as well as the concert hall. He early experimented with jazz, and gained from these investigations some fresh rhythmic ideas which found their way into his first popularly acceptable score, *Music for the Theater*. This is music of a native wit and personality.

But Copland has never clung to any one style of composition. His melodic vein is often thin, but his stylistic distinctions are striking, and unmistakably Copland. After his first and obvious attempts to be extreme and astonish the bourgeoisie, he became constantly simpler and clearer, if also a complete individualist, and one strongly affected by the neo-classicism of Stravinsky's late period. At this stage he cultivated an austerity of expression which for a time placed him almost aloof from the public.

It is significant that in his later period, especially in his ballet music, he has greatly enriched the melodic interest and atmosphere of his scores by the use of American folk melody. In this he has followed the example of Stravinsky, the composer who has had the greatest influence upon him, in every aspect of his art. In the realm of formal music his Third Symphony is the outstanding achievement up to date.

By the quality of his workmanship, the sincerity and adventurousness of his progress, Copland made himself the spearpoint of the development of the modern American school. And he has done this with an unostentatiousness and a desire for service to his art that will leave their mark on this whole period of native composition and open the way for a greater future to come.

He has gone far and traversed difficult distances since the day in January of 1925 when Walter Damrosch conducted his early symphony for organ and orchestra, and turned to the audience to say: "If a young man at the age of twenty-three can write a symphony like that, in five years he will be ready to commit murder."

In all these undertakings his work has been that of a leader who knows that he is participating in creative beginnings rather than ultimate achievements. Mr. Copland put the matter admirably in a chapter of his book, *Our New Music*, in these words: "Geniuses don't grow on little bushes. The great young American composer will not appear suddenly out of the West with an immortal masterpiece under his arm. He will come out of a long line of lesser men—half geniuses perhaps, each one of whom, in his own way and with his own qualities, will provide the way for our mature music." This is a clear reflection of Mr. Copland's sound sense, earnestness, and high purpose as a creative musician.

NOVEMBER 19, 1950

Firkusny Introduces Martinů's Third Piano Concerto

"News reached him of the death of Jan Masaryk. . . ."

THE first performance in this city of Bohuslav Martinů's Third Piano Concerto, with Rudolf Firkusny as the soloist, was given yesterday afternoon by the Boston Symphony Orchestra, Charles Munch, conductor, in Carnegie Hall.

This concerto has a special history, which affects the character of its music. For Mr. Martinů was at work upon the last movement when news reached him of the death of Jan Masaryk in Czechoslovakia. The lilt of the dance rhythms and melodic ideas, which are not those of folk song but emanate from a Czech composer, are interrupted by a climax and a pause, and the end of the movement, which has been one of music-making in the classic ideal of music, form, design, for their own sake, changes. The accent is, for the moment, tragical, after which the swift finale resumes its course, with an end which is defiant, almost martial—*pro patria*. Schumann said that rebellion can be concealed in the walls of a symphony and the police be none the wiser.*

Aside from this, at an initial hearing the concerto revealed itself as a work of the soundest craftsmanship and essential sincerity of musical thinking. There is now and again the flavor of Czech national idioms, though no approach to the quotation of folk song. The piano part is very fully written, with special demands upon the virtuoso, yet it is an integral part of the symphonic structure.

Mr. Martinů was fortunate in his interpreters—in the collaboration of Mr. Munch and Mr. Firkusny, who was a host in himself at the solo instrument, now blending into the orchestral ensemble, now leading with all appropriate authority and fire. At the end of this performance, composer, pianist, and conductor were called back repeatedly to the stage, and the orchestra rose in their honor.

Mr. Munch closed the Concert with a memorable—indeed, an overwhelming—performance of the César Franck Symphony in D minor. He communicated this naïve, mystical, incomparable score with quivering sensibility, glow of color, and noble passion throughout.

There is no symphony like it, however much the snobs and professional esthetes try to find important flaws in this transfigural song of the faith. The Gothic solemnity and shadow of the begin-

---

* Mr. Downes often used a variant of this statement, attributing it variously to Robert Schumann and to James Huneker. The full text as it appears in *Mezzotints* by Huneker is as follows:

"Because of its opportunities for soul expansion, music has ever attracted the strong free sons of earth. The most profound truths, the most blasphemous things, the most terrible ideas, may be incorporated within the walls of a symphony, and the police be none the wiser.

"Supposing that some Russian professional supervisor of artistic anarchy, really knew what arrant doctrines Tchaikowsky preached! It is its freedom from the meddlesome hand of the censor that makes of music a playground for great brave souls."—ED.

ning, the figurations of the strings which soar to the sky; the child-like simplicity of Franck, in communing with his God; the glory of the conclusion, when the horns call from afar, and themes heard in earlier pages return, passing like the procession of the quick and dead on the Last Day, before the Throne—these were thrillingly communicated.

This performance had the imprint of irresistible inspiration. It was perceptible that Mr. Munch could not remain objective or outside the music as he projected it, white-hot from his heart. He was shaken by it, and honor to him for that. With less emotion and less intensity, he could not so have communicated to us the wonder of the music.

FEBRUARY 23, 1951

Première of a Fifty-year-old Ground-breaker

Bernstein Conducts the Ives Second;
Then Plays Mozart Beautifully

IT WAS reserved for Leonard Bernstein, to his eternal credit, to give the first performance anywhere in its entirety of the Second Symphony of Charles Ives, at the concert of the Philharmonic-Symphony Orchestra last night in Carnegie Hall.

It is not necessary to emphasize the fact that this symphony, an astonishing work today, was completed just fifty years ago, and that it has lain that long awaiting a public hearing to prove the composer's originality. But it is testimony to Ives's complete conviction in his art, and audacity in expressing himself, to reflect upon the impression that this particular symphony, by no means the most daring of Ives's scores, would have made if it had been heard when it was completed at the beginning of this century.

As a matter of fact, the origins of the symphony date farther back than that. Mr. Ives commenced work upon it in 1897, and the finale is in part the material of an overture called *The American Woods*, which he completed in 1889. He was born in 1874. At the turn of the century America was scarcely aware of the mature music of Debussy or Richard Strauss. The Stravinsky of even *The Firebird* was undreamed of.

Mr. Ives did not wait for him, or indeed for any composer other than himself, to decide what should go into his scores. He has said of this Second Symphony, in characteristic fashion, that "it expressed the musical feelings of the Connecticut country around Redding and Danbury in the Eighteen Nineties—the music of the country folk. It is full of the tunes they sang and played then, and I thought it would be a sort of bad joke to have some of these tunes in counterpoint with some Bach tunes"—this citation of Bach apparently referring to the more serious melodies of his own creation and to the contrapuntal form of the symphony.

If this symphony were the work merely of a folklorist, if the score consisted only of references to old-time American tunes, it would have no particular individual or artistic significance. But these tunes, with their profound meanings to a creative artist, are matters of reference.

The symphony is an immense structure, especially in the first movement. The tonal speech, if you want to put it that way, is by turns rudely, tenderly, fantastically, and cantankerously Yankee. It is unvarnished and unsymmetrical, sometimes dour and ungracious, if sometimes discursive and sometimes for a moment falling into a formula of composition.

It is not a symphony to be easily estimated or put in a category at any time. The first movement alone, in its material and extensiveness and variety of treatment, is an immense symphonic fragment. The slow movement is the one most completely grasped at a first hearing, and it is of unique inspiration and a noble elevation of thought.

Because of poor health the composer could not be present to hear his long-silent symphony.

That symphony, followed by Aaron Copland's *El Salón México*, made the second half of the program. Mr. Bernstein arranged a delightful first half, consisting entirely of music by Mozart, and an unconventional selection, too. First came the overture to *Don Giovanni* with concert ending; then the delectable Three German Dances in *ländler* style; and, third, the exquisite and rarely played Mozart Piano Concerto in G major, K. 453, with Mr. Bernstein himself as both pianist and conductor of the performance.

It is seldom that a conductor who directs and plays the piano part in a concerto does more than apprise the audience of his capacity to do a stunt. But it was not so last night. We are constrained to remark that Mr. Bernstein played beautifully, with a fineness of tone, distinction of phrase, wholly within the boundaries of Mozart's aristocratic style.

MARCH 16, 1951

A Fine Performance and a Letter Induce a Revaluation of *Fidelio*

"If ever a work endured in spite of multitudinous glaring weaknesses . . ."

AN ATTENTIVE reader, Mr. F. Brunn, writes to ask if we weighed our words when we referred in a récent review to Beethoven's *Fidelio* as a "defective" opera and also remarked that "the real musical value of the opera begins only at the end of the first act." He makes some allowance for the haste in which a review of an evening performance must be written to make a morning edition; he does not overlook the possibility of there being no opportunity for correction of proofs. But it is clear that he deeply suspects us of being irreverent if not thoughtless in expressing such an estimate of an immortal opera by an immortal master.

We must say that we took pains to emphasize our opinion of the defectiveness of the libretto and the score of *Fidelio* in writing about it. We did this because a conviction growing through the years was not weakened but confirmed by the fresh impression of the opera on its return to the Metropolitan repertory. This was the effect of *Fidelio* upon us, in the face of the best, the most reverent, the most dramatic interpretation of the work we ever had heard.

All that could be done for *Fidelio* in interpretation was done. If Mr. Bing had nothing else to his credit, he could say that by means of daring and effective publicity, by excellent casting and thorough artistic preparation, he gave *Fidelio* the greatest success that it has had or is likely to have in this theater.

And the opera is tremendously worth that service. Mixed, as it appears to us, with an appalling amount of old-fashioned buncombe in book and score, it also contains in a unique manner an indestructible core of greatness. Its great climactic scene is such thrilling melodrama, and contains so much that is noble and pathetic, that at the moment you can forget all the rest. And even "the rest of it" you can welcome in a mood of sentimental appreciation of quaint things of the past. But if ever a work endured in spite of multitudinous glaring weaknesses, that work is Beethoven's *Fidelio*.

We know that Beethoven himself was never satisfied with it. Not merely untoward circumstances of the first production in Vienna in 1805, not even the paramount consideration, at the moment, of the impracticalness if not unvocalness of the writing for the singers, were responsible for the tortures the master underwent in his successive revisions of libretto and music. His discontent, arising from his inexperience of the theater and also, and primarily, his difficulty in securing any libretto which would suit his high moral as well as dramatic purpose in attempting an opera, had him defeated before he began.

For Beethoven, the tonal dramatist of the forthcoming Fifth Symphony, the prophet who in the *"Eroica"* had hymned heroism as no other man in the history of musical art, had too grand a morality, and was too vibrant with the creative forces then at work in art and society, to reconcile himself with the conventions and clichés of the sort of opera libretto then current in the land. At last he adopted the story of Bouilly's "rescue opera," *Léonore, ou l'amour conjugale* (1798). The plot was of a species popular in the years immediately following the French Revolution—in fact, emanating directly from an episode of the Revolution which had come close to Bouilly. His libretto, as we know, was set first by Pierre Gaveau, then used by the Italian Ferdinand Paër in an Italian version. Sonnleithner gave Beethoven a German version of the same which was revised twice, in a vain attempt to make it work, by Stephan von Breuning, and finally by Treitschke.

We know how terribly Beethoven struggled with the music. Many of the set pieces in the first version were cut out. Other numbers were substituted. The score was worked and reworked at different times between 1805 and 1814. There are those, thoroughly acquainted with the three separate versions of the opera, who advocate today a return to the original version of 1805. They feel it to be a more integrated creation than the final version of 1814. The 1805 version, as restored by E. Prieger, was done first in concert form in Breslau, and later, on November 20, 1905, the exact anniversary of the first performance, in Berlin, under the direction of Richard Strauss. Apparently it did not take hold. We do not know of later performances.

If we dismiss that attitude toward a great master which forbids questioning of anything he produces, it seems to the writer impossible to swallow *Fidelio* whole. In its form it is a *Singspiel*, and light bourgeois comedy in the opening scenes. In the final scenes it is heroic melodrama. The form, in the first place, does not sit naturally on Beethoven's shoulders, first of all for the reason that he is constantly striving to make a musical unit out of it. Now he is attempting grand arias and concerted pieces after the Italian model, and now writing in set ensemble pieces which in his hands constitute the reverse of dramatic characterization.

And the material he has to set! The twittering nonsense of Marzelline at the ironing board, coquetting with her quondam swain! The celebrated "canon" quartet, which for some reason is considered wonderful Beethoven! It is neither good Beethoven nor good opera. Four characters, each one having different problems and sentiments, follow obediently on each other's heels in this vastly respected piece, singing the same phrase. If that is music-dramatic characterization, we will eat our hat.

The father sings an aria about "gold," which, as he sagely observes, may do much to make a wedding happy. It is such a conventional piece that its plain omission, as has more than once been averred, would help the opera immensely. Ah! But in that case where will you give Rocco his aria?

What has Beethoven to do in this galley? How could we expect him to write music for these situations? He turns to the grand aria in the Italian manner. But the aria of the villain, Pizarro, is palpably a matter of "horror" machinery which convinces no one. The grand air of Leonore, *"Abscheulicher,"* is in different case, much nobler of accent, but so palpably a set piece in a certain manner that it does not blend with the dramatic progress.

One could multiply these and similar defects of book and score. The orchestra usually says much more than the voices, and is used by Beethoven in an epochal manner which affected all opera after him. In the dungeon scene, which also has its excrescences, we come to great music, to lightning flashes of genius. Beethoven is chanting as only he can chant of the dawn of liberty and the unconquerable human soul.

And then, at this well-chosen moment of the opera—a device adopted some years ago in Germany—we hear the greatest of all the overtures, "Leonore" No. 3, which Beethoven wrote for the second version of the opera. It says more, in greater concentration and intensity, in a perfect and incomparably purer form, than the whole opera which inspired it. The opera would have served its purpose if only as the matrix of the overture.

FEBRUARY 6, 1952

Beecham at His Best

And Also Introduces Us to a Diverting Novelty

WE KNEW last night, the instant Thomas Beecham stepped upon the platform at Carnegie Hall as guest leader of the Philadelphia Orchestra, that he was in top form. This would mean an exciting concert.

Sir Thomas bowed long and respectfully to the orchestra. He turned, bowed courteously, briefly, perhaps with a touch of condescension, to the audience. He picked up his baton, coquettishly, from the desk of the second violin near by, and addressed himself to the conducting of Mozart.

When he is formal and correct in his deportment, which fortunately is rare, one is not so sure of him. But when he twirls his baton delightedly in circles over his head, or thrusts it behind his back, picks a pianissimo delicately from the air, or heaves, most ungracefully, his solid British body at the orchestra for a climax, he is feeling good; and when he is feeling good we are sometimes prone to the belief that he is one of the most sensitively gifted and passionately inspired interpreters of this day. Therefore, last night, a thrilling concert!

Sir Thomas is justly famous for his Mozart. He is one of the very few conductors who play this music with equal sensitiveness and gusto. For it still seems to be the tradition that Mozart must be toned down, made miniature, never permitted passion or power. All the tides of life pour impetuously through his music in Sir Thomas's hands; nothing inhibits the winged flight of its art.

The Beethovenish energy summoned last night in the first movement of the "Haffner" Symphony was in no sense incongruous with the lyricism and tenderness of the movement that followed, or the sparkle, mischief, and delight of the finale. One movement was uncomfortable to us: the minuet, taken with excessive deliberation, heavy-footed, so that the measures that should dance did so in rubber boots.

Of all the Sibelius symphonies the one least understood and the most generally underestimated is the Sixth, chosen for this occasion. Sir Thomas gave the work the most clear and perceptive performance that we have heard. The symphony is a soliloquy, not an unhappy one, though tinged now and again with a somber thought. It is Sibelius's "forest murmurs." The sounds of the forest, heard so often in his music, are there persistently, and they accompany solitary reveries. The movements are happily free of classic formulas, "codas" and the like. They end in the most unspectacular and sometimes sudden manner, or they vanish, on a long sustained tone, as in the final measures, into silence.

This symphony is to be closely associated with the much shorter Seventh; in some ways it is a preliminary study for the latter work, with this important difference: the Sixth Symphony is freely spread out over a frame of considerable dimensions; the highly condensed Seventh Symphony is a concentration of four movements in one. It would not be easy to overpraise this performance. What was surprising, and remarkable, was the enthusiasm with which a work by no means of the obvious or dramatic kind was received.

A completely different affair was the first performance in this city, if we are not mistaken, of the suite from Lord Berners' ballet *The Triumph of Neptune*. Why have we had to wait so long to hear this diverting score? It parodies all sorts of composers in the most witty manner. It has imagination as well as farce in it. The audience laughed in the *Schottische* when there came sounds of barking from the back ranks of the orchestra—on cue, if not pitch! The bass Robert Grooters, invisible, sang with mock pathos *The Last Rose of Summer* in the movement of *The Sailor's Return*. A

Celtic tune used in *The Frozen Forest* is as Irish as the County Derry, and of a haunting poetry. Only a Briton could have penned the rousing finale—*Apotheosis of Neptune*. The performance was a triumph of drollery, extravagance, and finesse.

On the strength of all this, it was advisable to stay and find out what Sir Thomas would do with the concluding *Semiramide* overture. This proved good judgment. He made it electrical, beautiful, memorable.

MAY 3, 1952

Wozzeck in Paris

"Far and away the most revolutionary achievement"

Paris, May 2

THE French *première* of Alban Berg's opera *Wozzeck* was given here tonight in the Champs-Elysées Theatre with an effect that left an audience of music-lovers and connoisseurs from all parts of the world speechless for a moment after the last note had vanished into silence. Then the audience rocked the theater with its cheers.

This was one of the early offerings of the "Masterpieces of the Twentieth Century" Festival organized here to represent the achievements in art of the non-totalitarian nations of the Western world.

No more significant symbol of its recent developments in music could have been offered than Berg's opera. It is far and away the most revolutionary achievement in music drama of the modern age. No work has approached it for dramatic impact and psychology since its *première* in Germany in 1925. France is the last great European nation to hear it. America has heard experimental or inadequate performances in the theater. A masterly concert performance of the work was given by Dimitri Mitropoulos and the Philharmonic-Symphony in New York last season.

The interpretation by the artists of the Vienna State Opera and the Philharmonic Orchestra of Vienna, under the direction of Karl Böhm, is one of such illusion and atmosphere, such understanding, imagination, and consummate technique of the stage, that those who have heard the opera only in America barely know what it is about.

Whether it is a morbid and phosphorescent product of a period of European decadence and despair after World War I or whether it contains the seeds of a musical art of the future need not detain us here.

As it stands and speaks to us, *Wozzeck* is an opera that has no parallel for intensity of feeling and the sense of conflicting forces of the visible and invisible world. In perfection of form and integration of thought, it is a masterpiece.

It would not be easy to single out personal achievements in a cast that seemed to interpret as one person mysteriously initiated in the secret of Berg's score. The leading artists were, of course, Josef Herrmann, the Wozzeck, and Christl Goltz, the Marie. The hallucinated doctor was Karl Donch, and the drum major was Laszlo Szemere.

But who could be the supreme interpreter when at times the separate instruments of the orchestra are human voices and the voices on the stage become symphonic, or one imagines that nature herself is whispering of its presence, of vast formless things that control and manipulate the show?

MAY 9, 1952

———

Paris Cheers *Le Sacre* Thirty-nine Years Later

"There was just as much noise the last time,
but of a different tonality."

Paris, May 8

IGOR STRAVINSKY enjoyed a triumph of literally epochal significance tonight when the Boston Symphony Orchestra, Pierre Monteux conducting, performed his *Sacre du printemps* before a wildly cheering audience in the Champs-Elysées Theatre and history reversed itself.

For this was the same Igor Stravinsky who fled the violence of a Paris audience that denounced his music and actually came to blows in a disturbance near to mob violence at the *première* of the *Sacre du printemps* in the Chatelet Theatre on May 26, 1913, almost thirty-nine years ago.

On that turbulent occasion one man stayed in his place at the head of the orchestra, which could not be heard in the din, conducting without a superfluous gesture or expression on a face that showed only his intentness on the score. That man was Monteux. Stravinsky had disappeared. Diaghileff, producer of the *Sacre* and head of the Ballet Russe, was in his box, and did not emerge.

Monteux, his short, stocky body keeping its customary stance, his command of the orchestra steady and unflinching, saw the thing through to the end, and probably made no more signs of emotion or agitation of any sort than he did this evening. Turning after his brilliant performance, bowing to the audience and hardly smiling in response to its ovation, he kept looking through the auditorium for Stravinsky.

After minutes of cheering, Stravinsky, a small, quiet-looking figure in an everyday suit, rose from a place at the back of the hall, and the audience went wild again. They could not have enough of him, and at last got him on the stage, where Monteux was awaiting him.

What the old comrades-in-arms must have felt at this moment of crashing acclamation, what they must have been remembering as they faced the roaring crowd, can be imagined but not described. The work that affronted the public and aroused its violent indignation in a previous decade was now a classic monument deemed by many the most important symphonic creation of the twentieth century.

"There was just as much noise the last time," said Monteux after the show, "but of a different tonality."

But Stravinsky was not the only composer of the evening whose score was especially eloquent of the purposes of the International Exposition of the Arts of the Twentieth Century, of which this concert was a part. Darius Milhaud was seated quietly in a corner of the hall, his health not permitting him to rise and acknowledge the enthusiastic reception for his early suite from the ballet *Protée* —a score that this writer has long considered one of his best.

This impression was borne out this evening. With no books of reference at hand, it is nevertheless possible to recall a first American performance of the work in the second decade of this century when this new music of Milhaud intoxicated us by its audacity and laughter and assurance. One might even say its insolence, in its then very new polytonality, and orchestration and rhythmic novelty.

Milhaud had been in Brazil, at the French Legation there, and Brazilian rhythms, some of them akin to American jazz, were in the score. The music had then a pungency and a Rabelaisian gusto. What is more important, it has the same youth, brilliancy, and gusto today.

There were two other important scores during the evening. The first, which opened the program, was Vaughan Williams' poetical evocation of the Tudor past in his Fantasia on a Theme of Tallis, a work that familiarity never deprives of its unique beauty and atmosphere.

The other work, by a composer of America's young generation, was William Schuman's Third Symphony, a virile and splendidly constructed achievement. The symphony's forms are those of the eighteenth century; the content is very modern, with a fine tension and bite of counterpoint, and a confidence and zest in the writing that are contagious. Nor is the work one-sided in its character. There are passages of introspection and self-communion.

On a program with many celebrated names and highly individual music, this symphony of William Schuman gained an ovation.

NOVEMBER 19, 1952

A Frank Change of Mind about Honegger's
Jeanne d'Arc au bûcher

"Voices of the earth, confused and terrible, and voices
of heaven are in the air about her."

ONE of the most impressive performances we have heard the Philadelphia, or any other orchestra, give in this city in recent seasons was that of Honegger's *Jeanne d'Arc au bûcher*, under the baton of Eugene Ormandy, last night in Carnegie Hall.

As the composer's designation of *Joan of Arc at the Stake* as a "dramatic oratorio" implies, the Philadelphia Orchestra was not alone in its splendid deeds.

It was supplemented by two choruses, a big chorus of mixed voices from Temple University and the St. Peter's Boys' Choir, as well as a cast of distinguished soloists, some of whom spoke, others of whom sang their texts, and virtually all of them masters not only of singing but of superb French diction—and perhaps nothing is more important to the interpretation of a work so utterly French in form, idiom, spirit, from the root upward as this one.

Nor could the score remotely come into its own without a virtuoso chorus. For all that, the decisive elements in the interpretation were the magnificent orchestra and the dominating, co-ordinating, completely revealing concept of Mr. Ormandy, which can hardly be overpraised.

The culminating tribute to him must be in the fact that last night's reading of the work, in the perspective of its first performance in this city four seasons ago, caused a new valuation on this listener's part of the entire work. His reaction then is clearly remembered. He thought *Jeanne d'Arc au bûcher* a piece of accomplished, sophisticated musical theater, effective but superficial and without profound conviction or much communication of actual feeling. Last night every line of it struck home.

The net effect of it all was a work of profound feeling as well as dramatic power. *Jeanne d'Arc au bûcher* remains essentially a music drama in concert form. Its spirit is not only dramatic but theatrical in the highest sense of the word. It is invisible theater and French theater. It is also music and text, strongly felt and fused together with an effect almost of visual realization of the dramatic value of Paul Claudel's poem.

The work achieves its effect by most skillfully inclusive methods that impose upon the conductor an especial variety of technical and artistic problems. One of the most immediate and practical of these is the balance of all musical elements.

Jeanne d'Arc speaks her lines over a tumult of choral commentary. Voices of the earth, confused and terrible, and voices of heaven are in the air about her. The crowd savagely denounces her and howls for her execution or hails her apotheosis. The tirades of the prosecuting clergy are opposed to her utterances. A multitude of small individual parts woven into the fabric of this drama of poetry and tone have to be exactly adjusted, in tone volume and color, to the ensemble, while the orchestra must punctuate, comment upon, and convey the drama.

The music is a fabric into which many apparently disparate subjects are woven together. There are plain chant and folk song, brilliantly handled, variously harmonized in accordance with the situation, and all in the course of grand lines of a symphonic development. There are savage satire, ironical transformation of the themes, and a mystical effect with an old medieval chant, for instance, of which Pierné many years ago made use in his *Children's Crusade*.

The apotheosis, of course, is of Jeanne, at last yielding her body and freeing her soul in the flames, and the acclaim of humanity, with the final line: "Greater love hath no man than this—to give his life for those he loves."

The cast was wonderfully selected. Vera Zorina, who was the Jeanne d'Arc at the earlier performance, took the same role last night with greatly developed power of suggestion and also beauty of plastic line. Not only her voice, but her bearing, her arms, with a bracelet upon one of them singularly suggestive of the shining hilt of a sword, carried the tale.

Raymond Gerome's Frère Dominique was the perfect foil to this—a fine voice, a noble diction, a true artist. David Lloyd's multiple roles were each distinctive.

The choral singing was not a particle below the highest standards of the evening. In attack, shading, nuance, it was in the finest tradition of choral performance, but this was accessory to its fundamentally dramatic spirit and the manner in which the voices sometimes contrasted with the instrumental tone, and at other times blended into it so subtly that one was not sure where the vocal and the instrumental tone divided.

In the sum of it, we heard *Jeanne d'Arc au bûcher* last night for the first time in its complete meaning. This showed that it is a musico-dramatic masterpiece of a certain type which Honegger has here perfected with consummate technique and in a spirit far more enduring than any mere technical accomplishment can ever be. And we have, above all, Mr. Ormandy to thank for this revelation.

Sundry Thoughts on the *Première* of *The Rake's Progress*

"Stravinsky has stuck his thumb in the pies of Handel
and Mozart, Bellini and Donizetti, Verdi and
Moussorgsky, and pulled out their plums, crying:
'What a good boy am I!' "

THE long-awaited *première* of Igor Stravinsky's latest opera, *The Rake's Progress*, took place in the Metropolitan Opera House eight days ago. This *première* had all the flavor of a grand gala event, which it was.

And now the tumult and the shouting are over. But not the contentions of the Stravinsky and the anti-Stravinsky camps.

So we have again to thank Mr. Stravinsky for an argument, an issue, aside from the fact that in one particular if in none other he has made a definite contribution, by setting the text of a famous poet, to the cause of opera in English. How appropriate this setting is to the nature of the text, to what extent it exemplifies a fruitful union of English words and melodic writing, is yet to be determined. But another opera in English has aroused widespread attention and curiosity as to its nature and effectiveness, and this is certain to give additional stimulus to the cause of opera composed and not translated in the vernacular.

This may prove to be the work's greatest value. We are not of those who are convinced by its esthetic principle, which we consider false, or by its virtuoso devices of craftsmanship, which do not in our opinion make an opera that will endure in the theater and leave its impress upon music in the future. Aside from the question of how strong or weak Stravinsky's musical invention may be per se and therefore how successfully or otherwise it has fulfilled his express purpose, we think that the work is based upon an unsound artistic premise and that as a result it tries vainly to reconcile and integrate within itself disparate elements. The consequence, which we consider inevitable under the circumstances, is the shell and not the substance of an opera, and one without a true reason for being.

410

Mr. Auden's libretto is an achievement of distinguished crafts-manship in literary and poetical aspects, one that in these respects can only add laurels to his name. From a theatrical standpoint it is not so strong, so well knit, or so convincing in its dramaturgy. It shares with the Hogarth pictures, which suggested it, the motive of a morality play. It has not the Hogarthian vigor, directness, and realism which have made that master immortal.

For this libretto is on at least two planes, the one realistic, the other symbolic, and they get mixed on the stage. The character of the Rake is far more complicated, orally and emotionally, than anything Hogarth dreamed of.

He is a Faust with Freudian overtones, also a touch of Peer Gynt, Don Giovanni, and other literary and operatic characters—who make a strange stew of a bizarre and semi-symbolic progress to the tragical end. There are various overtones in this modernly couched libretto. There is the religious element, suggested in the Rake's very confession of faithlessness to his ideals in the brothel, and in the religious procession that winds around his body at the end of the prison scene.

The idea of Baba the Turk, the bearded lady from the circus whom the Rake in his final degradation makes his bride, is a new idea, and an extremely coarse one. Another Faustian touch is the scene in which Nick (our old friend Mephistopheles) fools the repentant Tom by presenting him a machine by which he will produce bread from stones or crockery and feed all impoverished mankind.

The investment in this machine apparently brings the Rake and his pseudo-wife to ruin, and the scene of the auction, which includes the bidding for Baba herself, who has apparently been quiet in mothballs for an act and an intermission and suddenly rises to denounce and dismiss the auctioneer, is one which can only mystify the beholder, who will have but the vaguest idea, if any, of the symbolism of the business.

Here and in other moments the poet-philosopher takes precedence over the opera librettist, and the result is not a good libretto from the standpoint of practical, neo-classic eighteenth-century operatic forms and styles, which Mr. Stravinsky intends his opera to be.

With this initial confusion of elements, we then come to Mr. Stravinsky's alleged objectivity, formalism, and neo-classic conception of opera, which, he has emphasized, he considers a form entirely different from the "music drama" of Weber or Wagner, Debussy or Moussorgsky. This is the basis of the doctrines advanced, as explanation and justification, for the objectivity and dryness of his musical substance. His proponents appear to point with pride to their master's eclecticism of style, to its derivation from many different sources, and the amalgam of all these elements into an art form which is nevertheless alleged to be stamped with the impress of Stravinsky's own creative personality: as though the fact that Stravinsky has stuck his thumb in the pies of Handel and Mozart, Bellini and Donizetti, Verdi and Moussorgsky, and pulled out their plums, crying: "What a good boy am I!" constituted a creative achievement.

This is a sophism as superficial as it is specious, proceeding directly from the fundamental fallacy of the kind of neo-classicism actually practiced, if not professed, by Stravinsky and his followers. Neo-classicism is not a species of imitation furniture. It does not consist of a fake simplicity, or the attempt to press the thought and the expression of modern man into the precise molds of old forms which were not old, but new and responsive, when they appeared to artistic demands of the age which begot them. To the best of our belief, Stravinsky's looking backward in the esthetic sense results in music which is "ersatz," artificial, unreal, and actually unexpressive. We know of no composer who has produced living and enduring art by hugging the past to his bosom, hiding his head, as it were, in the sands of bygone formulas and thus evading the issues and challenges of his day and the employment of new force and new ideas to meet them.

The unrealness of his theory is further demonstrated by the Stravinsky "melody." To say that there are no melodies, at least in outward appearance, in the score of *The Rake's Progress* is not true. There are a number of clearly set-forth melodies. But of what kind and texture? A real melody is an organic entity, born of germinal phrases which foliate and develop in response to the life force within them, and communicate expression that is quickly felt. Of course, there have been melodic expressions, ahead of their time, which have not been immediately recognized for their beauty and feeling. But when this occurred, the melodies, not immediately accepted by the great public, were in an unaccustomed idiom. We submit that such melodic elements as there are in this opera are short-breathed and unpropulsive, and oftenest compounded according to a system.

It is not astonishing that this score is most effective in those passages which are nearest the character of ballet, such as the choruses and the choreography of the prostitutes and the roaring boys of the brothel scene, in which the orchestra does some pretty figuration and Mr. Balanchine achieves some admirable effects of choreography. The lively scene of the auction of Tom's effects, and the amusing syllabification of Baba the Turk's nonsense, with a note to each syllable of the silly aria, are in Mr. Stravinsky's most effective vein of the satirical and sardonic.

Here and there is a moment—the leave-taking of Tom at the gate in the first scene; Tom's confession of faithlessness when he remorsefully confronts his own ruin in the brothel; a moment in the first part of Ann's soliloquy in the garden under the moon, as she decides to go to London to save Tom—in a Verdian aria with a cabaletta which ends triumphantly on a high C, in the most approved and old-fashioned operatic style.

But the moments of real feeling and inspiration are very few. We say nothing of the extremely bad prosody that reigns through most of the score, and such baldly apparent derivations as the beginning phrase of the trio of Chopin's funeral march, which makes the substance of one of Tom's arias. This chance reminder could be merely a "happenstance." We respectfully submit that, if only because of the banality of the progression, it should not be allowed to pass by a scrupulous master of style.

The grave scene at the end is the emptiest of all, and a good example of the way the whole opera, both in texture and music, wavers between various styles and point of approach. The *Freischütz* "Wolf's Glen" scene of the game of cards with the Devil, which decides Tom's fate, should be done either in the manner of twentieth-century neo-classicism of situation, text, and music, which it is not, or early nineteenth-century Weberish romanticism, which essentially it is.

To accompany this scene in the manner of eighteenth-century "recitativo secco" with punctuating chords of the piano, and continue it with meaningless piano exercises while the hellish dialogue goes on, means precisely nothing. It is not pleasurable to say that this tedious, labored, artificial score adds nothing to Stravinsky's achievements.

The sum and substance of it is a story which falls between many stools, philosophic, symbolic, legendary, and operatic, and ends by

413

plumping straight into nineteenth-century romanticism! The plot includes, with many a good old-fashioned operatic device, the card game in the churchyard at midnight, the sentimental outcry of Tom to the ever-womanly to save him, and the epilogue to this story of sin and its deserts *à la* Don Giovanni. This closes the show on a modernly satirical note which, in turn, is completely incongruous both in concept and in stage effect with the tragical scene in the madhouse which has immediately preceded it.

What there is in this score was done, we thought, the highest justice in Mr. Bing's production. He had a singing cast that was wonderfully prepared and of great individual efficiency. Miss Hilde Gueden's Ann led the cast from the vocal point of view, in the range and brilliancy of her song and its variety of effect. Her final scene had a degree of pathos and feeling which made that movement her great effect and moved us by her expression. Here, indeed, in this last scene the opera did the most toward leaving the ground, and here Eugene Conley was fully on a par with Miss Gueden in the skill, the sincerity and feeling of his delivery.

Blanche Thebom, however, very amusing, very effective in her satire and her apt characterization at Tom's breakfast table of the bearded and Impossible Woman, had a complete triumph.

Mack Harrell's Nick and Paul Franke's Sellem, the auctioneer, were also of their best.

The orchestra was in the hands of the experienced and admirable Fritz Reiner. The whole production had been supervised directly by Stravinsky himself, who, at the end of the performance, appeared repeatedly at the curtain, to long if not over-hearty applause.

And yet, with all the brilliant workmanship, virtuosity of execution, ingeniousness of effect, with the variety of styles and rhythms, and the excellently choreographic stage direction of George Balanchine, the opera remains a study in still-life; a structure that is as a house of cards which would fall apart at a touch, and which all the king's horses and all the king's men could not bring together again.

Heifetz: An Evening of Superlative Violin-Playing

"And a dramatic moment"

JASCHA HEIFETZ, who opened his recital last night in Carnegie Hall by playing the prelude of a Bach partita at a far livelier clip than the music demanded, continued with an evening of superlative violin-playing of which perhaps only he, of all living virtuosos, is capable.

The Bach excerpt was followed by the Nardini Concerto in E minor, and its performance was to this writer's mind an impeccable example of the classic style. By "classic style" is not meant a precision, coldness, and emotionless presentation—quite the contrary. Mr. Heifetz sang the slow movement as warmly, as humanly, and with as expressive a tone as that of the fabulous prima donnas of history; yet his interpretation made every melodic line, every smallest or most elaborate ornamentation distinguished and a triumph of proportion and taste.

The Beethoven sonata selected was the eighth one, in G. In this sonata Beethoven writes with a delicacy and fancy that have no duplication—unusual as it was to choose such a work for the spaces of Carnegie Hall. Here, too, there could be questions of preference of tempos and minor matters of interpretation. The effect, as a whole, was that of sovereign art, in which Emanuel Bay, the pianist, took a distinguished part.

Mr. Heifetz opened the second part of the program with Ernest Bloch's early Sonata for Violin and Piano. He had not played this work, if we are reliably informed, for seventeen years. How the earlier interpretation matched with that of last night, this writer does not know. But it is difficult to believe that on returning to the sonata Mr. Heifetz did not bring to it a ripened wisdom and a matured insight in communicating its passionate and richly colored music.

His style here was, of course, a complete contrast to everything done earlier in the evening. He was as rhapsodic, dramatic, sub-

415

jective in as great a degree as he had been the classicist in the communication of Nardini's music. The music mourned and denounced and was deep in reverie, by turns. The barbaric triumph of the finale ended in a mood of serenity and poetic meditation.

Regarding the physical difficulties of a score that is orchestral rather than violinistic in its nature, it need only be said that Mr. Heifetz was, as ever, in easy command of all the immense technical equipment that Bloch requires, not for purposes of soloist display, but for the communication of overwhelming emotion.

There followed a dramatic moment: the performance by one master violinist—Heifetz—of the work of another master of the instrument and of the composer's art—Fritz Kreisler—of Kreisler's Recitative and Scherzo for the violin alone. From the violinist's standpoint, and the composer's as well, the piece is superbly written. Playing it, Mr. Heifetz gave us as consummate an example of violin mastery and interpretive eloquence as this writer feels he ever can expect to hear.

Having done so, Mr. Heifetz followed his act of homage by quietly indicating with his bow Mr. Kreisler's presence in the auditorium. The applause compelled the older master to rise and be seen, to the thunderous demonstration of the audience.

Mr. Heifetz' simple and excellent arrangement of Rachmaninoff's song *Daisies*, and his electrical playing of the very amusing and extremely difficult and dazzling transcription by Castelnuovo-Tedesco of the *"Largo al factotum"* from the *Barber of Seville* brought the end of the printed program. And that, too, was the occasion for demonstrations of delight by the gathering that packed the hall.

M A Y   1 0 ,   1 9 5 3

Wonderful Town Is a Wonderful Pleasure

"Spontaneous, unfettered, and fertile"

LEONARD BERNSTEIN's *Wonderful Town* is a wonderful pleasure to hear and behold. The youthfulness and exhilaration of the music are companioned and fully matched by every artistic element of the

416

production. The critical practitioner whose customary beat, operatically speaking, centers about the Metropolitan, where they talk much and loudly of modern stage production of music drama, sighs with longing as he experiences the swift precision and perfect matching of libretto, music, action, décor, and timing, and the consequent virtuosity and spirit, release and laughter, of this well-nigh perfect show. It has the reckless mastery of means and the sure co-operation of artists, each expert in his or her part and all in accord in the joyous achievement of the common task.

As years file by, one is more and more painfully impressed by the degree to which the creative musician is at the mercy of his interpreters. Mr. Bernstein is, of course, extremely fortunate in all his collaborators and in the results of their skill and imagination—in the dances and musical numbers staged by Donald Saddler; in the brilliantly original sets and costumes by Raoul Pène du Bois; in the lighting of Peggy Clark; the orchestrations by Don Walker; the musical direction and vocal arrangements of Lehman Engel; and all other features of the production supervised by George Abbott.

We say nothing here, for we don't have to, of such refulgent luminaries as Rosalind Russell, the Ruth, and Edith Adams, her sister Eileen, among the principals of the cast. It is a galaxy of stars, any way you look at it—behind and before the curtain, from the lyric-makers, Betty Comden and Adolph Green, to the conductor, Lehman Engel. And it is utterly American in conception and execution, from crown to toe, in a way that is current and characteristic of our people, and not paralleled by any other musical theater, for better or worse, of the contemporaneous world.

We have seen certain approaches to this standard of opera production, mostly at the City Center, by the New York City Opera Company in its recent delightful production of the Rossini *Cenerentola,* under the stage direction of Otto Erhardt; and more frequently in the days when Laszlo Halasz was the musical director of that institution. But that is another story.

What vigor and delight in this fantasy of youth and mad antics, vertiginous music, and a cast egged on by the happy responses of the audience! The electricity shoots back and forth over the footlights in a show which projects such spirit, and is maintained with such ingenuity and taste, that it is not for an instant vulgar or banal or less than a triumph of invention, extravaganza, and comedy.

Everything fits, jibes, and "works." You have your sentimental tunes—and good ones, too. You have your dizzy and your mellifluous, haunting duets of the two girls, nostalgic and bewildered in the city. A quintet of persons trying hopelessly to relieve embarrassment by idiotic conversation is one of the cleverest passages in the show. So is the resounding conga, with its uproarious burlesque, and Rosalind Russell arranging her hair and reclining on top of as wild a group of Brazilian officers as you'd ever conceive this side of the equator—La Russell up there above the battle, sustained by strong masculine arms, serene and confident as Venus in her shell.

You have also a "number," for solo and chorus, which somehow escapes the corny and commonplace; likewise an Irish jig, and a "wrong-note rag," and such a crowd of hep-cats as never were on land or sea, except maybe in Greenwich Village of the nineteen thirties—a place traditionally fertile in characters. Here the characters are multiplied and caricatured, such as the lanky, long-haired, misty-eyed individual who carries a banner with the word "Peace" large upon it, and ends by beating up the football player after that husky soul, in full underwear, has been tackled—a beauty of a tackle—by a young village dame of equal prowess, agility, and pulchritude.

There is no need here to go back to the origins of this musical play, which Joseph Fields and Jerome Chodorov freely adapted from their comedy *My Sister Eileen*. Suffice it to say that, with all its exuberance and ostensible irresponsibility, the story of the two Ohio girls who come to New York seeking fame and fortune has perfect adaptability for musical and choreographic treatment. On the purely musical side, a composer and phenomenal musician, knowing his scores from Brahms to Bartók and from Shostakovich to Stravinsky, enriches his palette with many a pungent touch of dissonance and modern harmonic color, while yet keeping very clearly to the popular tone, the rhythmic vigor, the common human touch of our contemporaneous music of entertainment.

In this entertainment, choreography—not classic choreography but American choreography, born of the energy and gaiety and ways of our people—plays a strong and most exhilarating part. Mr. Bernstein, long before this, had written adroit and expert dance music for his ballet *Fancy Free* and other works. *Wonderful Town* is basically different from his earlier show, *On the Town*, which presaged this one. The new score is not only richer in its invention and warmer in its feeling, but it is vibrant throughout with the spirit of the dance. For this is no musical show with interpolated dance "numbers" to afford surcease from its ditties. This is an opera of which dance is warp and woof, an opera made of dance, prattle, and song—and speed. Its unflagging pulse is characteristic of its restless time and nervous environment. In days to come, it may well be looked upon in some museum exhibit as the archetype of a kind of piece which existed peculiarly in America of the neon lights and the whiz and zip of the mid-twentieth century. Very well! So it is, a reflection, with all its carefreeness and exuberance and irreverence, of this place and epoch, and the dynamic forces that are flashing dangerously about us.

The very overture, a rather long one in the traditional frame of a potpourri of the principal tunes of the show, seems more than a mere preliminary racket to be heard over the talking, rustling, and banging of an incoming audience. It seems a noisy, excited emanation of the audience itself, assembling for its pleasure.

We sense in it, before we see them, the commotion of the hustling crowd and the swift motley of the Village denizens milling about. The rising of the curtain is expected and hardly important since we are already so entirely aware of what is going on before it is lifted. The score takes everything in its stride as the action proceeds, hitting off character and situation with unerring facility; witness the repeated yawns of the brass between the senseless inanities of a drugstore clerk, an obnoxious reporter, and a girl who has picked up a book called *Moby Dick*—"something about a whale!"

The show stands for so much that is spontaneous and unfettered and fertile within us! Indeed, we are coming to believe that when the American opera created by a composer of the stature of the Wagners and Verdis of yore does materialize, it will owe much more to the robust spirit and the raciness of accent of our popular theater than to the efforts of our prideful emulators, in the upper esthetic brackets, of the tonal art of Bartók, Hindemith, and Stravinsky.

Unconventional Program-Making by Szigeti

"No consideration whatever to box-office appeal"

JOSEPH SZIGETI, as is his wont, arranged a program of violin music for his recital last night in Carnegie Hall that gave no consideration whatever to box-office or gallery appeal.

His list of eight compositions, involving two big works for violin unaccompanied, probably alienated in advance all but the hard core of his large and persistent following. It none the less revealed again the arresting and indisputable individuality of the interpreter, in ways that in the sum of it proved compelling.

For Mr. Szigeti always has something to say, in his own way, which is singularly worth saying. He is incapable of making a conventional program. Some say that he also is incapable of a truly appealing and sensuous tone—which is not true—and that he forgets loveliness and graciousness of style in his pursuit of the profounder and more austere aspects of the music that he discourses.

For ourselves, we would rather hear one of his programs, as he chooses its arrangement and interpretation, than a dozen by violinists of ways that are more suave and ear-tickling and far more adroit in their bids for popular acceptance; as witness last night.

The concert began with a Tartini sonata that had not been played to death, and was, therefore, a refreshing departure from precedent. It continued with the first-class performance of the late D major Sonata for violin alone of Prokofieff, composed in 1947, and one of that singularly tormented composer's latest productions.

Unhappy Prokofieff's circumstances may have been, yet the sonata, very skillfully written, is a joyous piece, composed with absolute mastery and with exuberance. The first movement is perhaps the strongest—one that would stand out happily by itself. But Mr. Szigeti made the performance of the whole sonata a monument of style and of virtuoso delivery.

He played after that the piece Prokofieff dedicated to him, the *Song without Words* of 1925. It is one of those melodies that have for us a false simplicity, a neat plausibility and overt sophistication —which don't ring true, coming from Prokofieff, in spite of the suave line and the ingenious harmonies that underlie it in the piano part. This is of course a personal impression. Who are we to interpret the mind of a composer?

After all this, and the artificial *Variation d'Apollon* from Stravinsky's ballet, came the plain tonics and dominants of Beethoven's F major Piano-and-Violin Sonata, of which the classic conformities of the opening movement might cause impatience, but not the slow movement, played with the utmost beauty of tone and simplicity of sentiment. In this and other performances Mr. Szigeti was aided materially by the sensitive and musicianly playing of his pianist, Carlo Bussotti.

And then one looked ahead with a gasp. The last half of this program, after the intermission, consisted solely of the Bach unaccompanied D minor Partita, ending with the chaconne. One sighed. This looked like rather a good deal of a thing.

Actually, the playing of the partita became the crown of the evening. One would have made the journey for that performance alone. We do not speak only of the chaconne, but of the earlier movements, too, such as the nobility and pathos of the saraband, the rousing energy and gusto of the gigue. The performance was a crescendo of excellence and of excitement.

We do not remember hearing in years the chaconne interpreted with such mastery and nobility, with such a wealth of thought and imagination, such a play of light and shade, fancy and reverie, intimacy and grandeur. And of course, as with Bach himself, the chain of variations seemed but as the enchained continuance of a single idea and the erecting, block by block, of an edifice that towered to the skies.

This was the act of a very great artist, wholly in love with his task, communicating the richness of his thought and experience, grown through many years. No doubt, after this, and all the applause, there were encores, but we left the hall, preferring to hear nothing else that would impinge upon the impression of that consummate interpretation of Szigeti.

Morel Conducts Elgar

"Great music-making"

ON THE evening of December 2 the Juilliard Orchestra, conducted by Jean Morel, gave the first concert of five "evenings" of the "Festival of British Music" held in observance of the year of the coronation of Queen Elizabeth II. This concert was more conspicuous for the remarkable playing of the Juilliard Orchestra, under the direction of Mr. Morel, than for the revelation of unsuspected masterpieces by any new composers of the British school.

For the Fifth Symphony of Edmund Rubbra, dated 1948, is tiresomely prolix, heavy-handed in its orchestration, and of a length and pretentiousness wholly out of proportion to the worth of its ideas. Far more contemporaneous in outlook, and skillfully written, is the Symphonic Suite for strings, of 1951, by Maurice Jacobson, heard for the first time in the United States.

In the second part of the program, Martha Flowers, with a beautiful voice and a striking personality, sang Benjamin Britten's settings of poems of Arthur Rimbaud, *Les Illuminations*, composed in 1939, to the vast satisfaction of the audience.

But the height of the accomplishment of the evening, one which makes the event stand out in the memory, was Morel's performance of nothing more nor less than the "Enigma" Variations of Edward Elgar! One would say of this work that it was too much of a thrice-told tale to particularly interest a hard-boiled concertgoer. The fact is that the exciting performance made us more fully aware of certain qualities of the music than we had been at any previous experience of it!

Was this the pontifical Elgar, composer laureate and V.I.P. of his art in Victorian England? Elgar was now addressing us in terms of untrammeled and unconcealed animation, and with a degree of tone color and dramatic accent that were transformative. If one took into consideration only the exterior characteristics of this performance—the contrasts of mood and style and dynamics, and the

422

blazing climaxes—it could be called another virtuoso display. But it was no such thing. It was great music-making, in the highest aspects that this activity can assume when it is creative.

The "Enigma" Variations are of German and Brahmsian descent —indeed, too German in the elaborate and rather superfluous coda that the conductor Hans Richter induced Elgar to add to the score in its original form. But the German technique, which so often becomes overweighted and thick, was clarified with beautiful balances and voice-leading, and was made the vehicle of feeling and imagination by a conductor of the first rank who should be more widely known to the American public than he is at the present time.

JANUARY 3, 1954

Berlioz: The Composer Who Never Grew Up

"Exquisite sensitiveness . . . incredible banality"

PURSUANT to last Sunday's remarks in this column upon the scarcity of performances of Berlioz's music in this year of his sesquicentennial, rumor reaches us of some special Berlioz performances projected for the second half of this season and at some summer festivals. Well, it were better late than never! This would be of great service to music-lovers. For it is part of the inherent paradox of Berlioz's life and art that we have not placed him yet in any definitive position as a composer. One reason for this is that he remains immune to inclusion in any classified list of creative artists; the other is that we still are not intimately acquainted with the body of his music.

It would be oversimplification to remark that there must be a good reason for this degree of neglect of a composer as voluminously publicized, by himself and by others, as Berlioz was in the course of the century that followed him. It is logical to assume that the reason for this must, in a measure, be in defects of his music; and that is true.

We do not believe for an instant the claim that Berlioz remains half understood because he is still ahead of his time and more original than even the twentieth-century criticism admits. His is not a perfect art, by any stretch of the imagination. Yet it is such an audacious and original art, and it has such vitality and passionate individuality, that in certain instances it has outlasted other music, better made, which received fully as much publicity as the compositions of Berlioz. We think especially of the Liszt symphonic poems, which represent the last new form that modern composition has produced.

Liszt developed this form with a considerably finer balance of elements and harmony of workmanship than Berlioz ever attained in the field of symphonic composition. But what has happened to *Les Préludes* or *Tasso* or other of the odd dozen productions of Liszt in this genre? He lives today on our orchestral programs by his two piano concertos and his remarkable three-movement "Faust" Symphony—the symphony which in its treatment of representative themes and in the divisions of the form comes nearest to the Berlioz program symphony, and is dedicated, as it happens, to Hector Berlioz!

Berlioz did not produce nearly as much music as either Liszt or Wagner, the other two of the triumvirate who were apostrophized and assailed in their century as the banner-bearers of "the music of the future." Berlioz, the least skilled of these three and the most limited in his quantity of production, stays with us, and refuses dismissal.

Why does this music, or that part of it which we know, persist in our ears? It is marred by patent incongruities of style, by which the exquisite sensitiveness and purity of some pages contrast with the incredible banality and commonplaceness of other pages right next door. Melodies that haunt us by their passionate feeling and by the noble curve of the instrumental song soar from his pages; the next moment we encounter a harmonic flatness and a sudden fall earthward.

These things have all been said before of Berlioz. Unfortunately they hold true, notwithstanding the efforts of his partisans to explain away bad workmanship by ascribing it to originality of method. This is begging the issue. One must value Berlioz for what he is, never for what he is not.

Berlioz was the most unprepared, and ill-educated, great composer who ever lived. But this, thanks to the quality of his genius, was his strength as well as his weakness. Would he ever have been the creator that he was if he had had thorough grounding in the technique and traditions of his art, and been taught, as Thomas Edison once remarked of his inventions, that all the things he had imagined weren't so? Was it Berlioz's misfortune, or was it divinely decreed by Providence, that of all teachers in the world he fell into the hands of the fantasy-ridden Lesueur as his instructor in counterpoint and composition at the Conservatoire? Lesueur was possibly the right man for less adventurous minds—Gounod was among his pupils—but he was too akin to Berlioz in his creative tendencies, one believes, to restrain and discipline his famous student.

For Berlioz, from one point of view regrettably, from another gloriously, never grew up. It is failure to advance, as all the other immortals did, that conditions his unqualified success in any single score, and his place in history. It is his strength that he remained the unadjusted, uncompromising, ill-balanced phenomenon of genius that he was from the beginning of his career. His nature was impressionable and acutely responsive to impressions in ways beyond description. Virgil, Shakespeare, Goethe taught him more, perhaps, than any of his teachers.

It was George Moore who said that we do not realize how like our destiny is to ourselves. Berlioz the musician, Berlioz the writer, the critic, the conductor, the dreamer and searcher for the ideal love that he never found in his life, was incorrigibly and defiantly himself, against all comers and circumstances. It is doubtful if his last music will be found to equal his earlier works in either workmanship or strength of inspiration. The vigor and nervous incandescence which characterized his earlier years and supported him in his endless and ferocious battle for the good and the great in art was not his in his last days, when life was bitter in his mouth— the bitterer, perhaps, because he was still youthfully irreconcilable to its lessons.

But there were some lessons which he fortunately never learned. One was the lesson of compromise, which he scorned. Another was the lesson of moderation and sound reasoning of the middle-of-the-road kind, of which he was equally incapable.

Would a different teacher and a different environment have made him a more complete artist? It is a very open question, never answered. If he had reached the consummative maturity that Wagner did? Somehow the idea does not fit. It seems exactly right, exactly his mission and destiny, that Berlioz, of all the composers in the history of his art, should remain unadjusted and unconquerable, the unique personification of flaming youth, rebellious, irreconcilable, indomitable; the challenger, even today, of the future.

OCTOBER 15, 1954

Shostakovich Finally Achieves Integration

The Tenth Symphony: Outspoken and Grossly Impolite

Two events gave special significance to the concert that Dimitri Mitropoulos directed as conductor of the New York Philharmonic-Symphony concert last night in Carnegie Hall. One was the first American performance of Shostakovich's Tenth Symphony. The other was the appearance as soloist, on the fiftieth anniversary to a day of his debut outside of Russia with the Berlin Philharmonic, of Mischa Elman, a sovereign master of his instrument.

The performance of the symphony was momentous, for this is obviously the strongest and greatest symphony that Shostakovich has yet produced. One would say that it is the first score in the symphonic form that proclaims the complete independence and integration of his genius.

He has appeared in earlier works as a singularly gifted, yet split creative personality. No doubt the creative problem was complicated rather than clarified for him by the fact that through special circumstances and events he became virtually the composer laureate of present-day Russia. In that capacity he had to compose, for example, his Seventh Symphony, the war symphony, which then symbolized the conflict and the struggle in which Russia and America were jointly engaged. It was excellent musical propaganda, but a second-class symphony. The inequalities, superficialities, and weaknesses of the Eighth and Ninth symphonies, which soon followed it, were all too apparent.

Precious persons, neo-classicist, perhaps even those musical devotees who dub themselves "intellectuals" will not be comfortable

426

in the presence of this powerful, outspoken, and at times grossly impolite symphony. But here is music with contour and force, with grand and broad lines, emotional tensions, and sincere and unconditional statement.

The feeling is matched by the strength and logic of the form. The dimensions, especially of the somber first movement, are spacious, and this first movement contains in germination all the main themes and developments of the movements that follow. And we know of no other composer producing today who would dare to write such an unhurried and inevitably developing movement.

The composer's method is one of broad brush strokes. For the most part it is in two-part counterpoint, with many instruments doubling the notes of each part, which means emphasis, and strong, sometimes shadowy, sometimes strident, contrasts of tone color. It is a style that goes directly to the mark, without sophistications to soften the utterance.

The first movement, the longest, is one of lament, sometimes introspective, profoundly melancholy, sometimes of a despairing emphasis. The second movement is very short, swift, furious, battle-drunk. The third is in a lugubrious waltz rhythm—in this, somewhat remindful of Mahler. But the expression is not Mahler. The essential ideas are but transformation of the melodic material of the first movement. It is true that in this score Shostakovich refers now and again to Tchaikovsky, as well as to Mahler and Prokofieff—Prokofieff especially in the exultant finale.

But these influences are no longer quoted. They are assimilated, and made part of an expression that is now wholly personal, and eminently racial and ancestral in its nature. Shostakovich, born of troubled times and confusing creative cross-currents, has gone through much to reach this symphony. It seems to us the sure token of his arrival at the master's estate, and it should precede more scores of his growing power.

There was immense and deserved applause for this symphony and for its magnificent performance.

When Mr. Elman appeared on the stage, after the intermission, he received a special greeting from the expectant audience. They listened and they rejoiced in the maturity and the grand sincerity of his playing. This was the Tchaikovsky Concerto, performed no longer by a young genius in the flush of his youth and temperament, but by a musician greatly learned through experience and thought.

The interpretation, by one particularly born to understand this superbly Slavic score, was that of a ripened artist whose heart and soul were in every note that he sounded.

In a box at this performance sat Andrei Vishinsky, his wife and daughter, who afterward went backstage to congratulate Mr. Mitropoulos and Mr. Elman. Mr. Vishinsky said that he would send this evening to Shostakovich a cable telling him of the brilliant performance and the strong effect of his symphony.

OCTOBER 17, 1954

A Door Opens

Marian Anderson Engaged for the Metropolitan

THE ANNOUNCEMENT of the Metropolitan Opera Association for the season of 1954–5 that makes history is not that of a new opera or a loudly trumpeted production. It is that of the engagement of Marian Anderson, the distinguished Negro contralto, who will make her first appearance in America's leading lyric theater as Ulrica in Verdi's *Masked Ball,* under the direction of Dimitri Mitropoulos. And Mr. Mitropoulos will make his first Metropolitan appearance as the conductor of that performance.

The engagement of Miss Anderson is a tardy tribute to her rank and achievement as an artist of international fame. The engagement comes late—at least fifteen years late. Miss Anderson's beautiful voice is not now in its prime. But we need not fear for the distinction of her performance. What is lost today in sheer vocal opulence is replaced by her authority and sensitiveness as an interpreter. What is to be discovered is her ability as an actress and dramatic interpreter on the stage, in an opera that she has never seen in performance on the stage of any opera house.

This will be Miss Anderson's first appearance not only at the Metropolitan but on the operatic stage. She has sung in most of the great concert halls of the world. Opera, until this time, has been a dream. Now the way has been opened for her in dramatic music.

The public of the greatest opera house in America will await eagerly the appearance of the singer who in years past has more than once been refused permission to appear in celebrated auditoriums for reasons other than art. On her part, she has declined to sing in some auditoriums where segregation was in force.

This year Rudolf Bing asked if Miss Anderson would be available for a number of Metropolitan appearances. It is characteristic of this singer's high intelligence and artistic scruple that Miss Anderson waited until she had found out to her own satisfaction and that of Mr. Mitropoulos that the Ulrica part would suit the range and quality of her voice before signing the contract.

Miss Anderson's first appearance in opera is also the first time, in the seventy-one years that have elapsed since the Metropolitan opened its doors in 1883, that a Negro singer has appeared on its stage in a principal role as a regular member of the company. Perhaps the most important aspect of her engagement is its effect upon the fortunes of other singers of her race. In other theaters than the Metropolitan many Negro artists have appeared. At the City Center, Negro composers, singers, and instrumentalists have repeatedly been engaged, including Lawrence Winters, Camilla Williams, and William Grant Still, the composer of the opera *Troubled Island,* given its *première* there in 1949. It is only at the Metropolitan that the white tradition, as one might call it, has endured up to the present day, although some years ago Mr. Bing brought in Janet Collins, a Negro dancer, to be the prima ballerina.

How far that policy is behind the times is obvious if one merely glances at the programs of recent seasons and notes the very important share that gifted Negro singers had in them. If it is fifteen years late for Miss Anderson to be recognized by the Metropolitan, it is as many years since it would have been appropriate for such a singer as Paul Robeson to make his appearance there. We do not speak here of Mr. Robeson's politics. We speak of his exceptional endowments as a singer and a dramatic interpreter. He could have been a highly impressive Boris, or Mefistofele, or Emperor Jones— the part that Lawrence Tibbett made famous in opera, and in which he achieved what we have always regarded as perhaps Mr. Tibbett's greatest individual impersonation. The character waited for such an artist as Robeson to give it a unique integration.

But other Negro singers, especially those of a younger generation, are with us. How about the young and exceptionally gifted coloratura soprano Mattiwilda Dobbs, who has sung at La Scala and at Glyndebourne? Her concert appearance in Town Hall last season fully supported the praise that she had received in opera houses abroad. Here, one would say, was a possible Queen of the Night in Mozart's *Magic Flute* who would certainly have surpassed some other singers who have taken that role at the Metropolitan Opera in seasons gone by.

An admirable baritone who already has made his mark in recital, in choral concerts, and with orchestras, including his appearance last April with the Philadelphia Orchestra, should be excellent operatic material—we mean, William Warfield. He and his wife, Leontyne Price, have made themselves internationally known with the *Porgy and Bess* touring opera company. Carol Brice, Dorothy Maynor, Roland Hayes—in his youth, when a lyrical tenor part such as Don Ottavio or perhaps Des Grieux would not have been outside his vocal and dramatic range of effective interpretation— are other names that come immediately to mind, of a list that is far from complete, of Negro singers whose talents should not be, or have been, absent from our opera stages.

But there will not be such hiatuses in our opera casts much longer. If Miss Anderson is the first Negro singer to appear at the Metropolitan, she certainly will not be the last. Mr. Bing's fearless action in engaging her has forever dismissed the taboo against Negroes on the Metropolitan stage. His statement of policy in this regard was of the most admirable simplicity. "I wouldn't hire anyone because he is a Negro, and I wouldn't refuse to hire anyone because he is a Negro, either." It would be purely a question of whether a singer was or was not right for a role.

"Ever since one was in high school," said Miss Anderson, in her characteristic third-person phraseology, "one wanted to sing opera —at the Metropolitan if that could be." Employing the same grammatical construction, it can be said that one thinks of many a Negro singer whose presence might enrich Metropolitan casts, for whom Miss Anderson's engagement will pave the way. It will hardly be considered a mature point of view, in the light of her achievement and that of other artists of her race, to reject contributions of intelligence and talent and character to the culture of America.

Blacher and Milstein

Some Masterly Concertos; Some Masterly Variations

THE concert given by the Philharmonic-Symphony Society last night in Carnegie Hall, when George Szell made his first appearance of the season as its guest conductor, was one of brilliant and admirable entertainment.

Its novel feature was the first performance in New York of a set of variations by Boris Blacher, the reputedly audacious and "ultra" composer of Russian ancestry long resident in Germany. The variations proved decidedly worth while, and not nearly so bad as persons shy of modernism had feared. And Nathan Milstein was the violin soloist. We have seldom heard him play with such *élan* and mastery as he evidenced in the two strongly contrasted violin concertos of Bach and Bruch, played as though each was his birthright.

He treated the solo part of the Bach concerto for just what it is— a single element of the orchestral fabric. From the modern point of view, this is not a concerto, but an ensemble of fine players making music together.

Mr. Milstein often joined with gusto and rhythmic figure in the tutti passages. His solo passages, when they arrived, were only an outgrowth of the thought of the score as a whole. When he did have the momentary ascendancy, he played with a modesty and a sturdy, forthright musicianship that forbade intrusiveness or overprominence of his part. The slow movement, of course, afforded him the most individually expressive opportunities, of which he made much, but always, again, as a strand of the tonal design.

His opportunity for the splendid romantic style came with the good old Bruch concerto, which, when it is played with the conviction, the sentiment and fire that Mr. Milstein bestowed upon it last night, remains today a superb masterpiece. Nothing was lacking in the masterly performance, and nothing was injected into that performance but strengthened and ennobled the music. Always it

431

struck fire. It had sentiment and imagination, but was never sentimentalized in the slow movement, where it is so often cheapened.

Not in a long time has the introduction been given its true sweep, color, and declamatory eloquence. The orchestra was now furnishing background, excitement, accentuation for the solo; and now, as the violinist swept up to a climax that unleashed the instruments, they seemed to shout "bravo" for his deeds. That is the way to play the Bruch concerto. And when it is played that way, we realize anew how original and how superbly made it is. Hardly is it necessary to add that at the end of this performance there were huzzas for Mr. Milstein and also for Mr. Szell, who had given his soloist the ideal support for his interpretation.

Boris Blacher's variations on the twenty-fourth caprice of Paganini have every resource of modern technique and take in their stride harmonic effects once thought audacious if not illegitimate. They are not in the least iconoclastic. They might be reckoned higher in the artistic scale than the lengthier and more sumptuous set of variations that Rachmaninoff has written for piano and orchestra upon the same theme; or they might be considered lower than the famous Brahms variations on this subject for the piano.

These comparisons are unnecessary. The variations have their own physiognomy. Blacher's writing is always expert and variegated, logical and clear in its thematic treatment, amusingly impudent here and diverting there, and always the writing is of an informed modern musician.

JANUARY 8, 1955

═══

Un Ballo in Maschera with Marian Anderson

"A thunderous ovation from the whole house"

HISTORY was made last night when Marian Anderson, the famous Negro contralto, as one of the fruits of her distinguished career, sang for the first time in the Metropolitan Opera House and for the first time in opera on any stage.

Miss Anderson's role was that of Ulrica in Verdi's *Un Ballo in Maschera* (*A Masked Ball*). It is a short but highly dramatic part, one that requires a dramatic personality as well as sumptuous singing. Miss Anderson received a thunderous ovation from the whole house when the curtain rose upon the second scene of the first act, showing Ulrica, the sorceress, stirring her magic brew while the crowd on the stage regarded her with broken exclamations of awe and reverence.

She proceeded with her first aria, the *"Re dell'abisso."* The passage suited well the dark and rich color of the voice, as the simplicity and eloquence of Miss Anderson's singing graced the song. At first, no doubt under the special tensions of the occasion, including the newness of the dimensions and vibrancies of the Metropolitan stage, she wavered a little in pitch. There was accompanying evidence of vacillation and unevenness of breath support in these measures. But before the air was finished the singer had demonstrated the same musicianship and instinct for dramatic communication that she had long since demonstrated on the concert stage.

As the act proceeded and the voice warmed, it gained in sonority and concentrated resonance. The first aria lies more comfortably for the voice in its middle register than the second one, the *"È lui,"* which asks more of range and dramatic delivery than the first.

Indeed, the two passages, the first in the dark tonality of C minor, the second in the brighter and more militant major key, significantly supplement each other. Miss Anderson drove this contrast home, at the same time that her voice took on its normal resonance and emotional appeal.

The climax of this scene was Ulrica's powerful, unaccompanied phrase that prophesies Riccardo's death—"not by a known enemy (*No—per man d'un amico*), but by the hand of a friend." These words were sung with such meaning that they made the whole scene. There was no moment in which Miss Anderson's interpretation was commonplace or repetitive in effect. In Ulrica's one half-act, by her native sensibility, intelligence, and vocal art, Miss Anderson stamped herself in the memory and the lasting esteem of those who listened.

There is no doubt that repeated appearances in this part and familiarity with the details of its dramatic action will give her unconditional authority and certainty of touch and expression that only experience can bring. At the end of the act the audience would not have enough of Miss Anderson, recalling her again and again before the curtain. Other leading members of the cast, appearing with her, made evident their gratification at Miss Anderson's success.

The performance was a fine one throughout in Richard Tucker's singing of the Riccardo role; in Leonard Warren's Renato—his voice equips him ideally for the delivery of the famous *"Eri tu"* of the last act; in the exhilarating certainty and effectiveness of Roberta Peters's Oscar, the page—a page equipped not only with voice, but also, may we say, with limbs such as all the women pages appareled as men should display in operaland.

Utterly magnificent was Zinka Milanov's Amelia, grand in manner, gesture, vocal sweep, and glory of tone. Then there were the conspirators, the Sam and Tom of Nicola Moscona and Norman Scott, accomplished vocalists and for the nonce comedians, who could have been even freer and more Rabelaisian in their jeering laughter—*"Ah, ha, ha"*—at Renato, confronted with his apparently guilty wife.

One does not ask why, when it had been specifically devised that the production would restore the Verdi plot to its original place, which was the Stockholm of the murdered Gustavus III, the program kept the old silly names of Sam and Tom for the conspirators of history, Count Warting and Count de Horn, and why Gustavus was not so identified on the list instead of Riccardo, governor of the Boston that Verdi had to name to please the censors when the opera was first produced.

But again, for all-around mastery and vividness that suffused not only the orchestra but also every detail of the performance, commend us to Mr. Mitropoulos's lyrical, blazing, volcanic interpretation of the score. The theater is evidently in his blood. A few of his tempos erred, perhaps, on the slow side, but who that heard will ever forget the torrent of orchestral tone that swept the voices and the drama itself forward on its crest, yet ignored no minor issue or detail of the whole?

Gluck's *Iphigénie en Tauride* Is Revived

"Impossible to listen with detachment"

ONE is inclined to .the belief that the greatest of Gluck's operas in the grand style is *Iphigénie en Tauride*, the last of his masterpieces, given in concert form last night by the American Opera Society in Town Hall.

The opera had not been heard in this city since its performance nearly thirty-eight years ago at the Metropolitan Opera House. It is in certain respects analogous, among Gluck's works, to *Götterdämmerung* among Wagner's. In both operas the composers write with an impetuousness and freedom arising from the fact that their theories are behind them, their experiments with the operatic form things of the past, their inspiration at a white heat and unrestrained by formal or technical considerations as the music drama progresses to its end.

One can condition this somewhat by reflecting that Gluck's third act, as the opera was presented last night, has its moments of obtrusive formalism. As a whole, *Iphigénie en Tauride* is gigantic not only in its formal arrangement but in the dramatic sweep and color of so many of its pages.

The opening immediately seizes the listener—the music of the storm, and Iphigénie's terrified narration of her dream of slaying her brother, Oreste. The storm itself, superbly orchestrated, must have been far wilder to its generation than Wagner's introduction to *The Flying Dutchman* in the next century.

But this is not mere orchestral background. For the storm, with the wailing wind instruments and the rhythmic shocks of the orchestra, is part and parcel of the tempest that rages in Iphigénie's heart. The opera goes forward on this principle, with the formal divisions of recitative and aria as such almost gone, and both styles combining or alternating as the dramatic need arises.

The chorus has a similar office. Now and again comes a grandly demarcated solo, and then Gluck speaks with nobility and energy of expression that he never surpassed. French declamation an Italian song go hand in hand in this score, modifying and ofter completely dispersing the formalism that lies at the basis of most operas of the eighteenth century.

There are passages that momentarily retard musico-dramatic development, such as those in which, somewhat excessively, Oreste and Pylade argue as to which shall be sacrificed by poor Iphigénie.

As a whole, this work impresses us as the most human, the most prophetic, the most exciting of Gluck's operas today. Such at least is the personal reaction. *Orfeo*, with its beautiful melodies, its dramatic suggestion, its abiding classic serenity, is very beautiful. Somehow it leaves us cool. But not so with *Iphigénie en Tauride*, to which it is impossible to listen with detachment.

It is a pleasure to add that the performance matched in dramatic spirit the nature of the opera. While all the singing was not of the same level, all of it was imbued with emotional intensity, if with different degrees of observation of the classic style. That style was most conspicuously projected by Leopold Simoneau, the Pylade, whose excellent French diction, brilliancy of tone, and sense of métier twice caused the house to burst into applause.

Mr. Hugh Thompson, the Oreste, was always a towering, tragic figure, one who put drama into his tones as well as his bearing and facial expression. Miss [Lucine] Amara sang her opening passages with very dramatic effect. Her second solo passage was distinguished for its tonal attractiveness and expressivity in song. The small chorus was always telling in its entrances and its dramatic pronouncements.

But a poorer vocal performance would have been more than balanced by the extremely effective and imaginative performance of the orchestra under the discipline and the inspiring baton of Arnold U. Gamson. He conducted for dear life, and the orchestra, which did so willingly, would have had to respond. The orchestra in a Gluck opera is of special importance, and no significance of Gluck's score went unnoticed, or was given less than the full power of delineation by the instruments.

Artur Rubinstein Plays at Carnegie

"Beethoven might have relished less respect
and more gallantry."

THE program given by Artur Rubinstein for his piano recital last night in Carnegie Hall was a formidable one, and no question about it. It was performed formidably—not invariably, perhaps, with plenary inspiration, but masterfully, as of course, and phenomenally in its greatest moments.

There were all the concomitants of the recital of one of the few blazing stars of the present pianistic firmament—the milling crowd jostling its way in; the seated audience that overflowed from the packed auditorium to those seated on the stage; the undercurrent of excitement, anticipation, and *sub rosa* comment by the expert and informed as the recital went on; the applause that crackled like gunfire and rumbled like cannon after a particularly felicitous exhibition of virtuosity. And the encores, in progress as we left the hall.

But Mr. Rubinstein was not there to shoot fireworks for mere display, or seek the quick favor of the gallery by some uncommon effect for effect's sake. He was in dead earnest; he brought all his immense artillery as pianist and musician to bear for the sake of the music he was presenting.

The first half of the program consisted of no less than the Beethoven E flat Sonata, Opus 31, No. 3, and the one-movement Liszt Sonata in B minor that takes more time for its exposition, development, and recapitulation than the four movements of Beethoven.

This Beethoven sonata was played with perfect correctness, musicianship, and respect. There was no attempt to make it something that it was not. So far as we are concerned, this pleasant sonata, with all of its Beethovenish side-effects, is very eighteenth-century. No doubt it was highly revolutionary in its time. Perhaps Mr. Rubinstein, in another mood, might have made it seem more daring and original than it sounded last night. He respected Beethoven. One wonders if, like a lady with her suitor, Beethoven might have relished less respect and more gallantry.

The music that carried the torch, in this first part of the concert, was Liszt's still discussable sonata, or symphonic poem for piano, with the astonishing transformations of the themes, and the drama, the panache, the sensuousness and rhetoric that Liszt has packed into this work. How much greater or lesser value does it have for us, purely as music, with the passing of the years? When it is played as Mr. Rubinstein played it last night, one is prone to remark that, whether it is music or something else, it is an extremely exciting experience.

He played that tremendous epic, the Chopin F sharp minor Polonaise, which should be played only by pianists of his stature. It is a vast fresco, crowded with detail, difficult to present in a manner that has the effect of unbroken unity. Mr. Rubinstein unified all its elements—not only the lordly polonaise, but also the sudden visions of the battlefield, with the hoofbeats, the roar of cannon; the nostalgic mazurka theme, interrupted by the sudden earthquake; the muttering basses, the wild sweeps upward, which bring the furious return of the polonaise; and at last the tragic echoes, somber, endlessly defiant, of the polonaise theme, stalking in the bass. This was grand playing.

The three études were the posthumous ones, if memory serves, which are not often heard and are on the same level as the sets of Opus 10 and 24, but which the pianist gave a distinction that these pieces seldom receive. This was especially so with the first of the three. A mazurka seldom heard was followed by the Fantaisie-Impromptu, which, for our choice, could well be spared as the second-class Chopin that it is.

The final performance of the program as printed was that of a "sonata in three movements," so-called, "dedicated to and written for Artur Rubinstein" by Stravinsky. These pieces, connected by the rumbling bass tones that replace the rolls on the drum that connect the three scenes of the Stravinsky ballet [Petrouchka], are about as near the *ne plus ultra* of pianist arrangement as we can conceive—a prodigious piece of what we shall call "pianostration." You hear all the colors, all the instrumental parts of the orchestral score. And Mr. Rubinstein's fingers do the rest.

The first two parts are very effective. The third part is too long and has too much in it. But the audience would have listened longer to the sheer fascination of the pianistic legerdemain. After that the encores began.

Berlioz's *Damnation of Faust* Is Revived

"Romanticism rampant, of the special Berlioz brand"

THE Boston Symphony Orchestra, Charles Munch, conductor, with the Harvard Glee Club and Radcliffe Choral Society, giving their one-hundredth performance together, united forces last night in Carnegie Hall for Mr. Munch's interpretation of Berlioz's *Damnation of Faust*. The work will be repeated next Saturday afternoon at the Boston Symphony's second concert of the week in this city.

For last night's occasion the hall was packed, and the performance was received with immense enthusiasm. Mr. Munch could congratulate himself and his musicians upon the effect of their notable revival of Berlioz's work, much neglected in late years in this city and last night brought to a triumphant summation.

The neglect of this *Faust* score is the more astonishing because of the singular freshness and inspiration of the music. There is nothing like it even in Berlioz. The lovely *L'Enfance du Christ* is in another genre. The love music of the *Romeo and Juliet* "dramatic symphony" is unique, lonely, and incomparable. But that work as a whole has by no means the sustained strength of the *Faust* score, or the headlong inspiration that flames in its every essential part.

Why is this? The answer, of course, is genius. There is another answer. It is, with apologies for the obnoxious term, romanticism rampant, of the special Berlioz brand; romanticism that created more original music in every decade of its existence than the whole "neo-classic" movement of our disillusionized half-century. It is the poetical and sensational tone painting of the man who was the arch-priest of dramatic effect and of sharp and confounding contrasts, and the inimitable master of modern instrumentation.

Here the orchestration is the investiture of the text and the illustrator of the dramatic idea. This is not a program symphony, like the "Fantastic," which shook the world in 1830. It is a cantata, and the text carries the burden of the drama. There is one surprise after another, not only in compound rhythms but in compound keys; haunting melodies, as wistful, tender, and tragic as those of Marguerite; a chorus that becomes in itself a dramatic catalyst; blinding flashes of instrumental inspiration, like those sudden lightnings of the orchestra in the *menuet* of the will-o'-the-wisps, and the sardonic parody of Mephistopheles's serenade by the skittering woodwinds, or its macabre brass in the wild ride. The conventional place is where it was unavoidable—the music of the ascension of Marguerite. This can readily be forgiven.

All these things were brought home to us afresh by Mr. Munch's performance. One did not have to agree with its every detail of "tempo" and "dynamics" and all the rest of its jargon to be smitten by the impact of Berlioz' blazing, extravagant, and most touching music.

The performance of the two choruses was a part of this achievement, and a very striking one. Of the soloists Mr. Singher was the master. We never heard him in better voice and more the master, free, secure, completely authoritative in every word and tone of his sardonic role. Mr. Gramm's Brander was admirably in the groove. It was not Mr. Poleri's night. The tessitura of his part was not comfortable for him. Nor was Miss Danco's performance exemplary in either tone quality or pitch. But the ensemble effect was an unforgettable demonstration of the genius and imagination of Berlioz.

MARCH 20, 1955

Slashing Attack

"At least sixty-per-cent agreement"

WE HAVE read with much relish and at least sixty-per-cent agreement the new book of Henry Pleasants, *The Agony of Modern Music,* which already has kicked up a lot of indignation, especially on the part of certain of our composers. It may well be that Mr. Pleasants writes in places with tongue in cheek, with the endeavor to be wantonly controversial, with the intent of frightening not the bourgeois, this time, but the more sophisticated and pretentious of the music-fanciers of the higher intellectual brackets of the present time. Certainly he oversimplifies his argument, and is disproportionate in his estimates of musical values. But when he attacks the snobbism, bluff, and propaganda so industriously pursued in the cause of professedly "modern" music, and its self-appointed high priests who confidently instruct the public in what its esthetic preferences should be, he does a valuable and refreshing job of debunking.

The contention at which the most denunciation has been leveled is Pleasants' assertion that the only modern music worthy of the name is jazz, and that no other music composed since 1920 can compare with it in vitality, significance, and real contemporaneousness.

Demonstrably the claim is excessive where serious composition is concerned. On the other hand, if one asks what kind of contemporaneous music has the most vitality, the most spontaneity, invention, and freshness of approach, the answer is obvious. Of course it is jazz, which has come up from the ground, and the genius of simple people. And of course there has not yet appeared in this country any orchestral or symphonic composition that has equaled in originality and authenticity such a work, for instance, as George Gershwin's *Rhapsody in Blue*—a highly imperfect piece, by the way, by an extremely gifted composer who did not know what to do with his superb ideas. But the ideas have carried and preserved it, just the same.

Nor is it logical to deny that the serious music of our period, on both sides of the water, proceeds from European traditions and usage, or that the product of our learned composers is anything but fundamentally emulative of foreign techniques and thought. How could it be otherwise in this America, descended from every foreign nation on earth, and the inheritor of their pasts? Naturally, inevitably, the American Mozart or Wagner has yet to arrive.

In the meantime, jazz wins by default. It is one thing to create a kind of music, simple in structure, informal in address, that will appeal immediately to the "masses" and another thing to attempt to enter the realm of thought and beauty known to a Haydn or a Beethoven.

Mr. Pleasants' main argument we think entirely sound and applicable to the problem. Haydn and Beethoven, and indeed every one of the great composers, wrote in ways that were hotly discussed, and in various quarters hotly contested, but that, in the main, had a strong and a rapidly growing appeal to music-lovers of many tastes and classes. Furthermore, and contrary to prevailing legend, virtually all the master composers, in a greater or lesser degree, received recognition and performance while they lived. And these masters, says Mr. Pleasants, served their public successfully, without compromise, and well.

He thinks that this is not now the case, and he supports his argument very effectively. It is the unreality of the contemporaneous composer's relation to his time, and his vain efforts, by pretense and propaganda, to conceal that unreality, and hence unproductiveness, which is at the bottom of the "agony of modern music."

Where we think this book unreasonable and lopsided in its conclusion is, for instance, in its *a priori* reasoning that there have been no important or really "modern" composers since Wagner, and that composers of the more serious and lofty objectives, as shown by the years since 1920, have no particular right to existence.

There are fertile and infertile periods in the history of every art, and it takes a thousand small composers to make a great one. Does Mr. Pleasants assume that an art has no past? Or that any living art fails to have its roots deep down in that past? Has there ever been a great composer unaffected by the thought and practice of masters who preceded him? Is it reasonable to reduce all the living composers of our day, old and young, to a dead level of epigonism? Granted that Wagner was immeasurably the most powerful creative genius in music of the last hundred years, which is the fact, there are, nevertheless, other creative minds that have given completely new material to music since he died.

These artists and dozens of lesser ones, who could be mentioned here, are contributing indefatigably to musical evolution. It may be added that the creative synthesis is a far more complex problem for the composer of this modern age than it could have been in any previous century. And we have yet to see the last half-century in any comprehensible perspective.

But for this very reason, if none others—and there are others— Mr. Pleasants' book appears as a very valuable corrective of current fallacies. It is a precipitant, let us hope, of sharper self-examination on the part of our composers and their effort to find sincere and individual expression in the tonal art.

In Praise of Four-Hand Piano-Playing

"Confession by one of the worst piano dabblers out of jail"

WHAT, one asks in some puzzlement, and some apprehension too, is to be the fate of the piano? Is the ultimate destiny to be that of the handyman of musical instruments, and its relegation to a second rank as a medium of personal and individual artistic interpretation?

Will the future see the appearance of new composers capable, as so many of their nineteenth-century predecessors were, of creating music specifically appropriate to the nature of this instrument and none other? If such composers do not appear, the piano will undergo the thinning of its repertory and will retreat in public favor, as some contend it already is doing. What, then, is the place of the piano in our culture of this twentieth century, and how will its social values compare with those of the glorious past, a century ago?

The piano, as an instrument of poetry, dramatic declamation, and sensuous song, embodied what appears unhappily as a concept of the past. It is today more often an instrument of percussion than of poetry. In the orchestra the piano is often used for effects of sheer rhythmical emphasis, while the particularity of hearing that formerly made orchestral composers fearful of employing the piano, with its neutral pitch, in combination with the strings with their variable pitch, today ignores those delicate tonal considerations as though they did not exist.

The results are for the future to reveal. But now another valuable use of the piano seems also to be dying out, especially since the coming of records, radio, and television. We mean the grand old practice of duet playing, or playing in larger ensembles, of arrangements of orchestral music and of other musical literature on one, two, and even three or more pianos.

It is the fashion to heap scorn and contumely upon those who will accept such substitutes as piano arrangements of music for combinations of other instruments. It is averred by the cognoscenti that a real musician could only scorn such a makeshift. In the first place, they reason, as all know, the piano arrangement for an orchestral work seldom presents its details, to say nothing of tonal balances and contrasts, as they were designed by the creator of the symphonic score. Secondly, the orchestral coloring, which is as different from a piano arrangement as a painting is from a pencil sketch, is hardly suggested. Ergo: the person who has played only the solo or ensemble piano arrangement of the master's symphony can have no definitive idea of its actual nature.

To which we answer, "Poppycock!" In the first place, an overture or a symphony, arranged by a first-class musician for the piano, gives the player a first-hand acquaintance with the form of the work and all its salient details. He sees the architecture of the symphony, it is true, in a black-and-white version. But one can add that if the only thing a composition possesses that attracts the listener is color and impressionism, it is likely to be a weak creation that will not stand for long the pressures of the years and of constantly changing taste. If the piece won't stand the so-called black-and-white exposure, it is seldom worth knowing intimately, anyhow; whereas intimacy with its plan and outline, fully attainable by pianists playing intelligently and co-operatively together, is perhaps better attained by this means than by any other that we know.

Confession being good for the soul, it may herewith be related by one of the worst piano dabblers out of jail that he gained more quickly a grip of the rhythmical counterpoint of the Stravinsky *Sacre du printemps* by vainly attempting its performance as arranged for piano duet, than he would have done if his examination of the work had been confined to reading the difficult orchestral score or, in the course of time, hearing many orchestral performances of it. He even ventures further: it would have helped more than one aspirant of the baton if he had first explored the score by this means before he took it into rehearsal.

If, in fact, we were asked to recommend the quickest way in which to become familiar with the contents of the masterpieces of the orchestral repertory, we would answer, by means, wherever available, of four-hand performance.

In years before we so much as heard a first-class orchestra, we were acquainted with the main elements of its repertory by way of the four-hand literature—the Bach of the suites and the "Brandenburg" Concertos; the "standard" Haydn symphonies; the dozen most famous ones of Mozart; Beethoven's nine and his principal

444

overtures, even concertos; Brahms's four; Schumann's four; the two principal symphonies of Mendelssohn and his overtures (including, of course, the magical one to *A Midsummer Night's Dream*); Liszt's tone poems; the three last symphonies of Tchaikovsky, etc. Most of these were familiar friends before we heard the wonder of their orchestral performance, with its miracles of tone color and power. These orchestral performances were not less but more appreciated for their belated discovery. And if anyone thinks it will be less than a lesson in musicianship to so much as attempt to solve the musical and rhythmical problems of a score by a Strauss, Debussy, or Hindemith, four hands at one piano—well, try conducting and be done with it.

In a former period it was a matter of course for the orchestral works of a prominent composer to be issued quickly in piano arrangements by his publishers. Is it that pianos are relatively so few in the modern home, where they have been replaced by record, radio, and television devices? Or is it that too few people now play in ensemble groups, or are able to do so?

It is too bad. Those potential lovers of music, every one of whom should have a working knowledge of the elements of piano-playing and sight-reading, are missing so much more than they know, as a result of these conditions, even as the composers themselves are missing listeners of curiosity and understanding. For the record or radio, presenting the masterly performance, can never replace the joy and the profit of four hands and a new score on the music rack, and the creative participation of all concerned on the piano.

BIOGRAPHICAL NOTE

OLIN DOWNES was born in Evanston, Illinois, on January 27, 1886.
At the age of eight he received his first instruction in piano. Five
years later he was given lessons in harmony and *solfège* at the National Conservatory of Music in New York. He was thirteen when
he heard a symphony orchestra for the first time.

His family then moved to Boston, and his study of piano continued with Carl Baermann. Later he studied theory with Homer
Norris, John P. Marshall, and Clifford Heilman; music history and
analysis with Dr. Louis Kelterborn.

In these Boston years of the early 1900's, the concerts of the Boston Symphony Orchestra were an experience of inestimable value
to him. He was always first on the "rush" line for students. With
unending fascination he listened to a vast range of great music
superbly interpreted.

In 1906—he was then twenty—he became Music Critic for the
Boston *Post*. He plunged into the absorbing activities of a music
critic. But his passion for the piano made him play, with an orchestra or chamber group, whenever there was an opportunity.

He presently became instructor in music courses at Boston University (1911), at the Harvard Summer School, and at the Chautau-
qua Institute. Then also began a career as lecturer which was to
take him, over the years, from coast to coast, with most of the major
symphony orchestras in the United States, and to many places in
Europe. He was eventually radio speaker and commentator for
many of the radio networks and stations including NBC, CBS,
WJZ, WOR and WQXR.

In 1924 he became Music Critic for *The New York Times*, succeeding Richard Aldrich.

Amid the rising tide of musical life in New York City and the
manifold duties this imposed, Olin Downes began trips to far places.

He wanted to experience music as produced in all its varieties outside the United States. In 1928 he reviewed the first Modern Composers Festival in Prague. Later trips took him to Moscow to hear the *Ur Boris* of Moussorgsky, and he advised Giulio Gatti-Casazza, Director of the Metropolitan Opera, on the desirability of producing this original version; to La Scala to hear Toscanini's *Lucia di Lammermoor*; to Vienna to hear Richard Strauss conduct his own operas; to Paris to hear the music of Ravel and Prokofieff, conducted by Koussevitzky; to Finland, in his devotion to the music of Sibelius. On one of his last trips, in 1952, he went to Belgium as a member of the jury for the Concours Musical International Reine Elisabeth de Belgique. He also covered, on this trip, the XXth Century Festival of Music in Paris; programs of the Florence (Italy) "May" Festival; the Festival of Contemporary Composers in Salzburg; and productions of his operas by Hindemith in Zurich, Switzerland.

His published writings included: Editor, *Select Songs of Russian Composers*, 1922 (Carl Fischer); Author, *Symphonic Broadcasts*, 1932, and *Symphonic Masterpieces*, 1934 (Dial Press); Contributor, Cobbett's *Cyclopedia of Chamber Music*, and Oscar Thompson's *Cyclopedia of Music and Musicians*, 1946 (Dodd, Mead and Company); Collaborator, with Elie Siegmeister, *A Treasury of American Song*, 1947 (Alfred A. Knopf); Author, *Ten Operatic Masterpieces; From Mozart to Prokofieff*, 1952 (Broadcast Music Inc., G. Ricordi, and Charles Scribner's Sons).

Among his services to the cause of music were: Director of Music for the New York World's Fair, 1939; Chairman, Executive Committee, the Rachmaninoff Fund, 1943–1949; Chairman, The New York Music Critics Circle; Director, Musicians Foundation, The Bohemians; Member, Jury, "Musical Talent in our Schools" series, jointly presented by *The New York Times* and Radio Station WQXR, 1950–'51, '51–'52, '52–'53, '53–'54, '54–'55; Member, International Jury, Concours Musical International Reine Elisabeth de Belgique, 1952; Vice-Chairman, International Committee, Sibelius Festival honoring the ninetieth birthday of Jean Sibelius, 1955; Director, American National Theatre and Academy, 1955.

Among the honors he received were: 1937—awarded Order of Commander of the White Rose by the Government of Finland for services to Finnish music through studies and writings on Jean Sibelius; 1939—honorary degree, Doctor of Music, the Cincinnati

Conservatory of Music; 1946—honorary membership, Chi Chapter, Pi Kappa Lambda, School of Music, University of Michigan; 1951— named Chevalier de la Légion d'Honneur by the Government of France for services to French music; 1955—a scholarship in his memory was established at the MacDowell Colony, Peterborough, New Hampshire.

His clubs were The Century Association, The Coffee House, and The Bohemians.

I. D.

ACKNOWLEDGMENTS

Olin Downes's published articles over the half-century of his writing in the Boston *Post* and in *The New York Times* were estimated at some 15,000,000 words.

Only 175,000 words were to be used in this book.

I am deeply grateful to the many friends who gave sustaining inspiration and fresh incentive in this arduous task. It is not possible to list the names of all who aided progress, each in his own way. A few, however, must be singled out for their share in the vast labor of love that went into the making of this book.

The New York Times made the source material available and gave generous and unfailing co-operation. The *Times*'s Information Bureau expedited the work of research and photostating.

The Boston *Post* at once graciously gave permission for use of the articles.

The research in Boston was helpfully forwarded by Mr. John N. Burk, who made available the files of the Boston Symphony Orchestra, and by Mr. Richard G. Hensley, Chief Librarian, Reference and Research Division, The Boston Public Library.

Research was also aided by Dr. Harold Spivacke, Chief of the Music Division, The Library of Congress, Washington, D.C., and by Dr. Carleton Sprague Smith, Chief of the Music Division, The New York Public Library.

Over many months, a group of friends and colleagues gave selfless and invaluable collaboration. Among them were: S. L. M. Barlow, Geo Bergal, Mrs. Alexander Brailowsky, Dr. Joseph Braunstein, Chalmers Clifton, Sidney Finkelstein, Mrs. Vladimir Horowitz, Dr. Henry Levinger, Goddard Lieberson, Arthur Kendy, Jean Morel,

Acknowledgments

Clara Rockmore, Mario Siletti, Henry W. Simon, Mrs. Roy Sinclair, Nicolas Slonimsky, Saul Taishoff, Virgil Thomson, and Mme Isabelle Vengerova.

It is not possible to evaluate a spiritual contribution, and I can only intimate the gratitude I feel for the devoted response of those who helped me in the making of this book.

IRENE DOWNES

INDEX

Index

Index

Index

Index

Index

Index

Index

Index

Index